D1596495

SSSP

Springer
Series in
Social
Psychology

SSSP

Bernard Weiner

An Attributional Theory of Motivation and Emotion

Springer-Verlag New York Berlin Heidelberg
London Paris Tokyo

Bernard Weiner
Department of Psychology
University of California, Los Angeles
Los Angeles, California 90024
U.S.A.

With 60 Figures

Library of Congress Cataloging in Publication Data
Weiner, Bernard.
   An attributional theory of motivation and emotion.
   (Springer series in social psychology)
   Bibliography p.
   Includes index.
   1. Motivation (Psychology)   2. Emotions
3.Attribution (Social psychology)   I. Title.
II. Series.
BF503.W44   1986   153.8   86-1807

Typeset by Publishers Service, Bozeman, Montana.
Printed and bound by R.R. Donnelley & Sons, Harrisonburg, Virginia.
Printed in the United States of America.

9 8 7 6 5 4 3 2 1

ISBN 0-387-96312-X Springer-Verlag New York Berlin Heidelberg
ISBN 3-540-96312-X Springer-Verlag Berlin Heidelberg New York

Better to attempt to light one small candle
than to curse the darkness

Confucius

Preface

For a long time I have had the gnawing desire to convey the broad motivational significance of the attributional conception that I have espoused and to present fully the argument that this framework has earned a rightful place alongside other leading theories of motivation. Furthermore, recent investigations have yielded insights into the attributional determinants of affect, thus providing the impetus to embark upon a detailed discussion of emotion and to elucidate the relation between emotion and motivation from an attributional perspective. The presentation of a unified theory of motivation and emotion is the goal of this book.

My more specific aims in the chapters to follow are to: 1) Outline the basic principles that I believe characterize an adequate theory of motivation; 2) Convey what I perceive to be the conceptual contributions of the perspective advocated by my colleagues and me; 3) Summarize the empirical relations, reach some definitive conclusions, and point out the more equivocal empirical associations based on hypotheses derived from our particular attribution theory; and 4) Clarify questions that have been raised about this conception and provide new material for still further scrutiny. In so doing, the building blocks (if any) laid down by the attributional conception will be readily identified and unknown juries of present and future peers can then better determine the value of this scientific product.

Engaging in this task requires a degree of both megalomania and courage—megalomania because one assumes that the work deserves the attention of others and has some belief that their judgments will be positive; courage because numerous errors of omission and commission often are more evident to an author than to readers or critics. The narcissistic aspect of this task will lead me to highlight the contributions of the attributional perspective; such a book is not the place to hide "light under a bushel." The more intrepid feature of my goal hopefully will enable me to write candidly about the shortcomings of the attributional approach that I advocate.

The empirical investigations described in this book conducted by my colleagues and me were funded by grants from the National Science Foundation, the Spencer Foundation, and the Public Health Service, National Institute of Mental Health.

I am grateful for their support and particularly to the National Institute of Mental Health for current funding, Grant #38014. In addition, I want to express my thanks to Franz Weinert and the Max-Planck-Institute, where this book was first started, and to Julie Verette, for her careful assistance.

Los Angeles, July 1986   Bernard Weiner

Contents

Chapter 1
Principles for a Theory of Motivation

In which the author tells why attributions provide the foundation for a theory of motivation. Twelve principles for a general theory of motivation are proposed.

In 1645, Miyamoto Musashi was contemplating the causes of his past success as a warrior. In *A Book of Five Rings* he mused:

> When I reached thirty I looked back on my past. The previous victories were not due to my having mastered strategy. Perhaps it was natural ability, or the order of heaven, or that other schools' strategy was inferior. (p. 35)

About 275 years later, and approximately 11,000 miles away, the editors of *Scientific American* were wondering why America was flourishing. They reasoned:

> The wealth and general prosperity of the country are largely due to the intelligence and energy of its people, but it can hardly be disputed that it is equally due to the natural wealth of the country. (Staff, April 1926, p. 228)

Unfortunately, battles are lost as often as they are won, and countries undergo economic decline as well as enrichment. During the recent financial recession in the United States, the *Los Angeles Times* reported:

> Timber industry experts blame high interest rates, the housing slump, tough logging regulation, and expansion of the Redwood National Park for their sorry state. Tim Skaggs, the union business agent, shrugged. "You could spend a lifetime fixing blame," he said, drinking coffee in his office on a dark and rainy day. (Martinez, November 1982, Part V, p. 1)

Even the coach of my favorite football team found it necessary to soul-search about causality following a series of losses. Again from the *Los Angeles Times* (Robert, November 22, 1982, Part III, p. 3):

> Here it is Thanksgiving week, and the Los Angeles Rams are looking like the biggest turkeys in town. Coach Ray Malavasi has eliminated bad luck, biorhythms, and sunspots as the reasons why his football team has lost 9 of its last 10 games. Now he's considering the unthinkable possibilities that: a) he has lousy players or b) they aren't really trying.

I am sure that the reader can readily supply other examples of causal search. Our daily newspapers are certainly a good source; we are constantly being told why the stock market rose or fell, why our cherished team won or lost, why a political party experienced victory or defeat, and on and on. But even more direct illustrations originate in our daily lives. How often have we wondered why we did poorly on some exam or at some job, why a particular person refused our request for a date, or, for many readers of this book, why a treasured manuscript was rejected for publication, or, when published, failed to reach the acclaim that was desired?

Why this constant pursuit of "why?" A number of explanations come to mind (see Forsyth, 1980). First, we might just want to know—to understand the environment, to penetrate ourselves and our surroundings. This interpretation, familiar to personality and motivational psychologists, is known as the principle of mastery (White, 1959). Second, it is clearly functional to know why an event has occurred. As Kelley (1971) stated, "The attributor is not simply an attributor, a seeker after knowledge; his latent goal in attaining knowledge is that of effective management of himself and his environment" (p. 22). Once a cause or causes are assigned, in many instances a prescription or guide for future action can be suggested. If the prior outcome was a success, then there is likely to be an attempt to reinstate the prior causal network. So, for example, if Mary went out with me because I had tickets to a sporting event that she enjoys, then I may purchase tickets to another game to be with her once more. Or, if success at an athletic event is believed to be due to hard work, then the triumphant person is likely to train hard again. The editors of *Scientific American* believed in 1926 that one cause of America's wealth was its natural resources. It was therefore incumbent on the population, they contended, to preserve those resources and to protect the environment, thereby ensuring future success.

On the other hand, if the prior outcome or event was undesired, such as failure at an exam, social rejection, political loss, or economic decline, then there is a strong possibility that there will be an attempt to alter the causes to produce a different (more positive) effect. The timber spokesperson quoted in the *Los Angeles Times* believed that the economic recession in 1982 was in part due to the expansion of the National Parks system, which prevented the cutting of trees used to start housing developments, thereby decreasing employment. The union agent therefore argued for less preservation and protection of the environment so that this failure could be overcome. Both the editors of *Scientific American* and the representative of the timber union, who hold opposing beliefs about environmental protection, surely would be guided in their actions by their views about causality—the latter approaching the forest with an ax, the former with an injunction. That people have conflicting beliefs about the causes of positive and negative outcomes such as economic prosperity and recession is self-evident; truth, like beauty, lies in the eye of the beholder. One can indeed "spend a lifetime fixing blame." This is the first of many encounters with a basic axiom of phenomenology advocated in this book: Causal beliefs and subsequent actions depend on "how it seems to me." Further, the distal environment is perceived quite differently by different people, and even disparately by the same person on separate occasions.

Desire for mastery and functional search, two of the generators of causal exploration, do not seem to specifically characterize one geographical area, or one period of human history, or even one species. The seventeenth-century Japanese warrior and today's union representative are engaged in the same endeavor: the attempt to assign causality. Indeed, one might argue that adaptation is not possible without causal analysis. The warrior needs to know why he is winning battles so he can survive the next one, just as the union representative needs to explain why the timber industry is doing poorly so he may urge wiser actions in the future. Because of the apparent pancultural, timeless aspect of causal search and explanation, and because of the evident adaptive significance of this mental activity, causal ascriptions might provide the cornerstone for the construction of a psychological theory.

That is what this book is about—the construction of a theory of motivation and emotion that, by virtue of the centrality of causal explanation, represents a *general* theory, applicable to a wide variety of phenomena, without apparent historical boundaries or the constraints of any particular social context. To claim that this conceptual goal has been reached would be prima facie evidence of madness, but to deny that a step has been made in that direction would be to conceal my thoughts.

There is a story about a cellist who never moved his finger off the same note during an orchestral piece. When after the concert the conductor asked why, the cellist replied that he had found the right note, while the rest of the orchestra was still looking! I will not be guilty of such blindness, but causal attributions do represent my main note. I hope this strategy of playing makes a contribution to the entire symphony.

Principles for Theory Construction

As indicated, this book describes a theory of motivation and emotion centered around the concept of causal ascriptions. How should one go about this task? What principles should be followed to guide construction of the theory? To answer these questions, one can first look to prior theories of motivation and examine what they have accomplished as well as what they have failed to do, what conceptual building blocks have been laid as well as what cul-de-sacs have been entered. During the 1930s and 1940s, the area of motivation was at the heart of psychology. At present, however, the field is not very robust; it is difficult "to stand on the shoulders of giants and see a little further." Some therefore argue that we should bury or overthrow the past. But the somewhat fashionable (although fading) call for "revisionism" or "radical revisionism" provides neither an alternative program for the future nor a first-hand illustration of how to solve our so-called crisis and build a science of psychology. Rather than completely renounce the past, it seems far better to pay homage to it, recognizing prior empirical, methodological, and conceptual contributions. The study of motivation has reached the point where the examination of history is both necessary and profitable.

The following principles, build on past knowledge, are offered to guide the construction of a theory of motivation. These beliefs at times overlap; no attempt is made to dispense with a rule because it is not independent of other rules.

A Theory of Motivation Must Be Based on a Concept Other Than Homeostasis

From the origins of the scientific study of motivation around 1920 until perhaps 1955, psychoanalytic (Freudian) and drive (Hullian) theories dominated the field. Both conceptions are grounded on the notion that individuals strive to reduce internal tension; their fundamental motivational principle is that any deviation from equilibrium produces a motivational force to return to the prior state of internal balance. The prototypical observation from which this tenet may be derived is that of the behavior of a newborn infant. When all biological needs are satisfied—that is, when internal equilibrium is attained and no tension from biological deficits exists—the infant rests. There is a state of sleep or quiescence. The onset of hunger or thirst, which signal biological needs that if unsatisfied may cause tissue damage, gives rise to activity such as reflexive sucking, which may reduce the need states. If the instrumental activity results in goal attainment, then there is an offset of the need and a return to the quiet state. But this tranquility is only temporary; because of the cyclical nature of needs, the behavior is reinitiated. Hence, disequilibrium cannot be avoided, and behavior fluctuates from rest to activity and again back to inactivity.

An array of clinical and empirical evidence supports the intuitively appealing homeostatic principle. There can be little doubt that, given a biological deficit, behaviors typically are instigated to reduce that deficit. After all, we generally eat when hungry (if food is available), drink when thirsty, and attempt to flee from pain. Furthermore, some psychogenic (as opposed to viscerogenic) need states can also be conceptualized according to homeostatic principles. For example, conflicting cognitions create a state of "mental disequilibrium" (e.g., I smoke and smoking causes cancer; I like Jane and the President whereas Jane dislikes the President). The individual then may bring the system back into balance by, for example, discounting the evidence that smoking causes cancer or devaluing his opinion of Jane.

Given the seeming robustness of the homeostatic principle, why should it not provide the foundation for a theory of human motivation? The major difficulty with this rule of conduct is that the greater part of human behavior cannot be subsumed within the concept of homeostasis. Human often strive to induce states of disequilibrium: We ride roller coasters, read scary mystery stores, seek new and exciting forms of entertainment, and quit comfortable jobs and even comfortable marriages for more challenge. Furthermore, the prominent psychogenic motivations, such as the desire to attain success, win friends, gain power, and help others, apparently fall beyond the range of homeostatic explanations. Such motivational concerns as hunger and thirst may even be overlooked when striving for achievement success, affiliative goals, or spiritual growth. As I am writing this, a leader of the Irish Republican Army is dying while on a hunger strike.

An additional, although somewhat less central point is that not all bodily needs instigate behavior. Theorists who posit automatic connections between internal disequilibrium and behavior have difficulty dealing with this fact. For example, oxygen deprivation may not be motivating unless accompanied by an awareness of this need or by an associated panic reaction. This is beautifully illustrated in the following story from Tomkins (1970):

> Consider anoxic deprivation. Almost any interference with normal breathing will immediately arouse the most desperate gasping for breath. Is there any motivational claim more urgent than the demand of one who is drowning or choking to death for want of air? Yet it is not simply the imperious demand for oxygen that we observe under such circumstances. We also are observing the rapidly mounting panic ordinarily recruited whenever the air supply is suddenly jeopardized. . . . We have only to change the rate of anoxic deprivation to change the nature of the recruited affect. . . Thus, in the Second World War, those pilots who refused to wear their oxygen masks at 30,000 feet suffered a more gradual anoxic deprivation. They did not panic for want of oxygen. They became euphoric. It was the effect of enjoyment which the more slowly developing anoxic signal recruited. Some of these men, therefore, met their deaths with smiles on their lips. (pp. 101–102)

To summarize, homeostatic mechanisms often govern viscerogenic or bodily needs and goal-oriented instrumental behavior. Some psychogenic needs may be guided by the same principles. Hence, the homeostatic analysis was an important conceptual advance in the history of motivation. But the concept of homeostasis cannot account for the variety of human actions, and biologically based needs may not instigate action unless accompanied by appropriate cognitions and/or emotional states. Moreover, my personal belief is that the behaviors best explained by homeostatic principles (eating, drinking, and pain avoidance) may be the least interesting aspects of human activity.

A Theory of Motivation Must Embrace More Than Hedonism

An axiom of virtually all the prior as well as extant theories of motivation is that organisms strive to increase pleasure and to decrease pain. The unassailable acceptance of hedonism, or what is known as the pleasure-pain principle, characterizes both psychoanalytic and drive theories, as well as the influential cognitive theories of motivation proposed by Atkinson (achievement theory), Lewin (field theory), and Rotter (social learning theory). Regarding this fundamental law of behavior, Freud (1920) stated: "The impressions that underlie the hypothesis of the pleasure principle are so obvious that they cannot be overlooked" (p. 1). In addition to these "impressions," hundreds of experiments document that reward (pleasure) increases the probability of repeating a response, whereas punishment (pain) decreases the probability of the response preceding the negative outcome. Homeostatic theories, derived from biology, and hedonism, derived from philosophy, are closely linked, for hedonic theorists assume that a return to a state of equilibrium produces pleasure.

There can be no doubt that the pleasure-pain principle guides human (and infrahuman) conduct; prior theories have not been remiss in having this principle as their foundation. But reward (pleasure) does not inevitably increase the likelihood of a response, nor does punishment (pain) assuredly decrease the probability of the reoccurrence of the punished behavior. For example, an expected reward for the performance of an intrinsically interesting activity (e.g., telling children they will get candy for playing a game they like) can, under some circumstances, reduce the interest in that activity. The children engage in the game less when reward is withdrawn because they come to believe that "playing" was due to the external reward (Deci, 1975; Lepper, Greene, & Nisbett, 1973). In addition, success is considered rewarding, yet if the task was easy, goal attainment reduces motivation and produces boredom (Atkinson, 1964). Finally, the absence of an anticipated reward produces increased motivation to attain the goal (Amsel, 1958) and may stimulate creative vigor.

In addition to the behaviors that are decreased by reward and increased by punishment, Freud pointed out that some of life's activities, including traumatic dreams, games of disappearance (peek-a-boo), and aspects of transference (reenacting significant conflicts with one's parents through the therapist) apparently do not increase pleasure. The pleasure-pain principle also cannot account for the focus of thoughts on, for example, past or present wrongs that others are perceived as having perpetuated (paranoia), goods that one does not possess but others do (envy), or the success of rivals (jealousy). One might contend that such deployment of attention has instrumental value in that goal attainment is promoted. That is, the unpleasant thoughts or behaviors serve the pleasure principle. Quite often, however, this is clearly not the case. What instrumental value is there in being obsessed over one's neighbors' more beautiful homes or their more considerate children?

If humans do not always act as hedonic maximizers, then other motivational principles are needed. As motivational psychologists progressed from the study of infrahuman to the study of human actions, nonhedonic aspects of thinking and acting became increasingly evident. One of the most important of these other "motive forces" is the desire to understand the environment and oneself, or what might be called cognitive mastery. This principle was introduced earlier when asking why individuals so often search for the "why" of an outcome. Cognitive mastery has been thought to instigate behaviors ranging from the acquisition of language to the selection of actions that can reveal information about one's capacities.

Motivational goals are often interrelated and complexly intertwined. For example, cognitive mastery or knowledge aids in goal attainment, which increases pleasure. Thus, it might be contended that mastery is subsumed under hedonic motivation. However, as already indicated, some knowledge has no apparent value for reaching end states. A different reason to believe that mastery is incorporated within the pleasure principle is that information search is influenced by the hedonic desire to increase self-esteem and to protect oneself from anxiety. For example, cancer patients tend to compare themselves with other, more seriously ill victims. This promotes the conclusion that life could be worse, a reassuring thought for the sick as well as the healthy (Taylor, 1983). Here again, mastery or knowledge seems to be in the service of hedonic goals. On the other hand, it is also the case that truth is sought even though the information might cause great displeasure. I am sure that the reader can remember being asked a question preceded by the phase, "Now, tell

Figure 1-1. Some of the consequences of maximizing truth rather than hedonism. © 1982 United Feature Syndicate, Inc.

me the truth..." although the questioner knew full well that the answer might "hurt" (see Figure 1-1). Hence, cognitive mastery cannot merely be encompassed within the pleasure-pain principle.

A Theory of Motivation Must Include the Full Range of Cognitive Processes

Before the advent of behaviorism, thoughts and other mental events played a crucial role in theories of human action. Behaviorism buried this belief with its conception of humans as machines or robots with input-output connections. Behaviorism no longer plays a dominant role in psychology, in part because a mechanistic approach to human motivation is not tenable. After all, we are not robots, machines, or hydraulic pumps. A broad array of mental processes, including information search and retrieval, short- and long-term memory, categorization, judgment, and decision making play essential roles in determining behavior. Just as behavior often is functional, aiding in goal attainment, cognitions also serve adaptive functions for reaching desired end states. Cognitive functionalism must play as central as part in a theory of motivation as behavioral functionalism.

Earlier cognitive conceptions of motivation, such as those formulated by Atkinson (1964), Lewin (1935), Rotter (1954), and Tolman (1925), focused on the expectancy of goal attainment as a major determinant of action. They unfortunately neglected a multitude of other mental structures and processes that influence behavior. This restriction greatly limits the capacity of these theories to account for human conduct.

A Theory of Motivation Must Be Concerned With Conscious Experience

Motivation has been inseparably linked with the study of overt behavior. Throughout the history of this field, well-known books have had behaviorally oriented titles such as *Principles of Behavior* (Hull, 1943), *The Motivation of Behavior* (Brown, 1961), and *The Dynamics of Action* (Atkinson & Birch, 1970). But we experience, feel, and think, as well as act. All these processes have a place within the study of motivation. A theory of motivation is responsible for examining the experiential state of the organism and the meaning of an action. Hence, the theory must embrace phenomenology and accept the position so clearly articulated by Lewin (1935) that organisms act on a perceived, rather than an objective, world.

Associated with this position is my belief that many (but not all) significant thoughts and feelings are conscious and known by the actor. As expressed by Gordon Allport, one should directly ask questions of an individual to gain information about him or her. We may not be aware of psychological processes, or the "hows" of psychology (how we learn, how we perceive, how we remember), but we are often aware of psychological content, or the "whats" of psychology (what we want, what we feel, for what reason we engage in an activity; see Nisbett & Wilson, 1977). If one focuses upon the highly conflicting actions of extreme emotional involvement, as did Freud, then repression and other dynamic processes may produce a discrepancy between the conscious and the "true" determinants of action. In addition, if attention is primarily directed to complex judgments, as exemplified in the work of decision theorists, or to inferences in esoteric, multistimuli situations, then the limits of human information processing may give rise to inaccuracies regarding self-observations. However, for the typical and prevalent aspects of being, that is, considering how life is spent and what is reflected upon, direct access to the determinants of motivation and emotion is quite possible. For most of us most of the time, a royal road to the unconscious is less valuable to the motivation researcher than is the dirt road to consciousness.

A Theory of Motivation Must Include the Self

This principle is closely related to the earlier contention that a theory must be concerned with consciousness and the subjective world, for the experience of the self is part of phenomenal reality. There are numerous indications that the self plays a fundamental role in human motivation: Many actions serve to sustain or enhance self-esteem; one's self-concept frequently determines one's thoughts and behaviors; individuals tend to maintain self-consistency in their actions; and self-perception provides one thread to the stability of personality and behavior over time. The concept of the self has been neglected in the study of motivation. It surely did not fit into behavioristic conceptions, which used lower organisms as their main source of experimental evidence. In addition, the cognitive theories of motivation focused on the more manageable concept of subjective expectancy, perhaps preferring to postpone a consideration of the subtle and vague role played by concern with the self. However, the self lies at the very core of human experience and must be part of any theoretical formulation in the field of human motivation.

A Theory of Motivation Must Include the Full Range of Emotions

One might anticipate that the study of motivation and the study of emotion would be intimately linked. In support of this expectation, a psychological journal exists with the title *Motivation and Emotion*, and psychology courses often carry the same name. Surprisingly, theories of motivation have incorporated only the pleasure-pain principle of emotion, even though this crude delineation is manifestly inadequate for describing feelings. Even the pleasures associated with aggression and sexual fulfillment, which formed the basis for the all-embracing notion of pleasure advanced by Freud, are quite likely to be distinct. I doubt that the emotion associated with the killing of father is akin to the pleasure of sleeping with mother! In addition, these feelings certainly are distinguishable from the emotions derived from occupational attainment or social success, such as pride or feelings of competence. In a similar manner, distinct "pains" surely are linked with unsatisfied hostility and unfulfilled sexual desires, and these doubtless differ from the feelings that accompany achievement failure or social rejection.

The theory of achievement motivation formulated by Atkinson (1964) does consider emotions characterized by labels other than pleasure and pain. Atkinson suggested that whether one approaches or avoids an achievement-related goal depends on the anticipated affective consequences of pride and shame. However, this conception does not acknowledge other emotions that are manifest in achievement contexts, such as happiness and unhappiness, anger and gratitude, and humiliation and pity. Thus, Atkinson's theory also fails to give emotions their rightful place in motivation.

Individuals experience a great diversity of emotions, which are intertwined with thoughts and actions. One of the goals of the theory presented in this book is to set forth precisely the relations between the tripartite division of psychology into cognition, affect, and behavior. In so doing, it will be demonstrated that motivation cannot be understood without a detailed analysis of emotion.

A Theory of Motivation Must Be Neither Too General nor Too Precise

From the fate of the psychoanalytic and drive theories, one can draw the conclusion that a theory must have some optimal level of breadth and precision. Perhaps the greatest virtue of the psychoanalytic conception of motivation was its range of convenience, its capability of addressing phenomena as disparate as war, wit, and neurosis. But in psychology the range of a theory correlates inversely with its ability to make exact predictions. Thus, the strength of the psychoanalytic conception also greatly contributed to its weakening position in the field of motivation.

In sharp contrast to the psychoanalytic approach, drive theory, as formulated by Clark Hull and Kenneth Spence, has limited breadth but, in certain contexts, great precision. Its rather exact theoretical predictions were most often tested with laboratory rats engaged in a simple behavior such as running down a straight alleyway for food. Unfortunately, these data are not of great value when attempting to generalize to complex human activities.

In sum, if theory is too broad (like psychoanalytic theory), then at this point in the history of motivation it will have little exactness; if too precise (like drive theory), then at this point in time the theory will have little breadth and generality. Hence, a careful path must be taken between the two-headed dangers of precision and generality.

A Theory of Motivation Must Be Built Upon Reliable
(Replicable) Empirical Relations

An adequate theory of motivation provides the opportunity for the creation of a
laboratory course or some other setting where a variety of derivations from the theory can be demonstrated *with certainty*. This is true in the natural sciences and
should apply to psychology as well. One of the reasons for the acceptance and
popularity of Skinnerian psychology is the demonstration that the frequency of a
response increases when an organism is rewarded for a particular behavior. Watching pigeons play ping-pong seems to be a sufficient antecedent for conversion to radical behaviorism!

Motivational theories are deficient in this respect. For example, regarding the
unequal recall of completed versus incompleted tasks, or what is known as the
Zeigarnik effect, Lewin (1935) stated, "All later experimental investigations were
built upon this" (p. 240). However, the differential recall observed by Lewin and
Zeigarnik is not a reliable finding. In a similar manner, Atkinson (1964) contended
that individuals classified as high versus low in achievement needs exhibit opposing
risk preferences when given tasks differing in perceived difficulty. This central
prediction from Atkinson's conception is not reliably found, and one suspects this is
partially responsible for the lessening influence of his conception. Further, differences in expectancy shifts between people labeled internal versus external in their
perceptions of control cannot reliably be demonstrated, although this is a fundamental prediction of Rotter's (1966) social learning theory.

One cannot build a theory on a weak "reference experiment," that is, an experiment that provides the standard for evaluating the theory. Motivational theories
must have reference experiments with results as certain as the outcome of mixing
two parts hydrogen and one part oxygen, or of giving a hungry rat food when it
engages in a particular behavior.

A Theory of Motivation Must Be Based on General Laws
Rather Than Individual Differences

Atkinson (1964) has been especially visible and persuasive among the motivational
psychologists who argue that individual differences play a central role in the study
of motivational processes. As already indicated, in Atkinson's theory of achievement strivings, persons labeled high in achievement needs are predicted to exhibit
different risk-taking behavior than persons low in achievement needs. Disparities
between individuals are therefore central to the testing of this conception. Atkinson's theory then falls prey to all the complex issues and obstacles faced by trait psychologists. For example, persons are not equally motivated to achieve in all
situations; in other words, there is discriminativeness in behavior. Individuals may
be highly motivated to achieve in tennis, but not in the classroom, or perhaps not
even at other sports such as baseball. Atkinson's theoretical formulation does not
recognize this possibility—individuals merely are classified as high or low in

achievement needs. It is not surprising that tests of this theory, which occur in many disparate situational contexts, often prove unsatisfactory.

In a similar manner, Rotter's current conception of social learning is linked with an individual difference labeled *locus of control*. However, individuals are not equally motivated to have or to relinquish control in all settings, and they might perceive control of reinforcement as possible in some situations but not in others. For example, perceptions of success as due to internal (personal) factors are uncorrelated with perceptions of failure as internally caused (see review in Weiner, 1980c). Specificity is not well integrated into the theory, and hypotheses using perception of control as a predictor variable are often disconfirmed. The classroom demonstrator in a laboratory course again would be embarrassed.

Indeed, one might claim that a *reliable* set of theory-generated findings that include individual difference measures has yet to be offered in the study of motivation. Here I am particularly thinking of studies using measures of drive (the Manifest Anxiety Scale), achievement needs (the Thematic Apperception Test), and locus of control (the Internal-External Scale). Others surely will disagree; the courts of science will have to render a final decision. But I would like to ask theorists of these persuasions, What single experiment are you willing to wager on as yielding differences between your designated groupings of people?

In sum, given the difficulties of personality measurement and the situational specificity of behavior, it will be more fruitful to search first for general laws rather than explore Person × Situation interactions. This can then be followed, if necessary, by the inclusion of individual differences to refine the generalizations that have been made or to uncover more complex associations that might have been overlooked.

An identical position has been expressed by many psychologists. For example, Festinger poetically stated:

> The philosophical ideas that explain [the ignoring of individual differences] are easy to locate. They are perhaps best expressed in the paper by Lewin on Aristotelian and Galilean conceptions of science. Too much concern with individual differences could create a mask that hid the underlying dynamic processes. These underlying processes had to be discovered. The kind of analogy that existed in our minds was something like the following. It would be hopeless to have tried to discover the laws concerning free-falling objects by concentrating on measuring the different rates of descent of stones, feathers, pieces of paper, and the like. It is only after the basic dynamic laws are known that one can make sense of the individual differences.
>
> The way I have always thought about it is that if the empirical world looks complicated, if people seem to react in bewildering different ways to similar forces, and if I cannot see the operation of universal underlying dynamics—then it is my fault. I have asked the wrong questions; I have, at the theoretical level, sliced the world up incorrectly. The underlying dynamics are there, and I have to find the theoretical apparatus that will enable me to reveal these uniformities. (Festinger, 1980, p. 246)

Although operating from a quite different theoretical perspective, Berlyne (1968) reached the same conclusion. He stated:

It is perfectly obvious that human beings are different from one another in some respects but alike in other respects. The question is whether we should first look for statements that apply to all of them or whether we should first try to describe and explain their differences. The behavior theorist feels that research for common principles of human and animal behavior must take precedence. This, he would point out, is how scientific inquiry must proceed....Until we can see what individuals of a class or species have in common, we cannot hope to understand how their dissimilarities have come about or even to find the most fruitful way to describe and classify these dissimilarities. (p. 640)

This is perhaps the only instance in this book where agreement with a behaviorist is found or admitted.

A Theory of Motivation Must Include Sequential (Historical) Causal Relations

The prominent theories of motivation, with the exception of the psychoanalytic approach, are ahistorical. These theories attempt to identify the immediate determinants of action, such as drive and habit, or expectancy and value, and specify the manner in which they influence behavior at a given moment in time. The antecedent historical conditions, or why an individual perceives the present situation as he or she does, is not necessary to predict behavior. What is essential is the specification of the present determinants of action.

One of the shortcomings of an ahistorical approach is that the influence of the components of the theory on one another have to be ignored. In expectancy-value theories, for example, if value is biased upward by high expectancy (one likes what one can get), or if high value biases expectancy upward (one expects to get what one likes), then a temporal sequence is implicated. In these instances, the magnitudes of the components in the theory cannot be determined simultaneously; respectively, value cannot be ascertained prior to expectancy, or expectancy prior to value. This is illustrated in Figure 1-2, along with the ahistorical expectancy-value approach.

The ahistorical analysis of motivational processes was enhanced by the growth of parametric statistics, particularly the analysis of variance. This technique enables investigators to determine which factors are affecting the dependent variable at a moment in time, and allows the mathematical relations between the independent variables to be specified. A newer approach in statistical analysis is causal modeling,

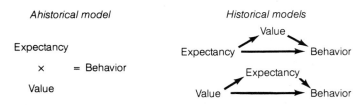

Figure 1-2. Ahistorical and historical approaches to motivation.

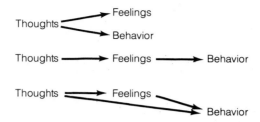

Figure 1-3. Some possible relations between thoughts, feelings, and action.

including path analysis. This methodology helps in uncovering the causal chain of influencing factors. Acceptance of a historical sequence suggests that one should search for the causal relations between the determinants of action.

One of the essential sequences examined in this book concerns the relations between thinking, feeling, and acting. I have already contended that a theory of motivation should include the full range of both thoughts and feelings. But how do these influence behavior? Many possibilities arise. It might be that 1) thoughts produce both feelings and behavior; or that 2) thoughts antedate feelings, whereas feelings give rise to action; or that 3) thoughts generate feelings, and thoughts and feelings together produce behavior. These possible permutations are shown in Figure 1-3. The historical position adopted in this book permits exploration of these different possibilities.

A Theory of Motivation Must Explain Rational and Irrational Actions, Using the Same Concepts for Both

Human behavior is varied and complex. Many behaviors are quite rational: Consciously selected strategies help control stress and anxiety (consider the current jogging craze), goal expectancies are calculated, information is sought and processed, and self-insight is attained. On the other hand, many aspects of our conduct are quite irrational: Plans that could control stress, anxiety, and smoking are abandoned; expectancies are biased; information is improperly utilized; and there is great personal delusion. Psychoanalytic theory has best explained some of the apparent unreasonableness in our lives, whereas the cognitive conceptions and decision theories are more adept at dealing with the sensibility of action, although these theories are increasingly pointing out the boundaries of rationality.

Kant contended that reason guides moral behavior, whereas the passions determine all other aspects of life. Psychological research, however, has documented that passions such as anger, pity, and sympathy in part direct moral actions, and a variety of intelligent judgments influence other motivated behaviors. The division suggested by Kant is therefore not justified. Rather, behavior has both ego (thinking) and id (emotional) components. Dichotomies between logically driven and emotionally driven actions are not justified. A theory of human behavior must be able to explain the moral and the amoral using the same principles. This belief reaffirms that an adequate theory must include diverse cognitions and emotions, as well as clarify the relations between the basic motivational components of reason, passion, and action.

A Theory of Motivation Must Be Able to Account for Achievement Strivings and Affiliative Goals

A theory has a focus and a range of convenience—observations that can be best explained, and observations to which the theory can be generalized. The focus of convenience of a theory of human motivation should be those activities that are most prevalent in everyday life. It would be unwise to base a general theory of human motivation on very uncommon behaviors. Hence, psychoanalytic theory, which is grounded on sexual and aggressive relations among family members, and Hullian theory, which examined the behavior of hungry and thirsty rats, developed conceptual frameworks inadequate to account for the modal activities of humans. Psychological theory and experimentation have been overly focused on the esoteric—on behaviors or thoughts that account for little of life's variance.

In our culture, two sources of motivation are most dominant: achievement strivings and social bonding. Freud recognized these with the more general terms of *Arbeit und Liebe* (work and love). Most preadults at a given moment are either in school, doing schoolwork, engaged in some other achievement-related activity such as sports or a hobby, or are with their friends of the same or the opposite sex. Adults typically are working in their selected occupation or are engaged in social activities with their friends or family. Of course, there are many other motivational pursuits: aggression, altruism, curiosity, lust, and power, to name just a few. But the most prevalent concerns are achievement success and social acceptance. Self-esteem has been documented to be determined by experiences of competence and incompetence in the achievement domain, and by acceptance and rejection in the interpersonal arena (O'Brien & Epstein, 1974). These topics therefore should be at the focus of a theory of human motivation.

If the above advice is followed, then the formulated theory undoubtedly will not readily account for the unconscious desires pointed out by psychoanalytic theory or behavior generated by food and water deprivation. This might seem to contradict a conceptual goal stated earlier, namely, the development of a *general* theory. The word *general* needs to be qualified to capture the current state of psychology: Any given conception cannot account for the supposed desire to sleep with mother and kill father, the longing for food when hungry and water when thirsty, and the strivings to accomplish success and enhance social networks. In light of this limitation, a reasonable strategy is to explain those behaviors that are most common, most usual, most exhibited. I believe these behaviors are the pursuits of social and emotional bonds and life accomplishments.

Summary

Twelve principles have been outlined that form the foundation for the general theory of motivation and emotion presented in this book. A theory of motivation must:

1. Be based on a concept other than homeostasis
2. Embrace more than hedonism
3. Include the full range of cognitive processes
4. Be concerned with conscious experience
5. Include the self
6. Include the full range of emotions
7. Be neither too general nor too precise
8. Be built upon reliable (replicable) empirical relations
9. Be based on general laws rather than individual differences
10. Include sequential (historical) causal relations
11. Explain rational and irrational actions, using the same concepts for both
12. Account for achievement strivings and affiliative goals.

I do have a confession. The principles listed above were not a priori axioms upon which a theory of motivation was constructed. Rather, a theory slowly emerged, and with it came a set of sometimes justifying, sometimes clarifying, often bootstrapped principles. The attribution theory presented in this book thus takes into account all the preceding 12 principles, although not with equal satisfaction.

Theoretical Overview and Plan of the Book

At the risk of shocking or discouraging the reader, the attributional theory of motivation championed in this book is presented in Figure 1-4. The chapters that follow examine in detail the individual paths or associations comprised within the conception. For now, the reader need not be concerned with the precise meaning of each relation. Rather, the entire theory is depicted at this time to aid in the understanding of the logical progression of the chapters.

Figure 1-4 shows that a motivational sequence or episode is initiated following an event outcome, particularly success or failure at an achievement-related activity or acceptance or rejection at a social encounter. In accordance with Principle 12, the theory is thus especially appropriate in the explanation of *Arbeit und Liebe*. In addition to the positive and negative affects that follow from these outcomes (see the arrows from outcome to the labels of "happy" and "sad"), Figure 1-4 reveals that under certain conditions (unexpected, negative, or important outcomes) a search for causality is instigated. In Chapter 2 of this book it is documented that people do indeed engage in such attributional activities. Chapter 2 also describes the typical causal ascriptions used to explain achievement-related success and failure, although the antecedents used to determine causal decisions (such as specific information and causal rules) are not discussed. Chapter 3 then progresses from description to

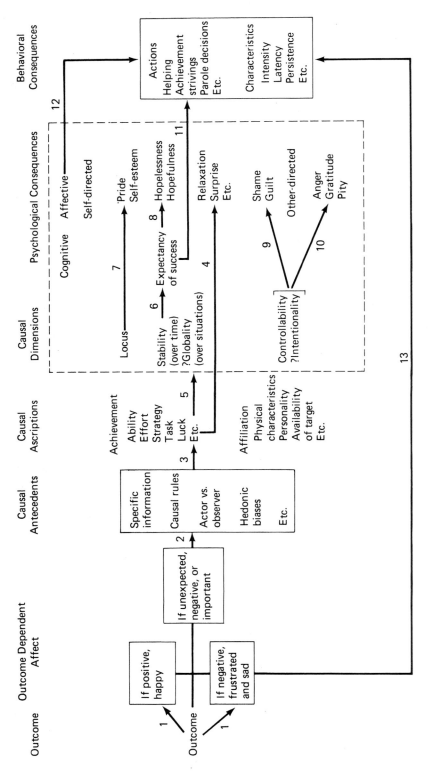

Figure 1-4. An attributional theory of motivation and emotion.

taxonomy. It is revealed that there is a simple organization of causal thinking, with three main proprerties (locus, stability, and controllability) surely represented in causal structure, while two other characteristics (intentionality and globality) perhaps are represented. Thus, causes of achievement-related success and failure, such as ability or luck, and causes of social acceptance and rejection, such as physical characteristics and the availability of the desired partner, can be described on the properties of locus (internal or external to the actor), stability (unstable or enduring), and controllability (controllable or uncontrollable). Qualitatively distinct causes across disparate motivational domains may then be compared and contrasted, thus aiding theoretical generality. I then examine the consequences of causal reasoning, advancing a genotypic analysis of thinking, feeling, and action. Hence, there is a progression from cognitive structure (Chapter 3) to the dynamics of behavior (Chapters 4 through 8). Chapter 4 presents the logic and empirical evidence supporting the belief that one of the basic properties of causes, namely, their perceived endurance or stability, influences expectancy of success. The reader may recall that expectancy of future success is a key cognitive component of action in the motivational theories of Atkinson, Lewin, Rotter, and Tolman. In Chapter 5 the discussion turns toward the emotions. Here it is documented that affective states are linked with causal explanations—feelings including pride, hopelessness, guilt, anger, gratitude, shame, and pity are related to causal structure. Thus, the theory includes a large range of emotions, as demanded in Principle 6. Chapter 6 then provides a theoretical integration, documenting that the components in the theory, particularly expectancy and affect, relate to achievement strivings. In Chapter 7, the theory is generalized beyond the achievement domain, and the topics of helping behavior, parole decisions, smoking cessation, and reactions to airline flight delays are examined. In Chapter 8 I turn toward relations in the theory that were previously neglected, focusing on feedback loops and bidirectional linkages. Finally, Chapter 9 presents a laboratory course in attribution theory; it is contended that each of the linkages in the theory is sufficiently robust that a classroom demonstrator can confidently replicate the associations in a classroom setting. Recall that this was one of the principles of theory construction. Indeed, throughout the book the consistency and the strength of the supporting data are highlighted. I believe that this degree of empirical confirmation does not characterize any other general conception of motivation.

Part I
The Components of the Theory

Chapter 2
A Description of Perceived Causality

In which causes are defined and spontaneous
attributional search is documented. The perceived
causes of success and failure, based on many empiri-
cal investigations, are determined, as are lay expla-
nations of wealth, poverty, and illness. The small
number of dominant causal explanations is noted.

Causal perceptions are instrumental to goal attainment and aid in the pursuit of cognitive mastery. Thus, they serve the two most basic motivators of behavior: hedonism and understanding. In addition, the search for causality does not appear to be constrained within any particular time and place in history. For these reasons, it was contended in chapter 1 that attributions of causality may provide the foundation for a general theory of motivation and emotion. As already intimated, the argument of this cellist is that a correct note has been found.

I therefore now turn to the topic of causes. A number of associated problems are addressed in this chapter. The first questions bear upon the definition of a cause: What is a cause? Does it differ from a reason? Is it something other than the assignment of responsibility? A second set of questions concerns the prevalence of causal explanations in everyday life: Are causes as common as have been hinted here? Do individuals always search for causality, or is this cognitive activity elicited only in certain contexts or only among certain persons? And how can the everyday existence of causal search be documented scientifically? Finally, a third general topic pertains to the content of causal perceptions: What are the salient causal ascriptions? Are some especially dominant? Do attributions about causality differ across content domains so that, for example, the causes of achievement success and failure are perceived to differ from the causes of economic outcomes (wealth and poverty)? Conversely, are elicited causes similar across activities? For example, are the perceived causes of exam success and a sporting victory the same? In this chapter the question of definition is first examined, followed more fully by a description of the when and the what (the elements) of causality.

A Working Definition

The analysis of causality has a long and a complex history; it would be unrealistic to entertain the idea that I might add to or clarify this established field of philosophical inquiry. I shall merely convey at the outset what I mean by the word "cause" (which is equivalent here to causal perception, causal attribution, and causal ascription).

The answer to a "why" question regarding an outcome is considered a cause (see Braithwaite, 1959; Kidd & Amabile, 1981). Causes elucidate such questions as: Why did I fail my exam? Why is Bill doing so well on this job, after he performed so poorly at the previous ones? Why did Jane refuse to marry me? Causes are constructions imposed by the perceiver (either an actor or an observer) to account for the relation between an action and an outcome. Note that causal ascription as used here refers to why an *outcome* has occurred, as opposed to why an *action* has taken place. Causes pertain to why Bill is doing well or poorly at his job, and not to why he is working at all. Later in this book there is a discussion of how one explains or accounts for failing to arrive for an appointment (an outcome), but why the appointment was made (an action) is not examined.

In the recent psychological literature it has been contended that causes should be distinguished from reasons (see Buss, 1978; Kruglanski, 1979; Locke & Pennington, 1982). Reasons, it is suggested, are justifications for an action and thus may be a particular kind of cause (see Davidson, 1963). For example, John may justify going out with Pam by pointing out her sincerity. He intends to go out with her, and the reason for the intent is described as a personality characteristic. On the other hand, causes need not justify an action. For example, an observer might explain John's attraction to Pam by noting that, although John does not recognize it, Pam resembles his mother. This is not a justification for an intended action; instead, it is an antecedent of a particular occurrence. The cause-reason distinction has merit (see Locke & Pennington, 1982); it will be seen that in this book we are concerned with causes, some of which might also be reasons.

The attribution of causality may also result in an assignment of responsibility. For example, assume that Mary did poorly in school because she rarely studied. Mary is held responsible (able to respond) and accountable for her inaction, inasmuch as the behavior was carried out "purposely," "knowingly," "recklessly," and/or "negligently" (see Fincham & Jaspers, 1980). Among the possible consequences of being held responsible are the invocation of some form of punishment from others and the potential experience of guilt. But it is evident that not all causes are attributions of responsibility, just as not all causes are reasons. Mary is not held responsible if the failure was caused by low aptitude or illness, which do not fulfill any of the inferential criteria (purpose, foresight, etc.) enumerated above. Hence, an attribution of responsibility presupposes one of causality, but not vice versa (see Shultz & Schleifer, 1983).

It must always be remembered that a cause is imposed or inferred by an attributor. Hence, the study of attribution is part of a phenomenological pursuit. One individual's positive judgment of responsibility (i.e., that a result was caused knowingly or recklessly) may be contradicted by the beliefs of another. Of course, that issue is at the heart of many court battles.

Causal Search in Everyday Life

An integral part of the attributional approach has involved studies to ascertain causal perceptions, particularly the perceived causes of success and failure in achievement-related situations. These investigations frequently induced success or failure, had research participants recall a real-life success or failure, or asked them to imagine a positive or a negative outcome given some task. At times, rather than have subjects focus on themselves, the success or failure of another person was considered. Following the experimenter-manipulated or real-life outcome, the research participants were asked about causality. On some occasions, a free-response format was used, with subjects generating their own causal inferences. In other investigations, a list of causes was provided, and the likelihood that each cause influenced the outcome was rated on some kind of scale. These studies generated data about the salience of particular attributions and were assumed to provide prima facie evidence for the importance of attributional thinking in everyday life (see reviews in Kelley & Michela, 1980; Weiner, 1980c).

It was only after many such investigations that psychologists began to raise doubts about the methodology being used. The basic dissatisfaction was that the experimental procedure was reactive; that is, the responses of the subjects were believed to be influenced by the experimenter's introducing the notion of causality (Bem, 1972; Enzle & Shopflacher, 1978; Wortman & Dintzer, 1978). Perhaps the research participants would not have made any attributions if they had been free from the prodding of the research investigators. That is, it was contended that causal thoughts were elicited by the procedure rather than emitted by the subjects. The investigators were accused of not addressing the issue of whether individuals engage in *spontaneous* attributional activities. As Smith and Miller (1983) clarified: "The skeptic will agree that perceivers produce attributional inferences on request . . . and yet deny that this ability is of much importance or is used frequently in the ordinary course of things" (p. 492).

Documentation of spontaneous attributional activity is a very difficult task. The experimenter must act as a transducer, observing and recording instances of everyday behavior, which are then coded for the presence of causal ascriptions (see Barker, 1965). One can readily imagine the tremendous difficulties associated with this procedure, including issues of time and subject sampling. However, these troubles would be associated with a request to demonstrate any thought content. For example, suppose that a group of psychologists argued that we characterize others with trait labels. To prove this, they might ask subjects to describe others and then code the responses for traits. This, however, is a reactive methodology; a skeptic might argue that in everyday life we do not waste time by labeling others. To demonstrate the spontaneous use of trait labels, some sort of observational and coding technique or indirect indicator would have to be developed (see Winter & Uleman, 1984). Perhaps, then, it has been unfair to ask for such "spontaneous" documentation only from attribution theorists.

Even if such a procedure could be mastered, it might still have low validity. The research participants may be thinking about causal attributions or trait descriptions, yet not exhibit or verbalize these thoughts. After all, causal communications and trait labels can have far-reaching interpersonal consequences. What, then, are some other possible alternatives that may be used to document spontaneous attributional activity?

Three methodologies are evolving in the 1980s. Each has specific advantages and shortcomings. One procedure, which has the advantage of not requiring experi-

menter intervention, involves the coding of written material from newspaper articles, business reports, letters, and personal journals. The remaining two methodologies require experimental intervention. In one procedure, subjects have been asked
to think aloud during or after task engagement, report what they had been thinking,
or interact with one another. Verbalizations are then recorded and coded for causal
attributions. Finally, in a more indirect method that involves different specific
procedures, causal search has been inferred from cognitive processes such as information seeking, free recall of previously read material, and sentence completion.

Twenty investigations using these research approaches to spontaneous attributional activity have been uncovered, with 14 published between 1983 and 1985. The
findings allow rather unequivocal conclusions and lay to rest the uncertainty about
the prevalence of attributional thinking in everyday life. In addition, there is agreement on the conditions that promote attributional search (see Weiner, 1985a).

Coding of Written Material

The coding of written material for particular psychological content has precedent in
psychology. Among the most well-known uses of this procedure was the attempt by
McClelland (1961) to score childrens' readers for need achievement. Coding of
written material was first used in the search for spontaneous attributions by Lau and
Russell (1980). These investigators examined 107 newspaper articles covering 33
major sporting events in eight different newspapers. The articles selected had to be
"long enough [so that they were not] . . . limited to descriptions of the game" (p. 31).
In addition, the articles "for the most part" were from the city of one of the teams
involved, and included six games of the baseball World Series. Hence, this was not
a random sample of all written sports-related material, and the events were likely to
be considered important in the city of the participants. This investigation therefore
did not address the question, How much written material in the sports page is
attributional? The answer to that question requires a different sampling procedure.
In fairness to Lau and Russell (1980), their investigation was concerned with the
kinds of attributions made and attributional antecedents, rather than with a
documentation of the absolute frequency of causal ascriptions in the sports pages.
Nevertheless, their data include frequency figures: 594 causal explanations were
identified in the 107 articles, or about 5.5 ascriptions per article.

Lau and Russell (1980) analyzed causal ascriptions separately for wins and losses
(outcome) as well as determining whether the outcome was expected or unexpected.
To operationalize expectancy, the odds in a game as established by a recognized
gambling agency were ascertained. If a favored team lost, an underdog team won, or
the predicted win or loss was much greater than the oddsmaker had anticipated, then
the event was considered unexpected. Lau and Russell did not find differences in
attributions for wins versus losses. However, unexpected outcomes elicited a greater
number of attempts at explanation than did expected results.

Lau (1984) later used this procedure to follow attributions for particular sports
teams over time. Thus, the events sampled were not independent. Again many attri-

butions were identified (2,269 in 176 articles, or 12.9 ascriptions per article). In direct opposition to the findings of Lau and Russell (1980), Lau reported no differences in attributional activity following unexpected versus expected outcomes, although there were more attributions made for a loss than for a victory. Furthermore, the differential attributional activity as a function of outcome increased over time (i.e., with nearness to the end of the sport season).

The coding of written material in the newspapers has not been limited to sports articles. Foersterling and Groenvald (1983) examined attributional statements regarding a political win or loss. In 1981, local elections were held in Lower Saxony, Germany. One party was the clear victor in terms of number of political seats gained. The editions of all the community newspapers in Lower Saxony published the day after the election returns were announced were analyzed for causal statements. Foersterling and Groenvald (1983) located 23 newspapers, which contained 123 articles covering the election. The authors identified 354 attributional comments, or about three explanatory statements for each article. Attributional statements also were examined separately regarding the winners and losers of the election. As Lau (1984) later reported, attributional activity was elicited more by failure than by success. Foersterling and Groenvald did not examine causal ascriptions as a function of the expectancy of the outcome.

A fourth investigation examining written material in the newspapers examined advice columns (Schoeneman & Rubanowitz, 1983, 1985). It was thought that advice columns:

> are nicely encapsulated commentaries on highly involving social interactions. . . . As an additional advantage, the explanations of correspondents and columnists alike center on "real-life" social situations, as opposed to the game-oriented outcomes on sports pages; this should enhance the ecological validity of attributions extracted from this source. (Schoeneman & Rubanowitz, 1983, p. 4)

Letters and replies were sampled from the two widely read advice columns of "Ann Landers" and "Dear Abby." Fifteen daily columns were randomly selected from each advisor, yielding approximately 30 letters and replies for each columnist.

This sampling procedure is subject to much greater biasing than the previous three studies. First, only a unique subset of individuals write such letters. Furthermore, fewer than 5% of these letters are chosen for publication, on the basis of unknown criteria. However, whether the letters published do or do not accurately portray the thoughts of the public, they do determine the amount of attributional material that the reader is exposed to in these advice columns.

Among the 61 letters, 200 instances of explanatory statements were identified, or about 3.3 per letter and reply (e.g., "She isn't able to do her job because she is drunk"). It is not possible to relate attributional material to outcome in these letters (the outcomes were predominantly negative) or to expectation.

Three additional investigations examining causal attributions made use of sources other than the newspaper. Bettman and Weitz (1983) scrutinized the novel source of corporate annual reports ("Letters to the Shareholders"), reasoning that these reports provide "fairly comparable sets of data from a broad sample of corporations" (p. 171). Whereas the public statements of well-known sports figures and politicians are likely to be subject to response withholding. Bettman and Weitz (1983) suggested that this might be less likely in corporate reports. Such statements, which are analyzed by the shareholders, must be accurate and avoid bias. They additionally reflect the thinking of many and are based on group decisions. However, none of these conditions preclude attributional biasing, and one suspects that the reports are likely to be less than entirely objective.

Reports from two years, one of economic prosperity and a second of economic decline, were chosen for analysis. Four industries were surveyed: metal mining, aircraft, scientific instruments, and telecommunications. A random sample of approximately 50 companies representing each industry were contacted for their reports, with a response rate greater than 95%.

The instances of causal reasoning in each report were identified according to the typical criterion: "A phrase or sentence in which some performance outcome, such as profits, sales, or return from investment, was linked with a reason for that outcome" (Bettman & Weitz, 1983, p. 173). For example, "Company sales increased because of new product introduction and creative advertising" was scored for the presence of attributions, whereas "Sales and prices increased" was not considered a causal explanation of success.

Bettman and Weitz (1983) identified 421 attributions, or 2.33 per "Letter." In contrast to the conclusions possible from the studies already reviewed, this figure might be considered representative of the mean amount of attributional content in all "Letters to the Shareholders." Bettman and Weitz also analyzed both outcome and expectancies as determinants of attributions. Within each "Letter," the companies addressed some positive and some negative outcomes. This contrasts with the exclusive win or loss experienced by a team in a sporting event or by a politician in an election. Expectancy was more difficult to determine. An indirect measure was derived from objective evidence related to the current performance of the company compared to its baseline performance during the previous year. Percentage change in profits was calculated, and the lowest one third of the companies were considered to be operating below expectations, whereas the highest one third in terms of percentage increments in profit were believed to be functioning above expectations. Bettman and Weitz found a significant expectancy effect consistent with other research: More causal reasoning was displayed when companies did worse or better than anticipated.

Another investigation, this one conducted by Salancik and Meindl (1984), also examined attributions in "Letters to the Shareholders." These investigators were primarily interested in the hedonic bias, or the tendency for the company to take more credit for success than blame for failure. Following Bettman and Weitz (1983), causal attributions in the reports of 18 corporations were examined, although in this study the reports spanned the years 1961 through 1978 and involved 324 "Letters." Approximately 10% of the selected pages contained a causal attribution. Attributions were not examined as a function of expectancy or outcome, although it appears from the data that more attributions were made for success than for failure, which contradicts prior findings. This latter finding was traceable to the hedonic bias, for far more internal attributions were reported for success than for failure.

A third investigation using archival material other than newspapers adopted methods from discourse analysis (Staton, 1984). Children in a sixth-grade class were required to write "dialogue journals" during the course of the school year. The journals contained private conversations between each student and his or her teacher that were written daily in class. They therefore "provided a record of the spontaneous thinking of children about the important events in their lives" (Staton, 1984, p. 1). Twenty-six such dialogues, obtained at two widely separated times during the school year, were scored for a variety of content material, including causal attributions. Staton (1984) reported that each dialogue contained about one causal attribution. This finding characterized both the statements of the children as well as those of their teacher. Nearly two thirds of the causal attributions involved negative outcomes; data regarding expectancy were not reported.

In summary, seven investigations have been conducted that examine causal thinking in written material, without experimental intervention. All suffer from possible shortcomings, such as response bias and unrepresentative sampling. Nonetheless, the set of data is persuasive. There is consistent evidence of a great deal of attributional exposure and thinking in everyday life, and this is exhibited in very diverse written material (Table 2-1). In addition, negative and unexpected outcomes appear to especially promote attributional thinking.

Coding of Verbalizations

The difficulties of documenting spontaneous attributional activity in everyday life were previously discussed. In spite of such obstacles, one ambitious study has been reported that unobtrusively recorded verbal interactions (Nisbett, Harvey, & Wilson, 1979; report in Nisbett & Ross, 1980). Nisbett et al. (1979) "bugged" 13 "haphazardly selected" conversations that included participants ranging from students to senior citizens. Nisbett and Ross (1980) summarized that:

> Statements expressing or requesting causal analysis were remarkably frequent, accounting for 15 percent, on the average, of all utterances. Even for the conversation in which causal analysis was least frequent (in the senior citizens' picnic), causal analysis accounted for 5 percent of all utterances" (p. 184)

Given the experimental difficulties and ethical problems in such research, it is not surprising that this is the only study of its kind reported. Rather, most studies of spontaneous causal thinking have involved some sort of known experimental intervention. What are free to vary are the reports of the subjects, which are not directed by the experimenter toward causal attributions. Four experiments have examined causal verbalizations during task performance (Brunson & Matthews, 1981; Carroll & Payne, 1977a; Diener & Dweck, 1978; Gioia & Sims, 1983), one study asked for retrospective reports of thinking that occurred during task performance (Anderson, 1983b), and four investigations analyzed causal thinking after task completion (Gilovich, 1983; Holtzworth-Monroe & Jacobson, 1985; Mikula & Schlamberger, 1985; Wong & Weiner, 1981). These studies primarily took place in achievement-related settings or pertained to explanations of achivement-related behavior, because situations had to be constructed or selected that encourage attributional search. If one asks for thoughts during a musical or when picking flowers, causal thinking is not likely to be prominent (although one might ask why the musician is playing so well or so poorly, or why the flowers are doing so well or so badly this year). Recall that the written material coded for attributions pertained to sporting events, political elections, corporate reports, marital problems, and school-related concerns, not social engagements or want ads. The research to be reported therefore is not a random sample of thinking, any more than the prior studies reviewed were a random sample of all written material. However, it will also be seen that the research included the study of attributions for interpersonal actions and for perceived social injustice.

The first investigation making use of spontaneous verbal reports to examine attributions (Carroll & Payne, 1977a) is noteworthy in that it also is one of the few investigations not occurring in situations where performance would result in immediate success or failure. Carroll and Payne (1977a) examined the role of attributions in parole decision making. They documented that, when making a parole decision, the parole officers search for the cause of the crime, primarily to determine the risk of the criminal to society. In one method of directly probing this process, verbal protocols were collected from parole decision makers as they examined actual case history material. It was observed that, "Having established the criminal history, the expert turns to look at the characteristics of the criminal that are interpreted diagnostically as predictors of future behavior and causally as postdictors of past crimes" (Carroll & Weiner, 1982, p. 240).

Spontaneous verbal reports in situations where success or failure were immediate possible outcomes were first examined by Diener and Dweck (1978), who induced children to fail at an experimental task. These children, like the parole officers in the Carroll and Payne (1977) research, were asked to "think out loud" while working. The verbalizations were then coded for a number of categories, including attributional statements. These children also were categorized as "helpless" or "mastery-oriented" on the basis of their scores on the Intellectual Achievement Responsibility scale. Subjects labeled as helpless tend not to ascribe success or failure to effort on this questionnaire, whereas mastery-oriented children select effort-related alternatives to characterize their typical attributional thinking.

Diener and Dweck (1978) reported that one third of the research participants classified as helpless spontaneously verbalized low ability ascriptions during task performance, whereas this did not characterize any of the remaining children labeled as mastery oriented. It must be noted, however, that Diener and Dweck only reported ability ascriptions, for other types of attributions were too infrequent to allow statistical comparisons. In addition, some statements coded for ability (e.g., "I am getting confused") seem questionably qualified as causal attributions, whereas uncoded reports related to effort expenditure seem to be causal ascriptions. Thus, it is not possible to determine the exact frequency of attributions in this investigation.

Brunson and Matthews (1981) repeated this procedure in an investigation that sought to contrast Type A (competitive achievement strivers) with Type B (less competitive) individuals. The research participants, in this case college students, were given four insoluble tasks. In addition, in one of the experimental conditions the failure was made particularly salient by having the participants repeatedly write the word "incorrect" on their papers. As in the Diener and Dweck (1978) investigation, the research subjects were asked to "think out loud" during their performance.

Disregarding higher order interactions between type of individual and salience of the failure reveals an average of approximately 2.5 attributional verbalizations for each subject. Only ability and task difficulty attributions were expressed, and a high salience of failure especially increased lack-of-ability verbalizations among the Type A subjects.

A final study coding causal verbalizations during task performance that attempted to overcome the limitations of a reactive methodology was conducted by Gioia and Sims (1983). Their research participants were recruited from volunteer business-people in the community. The general procedure was to have participants assume the roles of a manager and a subordinate employee and simulate performance evaluation. Both the manager and the employee had information regarding the performance of the employee (effective or ineffective) as well as his or her prior work history (good or poor). These two variables were combined to form four experimental conditions. The verbal interaction between the role-playing employer and employee was then recorded and coded for a number of verbal behaviors, including causal ascriptions. This methodology therefore has many precedents in psychology, particularly in the interactional analyses of Bales (1950).

Attributional material was subdivided into two categories: statements of causal attributions (e.g., "I have not put enough time in on it") and attribution-eliciting questions (e.g., "Why hasn't this objective been met?"). The data revealed frequent attributional requests by the manager and attributional statements by the employee, particularly in the case of failure. The reported data did not allow a determination of whether performance at variance with past history also increased attributional search.

Five additional investigations have also examined attributional verbalizations, but these utterances were not made during task performance. Anderson (1983b) asked subjects to recall what their thoughts had been after engaging in an experimental task; Gilovich (1983) confronted subjects with their outcomes on gambling bets and asked them to ruminate about the prior events; and Wong and Weiner (1981), Mikula and Schlamberger (1985), and Holtzworth-Munroe and Jacobson (1985) created a series of hypothetical situations and asked the subjects what they might think about after the event. These studies therefore provide less direct evidence for spontaneous attributional search, although the responses of the subjects are not directed by the experimenter toward attributions.

Anderson (1983b) gave subjects information about the relation between risk-taking behavior (high or low) and fire-fighting effectiveness (high or low). The data were presented either concretely (two case histories) or abstractly (a summary of 20 cases). The subjects first indicated the strength of the relation between risk taking and job effectiveness. They then were asked to "list all of their thoughts that they could recall while looking over the initial data" (Anderson, 1983b, p. 103).

Following this, the subjects reported which of eight causal thoughts had occurred to them while examining the data. Anderson (1983b) found that 58% of the participants revealed some causal thinking when freely responding, and approximately five of the eight items were claimed as describing their thoughts. Furthermore, causal thinking was more evident given concrete than abstract data. Anderson believes this to be the case because concrete information is more readily assessible from memory and more easily imaginable, thus promoting causal inferences about the relation between personality and job performance.

Rather than examining the recall of prior thoughts, Gilovich (1983) analyzed current thinking about a prior event. Subjects first placed bets on sporting events and either won or lost money. About 1 week later, the subjects settled their bets with the experimenter and "provided tape-recorded accounts of their thoughts about the games" (Gilovich, 1983, p. 1112). Inasmuch as the subjects were directed to think about the prior outcome, this investigation may not be tapping "spontaneous" causal thinking. It is therefore equivocally included in this review, in part because Gilovich was guided by spontaneous attribution research and examined causal explanations separately for wins and losses as well as for expected versus unexpected outcomes. As is consistent with prior findings, causal search (operationally defined as the amount of time spent discussing the game) was greater for losses than for wins. Other data in the publication suggested that the increased causal search provided the opportunity to "explain away" the loss by finding random or "fluke" causes. There were, however, no differences in causal thinking as a function of the expectedness of the outcome.

The study by Wong and Weiner (1981) departed from most prior research by primarily using imaginative or role-playing procedures. Wong and Weiner suggested that when one is engaged in an achievement activity, attention is predominantly focused on the task demands. Because immediate consciousness is limited, Wong and Weiner contended that the procedure first used by Diener and Dweck might underestimate causal thinking. That is, although subjects might not verbalize causal thoughts during task performance, they might do so after performance feedback, when not actually engaged in the task.

To examine this possibility and to overcome the perceived shortcomings of the Diener and Dweck procedure, Wong and Weiner (1981) asked subjects what they might think about after an achievement-related outcome. In one of five experiments, for example, subjects reported their thoughts following expected or unexpected success or failure at a hypothetical exam. After a description of each of the four possible Expectancy × Outcome conditions, the subjects were asked, "What questions, if any, would you most likely ask yourself?" This clearly is a reactive methodology, for questions were elicited. However, the content of the questions (attributional, action-oriented, etc.) was free to vary. This series of studies revealed a great deal of attributional activity, with causal search more evident after failure than after success, and after unexpected than after expected outcomes. Unexpected failure particularly instigated attributional search.

Mikula and Schlamberger (1985) then followed the paradigm of Wong and Weiner but examined attributions in situations of social injustice. They described a hypothetical situation of a student being unjustly treated by a teacher and asked subjects to write down "all questions and thoughts coming to mind in the described situation." In addition, two experimental conditions were created by varying the degree of involvement of the respondent. In one condition they were to put themselves in the place of the student, whereas in a second condition they merely were to assume that they observed the event. Mikula and Schlamberger (1985) found about 1½ attributions in the reports of subjects assuming that they were the "victim," and somewhat less than one attribution in the reports of the observer subjects. Thus, again attributional activity is found, with attributions increasing as a function of degree of personal involvement.

Finally, Holtzworth-Munroe and Jacobson (1985) made use of this simulational methodology to examine the attributions of happily and unhappily married couples. They presented hypothetical positive and negative events, which they described as frequently or infrequently occurring, and asked the subjects to "list your thoughts and feelings if these events were to occur today or tomorrow." These events included "spouse hugged or kissed me," "spouse nagged me," and so on.

The findings revealed a greater number of thoughts for negative than for positive partner behavior. However, contrary to the expectancy disconfirmation position, most attributions were reported by unhappily married couples given a frequent negative event. In all conditions, however, spontaneous attributional activity was again reported.

Indirect Attributional Indexes

Three additional investigations examined spontaneous attributional search indirectly, rather than coding written or verbal statements. In these studies, the experimenters assessed indexes presumed to be influenced by causal thinking, including selection of information, free recall, and the content of sentence completions.

Pyszczynski and Greenberg (1981) created one of the infrequent nonachievement-related contexts used in the study of attributional search. Their subjects were first led to believe that the experiment was concerned with "getting acquainted" processes and personality impressions. The subjects then had the opportunity to observe a confederate comply with or refuse to do the experimenter a favor that was either easy or very time consuming. Before performing the next phase of the experiment, which supposedly would ask something about the personality of the confederate, the experimenter permitted the subjects to read some personality-related answers that the confederate previously had given on a questionnaire. A few of the items on the questionnaire would help the subject explain the previously observed behavior of the confederate (e.g., "Do you find it difficult to say 'no' to people?"). Other items were irrelevant to the prior observation (e.g., "What are your hobbies?"). The dependent variable was the type of information that the subjects selected. The investigators contended that this measure "reflects subjects' motivation to engage in causal analysis without forcing them to do so" (p. 32).

The data revealed that attribution-relevant information was most sought when prior expectancies were disconfirmed, that is, when the confederate agreed to help given a difficult request or refused to help given an easy request. Although not as open-ended as many of the investigations already reviewed, this study certainly represents a nonobtrusive and novel approach to the documentation of attributional search.

The second study in this grouping using indirect indexes (Clary & Tesser, 1983) inferred attributional thinking from free-recall data. Subjects were exposed to a general description of an actor and then received additional information consistent or inconsistent with that description. For example, subjects read about a person known for his independent behavior who agreed to go to a movie his friends wanted to see rather than go by himself to a concert given by one of his favorite musical groups. The subjects then retold the story they had read, under the guise that the experimenter was interested in "informal social communication."

The results revealed that subjects exposed to an expectancy-disconfirming story were more likely to include an unread explanation in the retelling than those receiving an expectancy-confirming story. These explanations were frequently excuses or justifications. In addition, the disconfirmed stories produced a higher usage of causal conjunctions (e.g., "because") than did the confirmed vignettes.

Hastie (1984) employed a variant of this "incongruity" procedure in his study of causal thinking. Subjects were presented with a trait description of a person (e.g., intelligent or unintelligent) and a set of behaviors primarily congruent or incongruent with that trait (e.g., won or lost a chess game). The traits and behaviors were paired, with subjects required to generate a sentence completion following each pairing. The contents of these completions were then classified into coding categories. Hastie reported that 24% of the completions were causal explanations. In additions, an incongruent act was more likely to elicit an explanation as a continuation than was an act congruent with the trait description.

Summary and Conclusions

Twenty studies have been conducted that attempt to document spontaneous attributional activities (Table 2-1). To the best of my knowledge, this is a complete listing of the research investigations on this topic. All the studies report a great amount of causal search. Although a critic might question the inclusion of one or two of these investigations, it appears that the issue of the existence of spontaneous attributional activities can be put aside.

The topic under investigation therefore should not be whether there is attributional research, but rather under what conditions it is most promoted. There is reasonable consensus in the reviewed research (six of the nine pertinent publications) that search is elicited by an unexpected event: a win by an underdog, a loss by a favored team, more or less profits than anticipated, unexpected academic success or failure, unusual willingness or unwillingness to help, and inconsistent behavior. One's belief in an expectancy principle is certainly enhanced by the great variety of specific contexts that have been examined. There also is reasonable documentation (7 of the 10 pertinent publications) that nonattainment rather than attainment of a goal (political loss, defeat in a sports contest, examination failure, poor job performance and negative interpersonal behavior) promotes attributional search. These are primarily achievement-related outcomes, but nevertheless one is impressed by the variety of specific contexts in which this principle appears to be operative.

Why should unexpected outcome and failure stimulate causal thinking? Concerning unexpected outcome, it has been demonstrated that novel events promote exploration (Berlyne, 1960). For example, head turning is a reaction to a novel stimulus such as a loud noise. This orienting response is a reflexive search for more information. Attributional search thus can be considered one instance of the more general class of exploratory behaviors that are elicited in the face of uncertainty (including unexplained internal arousal; see Schachter & Singer, 1962). Exploratory behaviors have been accounted for with two different motivational principles contrasted in chapter 1 (this volume): functionalism (Berlyne, 1960) and mastery (Heider, 1958; White, 1959). That is, one might explore to promote adaptation and survival (functionalism, which often is linked with hedonism) or to better understand oneself and the environment (mastery).

Concerning nonattainment of a goal as a facilitator or attributional thinking, the law of effect captures the idea that organisms are motivated to terminate or prevent a negative state of affairs. Effective coping importantly depends on locating the cause(s) of failure. In this case, attributional search more clearly serves an adaptive, and therefore hedonic, function.

The remaining antecedents of attributional activity identified in this review do not clearly fall within the functional or mastery principles. It appears in service neither of adaptation nor of knowledge gain for some individuals to focus on low-ability causal attributions during failure. Inasmuch as attributional thinking is considered part of cognitive functionalism (Weiner, 1980c), such dysfunctional actions are difficult to explain. However, it also is evident that much further documentation is needed before individual differences in helplessness or Type A behavior can be accepted as antecedents of attributional search (as opposed to influencing what cause is selected, once a search has been initiated).

The demonstration by Anderson (1983b) that concrete rather than abstract information stimulates attributional activity also apparently falls beyond the functional and mastery motivational interpretations. This study calls attention to the possibility that a great number of informational variables, such as salience or interest, might enhance attributional search.

Might there be other antecedents of attributional activities that have not yet been experimentally documented? It seems intuitively reasonable to suggest that not all unexpected events or deprivations will give rise to attributional search. This search requires time and may place cognitive strain on an organism. Hence, important outcomes such as academic failure, job ineffectiveness, political loss, marital problems, personal injustice, and, for some, the loss of a World Series baseball game by a favorite team seem especially likely to give rise to "why" questions. These were the situational manipulations in many of the reported research studies. However,

Table 2-1. Investigations of Spontaneous Attributions

Experiment and Paradigm	Subject Matter and Place	Attribution Frequency	Attributional Determinants		
			Outcome	Expectancy	Other
Archival					
Lau & Russell (1980)	Sporting events (in newspaper)	5.5/article	NS	Unexpected > expected[a]	
Foersterling & Groenvald (1983)	Election results (in newspaper)	2.8/article	Failure > success		
Bettman & Weitz (1983)	Corporate reports	2.3/report	NS	Unexpected > expected	
Salancik & Meindl (1983)	Corporate reports	10% of pages	Success > failure(?)		
Schoeneman & Rubanowitz (1983)	Advice columns (in newspaper)	3.3/letter			
Lau (1984)	Sporting events (in newspaper)	12.9/article	Failure > success	NS	Repeated outcomes
Staton (1984)	School concerns (personal journal)	1.0/dialogue	Failure > success		
Verbalizations					
Carroll & Payne (1977)	Parole decisions				
Diener & Dweck (1978)	Achievement failure				Individual differences in mastery
Nisbett, Harvey, & Wilson (1979)	Varied				

Brunson & Matthews (1981)	Achievement failure			Individual differences in Type A, salience of failure
Wong & Weiner (1981)	Achievement outcome	Failure > success	Unexpected > expected	
Gioia & Sims (1981)	Job performance	Failure > success		
Gilovich (1983)	Gambling outcomes	Failure > success	NS	
Anderson (1983b)	Achievement histories	Failure > success		Concrete vs. abstract information
Mikula & Schlamberger (1985)	Injustice			Personal involvement
Holtzworth-Munroe & Jacobson (1985)	Marital events	Failure > success	Expected > unexpected(?)	
Indirect indexes				
Pyszczynski & Greenberg (1983)	Helping behavior		Unexpected > expected	
Clary & Tesser (1983)	Consistency of behavior		Unexpected > expected	
Hastie (1984)	Social impressions		Unexpected > expected	

[a] Unexpected outcomes generated more searches for causal attribution than did expected outcomes.
NS, not significant.

importance has not been systematically manipulated in experimental studies. One might hypothesize, for example, that information pertinent to the self is likely to engage attributional processes (see Berscheid, Graziano, Monson, & Dermer, 1976).

This discussion advances some possible guides for future research. There is no longer any justification for merely demonstrating spontaneous attributional activity. There also seems little need to continue to concentrate on negative and unexpected outcomes. Thus, new directions are needed. And, most importantly, critics who intimate that there is not a great deal of causal search in everyday life are wrong. If one only reads the sports pages and advice columns at breakfast (which captures my reading habits), about 20 attributions probably will be encountered. Imagine then what happens during election time, or if one also owns stocks!

The Content of Causal Thinking

The evident fact that humans ask causal attribution questions has been documented with acceptable scientific procedures. But what are the answers to these questions? What are the perceived causes of success and failure at school, in sports, for winning or losing an election, or for being accepted or rejected for a social engagement? Of course, the answers will depend on many factors, such as the particular event under consideration; the outcome; the information known by the attributor, such as past success history and social norms; who is responding; and on and on (see the first box in Figure 1-4). There is a huge literature on this topic, referred to as the "attribution process" by Kelley and Michela (1980). Attributional inferences have constituted the most studied aspect of perceived causality and include the two popular themes of attributional differences between actors and observers and self-enhancing or motivated attributional biases. The determinants of causal inference are not of concern here, inasmuch as the focus of this book is on the consequences, rather than the antecedents, of attributions. Instead, what is now under examination are the causes available to serve as adequate explanations. I therefore now move on to this third step in the sequence depicted in Figure 1-4 (outcome → causal antecedents → causal ascriptions).

The Perceived Causes of Achievement Success and Failure

By far the majority of investigations of causal perceptions have occurred in the context of achievement-related situations. As indicated at the outset of this chapter, the circumstances examined typically involve success and failure in an academic setting and make use of college students as subjects. However, the achievement-related tasks have included sporting events, occupational performance, and games.

It often happens in science that research starts at a particular point and then backtracks because some important, logically prior question has been overlooked. For example, investigations examined the causes of success and failure well before it was documented with appropriate scientific procedures that individuals do in fact engage in spontaneous attributional search. The examination of such attributional activity was not undertaken until it was pointed out to be a logically prior issue.

There was a similar omission of a logically prior issue in research examining the perceived causes of success and failure. Rather than fully considering all possible causes, in the initial studies participants rated the importance of only four causes: ability, effort, task difficulty, and luck. More specifically, subjects thought about or were induced to succeed or fail at some task and respectively rated the relative contribution of high or low ability, high or low effort, ease or difficulty of the task, and good or bad luck. These four factors were examined because early in the study of attributional processes my colleagues and I (Weiner et al., 1971) prematurely concluded that they were the main perceived determinants of success and failure. This judgment was based on no data whatsoever, but in part was guided by the compelling logic of Heider (1958). Subsequent investigators accepted this analysis and did not consider broadening their attributional net to include other possible subjective causes of achievement-related outcomes. So dominant was this restricting position that Whitely and Frieze (1983) were able to find 41 investigations of causal perceptions examining only these four causes. Moreover, this coverage was not complete because children were not included as research participants among the studies examined, and the research had to meet special qualifications imposed by Whitley and Frieze to be included in their meta-analysis.

More recently, a greater range and diversity of perceived causes than merely ability, effort, task difficulty, and luck have been documented. Two research procedures have been followed. In one, subjects are provided only with outcome information, namely, whether success or failure has taken place. The outcome might be imagined, induced, or have occurred in a real setting, and might pertain to the subject or to another who is being judged. The subjects are then asked to explain the outcome, using a free-response procedure in which they merely list the possibilities that come to mind. In a related methodology, subjects are provided with an expanded list of causes and rate the contributions of each cause to the outcome. These causes often were ascertained by means of pilot research using a free-response methodology and represent the dominant perceptions or embracing categories.

A summary of 10 studies that I uncovered, which were reported in eight articles, is presented in Tables 2-2 and 2-3. Table 2-2 reveals the source of the data, the characteristics of the sample and task, and special considerations that bear upon the data. Table 2-3 shows the rank-order importance of the causal attributions for success in the investigations. The data for failure tell an identical study and are not included here.

The message of Table 2-3 is clear. The potential causes of an achievement-related outcome are infinite, and in most studies there is an idiosyncratic, salient cause of success such as personality, charismatic style, cheating, or arousal during the test. Unique responses are not represented sufficiently in the lists, for these causes frequently are classified as "miscellaneous." Over all the investigations, however, the perceived causes of success at achievement-related activities overlap; they are ability, immediate and long-term effort, task characteristics, intrinsic motivation, teacher's competence, mood, and luck. Thus, Weiner et al. (1971) were more guilty

Table 2-2. Investigations of the Perceived Causes of Success and Failure

Experiment	Subjects	Perspective	Task	Special considerations
Frieze (1976)	College students	Self and other	Hypothetical school and game performance	Data combined across the two situations and across perspectives
Elig & Frieze (1979)	College students	Self	Anagrams	Data combined across outcome
Frieze & Snyder (1980)	First- through fifth-graders	Other	Hypothetical academic test, art project, sports, and game	Data combined across four task conditions
Cooper & Burger (1980)	Teachers	Other	School performance of students	Data combined across outcome
Burger, Cooper, & Good (1982)	Teachers	Other	School performance of students	
Anderson (1983a)	College students	Other	Variety of hypothetical situations	
Willson & Palmer (1983)	College students	Self	School exam	Two independent studies
Bar-Tal, Goldberg, & Knaani (1984)	Seventh-graders	Self	Academic test	Advantaged students in Study 1; disadvantaged students in Study 2

Table 2-3. Rank-Order Salience of the Perceived Causes of Success in Ten Free-Response Investigations

Frieze (1976)	Elig & Frieze (1979)	Frieze & Snyder (1980)	Cooper & Burger (1980)	Burger, Cooper, & Good (1982)	Bar-Tal, Goldberg, & Knaani (1984)	
					Sample 1	Sample 2
Effort	Task	Unstable effort	Typical effort	Ability	Test preparation	Test preparation
Ability	Ability	Ability	Academic ability	Immediate effort	Effort for study	Concentration during study
Luck	Stable effort	Interest	Immediate effort	Stable effort	Concentration during study	Effort for study
Other persons	Mood	Task	Attention	Attention	Teacher's ability	Self-confidence
Mood	Intrinsic motives	Stable effort	Task	Subject matter	Interest	Attentive reading
Task	Unstable effort	Other's unstable effort	Instruction	Directions and instruction	Arousal during test	Arousal during test
Stable effort	Personality		Prior experience	Other students	Will to succeed	Cheating
	Luck		Attitude		Cheating	Test difficulty
					Help in home	Teacher ability
					Ability	Liking teacher

Anderson (1983a)	Willson & Palmer	
	Study 1	Study 2
Behavioral preparation	Effort	Effort
Experience and skill	Luck/chance	Ability
Effort level	Task characteristics	Task characteristics
General knowledge	Interest	Interest
Intelligence		
Physical attributes		
Memory		
External factors		
Charismatic style		

of the sin of omission than of commission when they designated ability, effort, task difficulty, and luck as the most common causal perceptions. Furthermore, within this already delimited list, ability and effort predominate. In nearly all the reported investigations, how competent we are and how hard we try are the most frequently given explanations of success and failure. Hence, a conceptual analysis of the similarities and differences between ability and effort, and their linkages to emotions and motivated behavior, lies at the very heart of the attributional theory to be presented in this book.

Cross-cultural investigations, using a somewhat different methodology and not confining causality specifically to achievement success and failure, find similar results (Triandis, 1972). In Table 2-4 it is shown that, in three of the four cultures examined by Triandis (1972), ability and effort were judged as the most important causes of success and failure. This was not the case with the Indian culture, thus suggesting that cross-cultural comparisons provide an interesting avenue for further study.

Perceived Causality in Nonachievement-Related Contexts

Causal search is especially prevalent in achievement-related contexts because of the frequency of success or failure and because of the importance of achievement outcomes in many cultures. But attributions certainly are not confined to these contexts. Pertinent investigations have concerned interpersonal situations (Anderson, 1983a; Folkes, 1982); political elections (Kingdon, 1967); the onset of illness or accident-induced medical problems (Bulman & Wortman, 1977; DuCette & Keane, 1984; Lau & Hartman, 1983; Rudy, 1980); affluence, poverty, and unemployment (Feather, 1974; Feather & Davenport, 1981; Forgas, Morris, & Furnham, 1982; Furnham, 1982a, 1982b, 1983); and even a study of the perceived causes of passing and failing a driver's test (Mark, Williams, & Brewin, 1984). This surely is far from a complete listing.

The specific descriptive responses to attribution questions in these situations are not of prime interest here, but nevertheless will provide the reader with some notion of typical attributional thinking in other contexts. Table 2-5 therefore summarizes the perceived causes of wealth and poverty, and attributions for a common as well

Table 2-4. The Antecedents of Success Presented According to the Rank Order of Their Frequencies (adopted from Triandis, 1972)

American	Greek	Indian	Japanese
Hard work	Patience	Tact	Effort
Ability	Willpower	Leadership	Willpower
Effort	Ability	Huge army	Patience
Devotion	Effort	Planning	Ability
Patience	Courage	Unity	Inquiring mind
Planning	Cooperation	Discipline	Cooperation
Preparation	Progress		Courage

Table 2-5. Summary of Perceived Causality in Selected Domains

Wealth	Poverty	Sickness
Family background	Individualistic	Common illness
Inheritance	Lack of effort	Being worn out
Good schools	Lack of intelligence	Exposed to germs
	Won't move to new	Weather
Social factors	places	Poor eating habits
Unions	Lack of thrift	Stress and nerves
High wages in certain	Loose morals and	
trades	drunkenness	Surgery
		Bad habits
Individual effort	Societal	Heredity
	Policies of government	Physical history
Luck and risk taking	Influx of immigrants	Personality
	Weak unions	Stress
	Prejudice and	Fatigue
	discrimination	
	Taken advantage of	
	by rich	
	Poor schools	
	Fatalistic	
	Bad luck	
	Sickness and physical	
	handicap	

as a serious illness. These summaries are based on the citations given above. The perceived causes of wealth and poverty are grouped into categories, followed by examples of salient causes within those categories.

Table 2-5 reveals a potpourri of causes that should strike the reader as familiar, such as family background as a cause of wealth and exposure to germs as a cause of illness. In addition, if wealth is considered an achievement success, and poverty an achievement failure, then it will be noted that the causes do somewhat resemble those in Table 2-3. For example, effort and good luck are perceived as causes of wealth, and lack of effort, low ability, and bad luck are thought to be causes of poverty. However, again it can be noted that each particular domain is characterized by some unique causes, such as "influx of immigrants" being perceived as a cause of poverty.

Conclusions About Perceived Causality

Based on the information presented in this chapter, the following conclusions can be reached with some certainty:

1. Individuals search for and can readily supply attributions across a wide variety of motivational concerns. Unexpected failure at an important event is especially likely to elicit causal thinking.
2. A virtually infinite number of causal ascriptions are available in memory.
3. The activated causal ascriptions differ given distinctive activities and motivational domains. For example, the causes of poverty differ from the causes of failing at an exam (although there may be some overlap in explanations, such as lack of effort). On the other hand, causal ascriptions are similar within a motivational domain. For example, the causes of failure at an exam and failure at a sporting event are alike (although there may be some unique explanations for each activity, such as physical strength, which only applies to sporting events). A principle of stimulus generalization seems to be operative, such that the more similar the activities under consideration, the more similar are the causal explanations for positive and negative outcomes.
4. Within any particular activity, a relatively small number of causes from this vast array are most salient. For achievement-related activities, and within most cultures that have been examined, the dominant causes are ability and effort. There appears to be an economy or a simplicity to causal thinking.

With these hurdles of credibility and description now passed, we may get on with the task of theory construction. I will assume that the initial task of description is reasonably settled, with room for future selective investigations regarding the prevalence of attributions, the determinants of causal search (including individual differences), the salient causes of positive and negative events in nonachievement-related contexts, and cross-cultural comparisons of perceived causality.

Chapter 3
The Structure of Perceived Causality

In which the proposition that causes have three fundamental properties or dimensions is logically argued and empirically supported. There is a pleasing simplicity to the organization of causal thinking.

In this chapter I move from description to a taxonomy of causal structure. This is the first step toward "authentic" theoretical analysis, although classification is the least advanced aspect of conceptualization. The remainder of the book then progresses from structure (causal classification) to dynamics or to a genotypic analysis of emotion and motivation. This represents a higher level of scientific theorizing. This ordering of description-taxonomy-dynamics (causes, causal structure, causal consequences) captures a general developmental sequence evident in the growth of other theories, particularly in the study of personality.

A reasonable question to raise is, Why does one want to create a taxonomy or classification system for perceived causes? What purpose or role does this play in the goal of theory construction? In response, consider that within any particular activity a myriad of distinct causal explanations are possible. Furthermore, the causes of, for example, success and failure at achievement-related activities, such as ability and effort, may be quite unlike the perceived causes of social acceptance or rejection, such as personality or physical characteristics. One puzzle that arises is the relationship or the comparability between the various causal explanations: In what ways are ability and effort, or ability and physical beauty, alike, and in what ways do they differ? A taxonomy enables this question to be answered, for when finding the underlying properties of causes one no longer is confronted with incomparable qualitative distinctions. Rather, quantitative comparisons can now be made. This facilitates empirical study so that other relations may be uncovered that contribute to the meaning and significance of a cause. A taxonomy also permits the imposing of order; parsimony is certainly one of the accepted goals of science.

One of the best examples of the usefulness and importance of a taxonomy of verbal labels in psychology involved the use of the Semantic Differential Scale (Osgood, Suci, & Tannenbaum, 1957). By identifying three underlying properties or dimensions of meaning, Osgood and his collaborators were able to compare the denotations of distinct words and an array of research was then generated, including cross-cultural linguistic analyses. The same heuristic value may follow from an identification of the underlying properties of perceived causes. The possibility that a finite number of properties might describe causes is therefore of prime importance.

In this chapter I outline two approaches to the studies of the underlying properties or structure of perceived causes. The method that was first employed is best labeled as dialectic (see Rychlak, 1968) and characterizes the work of my colleagues and me (Rosenbaum, 1972; Weiner, 1979; Weiner et al., 1971). The general procedure was to group logically a set of causes (thesis), discover an apparent contradiction in reasoning by demonstrating that causes within the same grouping differ in some respect (antithesis), and then resolve the inconsistency by postulating an additional causal dimension to capture this dissimilarity (synthesis). This approach was guided by the prior intuitive analysis of Heider (1958). The second method, which emerged with a dissertation by Passer (1977), is best labeled as experimental or empirical. The empirical procedure has involved an analysis of responses from subjects primarily using the quantitative methodologies of factor analysis or multidimensional scaling. A pleasing simplicity to attributional structure that also was evident in causal salience will be unraveled—a few basic dimensions underlie the organization of explanation in all motivational domains.

The Logical Analysis of Causal Structure

The first systematic analysis of causal structure was proposed by Fritz Heider (1958). Rightly called the originator of attributional thinking, Heider has been in the background of much of the thinking that led to the present theory.

The most fundamental distinction between causes made by Heider (1958) was stated as follows: "In common-sense psychology (as in scientific psychology) the result of an action is felt to depend on two sets of conditions, namely factors within the person and factors within the environment" (p. 82). A simple example taken from Heider (1958) clarifies the person-versus-environment differentiation. Assume that one has successfully rowed across a lake on a windy day. The final outcome (reaching the other side) can be perceived as due to factors within (internal to) the person (ability, effort, strength) and/or external or environmental factors (wind, waves). In a similar manner, success at a task can be conceived as due to personal factors (ability, study habits) or factors residing in the environment (an easy task, a good instructor). Heider leaves open the question whether internal and external are discrete categories or anchors of a causal continuum. It will be presumed throughout this book that causes such as ability or wind are conceived as located on a bipolar continuum anchored with the labels *internal* and *external*. However, it has also been contended that humans think in terms of dichotomous constructs (internal or external), rather than continua (degree of internality-externality; Kelly, 1955). Hence, this issue certainly is not settled. For ease of presentation, I will often discuss causes as though they were dichotomously categorized.

Since the early 1950s, but particularly after 1965, psychologists have embraced an internal-external distinction. Collins, Martin, Ashmore, and Ross (1973) pointed out that two different topics are subsumed within this classification:

1. The extent to which behavior is a function of internal versus external determinants; and

2. Beliefs among persons regarding internal versus external determinants of action.

Among the early analyses of the first issue is the well-known book *The Lonely Crowd* (Riesman, Glazer, & Denney, 1950), which suggested an inner-directed and an other-directed typology. There has also been a spate of related work originally traced to Jung, but more recently associated with Eysenck (1970), contrasting introverts and extraverts. Collins et al. (1973) also noted that comparisons between normal and obese individuals, whose respective eating behaviors have been suggested as being guided by internal versus external cues (Schachter, 1971), also fall within this rubric.

However, the domination of the internal-external distinction arrived in psychology with the work of Rotter (1966), who was concerned with causal beliefs. Rotter (1966) stated:

> An event regarded by some persons as a reward or reinforcement may be differently perceived and reacted to by others. One of the determinants of this reaction is the degree to which the individual perceives that the reward follows from, or is contingent upon, his own behavior or attributes versus the degree to which he feels the reward is controlled by forces outside of himself and may occur independently of his own actions. . . . When a reinforcement is perceived by the subject as . . . not being entirely contingent upon his action, then, in our culture, it is typically perceived as the result of luck, chance, fate, as under the control of powerful others, or as unpredictable because of the great complexity of the forces surrounding him. When the event is interpreted in this way by an individual, we have labeled this a belief in external control. If the person perceives that the event is contingent upon his own behavior or his own relatively permanent characteristics, we have termed this a belief in internal control. (p. 1)

The classification of individuals into internals and externals became a dominant focus in psychology. Hundreds of studies related scores on a measure of this proposed personality dimension to other psychological indexes.

A number of subsequent distinctions were guided by the contrast between a perception of internal versus external control. Most closely related to Rotter's contribution was the typology offered by de Charms (1968), which classified individuals as origins (internally directed) or pawns (externally driven). In addition to these classifications of persons, environments also have been categorized with associated concepts such as those promoting freedom versus constraint (Brehm, 1966; Steiner, 1970), or fostering intrinsic as opposed to extrinsic motivation (Deci, 1975; Lepper, Greene, & Nisbett, 1972).

The discussion concerning what Rotter (1966) labeled *locus of control* was provided to justify the assertion that the logical analysis of the structure of causality began with an internal-external dimension. This simple classification allows one to consider where causes are perceived on an internal-external continuum. Thus, not only does effort qualitatively differ from the wind as a cause of rowing success, but one can specify the precise way in which they differ—in other words, how they are perceived in terms of locus of causality. Even if only discrete internal and external categories are accepted, rather than an internal-external continuum, it can be determined that both ability and effort are perceived as internal to the person, whereas wind is an external cause. Thus, qualitatively distinct causes can be grouped as "the same" or "different."

A Second Causal Dimension

The argument was then made by Weiner et al. (1971) that a second dimension of causality was required. The reasoning was that, among the internal causes of behavior, some fluctuate while others remain relatively constant. For example, as Heider had previously noted, ability (or, more appropriately, aptitude) is perceived as a constant capacity, whereas such causal factors as effort and mood are perceived as more variable, changing from moment to moment or from one time interval to the next. Among the external causes the same reasoning applies: Success in rowing across the lake may be perceived as due to the narrow width of the lake or the presence of wind. The structure of the lake is fixed, but the wind might vary from hour to hour or from day to day. In a similar manner, success or failure at an exam might be perceived as dependent on the university's grading policy, a relatively fixed external criterion, and/or on lucky or unlucky guessing during the exam, a fluctuating external cause. Because causes within an identical grouping (internal and external) differ in some respect, an additional causal dimension is needed to capture this dissimilarity.

Weiner et al. (1971) characterized causes we thought were most dominant in achievement-related contexts, namely, ability, effort, task difficulty, and luck, within a 2 × 2 categorization scheme (Figure 3-1). In addition to representing four causes within two dimensions, this classification system shed light on some of the shortcomings of Rotter's dichotomy. Rotter (1966) had defined internal control as the perception that rewards are determined by skill (ability), whereas an external orientation in part indicates that reinforcements are perceived as decided by luck or fate. Figure 3-1 points out that ability and luck differ not only in locus, but also in stability. Thus, the Rotter classification system is deficient or inadequate in that it blurs two dimensions of causality. Some of the consequences of this confusion are examined in detail in Chapter 4.

The specific causes listed in Figure 3-1, although appropriate because they were thought to be dominant in achievement-related contexts, nevertheless were a somewhat unfortunate choice. It is now realized that ability may be perceived as unstable if learning is possible; effort is often perceived as a stable trait, captured with the

	Internal	External
Stable	Ability	Task difficulty
Unstable	Effort	Luck

Figure 3-1. A 2 × 2 scheme for the perceived causes of achievement outcome. From *Perceiving the Causes of Success and Failure* by B. Weiner et al., 1971, Morristown, NJ: General Learning Press. Copyright 1971. Reprinted by permission.

	Internal	External
Stable	Aptitude	Objective task characteristics
Unstable	Temporary exertion	Chance

Figure 3-2. Locus × Stability classification scheme, with the entries within the cells altered.

labels *lazy* and *industrious*, and the intent to work hard or not may be quite enduring; tasks can be changed to be more or less difficult, and the perceived difficulty of a task is in part dependent on one's ability and expenditure of effort; and luck may be thought of as a property of the person (lucky or unlucky). Thus, the causes within the cells did not truly represent the classification system (i.e., they did not conform with the phenomenology of the naive attributor). This shortcoming had serious and negative methodological consequences (see chapter 4). A less ambiguous classification scheme is shown in Figure 3-2. As suggested in Figure 3-2, *aptitude* better captures a fixed capacity than *ability*; *temporary exertion* better describes unstable effort than the mere label *effort*; *objective task characteristics* are not dependent on ability and effort and do remain constant; and *chance* is more indicative of an environmental determinant than is *luck*. Hindsight, however, is better than foresight, and the problems so evident now were not fully recognized in 1971.

The classification system shown in Figures 3-1 and 3-2 permits more sophisticated comparisons between causes than merely having one dimension of causality. Assume, for example, that some causes of academic, sports, and social success and failure are rated on the two dimensions of locus and stability with the use of a six-point scale, the score of 1 representing internal and 6 representing external locus, and 1 representing a stable and 6 an unstable cause. Before examining the data in Table 3-1, I suggest that the reader decide the dimension scores of these causes. My hypothetical ratings of the causal perceptions (which will probably not be too different from your ratings) are shown in Table 3-1.

Table 3-1 indicates that ability, effort, and physical beauty are perceived as internal causes, whereas the width of the lake and wind are external in locus. Further-

Table 3-1. Hypothetical Ratings of Causes on the Locus and Stability Dimensions

Causes	Locus[a]	Stability[b]
Ability	1.2	1.5
Effort	1.2	4.5
Width of the lake	6.0	1.0
Wind	6.0	5.2
Physical beauty	1.1	1.5

[a] 1 = internal.
[b] 1 = stable.

more, ability, the width of the lake, and physical beauty are perceived as fixed, whereas to some extent effort, and to a greater degree the wind, are unstable or variable. One might then suggest that ability and physical beauty, respective causes of achievement and social success, are perceived similarly; that is, they have like denotations. In addition, they are more similar than ability and effort on the causal dimensions, although the latter two causes more closely pertain to achievement outcomes. Many other comparisons within Table 3-1 are possible. Without a classification system or dimensional categorization, one would not be able to contend that ability and physical beauty are "alike," or that the width of the lake and effort differ by a certain "amount," inasmuch as these causes differ qualitatively. However, the isolation of the underlying properties of causes permits a quantitative, more exact determination of their similarities and differences.

A Third Causal Dimension

A third dimension of causality was established with the same deductive reasoning that led to the naming of the stability dimension. Causes were first identified within each of the four cells shown in Figures 3-1 and 3-2. The causes within a cell were then discriminated on a particular property, and this property was used to describe all the remaining causes.

A third dimension of causality was first suggested by Rosenbaum (1972). He recognized that mood, fatigue, and temporary effort, for example, all are internal and unstable causes. Yet they are distinguishable in that effort is subject to volitional control—an individual can increase or decrease expenditure of effort. This is not typically true of mood or the onset of fatigue, which under most circumstances cannot be willed to change. The same distinction is found among the internal and stable causes. So-called traits such as laziness, industriousness, and tolerance often are perceived as under volitional or optional control. This is not characteristic of other internal and stable causes of success and failure such as mathematical or artistic aptitude and physical coordination.

The identification of this dimension, now called controllability (Weiner, 1979), enlightened and solved some issues while creating other difficulties. Among the topics illuminated was again the distinction by Rotter between internal versus external perceptions of control of reinforcement. Within the three-dimensional taxonomy, two of the proposed independent causal properties are labeled locus and control. A cause therefore might be internal, yet uncontrollable. Art aptitude and physical coordination, as already indicated, are examples of such causes. Failure ascribed to poor aptitude reveals that this outcome is perceived as determined by skill and ability, which according to Rotter would also indicate that the task outcome is perceived as subject to internal control. Yet aptitude, which often is perceived as genetically inherited, will not be considered controllable. Thus, confusion is again evident in the Rotter classification. To avoid confounding, throughout this book the locus dimension is labeled *locus of causality*. Locus *and* control, not locus *of* control, describe causal perceptions.

By introducing the property of control into the taxonomy, the expanded causal structure is able to make contact with a concept that has received much attention in psychology. Many investigators have concluded that feelings of personal control, or the belief that one can overcome barriers effectively and act upon the environment, is an extremely important belief that deters depression, maladaptive stress reactions, and a variety of other undesirable psychological states and consequences (see Langer, 1983).

However, a major problem was created that must now be introduced. The issue concerns the factorial nature of the taxonomy, or the idea that there are eight identifiable causal distinctions or "cells." Eight causal distinctions may not be possible. It will be recalled from Figures 3-1 and 3-2 that all the causes could be classified as internal or external, and as stable or unstable. Logically an internal cause could be stable (e.g., aptitude) or unstable (e.g., fatigue), and the same is true of external causes (contrast the width of the lake with the wind as perceived causes). But thus far in this chapter in the discussion of controllable versus uncontrollable causes, distinctions were made only among internal causes. For example, aptitude was contrasted with laziness, for although both are internal and stable, only the latter is perceived as controllable. In a similar manner, contrasts were made between fatigue and temporary exertion, both being internal and unstable, with only the latter considered controllable. The *internal* causes are more specifically represented in Figure 3-3 with examples of causes of success and failure in achievement-related contexts.

But what about the external causes? From the perspective of the successful or failing person, external causes seem by definition to be uncontrollable, for they are not willfully changed by the actor. If they can be altered, then personal effort or some other internal factor is involved, and the cause is more accurately classified as either internal or involving some interaction between the person and the situation. If external causes are by definition uncontrollable, then causal perceptions have the structure illustrated in Figure 3-4, which includes only six distinctions. Although all external causes are then uncontrollable, not all uncontrollable causes are external.

However, a decision to label all external causes as uncontrollable may be ill-advised, inasmuch as causes external to the actor may be perceived as controllable by others. For example, assume that a student failed an exam because of perceived lack of help from negligent friends, or because the teacher was biased. These external causes are uncontrollable by the student, but they are perceived by the student

	Stable	Unstable
Uncontrollable	Aptitude	Fatigue
Controllable	Long term effort Laziness Industriousness	Temporary exertion

Figure 3-3. Internal causes of success and failure, classified according to stability and controllability.

Figure 3-4. Structure of causal perceptions when external causes are seen as uncontrollable.

as subject to volitional change by the friends or the teacher. The student would hold these individuals responsible for his or her failure.

Consider, more specifically, an economist viewing the unemployment of a particular group of individuals, such as adolescents or women. He or she attributes this negative outcome to four causes external to these groups, shown in Figure 3-5. Figure 3-5 reveals quite credible *external* causes that are perceived as controllable. The obviously difficult problem that remains to be solved is whether controllability implies "controllable by me" or "controllable by anyone."

The unemployed do not perceive that they have personal control over the prejudice of others or over support from the government, but they as well as the economist do see these barriers as controllable by others. For the present, it therefore seems more expedient to accept "controllable by anyone" as the definition of controllability. This definition will be adhered to throughout this book, even though some problems are thereby created.

Review

The logical analysis of causality yields three dimensions: locus, stability, and controllability. Each of these properties is conceived as a bipolar continuum, labeled at the extremes with the phrases internal-external, stable-unstable, and controllable-uncontrollable. For present purposes, however, we assume that causes fall within discrete categories such as internal or external. Table 3-2 presents eight causes for achievement failure and eight causes for social rejection that intuitively represent the meanings of these dimensions. As shown in Table 3-2, one can fail because of such internal causes as low aptitude or lack of effort, or because of external causes such as a biased instructor or friends who failed to help. For illustrative purposes,

	Stable	Unstable
Controllable	Prejudice of people doing hiring	Temporary lack of governmental support
Uncontrollable	Jobs replaced by machines	Temporary recession

Figure 3-5. Perceived external causes of unemployment.

Table 3-2. Perceived Causes of Achievement Failure and Social Rejection on the Basis of a Locus × Stability × Controllability Classification Scheme

Dimension Classification	Motivational Domain	
	Achievement	Social
Internal-stable-uncontrollable	Low aptitude	Physically unattractive
Internal-stable-controllable	Never studies	Always is unkempt
Internal-unstable-uncontrollable	Sick the day of the exam	Coughing when making the request
Internal-unstable-controllable	Did not study for this particular test	Did not call sufficiently in advance
External-stable-uncontrollable	School has hard requirements	Religious restrictions
External-stable-controllable	Instructor is biased	Rejector always prefers to study at night
External-unstable-uncontrollable	Bad luck	Rejector must stay with sick mother that evening
External-unstable-controllable	Friends failed to help	That night the rejector wants to watch television

in the social situation the external causes primarily refer to the rejector. Hence, one can be rejected for a date because of internal causes such as appearance or because of such external factors as the rejector preferring not to go out. The dimensions equally apply in the achievement and affiliative contexts and permit direct comparisons between phenotypically distinct causes across disparate motivational domains.

The Empirical Approach

The logical analysis of causal structure has an inherent flaw: Casual dimensions are derived from attribution theorists, rather than from their subjects. It is conceivable that each attribution theorist might derive his or her own rational scheme of causal organization and that these postulated structures will not be identical between theorists nor the same as those of the layperson. Although I am persuaded by the organization already proposed (since I and others suggested it), one could point to our prior description of perceived causality as a warning signal. Whereas Weiner et al. (1971) intuited that ability, effort, task difficulty, and luck are the main perceived causes of success and failure, documentation from research participants yielded somewhat different conclusions. Direct evidence therefore also is needed concerning the organization or the interrelationships within a causal structure.

The problem of inferring an underlying organization or structure in the field of psychology is of course not unique to attribution theorists. Indeed, this problem has been at the very heart of the field of personality. For many years personality psychologists sought to identify the basic traits or instinctive propensities of human beings. Initially, logical and intuitive methods were used in this pursuit, and the number of suggested personality traits varied from four temperaments (based on the alleged four bodily humors) to literally dozens of so-called fundamental dispositions. Faced with this disagreement among theorists, the field turned toward empirical approaches. The technique most widely adopted was that of factor analysis. It is not necessary here to examine this mathematical procedure; it is sufficient to indicate that subjects typically rate a number of personality trait descriptors, and the intercorrelations between the ratings provide the data that reveal the identity of the more basic dispositions. Out of the myriad of human qualities, underlying characteristics such as introversion-extraversion or warm-cold have been suggested on the basis of the empirical findings. Attribution theorists (Foersterling, 1980a; Meyer, 1980; Meyer & Koelbl, 1982; Wimer & Kelley, 1982) also have made use of this well-known procedure to determine underlying causal structure. In this case, subjects rate specific attributions, and these intercorrelations provide the data to determine causal structure.

In addition, a more recently developed method, multidimensional scaling, also has been prominent in the search for attributional dimensions. The data in multidimensional scaling investigations are measures of proximity between pairs of objects. Subjects are asked, for example, to rate how similar are effort and ability, effort and luck, and so on. This measure determines the degree to which two causes are perceived as alike. These data then are represented spatially as in a map. The positions in this space permit the experimenter to interpret or to propose an underlying structure or organization for the spatially depicted stimuli. As already intimated, this procedure has been used relatively often in the search for attributional structure (Falbo & Beck, 1979; Lee, 1976; Michela, Peplau, & Weeks, 1982; Passer, 1977; Passer, Kelley, & Michela, 1978; Stern, 1983).

Research using multidimensional scaling does not merely differ technically from research using factor-analytic procedures, but rather entangles basic unknowns regarding causal structure. In multidimensional scaling procedures, participants are required to make direct comparisons between causes. These responses then provide the input for a scaling solution, which should reveal perceived causal structure. This structure or cognitive schema is spontaneously called forth by the layperson, for it is inferred from direct similarity estimates (although it must still be inferred or labeled by the experimenter).

On the other hand, with a factor-analytic technique, subjects rate a number of causes of outcomes, and an underlying causal structure is inferred from the pattern of intercorrelations. The associations between the causes are statistical in origin. This structure may or may not be salient or knowable by the respondents.

At issue here is the fundamental question of whether the dimensions are higher level theoretical constructs imposed by the attribution theorist to organize the causal perceptions of the layperson (see Schütz, 1967, p. 59) or whether causal structure is also part of naive or everyday psychological understanding. As Heider (1958) noted, "There is no a priori reason why the causal description [scientific language] should be the same as the phenomenal description" (p. 22). This is an issue we must be aware of when evaluating the data.

Still a third method to determine attributional structure makes use of categorization, or concept attainment. In categorization or concept attainment research, subjects are instructed to place a number of complex (i.e., multipropertied) stimuli into distinct categories. The classification reveals the common underlying attributes of the objects that are placed together. In the pertinent attribution research, subjects are asked to place causal attributions into distinct categories; attributions classified similarly thus share a common property. Only one investigator (Stern, 1983) has made use of this procedure. Thus, factor-analytic and multidimensional scaling procedures have provided the bulk of the data in this area.

In the brief summaries of the empirical search for causal structure that now follow, 7 of the 10 pertinent investigations already cited are reviewed. The research of Foersterling (1980a) and Lee (1976) is omitted because these investigators only examined ratings of ability, effort, task difficulty, and luck. In addition, the study by Falbo and Beck (1979) is not included because it is so flawed methodologically (see Michela, Peplau, & Weeks, 1982; Weiner, 1979, 1983).

Before presenting this detailed review, a basic rule guiding my conclusions must be made explicit. Given both qualitative and disparate quantitative methods, the reader should not be surprised to learn that there has been some disagreement among the investigators (although it will be documented that the correspondence of views is quite substantial). In addition, considering the empirical procedures, the possibility of a unique subject population, a unique set of stimuli, or a unique situation upon which the subjects' responses are based increases the likelihood that a dimension might be found in a particular research study, yet will not prove reliable between investigations. In the face of potential inconsistency, it was decided that a high degree of reliability in the findings between investigations had to be demonstrated before concluding that a causal dimension had been empirically identified. Furthermore, a high degree of agreement between the empirical and the logical procedures then had to be demonstrated before concluding that a causal dimension indeed had been determined.

Factor-Analytic Studies

The three factor-analytic studies form a curious grouping. Two of them (Meyer, 1980; Meyer & Koelbl, 1982) are very similar, whereas the investigation conducted by Wimer and Kelley (1982) could not be more unique.

In the Meyer (1980) investigation, causal responses were gathered to 16 hypothetical exam situations that varied in outcome (success or failure) as well as according to information known to influence causal ascriptions (prior achievement history, social norms, and task importance). Thus, for example, a person having a history of past success was described as succeeding at an important exam while others failed this exam. Nine causes with bipolar anchors were rated as determining the outcome. A factor analysis of the ratings was employed, and different factor solutions were examined. The best solution isolated three factors, labeled stability, locus, and control. The rank-order loadings of each of the causes on the three dimensions are shown in Table 3-3. The general placement of the anchoring causes should now be familiar: Intelligence and study habits are perceived as stable, whereas mood and luck are unstable; exam preparation and study habits are internal, whereas teacher effort and exam difficulty are external; exam preparation and mood are perceived as controllable, in contrast to luck and test-taking ability, which are believed to be uncontrollable. (The classification of mood as controllable is inconsistent with some previously reported research.)

The research reported by Meyer and Koelbl (1982) was quite similar, although some changes were introduced. First, high-school students rated the causes of their own exam performance. Thus, the context was real rather than simulated, and ratings were of oneself rather than of a hypothetical other. Second, no information other than actual exam outcome was introduced. Third, again nine causes were rated as explaining why the student perceived himself or herself as succeeding or failing, although in this study anxiety and background were included among the possible determinants of exam outcome.

A factor analysis of the rating data yielded four factors: Three were identified as locus, stability, and control, but the fourth factor could not be named. The unnamed factor was anchored by the causes *anxiety* and *mood* at one end and *luck* and *task difficulty* at the other. The rank-order loadings of the causes on the first three dimensions also are shown in Table 3-3. It is evident from this table that the two studies guided by Meyer yielded consistent data.

The investigation by Wimer and Kelley (1982), as indicated earlier, was of a different ilk. These psychologists "wanted a set of sentences that would produce a wide range of attributions" (p. 1143). Thus, instead of confining the judged events to achievement outcomes, the research participants were given descriptive sentences such as:

Harry committed suicide.
Larry has been going to church every Sunday for over 10 years.
After a hard day at work, Dan takes off his coat, tie, shoes, and makes himself comfortable with a beer.
Mike laughed at the clown.

It is evident from this small sampling that many of the situations judged are actions, which elicit justifications or reasons. In addition, at times the sentence stems refer to emotional states, which are neither outcomes nor actions.

Subjects then wrote the attribution that "was the most likely cause for the event described." These attributions were then rated on 44 scales provided by Wimer and Kelley. These descriptions of the attributions were far-ranging (as they must be, given the array of situations). For example, among the causal descriptions were:

The cause puts blame on the other person.
The cause is mostly unconscious.
The cause is weak or minor.
The cause involves the person's thinking.

Table 3-3. Rank-Order Listing of Causes According to Their Loadings on the Dimensions of Stability, Locus, and Control

Stability		Locus		Control	
Meyer (1980)	Meyer & Koelbl (1982)	Meyer (1980)	Meyer & Koelbl (1982)	Meyer (1980)	Meyer & Koelbl (1982)
General intelligence	Teacher	Preparation for exam	Study habits	Preparation for exam	Preparation for exam
Study habits	Ability	Study habits	Preparation for exam	Mood	Study habits
Test-taking ability	Background	Test-taking ability	Luck	Study habits	Teacher
Teacher ability	Study habits	Intelligence	Background	Teacher effort	Mood
Teacher effort	Anxiety	Mood	Ability	Exam difficulty	Luck
Preparation for exam	Difficulty of test	Luck	Anxiety	Teacher ability	Anxiety
Difficulty of exam	Luck	Teacher ability	Mood	General intelligence	Exam difficulty
Mood	Preparation for exam	Teacher effort	Teacher	Luck	Ability
Luck	Mood	Exam difficulty	Exam difficulty	Test-taking ability	Background

Wimer and Kelley (1982) reported five main dimensions based on a factor analysis of the ratings. The factors were good-bad, simple-complex, the person, enduring-transient, and motivation. The person factor describes the internal pole of a locus dimension (these investigators also reported that "other persons" was one of the minor factors isolated). In addition, enduring-transient appears to resemble causal stability (unchangeable-changeable also was among the minor factors identified). However, Wimer and Kelley found that endurance refers to the length of time that the cause impinges on a person. Hence, both luck and task difficulty, for example, are perceived as transient inasmuch as they influence the person at just one moment in time. The correspondence between this dimension and causal stability is therefore problematic.

Given the disparate stimulus stems and causal descriptions, it is difficult to evaluate the relevance of this study to a taxonomy of outcome perceptions (causes), and virtually impossible to compare the findings with the two Meyer studies. Nonetheless, among the dimensions identified, one or two appear to overlap with the properties posited by Meyer (1980) and Meyer and Koelbl (1982).

Multidimensional Scaling Research

The four studies using multidimensional scaling techniques varied widely in the situation under study. Passer (1977) examined the causes of academic success and failure; Passer et al. (1978) were concerned with the perceptions of negative interpersonal behavior among married couples; Michela et al. (1982) considered the perceived causes of loneliness; and Stern (1983) returned to the achievement domain but included positive and negative outcomes at both academic exams and sports. The difference in content domains, and therefore in the specific causal perceptions under examination, certainly raises fear of disagreement among the investigations. On the other hand, consistency of the data between studies examining such different content domains would provide strong evidence for the existence of a general structure of causality.

Passer (1977) conducted the first of these investigations as well as the initial systematic empirical study of causal structure. Passer started by developing a list of the most salient perceived causes of success and failure in the academic achievement domain. Then one-half of the subjects in his experiment were presented with all possible pairings of the 18 most salient causes and judged their degree of similarity. This was done separately for success and failure. The remaining one half of the subjects rated each cause on 14 bipolar scales to aid in subsequent labeling of any emerging dimensions. The 14 scales included active-passive, strong-weak, stable-unstable, intentional-unintentional, and others. Thus, for example, subjects rated whether ability and effort were perceived as active or passive, strong or weak, and so on.

Passer reported comparable but not identical results for the two outcome conditions as well as for his male and female respondents. Figures 3-6 and 3-7 show the scaling solutions given failure and success, respectively, for the female subjects. Two dimensions emerged for failure: 1) intent (anchored with the intentional causes *never studies hard* and *lazy* versus the unintentional causes of *nervous* and *bad*

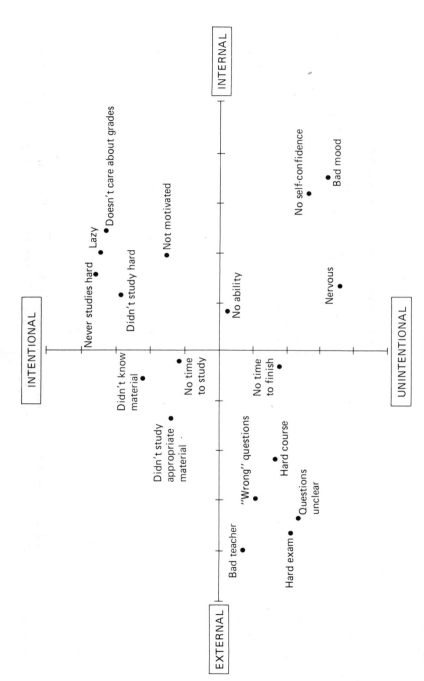

Figure 3-6. Two-dimensional solution for the perceived causes of failure among females. From *Perceiving the Causes of Success and Failure Revisited: A Multidimensional Scaling Approach* by M. W. Passer, 1977. Copyright 1977. Reprinted by permission.

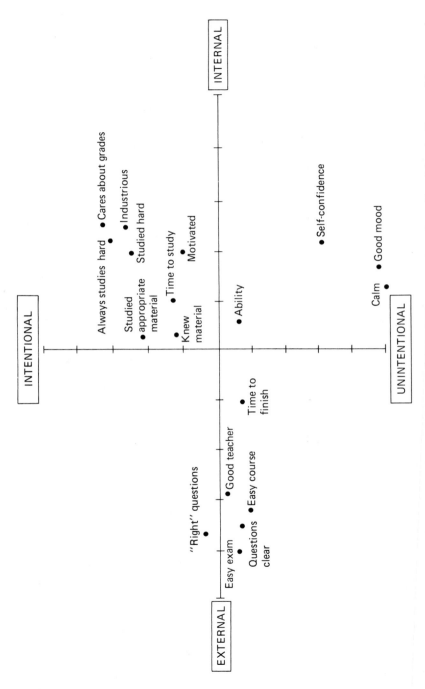

Figure 3-7. Two-dimensional solution for the perceived causes of success among females. From *Perceiving the Causes of Success and Failure Revisited: A Multidimensional Scaling Approach* by M. W. Passer, 1977. Copyright 1977. Reprinted by permission.

mood) and 2) locus (anchored with the external causes of *bad teacher* and *hard exam* versus the internal causes of *bad mood* and *low self-confidence*). The loadings of the causes on the intent dimension correlated highly with the scales designated as intentional-unintentional and controllable-not controllable. It is thus uncertain whether this dimension is best labeled intent or control, but control seems to be the more appropriate descriptor. The loadings on the locus dimension correlated highly with scales such as person-situation and inside-outside of the person.

For success, only the locus dimension was clearly discernable. The intent (control) dimension of causality did emerge among the internal causes, and distinguished between *always studies hard*, on the one hand, versus *calm* on the other. It is not possible to reconcile why this dimension differed in the success and failure conditions.

The multidimensional scaling procedure was then brought to bear on perceived causes of marital conflict (Passer et al., 1978). Making use of a hypothetical scenario, Passer et al. (1978) asked college students to imagine that "One member of a married couple has actively done something, and this behavior has displeased or upset the other member" (p. 953). Thirteen possible explanations were then provided, each preceded by the stem "My partner did it because . . ." The causes included, for example:

He/she is a selfish person.
He/she thought it would be in my best interest.
He/she wanted to change my behavior.
Some unusual situation occurred.

As in the prior study, subjects indicated the similarity of the various pairs of causes and again rated each cause on a number of bipolar scales to aid in identifying the underlying structure of causality. The bipolar scales included good-bad, moral-immoral, accidental-deliberate, temporary-permanent, outside-inside actor, and others.

The similarities of the causes were rated from the perspectives of the actor (the one who caused harm) and the person being harmed (the partner). Somewhat different solutions emerged in these two conditions (Figures 3-8 and 3-9). For the actor, two dimensions were isolated and labeled attitude toward partner and intention. The former factor loaded highly on scales such as good-bad and moral-immoral, whereas the latter factor correlated with such scales as accidental-deliberate and voluntary-involuntary. For the partner condition, again an attitude dimension emerged with a similar pattern of correlations as in the actor judgments. However, the second dimension was labeled circumstances or states versus actor traits. This dimension is a combination of the locus and stability properties, correlating nearly $r = .80$ with the scales of outside-inside of actor and temporary-permanent. Traits typically are considered both internal and stable properties of a person (Greenberg, Saxe, & Bar-Tal, 1978).

The next investigation in this grouping also was done in an interpersonal context, focusing on the causes of loneliness (Michela et al., 1982). The procedure should by now be familiar: 13 causes of loneliness, determined from prior research, were judged on similarity, and bipolar scales were also rated for each cause. The scales

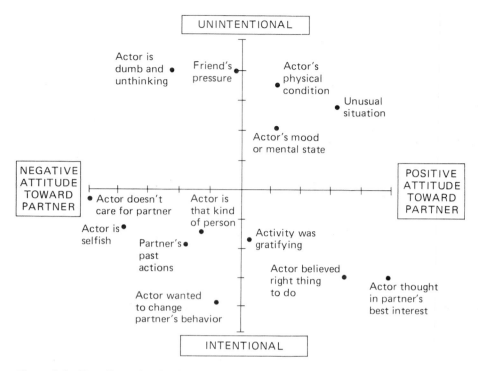

Figure 3-8. Two-dimensional solution for the perceived causes of marital conflict among actors (person doing the harm). From "Multidimensional Scaling of the Causes for Negative Interpersonal Behavior" by W. M. Passer et al., 1978, *Journal of Personality and Social Psychology, 36*, p. 955. Copyright 1978. Reprinted by permission.

were of the commonly believed properties of causal ascriptions, including temporary-permanent, reflects-does not reflect on the person, and controllable-not controllable. A two-dimensional scaling solution was reached (Figure 3-10). The first dimension was labeled locus (anchored at the internal end with *shyness* and *fear of rejection*, and at the external extreme with *other's lack of trying* and *other's fear*). The second dimension was called stability (anchored at the stable pole with *physically unattractive* and *unpleasant personality*, and at the unstable end with *lack of knowledge* and *lack of opportunities*). The addition of a controllability dimension did not improve the fit of the data.

Concept Formation (Categorical Sorting)

One further set of empirical studies is pertinent to the organization of causality (Stern, 1983). In addition to a multidimensional scaling procedure, Stern employed novel methodologies in which the underlying structure also is directly provided by the judgments of the subjects.

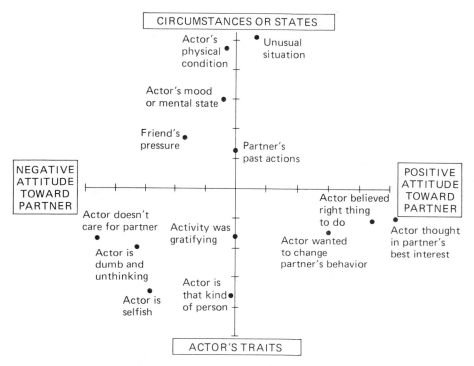

Figure 3-9. Two-dimensional solution for the perceived causes of marital conflict among partners (person who has been harmed). From "Multidimensional Scaling of the Causes for Negative Interpersonal Behavior" by W. M. Passer et al., 1978, *Journal of Personality and Social Psychology, 36*, p. 955. Copyright 1978. Reprinted by permission.

In four independent investigations, Stern (1983) had her research subjects perform a variety of concept formation tasks. The subjects most often received 16 cards, on each of which was typed one of 16 causes of success or failure at either an academic test or a sports-related task (gymnastics performance; see Table 3-2).

In the simplest procedure, called free-sort, subjects merely placed the 16 cards (causes) into as many or as few categories as they felt appropriate to distinguish the causes from one another. In a second experiment (sort-resort), the subjects were required to place all 16 causes into two logically distinct piles. They had the opportunity to do this again and repeated the procedure until they had no more organizational rules on which to sort the causes. In yet a third procedure, the research participants first placed the causes into two piles and then resorted each individual pile again into two smaller categories (sequential sort). This continued until they no longer had any properties available on which to distinguish the causes. In perhaps the most unique experiment, called graph building, subjects united all the causes with connecting lines in a figural representation, designating the two most similar causes with a "1," the next most similar pairing "2," and so on, until all the causes

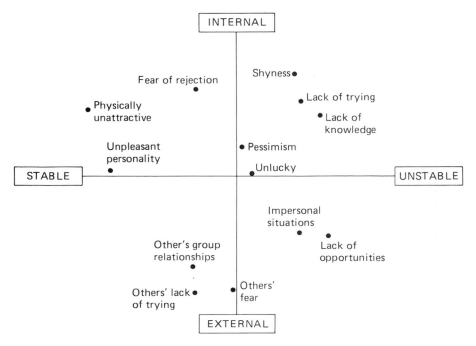

Figure 3-10. Perceived dimensions of 13 causes of loneliness. From "Perceived Dimensions of Attributions for Loneliness" by J. L. Michela et al., 1982, *Journal of Personality and Social Psychology, 43*, p. 932. Copyright 1982. Reprinted by permission.

were interconnected. In addition, a different group of subjects made similarity judgments while others rated the causes on bipolar scales. Clearly, Stern (1983) has conducted the most ambitious of the empirical investigations to date.

To analyze the data in the concept formation studies, Stern (1983) created a correlation matrix of the similarity of causes based on the logical analysis presented earlier in this chapter. Her 16 causes and their a priori similarity scores are shown in Table 3-4. In this matrix, if a priori dimensional categorizations are similar on the three dimensions of locus, stability, and controllability, then a score of 3 is given. A score of 0, on the other hand, indicates dissimilarity on all the dimensions. Hence, for example, innate intelligence and superior coordination "correlate" 3, inasmuch as they both were classified a priori as internal, stable, and uncontrollable. On the other hand, innate intelligence and help from a teaching assistant are shown to correlate 0, inasmuch as help from a teaching assistant is perceived as external, unstable, and controllable.

The concept formation decisions were also transformed into numerical values depending on the grouping of the causes. The correlations in the four methods between the a priori score and the subjects' data averaged approximately $r = .60$. Thus, subjects perceived the same similarities and differences between causes as

Table 3-4. Target Matrix for Causes of Positive Academic and Athletic Outcomes[a]

	Innate Intelligence	Healthy	Studies Hard	Good Time Allotment	Superior Coordination	"Up"	Practices	Excellent Concentration	High Pass Rate	Lucky	Good Professor	TA Help[b]	Easy Routine	Bus Early	Good Coach	Supportive Team
Innate intelligence		2	2	1	3	2	2	1	2	1	1	0	2	1	1	0
Healthy			1	2	2	3	1	2	1	2	2	1	1	0	2	1
Studies hard				2	2	1	3	2	1	1	2	1	1	0	2	1
Good time allotment					1	2	2	3	0	1	1	2	0	1	1	2
Superior coordination						2	2	1	2	1	1	0	2	1	1	0
"Up"							1	2	1	2	0	1	1	2	0	1
Practices								2	1	0	2	1	1	0	2	1
Excellent concentration									0	1	1	2	0	1	1	2
High pass rate										2	2	1	3	2	2	1
Lucky											1	2	2	3	2	1
Good professor												2	2	1	3	2
TA help													1	2	2	3
Easy routine														2	2	1
Bus early															1	2
Good coach																2
Supportive team																

Note. From A Multimethod Analysis of Student Perceptions of Causal Dimensions by P. Stern, 1983. Copyright 1983. Reprinted by permission.
[a] Numbers indicate the extent of correlation based on an a priori categorization scheme.
[b] TA, teaching assistant.

emerged from the a priori logical analysis. Although this correlation leaves much variance yet to be accounted for, it must be considered quite high given the alternate and novel procedures that were used.

Stern then correlated the causal scores on each dimension within one method with the scores received given the other methods. This multitrait, multimethod procedure is well known in personality testing and is used to separate the variance due to the method employed from the "true" variance. Prior studies of causal structure were unable to do this because they were confined to a single methodology.

This matrix, which includes the similarity judgments, is shown in Figure 3-11. Values within each cell diagonal show the correlation of the dimension ratings between methods; off-diagonal cells indicate correlations between different dimensions given dissimilar methodologies. It is quite evident that the numerical values on the diagonal are consistently near the $r = .90$ level and well exceed the correlations in the nondiagonal intersections. Thus, different methods yield identical dimensional scores.

Summary

It is now possible to summarize the empirical research and reach some conclusions regarding the structure of causality or the organization of explanation. Complex meta-analyses of many studies by many independent investigators are not possible, inasmuch as an insufficient number of studies have been conducted. A simple yes or no vote will have to suffice. In addition, it is evident that just a few investigators, often working together, have been the main contributors.

Table 3-5 provides a brief overview of the empirical research. It is immediately evident that all the studies with the possible exception of Passer et al. (1978) identified a locus dimension of causality. Given the prominence of the internal-external psychological distinction, this finding perhaps increases one's belief in the entire set of data. Turning to the stability dimension, Table 3-5 indicates that all investigators with the exception of Passer (1977) and perhaps Passer et al. (1978) and Wimer and Kelley (1982) found a temporary-enduring or a fixed-variable property of causality. Finally, all the investigators save Michela et al. (1982) and Wimer and Kelley (1982) described a dimension called either control or intent. In three investigations other dimensions have emerged, but they are not manifest in more than one between-experimenter study.

The data therefore unambiguously support the contention that there are three dimensions of perceived causality. These dimensions are reliable, general across situations, and meaningful. Other dimensions are either unreliable (perhaps this suggests that they are specific to a particular context) or are not clearly meaningful, such as the unnamed factor uncovered by Meyer and Koelbl (1982). In addition, these three factors are entirely consistent with the dimensions derived from logical procedures. Logical and empirical, deductive and inductive, factor-analytic and multidimensional procedures—all roads seem to be leading to Rome.

It is also the case that the structure of causality is not merely a convenient classification system imposed by attribution theorists. The factor-analytic, multidimen-

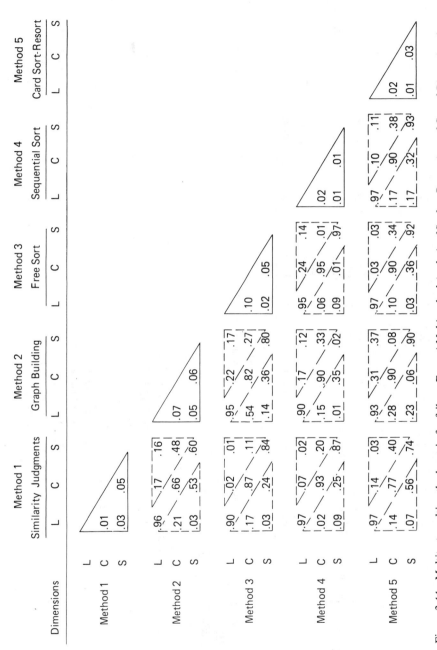

Figure 3-11. Multitest, multimethod matrix for failure. From *A Multimethod Analysis of Student Perceptions of Causal Dimensions* by P. Stern, 1983. Copyright 1983. Reprinted by permission.

Table 3-5. Empirical Studies of Causal Dimensions

Experiment	Procedure	Domain	Locus	Stability	Control (Intent)	Other
					Dimensions	
Meyer (1980)	Factor analysis	Achievement (hypothetical exam of others)	X	X	X	
Meyer & Koelbl (1982)	Factor analysis	Achievement (examination performance)	X	X	X	Unnamed
Wimer & Kelley (1982)	Factor analysis	All	X[a]	X?		Good-bad; complex-simple motivation
Passer (1977)	Multidimensional scaling	Achievement (hypothetical exam performance)				
		Failure	X		X	
		Success	X		X[b]	
Passer, Kelley, & Michela (1978)	Multidimensional scaling	Marital conflict (hypothetical other)				
		Actor			X	Attitude toward partner
		Partner	X? or X?			Attitude toward partner

Study	Method	Loneliness (hypothetical other)	Achievement (academic and sports)
Michela, Peplau, & Weeks (1982)	Multidimensional scaling	X	X
Stern (1983)	Correlation with a priori scheme using concept formation tasks		
	Free-sort	X	X
	Sort-resort	X	X
	Sequential sort	X	X
	Graph building	X	X
	Multidimensional scaling	X	X

[a] Unipolar.
[b] Only internal causes.

sional scaling, and concept formation procedures yield comparable data. The dimensions therefore are part of lay psychology. There is a relative simplicity in the organization of causal thinking, just as there is in the selection of causes, that is available to the naive or amateur attributor. Individuals think in terms of three broad categories, grouping qualitatively distinct explanations within the same rubric on the basis of shared causal properties.

Some Challenges

Although the rational and the empirical approaches converged and identified the same three causal dimensions, a number of pertinent issues nevertheless remain to be addressed.

Might There Be Fewer Than Three Dimensions?

This question is guided by a reliable finding that the dimensional ratings of causes are correlated. Consider, for example, a representative study by Anderson (1983a). Anderson had subjects generate causes for success or failure in both achievement and interpersonal social contexts. The 63 most dominant causes were then rated by other subjects on the three causal dimensions, as well as on intentionality. These ratings were intercorrelated, and the resulting data are given in Table 3-6. The correlations in Table 3-6 are higher than those reported in other investigations, but they therefore more dramatically call attention to the lack of empirical independence of the dimensions. This pattern of data suggests that there may be fewer than three underlying causal properties.

A number of arguments can be marshaled against this position. Many causal perceptions, particularly in social contexts, implicate traits. For example, an individual may be rejected for a date because he or she is thought to be aggressive, or boring, or arrogant. As already indicated, traits tend to be perceived as both internal and stable (see Greenberg et al., 1978). Inasmuch as a preponderance of causal ascriptions

Table 3-6. Intercorrelations of the Perceived Dimensionality of Causes

	Stability	Intentionality	Controllability
Locus	.66	.67	.68
Stabilty	— —	.43	.45
Intentionality		— —	.90
Controllability			— —

Note. From "The Causal Structure of Situations: The Generation of Plausible Causal Attributions as a Function of the Type of Event Situation" by C. A. Anderson, 1983a, *Journal of Experimental Social Psychology, 19*, p. 198. Copyright 1983. Reprinted by permission.

in interpersonal contexts fall within an internal-stable quadrant, the locus and stability dimensions will be correlated in ratings of causes.

However, as also noted by Anderson (1983a), a failure of orthogonality at the empirical level does not invalidate separation at the conceptual level. For example, height and weight are positively correlated—tall people tend to be heavier than short people. Nonetheless, height and weight are distinct characteristics, and certainly tall, light individuals as well as short, heavy ones can be identified. The empirical correlation based on actual subject samples does not invalidate the conceptual distinction.

In addition, as Passer et al. (1978) pointed out, there is good reason to have an unequal distribution of causes in a multidimensional causal space. Figures 3-8 and 3-9 show much greater differentiation on the dimension of attitude toward partner given intentional than unintentional causes, and given traits rather than states (compare the range of causes below versus those above the dimension line). Passer et al. (1978) reasoned:

> The logic of these patterns seems fairly clear: Behavior attributed to unintentional causality or to external circumstances and states is less reflective of a person's underlying attitudes than behavior attributed to that person's intentional actions or dispositional nature. (p. 961)

They went on the conclude:

> There is no necessity that the elements used in multidimensional scaling be distributed evenly over the space identified by the analysis. In fact, there may be psychological reasons, as illustrated here, for certain regions of the space not to contain any elements. (p. 961)

In sum, correlations between the causal dimensions, or uneven distribution in multidimensional space, do not invalidate the conceptual distinctions that have been made, nor do they support the contention that fewer than three dimensions are needed.

Might There Be More Than Three Dimensions?

As more dimensions are uncovered, it becomes increasingly difficult to meet the logical criterion posited as necessary for the identification of still another dimension. The three dimensions already introduced have governed the status of taxonomic thinking. But a credible argument *perhaps* can be made for still a fourth or even a fifth causal dimension, although again very complex issues are raised and not solved.

Consider, for example, effort versus strategy as perceived causes of success and failure. One might succeed because of hard work or because of proper strategy while studying, or fail because of insufficient effort or poor strategy. Both causes clearly are internal and can be volitionally changed. In addition, both might be either stable (long-term exertion or enduring strategy) or unstable (temporary exertion or fluctuating strategy). Failure because of lack of effort also meets the criteria for inferring responsibility, because not trying is carried out "purposively," "knowingly," "recklessly," and/or "negligently" (Fincham & Jaspers, 1980). But these criteria are not met if poor strategy is given as the cause of failure. One does not purposely or knowingly use bad strategy. The dimension that perhaps best describes the contrast between effort and strategy has been labeled intentionality (Weiner, 1985b) and was identified in some of the reviewed empirical investigations. One might intend not to try and can usually supply a reason for this inaction, but one does not intend to apply a poor strategy.

Intent and control generally covary quite substantially (Table 3-6). We intend to do what is controllable, and typically we can control what is intended. But there are some important instances in which intent and control do not vary together. For example, an overachiever might state that she intends to take some time off from work, but cannot control her working habits. Or an underachiever might plead that he intends to work but cannot control the inner thoughts that interfere with his concentration. Furthermore, an obsessed thief might plead that he did not intend to steal, but could not control the desire when he saw some expensive jewelry. Or a driver might not have intended to kill a pedestrian, but should have controlled his speeding. The distinction between intent and control lies at the heart of the differentiation between murder and manslaughter.

It seems, then, that it is reasonable to separate control from intent and consider them both dimensions of causality. A difficult conceptual problem, however, is created when intent is posited as a dimension of causality. Causes can be considered internal, or stable, or uncontrollable, but a cause is not intentional. Intent describes an action, its anticipated consequences, or a state of an organism. One might refer to ability as internal, or stable, but can it be called unintentional? It seems not; intent does not appear to be a characteristic of a cause. Solving this difficult philosophical problem is beyond the scope of this book and even further beyond the capability of this writer. Thus, the possibility of an intentionality dimension of causality will be put aside, although I occasionally return to it at various points throughout the book. For now, it is suggested that both controllability and intentionality be subsumed under the controllability label.

A logical analysis of causality provided by Abramson, Seligman, and Teasdale (1978) has revealed another potential dimension of causality. The contention of these investigators, which has been uncritically accepted by many, is that some causes are specific to a situation, whereas others generalize across settings. For example, an individual may perceive failure at mathematics as due to low math aptitude (specific) or low intelligence (general). Intelligence will be perceived as influencing performance in a greater variety of activities than math aptitude. For the area in which these investigators are active (depression), a specific-general distinction is of prime importance because depressed individuals apparently exhibit low expectations and negative affect across many diverse situational contexts.

The argument in favor of a distinction between general and specific causes certainly seems rational and cannot be faulted on the grounds of face validity. To elevate this distinction into a dimension, however, does raise some problems. First, a specific-global property has not emerged in any empirical analysis. If, for example,

I ask the reader to judge the similarity of luck and ability, the specificity or generality of each would not very likely be taken into account in this judgment, for more information is required for that property to play a part in the comparison. This is not so clearly the case for other dimensions: Luck and ability can readily be compared on locus, stability, and control without additional elaboration. But, considering ability and luck, which one is specific and which one is general? Additionally, the precise meaning of the generality dimension is not clear. Assume, for example, that hot weather is perceived as a cause of failure because it interfered with concentration. Is this a global cause, inasmuch as it could have interfered with any exam performance and a variety of other activities, or is it quite specific in time and space, with few implications for other aspects of behavior? Part of the confusion, it seems to me, stems from the investigators merely presuming a "new" dimension without serious consideration given to the meaning or the implication of this pronouncement, and without attention to the empirical foundation of causal structure.

When personality psychologists discuss traits, both the temporal aspects (test-retest reliability, or consistency over time) and generalizability (cross-situational consistency) are considered. In a similar manner, causes can be construed logically in terms of their consistency over time (causal stability, or temporal generalization) and across situations (globality, or stimulus generalization). It therefore seems warranted to entertain the possibility that both stability and globality might be included within a single generalizability dimension, even though the empirical findings do not support such a category enlargement.

For present expediency, it is suggested that the basic causal properties be conceived as follows (although it must be kept in mind that this conceptualization could create some problems):

1. Locus (internal-external)
2. Stability
   Fixed-variable
   Specific-general (?)
3. Controllability
   Controllable-uncontrollable
   Intentional-unintentional (?)

Why Are There Three Dimensions?

It is said that Freud sensed something mystical about the number three, which he incorporated into his thinking about the structure (id, ego, and superego) and the dynamics (conscious, preconscious, and unconscious) of personality. There are, of course, three in the Trinity, and Jonah spent three days in the belly of the whale. I doubt, however, that Osgood et al. (1957) had the same feeling of the occult when they uncovered three dimensions of meaning.

I have no answer to the question of "why three?" as opposed to five, or eight, or whatever number of causal dimensions. At the outset of the pursuit of causal structure, no a priori hypothesis about the number was formulated, and there was no particular attraction to finding three dimensions. Later in this book it is documented that these dimensions have great psychological significance and perhaps evolutionary importance, but the specification of just three properties of causality is neither personally motivated nor a fixed belief.

Research Topics

The existence of causal ascriptions, the conditions that promote causal search, and the causes available from memory (topics discussed in chapter 2) have been reasonably documented and determined. Those topics are not ripe for additional empirical study, although some research issues that were pointed out remain to be more fully examined. Conversely, a large number of research topics and unsolved problems are raised by the dimensional analysis. Some of these, including whether there should be a continuous or dichotomous classification of causes and the incorporation of the dimensions of intention and globality have already been identified as in need of further study. In the following pages some other research topics are introduced. They are not presented in any specific order, and the reader more concerned with general motivational questions than with a detailed analysis of attributional concerns could merely skim this section.

Differential Activation of Dimensions

Disparate personal concerns or situational contexts might activate different elements of cognitive (causal) structure. For example, assume that a student is worried about an upcoming exam. A prior exam failure was ascried to lack of ability and to the very difficult objective characteristics of the test. Although these explanations differ in locus, this student may perceive them as similar, for both raise doubts about future success. That is, the stability rather than the locus dimension is activated. On the other hand, another student with the same exam experience and causal ascriptions may be more concerned about maintaining self-esteem. These causes might then be perceived as quite distinct; the locus rather than the stability dimension is more salient. In the above example, disparate aspects of causal structure may be activated, leading to divergent meanings of the causes.

It is also likely that disparate aspects of causal structure are aroused in dissimilar situations. For example, a key determinant in criminal sentencing is the intent of the accused, which is distinguished from controllability (as evidenced in the previously mentioned distinctions between murder and manslaughter). Whereas an intent-control differentiation may be central in moral contexts, it might be of little value or importance in achievement-related situations. Hence, the same parts of the causal structure may not be activated in these two contexts.

Structure or underlying cognitive organization therefore should be distinguished from an activated schema. The causal structures associated with locus, stability, and controllability are available and accessible, but are not likely to be indiscriminately aroused in all situations. The conditions that promote the activation of varying aspects of causal structure remain to be examined.

Dimensional Description of Situations

Situations also influence which causes are elicited and, therefore, the dimensional characteristics of environments. To examine this topic, Anderson (1983a) ascertained the dominant perceived causes of success and failure in both achievement and interpersonal contexts. As indicated previously, other subjects then rated these causes on the causal dimensions, including globality and intentionality.

Anderson (1983a) found that social success and failure are perceived as due more to internal and stable factors than are achievement-related outcomes. The causal significance of traits primarily accounted for these differences (although this finding may not be replicable; see Feather, 1983). Inasmuch as causal dimensions have far-reaching behavioral and emotional implications, these data might provide important clues to understanding the situational determinants of the dynamics of action and why, for example, affiliative contexts could promote more feelings related to humiliation and embarrassment than achievement-related contexts.

Cross-Cultural Considerations

Among the environmental factors that should influence causal ascriptions is the culture of the perceiver. This area is badly in need of research and contrasts with the extensive cross-cultural work by Osgood and his colleagues (see also Bond, 1983).

It seems to this writer that the basic properties of causality will be pancultural. Each culture must assign causality and determine, for example, if hunting failure was due to unfavorable external conditions (perhaps resulting in a decision to move) or due to a poor hunting leader (perhaps facilitating a change in leadership). Decisions must also be made about the stability of current hunting outcomes and the controllability of the factors that influence survival. Thus, it would not be surprising if the three dimensions found in our culture also characterize other cultures. This expected consistency contrasts with specific causal perceptions, which are likely to be quite different in the various cultures because of the disparate ongoing activities. It is obvious, however, that empirical work is needed to confirm or disconfirm these naive beliefs.

A related area of inquiry concerns the dimensional placement of specific causes in different cultures. It has been documented in many studies with American participants that ability and effort, for example, are perceived as internal or personal properties, whereas such causes as task difficulty and teacher characteristics are perceived as external to the judging student. But it is not known if these classifications are descriptive of other cultures. For example, an American might perceive aptitude as an internal cause of success, whereas someone from an Eastern culture might believe it to be a gift from God, an external cause. Success ascribed to this factor therefore may generate quite different affective experiences in the two cultures. The American might feel proud, whereas the oriental might experience gratitude or even humility. In sum, pertinent cross-cultural data could provide insights about the mechanisms that mediate disparate behavioral and emotional reactions across cultures.

Table 3-7. Mean Ranking of the Causes on the Three Dimensions by Advantaged and Disadvantaged Students

Causes	Locus of Causality		Stability		Controllability	
	Disadvantaged Ranking[a]	Advantaged Ranking	Disadvantaged Ranking	Advantaged Ranking	Disadvantaged Ranking	Advantaged Ranking
1. Concentration	1	11.5	14	10.5	9	6
2. Preparation	11.5	13	10	12.5	4	4
3. Test difficulty	19	18	17	22	23	23
4. Studying effort	5.5	5	5	7	2	1
5. Teacher	24	24	11	15	17	20
6. Interest	14	8.5	9	12.5	7	11.5
7. Attention	4	7	3	3.5	1	2
8. Liking the teacher	16	17	18	19.5	15	14
9. Mood	9	11.5	2	8	19	17
10. Luck	21	22	21	21	24	24
11. Motivation	5.5	3	1	1	3	5
12. Help in home	21.5	21	13	6	13	13
13. Ability	8	4	8	3.5	12	15
14. Effort during test	2	2	4	5	5	3
15. Home conditions	23	20	2	2	10	9
16. Subject difficulty	18	19	20	18	18	19
17. Self-confidence	13	10	17	9	14	11.5
18. Memory	3	1	15	14	11	7
19. Cheating	17	15	22	24	6	8
20. Will to prove	10	8.5	7	10.5	8	10
21. Health	11.5	14	23	23	20.5	22
22. Arousal	7	6	16	16	16	16
23. Load	20	23	19	17	22	21
24. Fatigue	15	16	24	19.5	20.5	18

Note. From "Causes of Success and Failure and Their Dimensions as a Function of SES and Gender: A Phenomenological Analysis" by D. Bar-Tal et al., 1984, *British Journal of Educational Psychology*, *54*, p. 57. Copyright 1984. Adapted by permission.
[a] 1 = internal, stable, uncontrollable.

In one investigation, Bar-Tal, Goldberg, and Knaani (1984) examined causal perceptions among Israeli children from Asian-African families who also were "disadvantaged," and among children from European-American families who also were classified as "advantaged." These children were provided a list of 24 causes for success and failure at school and rated these causes on the three dimensions of locus, stability, and controllability. The causes and their rank ordering on the dimensions are shown in Table 3-7. The correlations between the rankings within each dimension, for both boys and girls, are shown in Table 3-8. It is evident from Table 3-8 that the correlations are substantial and begin to approach unity for the locus and controllability dimensions. Thus, in these two disparate samples (but from the same school environment), the causes had identical dimensional meaning. Similar rank-order findings have been reported by Chandler and Spies (1984), using four different population samples in America.

A similar investigation was conducted by Betancourt and Weiner (1982). We examined dimensional perceptions of eight causes of achievement success and failure among both Chilean and American subjects. These causes had been classified a priori into one of eight cells in the usual Locus × Stability × Controllability matrix. The comparative ratings of the causes in the two cultures are shown in Figure 3-12. Figure 3-12 reveals great similarities in the ratings, although some cultural differences were exhibited. Chileans perceived the external causes as more external, the stable causes as less stable, and the controllable causes as less controllable than did the Americans. However, this experiment suffered from the fact that participants in both samples were college students. This population seems to be universally homogeneous. Similar studies need to include other cultures and broader samples. This could produce an atlas listing many causes in many contexts across many cultures, with the causes rated according to their dimensional properties. This research is difficult to conduct because comparable situations must be created and causes pertinent to each culture must be provided. I perceive this attempt as one of the more important and formidable future research directions. Beate Schuster, of Germany, is now undertaking this project.

Table 3-8. Correlations Between the Ratings of the Four Groups Within Each Dimension[a]

Groups	Locus of Causality	Stability	Controllability
Advantaged boys–advantaged girls	.89	.73	.94
Advantaged boys–disadvantaged boys	.90	.73	.91
Advantaged boys–disadvantaged girls	.92	.75	.94
Advantaged girls–disadvantaged boys	.93	.88	.92
Advantaged girls–disadvantaged girls	.94	.90	.91
Disadvantaged boys–disadvantaged girls	.98	.93	.94

Note. From "Causes of Success and Failure and Their Dimensions as a Function of SES and Gender: A Phenomenological Analysis" by D. Bar-Tal et al., 1984, *British Journal of Educational Psychology, 54,* p. 58. Copyright 1984. Reprinted by permission.
[a] The df is 22 and all the correlations are significant, $p < .001$.

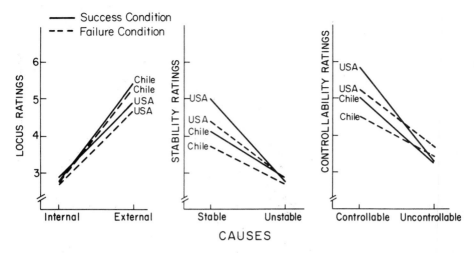

Figure 3-12. Dimensional ratings of causes in two cultures. Left panel, high ratings indicate externality; middle panel, high ratings indicate stability; right panel, high ratings indicate controllability. From "Attributions for Achievement-Related Events, Expectancy, and Sentiments: A Study of Success and Failure in Chile and the United States" by H. Betancourt and B. Weiner, 1982, *Journal of Cross-Cultural Psychology*, *13*, p. 368. Copyright 1982. Reprinted by permission.

Dimensional Salience As an Influence on Causal Decisions

It is likely that dimensional focus or centrality will influence particular causal explanations (see Wong & Weiner, 1981). If an individual is prone to search for external and uncontrollable causes of an event before considering internal and controllable causes, then it is likely that an acceptable external, uncontrollable cause will be found. This might characterize the individual especially concerned with maintenance of self-esteem in situations of failure. Such a person would prefer to conclude that "It is not my fault" rather than that "I am to blame." A great void exists regarding the strategies that people use in attributional search and the influence of different heuristics and dimensional thinking on causal ascriptions.

Variability in the Dimensional Location of a Cause

Attributional decisions represent phenomenal causality—it is the causal world as perceived by the viewer. As intimated earlier, perceived causality certainly will differ from person to person and within a person on different occasions. This is true not only for any specific causal inference, but also for the meaning or dimensional location of the presumed cause of an event. For one individual, luck may be perceived as an external, unstable cause of success; for another, luck is conceived as an enduring personal property; for yet another, good luck on one occasion gives rise to the belief that bad luck will follow, so that luck is unstable but not random. Although the interpretation of specific causal inferences might vary over time and between people, the underlying dimensions on which the cause is "understood" is presumed to remain constant. That is, dimensions are invariant; the location of a specific cause on the dimensions is variable.

A specific cause also might convey different meanings in diverse contexts. For example, it has been indicated that effort expenditure as an outcome determinant might be perceived as akin to temporary exertion (unstable) or looked upon as reflecting a trait (stable). In support of this belief, effort appears to be interpreted differently in situations of success and failure. Success ascribed to high effort may promote the belief that expenditure of effort is stable. According to reinforcement principles, behavior that results in goal attainment is likely to be repeated. This also may be a "naive" law of action held by the layperson. On the other hand, failure ascribed to lack of effort typically motivates an individual to work harder. The behavior that resulted in nonreward (lack of trying) should be subject to extinction. Thus, expenditure of effort may often be considered unstable in situations of failure if lack of trying is the perceived cause of the negative outcome. In sum, effort ascriptions could connote stability given success, but instability given failure (see Dalal, Weiner, & Brown, 1985).

Variability in the dimensional location of a cause is therefore to be anticipated. This is not a shortcoming of dimensional analysis, but rather a principle of phenomenal causality. What antecedents determine the dimensional location of a cause is a broad and complex problem that remains to be addresssed.

Dimensional Complexity

There is a complexity in dimensional judgments that is more real than apparent. Thus far the discussion has been simplified by confining perceived causality to a single cause. But assume a situation in which a student fails and ascribes that outcome to low aptitude and bad luck. How is the stability of the causal configuration determined? Are the causes weighted equally or differentially? For example, is ability perceived to be of special importance in achievement-related contexts, so that it "masks" the contribution of luck when determining the locus or the stability of causal configuration? In a similar manner, might physical attractiveness be given special importance by someone rejected in an affiliative encounter? It is not known how causal perceptions are integrated to yield an overall dimensional judgment.

Trait Versus State: The Search for Invariance

The classification of causes as stable (invariant) or unstable (variant) is remindful of a distinction among personality psychologists between traits and states. Dispositions or traits summarize many occurrences—a trait implies than an action has been repeatedly manifested over time. A state label, on the other hand, is used to identify a behavior that is performed only occasionally, perhaps as a reaction to particular environmental circumstances. Allen and Potkay (1981) summarized:

> The "person on the street" has distinguished between state and trait, giving the
> label "mood" (state) to that which appears ephemeral and due to temporary condi-
> tions and giving the label "trait" to that which appears to be due to relatively per-
> manent internal dispositions. (p. 917)

Traits therefore are thought to be more predictive of future behavior than are states.
A person labeled as "dominant" will be expected to act dominantly in the next interaction but a person acting out of anger may not be expected to act "angry" in the
future.

Attribution theorists such as Heider (1958) and Jones and Davis (1965) have contended that people seek the underlying invariances in behavior (traits) in their
attributional search. Many others have followed this suggestion, contending that an
attribution is not "complete" or "satisfactory" unless a stable cause has been found.

Although stability is thought to aid in subsequent prediction, it also is the case that
unstable attributions are quite suitable to provide understanding and closure. Calling
off a picnic because of rain, having a date broken because the partner becomes ill,
or failing because of poor study strategy all are unstable causes, yet they provide
satisfactory explanations. The attributor need not search only for the "underlying
invariances"; this seems to be an unnecessary restriction postulated by some attributional experts. However, this is an issue that deserves research; at present, there is
no empirical evidence to support the belief that there is a focus during the search
process on stable causes.

Conclusion

In the closing statement of their factor-analytic investigation of causal dimensions,
Wimer and Kelley (1982) concluded:

> We began this study with a sense that, given a sufficiently broad sampling of events
> and rating scales, we might identify the main causal distinctions people make, at
> least as they relate to a person's actions and outcomes. We are now humbled by the
> complexity of the problem. People can make whatever distinctions their language
> permits and the causal structures of their world make important. At least for the
> time being, the question of their most important distinctions must be answered for
> each major domain in everyday life. (p. 1161)

I feel less humbled. The data unequivocally support the contention that there are
three underlying and very general dimensions of causality that transcend situations
and motivational contexts. Of course, a great many questions remain to be
answered, such as the situational and cultural determinants of structure and structural activation, and the cognitive processes involved in decisions regarding the
properties of causality. Many interesting questions are ready for systematic exploration. But there is clarity and simplicity in causal organization and in the layperson's
taxonomy of explanation.

Chapter 4
Perceived Causality and Goal Expectations

*In which a general psychological law is proposed
linking perceived causal stability with expectancy
change. Field and experimental studies support this
position, and aspects of the reinforcement literature
are reinterpreted.*

The foundation needed for more advanced theory construction has now been completed. As summarized in Fig. 1-4, an attributional theory of motivation begins with
a completed event, an outcome. If that outcome is unexpected, important, and/or
involves nonattainment of a desired goal, then a causal search is likely to be immediately undertaken. A large number of variables affect the results of this search,
including past history information, causal rules, and communications from others.
These factors influence what causal decision is reached, that is, which of the many
available causes is identified as appropriate to explain the outcome. Each motivational domain and specific activity within that domain has an extremely large number of plausible explanations for outcomes, but a few among these are most
dominant. Figure 1-4 lists the most salient causes within achievement- and
affiliative-related contexts, headed by the very prominent explanations of high or
low ability and high or low effort as determining success or failure. The causal judgment is located within a three-dimensional space representing the properties of
causes. The three dimensions are locus, stability, and controllability. The dimensional analysis gives the causes meaning or significance.

Concretely, assume that John's girlfriend Mary says no when he asks her to go to
a movie with him. This response initiates a causal search, inasmuch as goal attainment has been thwarted and the answer was unexpected. To aid in reaching a causal
decision, he asks, "Why not?" Mary is then likely to offer an explanation, such as,
"I hurt my back playing volleyball." John, in turn, may or may not accept this as the
true cause; he may remember that Mary does not think she will like this particular
movie, or had mentioned that a good program was on television, or that she has to
study for an exam. If the injury explanation is accepted, then the connotation or
meaning for John is that the cause is external to him (and internal to Mary), unstable
and uncontrollable. (Many people do not communicate the truth in situations of
rejection, although the false reason given is quite often believed; see Folkes, 1982;
Weiner, Amirkhan, Folkes, & Verette, in press).

To provide a further example, assume that Bill failed an important exam. Upon
receiving the grade he wonders, "Why did I do so poorly?" He notes that other stu-

dents received better grades than he did, although he studied a great deal. Bill concludes that he has low ability. Low ability is likely to be categorized as internal, rather constant, and primarily uncontrollable.

I now move from this description and taxonomy to a more complete theoretical analysis. My intent is to specify the theoretical linkages between causal attributions and other thoughts, feelings, and actions—the three aspects of psychological life.

Expectancy of Goal Attainment

The question, then, is what relations to pursue. After all, in the field of motivation thousands of empirical investigations have been conducted involving many, many independent and dependent variables. Which research is following the royal road, and which will fall by the wayside because it represents trivial concerns or because it has entered a cul-de-sac?

It is evident that some themes throughout the study of motivation are considered more central or more important than others and keep appearing. One such focus is goal expectancy. Every major cognitive motivational theorist, including Tolman, Lewin, Rotter, and Atkinson, includes the expectancy of goal attainment among the determinants of action. Indeed, the hypothesis that organisms are guided by anticipations (expected rewards) was crucial in distinguishing cognitive from mechanistic theories (see Tolman, 1932). It would therefore seem prudent to search for some connection between attributional thinking and goal expectancy.

Two possibilities come to mind. On the one hand, the influence of causal variables on the absolute expectancy of goal attainment could be ascertained. Heider (1958), for example, reasoned that goal expectancies in achievement-related contexts are determined by perceived ability and planned expenditure of effort relative to the perceived difficulty of the task. The higher one's perceived ability, the greater the planned exertion, and the easier the task, the greater the certainty of future success. This is an enticing analysis to follow, inasmuch as attributional concepts already are introduced.

Other theorists, however, have had completely different notions about the antecedents of goal expectancy. Tolman (1932), for example, working with animals, stipulated that expectancy is a function of the primacy, frequency, and recency of reinforcement. According to Rotter, Chance, and Phares (1972), expectancies are determined by the percentage of reinforcements of a particular response in a particular situation, the percentage of reinforcement of this reponse in similar settings, and individual differences in the belief that reinforcements are under personal control. For Atkinson (1964), expectancy is influenced by the number of individuals against whom one is competing, prior reinforcement history, or merely information from others (e.g., "You have a high chance of solving this problem"). It therefore is evident that consensus does not exist, although all these investigators would agree that past reinforcement is an important determinant of goal expectancy.

Even the belief in past reinforcement history is not without complexity, however. Are the historical antecedents the number of past reinforcements or the percentage of reinforced responses? Are early or recent successes given special importance in determining goal expectancies? Does the pattern of reinforcements influence expectancy, even with the number and percentage of rewards held constant? How does learning between trials, or the relation of between-response activities to response-linked outcomes, influence goal anticipations? These all appear to be difficult problems requiring mountains of research, which nonetheless will not immediately yield findings that may be generalized across a diversity of situations. Indeed, the lack of empirical consensus at this time is evidence that answers have not been reached regarding the determinants of expectancy of success. It therefore does not seem fruitful, at least initially, to search for the influence of causal ascriptions on the absolute level of expectancy.

A second possibility is first to find relations between attributions and *changes* in expectancy, and then later use this information to ascertain the relation between causal ascriptions and absolute expectancy level. Perhaps changes in goal expectancy, as opposed to absolute expectancy level, are more amenable to a general statement or law that will transcend the situational context. This may be particularly likely if only the direction and not the absolute magnitude of change is the prime concern. For many human endeavors, prediction of just the direction of expectancy shift ("Does she think her chances of success in the future have increased, remained the same, or decreased?") will facilitate our understanding of motivation and emotion.

Theories of Expectancy Change

Three psychological areas of investigation are directly related to changes in goal expectancy. One set of investigations is associated with research on level of aspiration; the second concerns the effects of outcomes at chance tasks on probabilities of future success; and the third is linked with resistance to extinction and beliefs about locus of control. The first two areas of study developed independently and apparently had little in common. Level-of-aspiration research was guided by Lewinian theory and a desire to understand developmental processes, whereas studies of chance were incorporated within game theory and the analysis of adult decision processes. However, in both research traditions success and failure were observed and/or manipulated. In addition, expectancies following an outcome were directly assessed by asking the research participants for their estimates of future success, or were indirectly inferred from behaviors such as betting, choice, or persistence (resistance to extinction).

These investigations left an important empirical legacy, which was incorporated within social learning theory by Julian Rotter (1954, 1966) and later into attributional thinking. The creative work of Rotter toward synthesizing these diverse fields included investigations that combined the study of skill-versus-chance perceptions with the manipulation of schedules of reinforcement. Ultimately, Rotter's analysis proved to be a key step in the formulation of a general law regarding expectancy change.

Level of Aspiration

The most widely accepted definition of level of aspiration is "the level of future performance in a familiar task which an individual, knowing his level of past performance in that task, explicitly undertakes to reach" (Frank, 1935, p. 119). Level of aspiration can therefore be considered a decision or a choice among alternatives of differing difficulty; the individual must decide, for example, how many rings he or she will toss over a peg in the next series of trials, or from what distance he or she will stand when tossing the rings (considering the experimental paradigm most frequently used by level-of-aspiration researchers).

A number of quite replicable findings emerged from this research. Among the most important for present purposes is that subsequent aspiration level is in part dependent on the prior outcome. In the vast majority of instances, aspiration level increases after goal attainment (success) and decreases if a prior aspiration was not fulfilled (failure). These so-called goal discrepancies are referred to as "typical" aspiration shifts. However, "atypical" reactions are also sometimes observed. In these instances, there is a decrease in aspiration level following success and an increase after a goal has not been met. For example, Lewin, Dembo, Festinger, and Sears (1944) noted:

> In the case of nonachievement which is linked, for instance, to outside disturbances, the subject is not likely to lower this aspiration in the way that he would if he believed that the nonachievement reflected a genuine decrement in his performance ability. (p. 367)

All aspiration theorists (e.g., Atkinson, 1964; Festinger, 1942; Lewin et al., 1944; Rotter, 1954) assume that aspiration level is in part determined by the subjective expectancy of success. The higher the expectancy, the higher will be the aspiration level. Thus, for example, the tendency to raise aspiration level from five to six rings over the peg, after five rings have been successfully thrown, is assumed to reflect additional confidence of success after goal attainment. Conversely, decrements in aspiration level following failure are presumed to reflect lowered expectations. Indeed, at times aspiration level has the same connotation as subjective expectancy of success. As Zajonc and Brickman (1969) noted, "In some cases level of aspiration has been obtained not by asking subjects to state their goals, but by indicating what level of performance they expect to attain on the next trial" (p. 148).

Substituting, then, expectancy change for aspiration level, a general statement regarding goal anticipations can be offered: In skill-related situations (such as ring tossing), increments in expectancy follow success, whereas expectancy decrements follow failure. This conclusion is not based exclusively on level-of-aspiration research; these changes also have been documented in contexts where expectancy is directly measured rather than inferred from statements about goal aspiration (see, for example, Diggory, Riley, & Blumenfeld, 1960; Montanelli & Hill, 1969; Zajonc & Brickman, 1969). This summary is not the complete story, as illustrated in the observation by Lewin et al. (1944) of atypical shifts. It will, however, serve as a very useful first step linking performance outcomes (success and failure) to respective changes (increase or decrease) in the direction of expectancy shifts given achievement-related contexts.

Expectancy Change at Chance Tasks

A quite divergent pattern of data emerged from research on the subjective probability of success at games of chance. Here, one often observes what is called the "gambler's fallacy." That is, a loss is expected after winning, and a win is anticipated after losing, even though the outcome at games of chance are objectively independent (see Cohen & Hansel, 1956). A related phenomenon in games of chance is labeled the "negative recency effect." This is illustrated in the increased expectancy of a "heads" after appearance of a "tails" on a coin toss. Indeed, the belief in the appearance of a heads increases with the number of consecutive occurrences of tails, until there are questions raised about the fairness of the game (Lepley, 1963). In sum, in games of chance atypical shifts are frequently observed.

These findings in chance tasks have been documented many times and can be accepted as empirical truths. However, there are again some exceptions to the general rule. At times, gamblers exhibit the belief that they will continue to win or that they are in the midst of a losing streak in which they anticipate future repetitions of a loss. At this point they often decide to leave the game. Thus, typical shifts can also be observed in chance settings.

Expectancy Shifts at Skill Versus Chance Tasks: The Social Learning Theory Integration

In skill-related tasks, then, expectancies tend to increase after success and to decrease after failure. These are called typical expectancy shifts. On the other hand, in chance tasks there are frequent occurrences of atypical shifts or what is called the gambler's fallacy: The future is perceived as having a reasonable likelihood of differing from the past. There also are less frequent instances of the opposite pattern of data: atypical shifts at skill-related tasks and typical shifts at chance tasks. These data are summarized in Figure 4-1. The problem faced is to create a conceptual framework able to incorporate all these observations.

Social learning theorists attempted to do just that. As one step in this endeavor, experiments were conducted that manipulated both skill and chance perceptions

	Task Characteristic	
	Skill	Chance
More common observation	Typical shift	Atypical shift
Less common observation	Atypical shift	Typical shift

Figure 4-1. Observation of expectancy change at skill and chance tasks.

within the identical situational context. For example, Phares (1957) instructed one half of his subjects that performance at a matching task was only a matter of luck, while subjects in a second experimental condition received information that performance at the same task was determined by skill (visual acuity). In this task, the research participants had to determine whether two colors or two lines were identical. Subjective probability of success was inferred prior to each trial from the amount that the subjects were willing to bet on their next response. There was a fixed order of partial reinforcement given in both experimental conditions that was entirely predetermined by the experimenter, regardless of the responses made by the subjects.

The data revealed that typical expectancy shifts were more frequent and of greater magnitude in the skill condition, whereas atypical shifts were more evident in the chance condition. However, there were some observations of atypical shifts in the skill setting and of typical shifts in the chance setting. The data therefore were entirely consistent with the scheme in Figure 4-1.

To explain these data, Rotter and his colleagues used principles from social learning theory and the concept of locus of control introduced in the prior chapter. They reasoned:

> It is a matter of common sense that most individuals who find a $5 bill on a given street would not return and walk up and down the street many times to find more $5 bills . . . [that is, the expectancy of the behavior producing a reward has not increased]. On the other hand, should someone take up ping pong and be told that he plays an excellent game for someone just learning, he is quite likely to increase the number of times he plays ping pong [that is, the expectancy of the behavior producing a reward has increased]. In the first place, the reinforcement appears to be a matter of chance . . . and in the second instance, the reinforcement appears to be dependent on some characteristic or quality of the person which he can label as skill. (Rotter, Seeman, & Liverant, 1962, p. 474)

In sum, the magnitude of expectancy change following a success or failure was postulated to be influenced by the perceived locus of the event, with internal or personal causal ascriptions for an outcome producing greater and more typical shifts than environmental or external perceptions of control (causality).

This theory therefore could explain the predominant typical shifts observed in skill settings (internal control) and the atypical shifts evident in chance settings (external control). In addition, given that some individuals might perceive skill tasks as determined by chance, and chance tasks as affected by personal factors, occasional reversals in the usual pattern of data could be accounted for.

A Confound

In the previous chapter it was reasoned, however, that Rotter and his colleagues gave insufficient attention to the richness of causal explanation and confounded dimensions of causality. Ability (skill), in addition to being perceived as internal, also is relatively stable. In the experiment by Phares (1957), it certainly is likely that the possession of visual acuity would be perceived as a traitlike characteristic in the skill instruction condition. On the other hand, in addition to being perceived as external, luck is unstable. Hence, ability and luck differ in subjective stability and not just on the locus dimension of causality (see Figure 3-1). The observed differences in expectancy shifts given skill versus chance tasks (or perceptions), which can be regarded as an empirical fact, may then be ascribed to either the locus (ability as internal versus luck as external) or the stability (ability as stable versus luck as unstable) dimension of causality.

Rotter and his colleagues erred in selecting locus rather than stability as the causal property linked with expectancy and expectancy change. Although it will now be documented that the social learning theorists lost this battle (the specific attributional property related to expectancy), they indeed won the larger war (discerning that expectancy shifts could be explained with causal constructs).

An Attributional Approach to Expectancy Change

The attributional position is that the stability of a cause, rather than its locus, determines expectancy shifts. If conditions (the presence or absence of causes) are expected to remain the same, then the outcomes experienced on past occasions will be expected to recur. A success under these circumstances would produce relatively large increments in the anticipation of future success, and a failure would strengthen the belief that there will be subsequent failures. On the other hand, if the causal conditions are perceived as likely to change, then the present outcome may not be expected to repeat itself in the future, or there may be uncertainty about subsequent outcomes. A success therefore would yield relatively small increments, if any, and perhaps decrements in the expectancy of subsequent success, whereas a failure need not necessarily intensify the belief that there will be future failures.

Just as with social learning theory, these principles are able to explain all the data thus far presented. Success and failure at skill tasks are usually ascribed to ability and effort. Ability is thought to be a fixed property, such as visual acuity, and the belief that success was caused by hard work usually results in the intent to work hard again in the future. Inasmuch as the causes of a prior success are perceived as relatively stable given skill-related tasks, future success should be anticipated with greater certainty, and there will be increments in aspiration level and expectancy judgments. Occasionally, however, outcomes at skill tasks are ascribed to unstable factors, such as the "outside disturbances" noted by Lewin et al. (1944). In addition, if failure is attributed to low effort, then the failing person may plan to work harder in the future. In these situations, there would be atypical or minimal shifts in expectancy following the outcome.

On the other hand, success or failure at a chance task tends to be ascribed to an unstable factor. The person is likely to reason, "I had good (or bad) luck last time, but that may not happen again." Expectancy or level of aspiration therefore should not rise and indeed could drop following a positive outcome or rise after a negative outcome. On occasion, however, given a chance task, one might conclude that he or she is a lucky or unlucky person (a trait), or is "riding a winning (or losing) streak."

In these instances, the cause of the outcome is perceived as stable, so that typical shifts are displayed. In sum, the attributional position also can account for the pattern of data summarized in Figure 4-1.

An Experimental Comparison of the Competing Theories

Numerous laboratory investigations relating causal stability to expectancy were conducted in the 1970s. Some of these, including an investigation by Weiner, Nierenberg, and Goldstein (1976), were crucial in that direct comparisons were made between the social learning and the attributional positions.

Weiner et al. (1976) gave subjects either 0, 1, 2, 3, 4, or 5 consecutive success experiences at a block-design task, with different subjects in the six experimental conditions. Following the success trial(s), expectancy of success and causal ascriptions were assessed. Expectancy of success was determined by having subjects indicate "how many of the next ten similar designs you believe that you will successfully complete" (Weiner et al., 1976, p. 61). To assess perceptions of causality, subjects were required to mark four rating scales, which were identical with respect to either the stability or the locus dimensional anchors but differed along the other dimension. Specifically, one attribution question was, "Did you succeed on this task because you are always good at these kinds of tasks, or because you tried especially hard on this particular task?" *Always good* and *tried especially hard*, the anchors on this scale, are identical on the locus of causality dimension (internal), but they differ in perceived stability, with ability a stable cause and effort manipulated by the wording of the question to connote an unstable cause. In a similar manner, judgments were made between *lucky* and *tried especially hard* (unstable causes differing in locus), *these tasks are always easy* and *lucky* (external causes differing in stability), and *always good* and *always easy* (stable causes differing in locus).

In sum, there were two judgments for each causal dimension. These two ratings were then added to yield an overall dimension score. In this manner, causal perceptions were independently determined for both the locus and the stability dimensions of causality. Then, within each of the success conditions, the subjects were classified as high (above the median) or low (below the median) in perceived stability of the causal judgment and perceived locus of causality of the outcome.

Table 4-1 shows the mean change in expectancy of success (relative to the baseline group, which received no success before the expectancy judgment) as a function of the number of success experiences and the dimensional classifications. As anticipated on the basis of the skill research literature, expectancy of success generally increases with the number of prior successes. More important for the present discussion, Table 4-1 reveals that the increase in expectancy of future success is directly related to the perceived stability of the cause of the prior outcome—high stability is linked with higher expectancies than is low stability, particularly on the early trials. On the other hand, Table 4-1 also shows that perceptions of the locus of causality are much more weakly (and insignificantly) related to stated expectancies of success. The results therefore support the attributional conception and contradict predictions from social learning theory.

Table 4-1. Mean Expectancy Difference Scores (Trial Minus Baseline) for Subjects Classified on the Causal Dimensions of Stability and Locus, as a Function of Number of Success Trials

Causal Dimensions	Trials				
	1	2	3	4	5
Stability					
Stable	1.09[a]	1.09	1.73	1.91	1.82
Unstable	−.19	−.49	.91	1.11	1.91
Difference	1.18	1.58	.82	.80	−.09
Locus					
Internal	.82	.64	1.61	1.51	1.73
External	.11	.01	1.09	1.56	2.01
Difference	.71	.63	.52	−.05	−.28

[a] Positive numbers indicate a higher expectancy on that trial relative to a presuccess trial.
Note. Data from "Social Learning (Locus of Control) Versus Attributional (Causal Stability) Interpretations of Expectancy of Success" by B. Weiner et al., 1976, *Journal of Personality, 44.* Copyright 1976. Reprinted by permission.

Other Experimental Research

The Weiner et al. (1976) investigation has been reviewed in some detail because it clearly pitted the social learning position against the attributional position regarding the determinants of expectancy of success. As already intimated, many other laboratory investigations conducted in the 1970s also tested the attributional conception. Before reviewing this research, it is necessary to make explicit my approach to these studies. As in the examination of causal dimensions, I will be attempting to discern the cross-study consistency in the data. An "amateur" meta-analysis is conducted that allows the reader, as well as the writer, to feel confident about the general conclusions that are reached. However, a note of caution is necessary concerning the quality of the individual research studies: As wisdom about causal attributions and attributional research increased, the shortcomings of prior investigations became evident. The problems particularly pertain to the classification of causes on the stability dimension. I acknowledged earlier that effort is likely to be perceived as more unstable given failure than success, and that there might be disagreement between individuals concerning the relative placement of a cause on a dimension. These possibilities were overlooked by earlier researchers. I believe that as a consequence of neglecting the phenomenology of the subject, many investigators may have underestimated the association between causal stability and expectancy. This further increases the need for a more encompassing data analysis, bringing many studies to bear upon a conclusion.

Correlational research. The laboratory research falls into two distinct groupings. One set of investigations is correlational, although there is an experimental intervention. Success and/or failure at some task is manipulated, and subjects indicate their attributions for the outcome as well as their subjective expectancy of future success (Hendrick & Giesen, 1975; Inagi, 1977; Kojima, 1984; Kovenklioglu & Greenhaus, 1978; McCaughan, 1978; McMahan, 1973; Meyer, 1970; Singer & McCaughan, 1978; Weiner et al., 1976). The attributions are then correlated with reported expectancy of success. Among the variations between these studies are the age and nationality of the subjects, the types of tasks used to induce success and failure, the method of assessing causal attributions, and the index of future expectancies (see Table 4-2). Of the nine correlational studies cited, only six are included in Table 4-2. The reported data in the three excluded investigations do not permit conclusions pertinent to the present discussion.

Table 4-3 shows the correlations in four of these six studies. The data from Meyer (1970) were not reported as correlations and are therefore separately depicted in Figure 4-2, and the data from Weiner et al. (1976) have already been presented in Table 4-1. What is most evident and certain from Tables 4-1 and 4-3 is that, given success, attributions to ability correlate positively with expectations, whereas ascriptions to luck correlate negatively with future hopes. That is, the more one ascribes success to ability and the less one ascribes success to luck, the more positive are future anticipations. Given failure (here the data in Figure 4-2 also are relevant), attributions to ability correlate negatively with predictions for the future, whereas ascriptions to effort and, to a lesser degree, luck relate positively to anticipations of

Table 4-2. Correlational Studies Relating Attributions to Expectancies

Investigator	Subjects	Task	Attribution Measurement	Expectancy Measure
Meyer (1970)	German high-school students	Digit-symbol substitution	Percentage rating	Probability of future success
McMahan (1973)	American grammar, high-school, and college students	Anagrams	Paired comparison	Confidence of future success
Weiner, Nierenberg, & Goldstein (1976)	American college students	Block design	Within-dimension scale rating	Level of anticipated performance
Inagi, 1977	Japanese college students	Puzzle	Percentage rating	Probability of future success
Kovenklioglu & Greenhaus (1978)	American college students	Test	Paired comparison	Level of anticipated performance
Kojima (1984)	Japanese high-school students	Digit-symbol	Percentage rating	Probability of future success

Table 4-3. Correlations Between Attributional Judgments and Expectancy of Success

Investigator	Outcome									
	Success					Failure				
	Ability	Effort	Task Difficulty	Luck	Stability[a]	Ability	Effort	Task Difficulty	Luck	Stability
McMahan (1973)[b]	.39	−.27	.16	−.27		−.27	.35	−.08	.05	
	.54	−.14	.15	−.42		−.22	.38	−.30	.17	
	.31	.01	−.01	−.34		−.33	.16	.03	.11	
Inagi (1977)[c]						−.38	.18	.03	.43	−.48
Kovenklioglu & Greenhaus (1978)[d]	.40	−.22	.06	−.25	.39	−.36	.33	−.04	.12	−.38
Kojima (1984)[e]	.24	−.09	.13	−.16	.30	−.33	.32	−.20	.08	−.39
						−.29	.08	−.02	.23	−.24

[a] A combined score of the stable minus the unstable ascriptions.
[b] Only the first trial data for his three subject groups are taken; stability indices were not reported.
[c] Data from the success condition were not reported.
[d] Data reported from two different testing periods.
[e] Correlations reported for failure only.

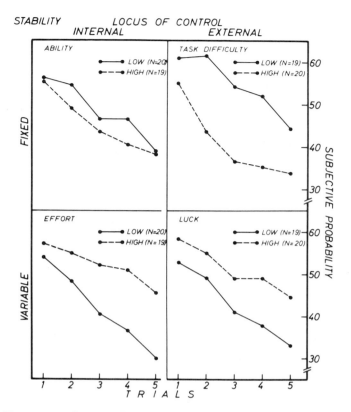

Figure 4-2. Expectancy of success following failure as a function of above-versus below-median ascriptions to four causal factors. High ascription indicates lack of ability, a difficult task, lack of effort, and bad luck. From *Selbstverantwortlichkeit und Leistungsmotivation* by W. U. Meyer, 1970 (reported in Weiner, Heckhausen, Meyer, & Cook, 1972). Copyright 1970. Adapted with permission.

success. Hence, the more one ascribes failure to lack of trying and bad luck, and the less to low ability, the higher the hopes for the future. Note that effort and ability are internal causes of achievement outcomes, yet they have opposite relations to expectancy of success in situations of failure. This contradicts the approach of social learning theory. Conversely, the overall pattern of data conforms closely to attributional predictions, inasmuch as ability is a stable cause of success and failure, whereas luck is unstable. In addition, effort is also perceived as unstable in most situations involving failure.

Of particular interest among this group of investigations is the study by Inagi (1977), for he also contrasted the attributional with the social learning position among a Japanese subject population. Attributions for failure were combined to yield indexes of both stability and locus of causality. The relations between these

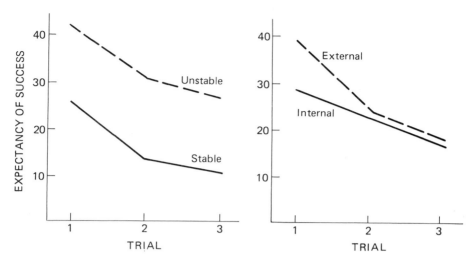

Figure 4-3. Expectancy of future success related to causal stability (left panel) and causal locus (right panel). From "Causal Ascription and Expectancy of Success" by T. Inagi, 1977, *Japanese Psychological Research*, *19*, p. 25. Copyright 1977. Reprinted by permission.

two causal dimensions and future anticipations of success are depicted in Figure 4-3, which shows clearly that stability, but not locus, is systematically related to expectancy of success. An identical pattern of data subsequently was reported by Kojima (1984).

Manipulating causal ascriptions. The second procedure examining the relation between causal ascriptions and expectancy is experimental, in that attributions as well as outcomes are manipulated (see Fontaine, 1974; Heilman & Guzzo, 1978; Neale & Friend, 1972; Pancer & Eiser, 1977; Rosenbaum, 1972; Valle, 1974). These investigations differ in their method of inducing causal attributions (e.g., instructions from the experimenter, communications from confederate subjects, description of a hypothetical situation), as well as in their situational context (see Table 4-4). Table 4-4 reveals that four of the six studies cited above are hypothetical; that is, subjects act as observers in make-believe settings rather than judge their own future performance. Thus, in contrast to the correlational research, these experimenters have for the most part traded the reality of the situation for purity in the causal manipulation and the increased amenability to infer the direction of causation.

Unlike the correlational studies, the investigations that manipulate causal ascriptions are too diverse to present in a table format, and the dependent variables are only conceptually comparable. A very brief summary of these papers therefore is provided.

• Rosenbaum (1972) informed subjects that a supervisor and a subordinate produced a high- or a low-quality "project," with eight different reasons provided in

Table 4-4. Experimental Studies Relating Attributions to Expectations

Investigator	Subjects	Task	Manipulation Method	Expectancy Measure
Rosenbaum (1972)	American college students	Unspecified "project" (hypothetical)	Causes given in description	Expected project outcome
Neale & Friend (1972)	American college students	School exam (hypothetical)	Causes given in description	Anticipated grade
Fontaine (1974)	Australian college students	Unspecified "tasks"	Fictitious ascriptions of others	Expected score
Valle (1974)	American college students	Sales (hypothetical)	Causes given in description	Performance anticipation
Pancer & Eiser (1977)	British college students	Anagrams	Fictitious information from others	Performance prediction
Heilman & Guzzo (1978)	American college students	Job performance (hypothetical)	Causes given in description	Predicted personnel action

the experimental conditions (e.g., tried hard, does not have the ability). Figure 4-4 shows that stable effort and stable ability, relative to unstable effort and a temporary lapse in ability, augment the expectancy that the prior outcome, whether success or failure, will occur.

• Neale and Friend (1972) indicated that students performed well or poorly on an exam, and ability, effort, task, and luck information was provided. High ability, high effort, and the absence of good luck as the prior causal pattern was associated with high expectations following a success, whereas being considered high in ability, expending little effort, and experiencing bad luck was related to high expectancies for the future given failure.

• Fontaine (1974) induced subjects to believe that they would be performing some tasks, and the subjects were told why similar research participants had succeeded or failed. Fontaine concluded, "High expectancies were associated with comparison group success and attribution to stable factors (ability and task ease), while lowest expectancies were associated with attributions to stable factors and comparison group failure" (p. 492). The data, shown in Figure 4-5, closely mirror the findings of Rosenbaum (1972).

• Valle (1974) described successful sales projects and reported systematic and reliable positive relationships in four studies between future performance anticipations and perceived stable causes for success and unstable causes for failure.

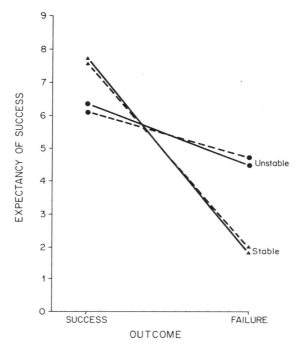

Figure 4-4. The effects of causal stability on expectancy of success following hypothetical success and failure. From *A Dimensional Analysis of the Perceived Causes of Success and Failure* by R. M. Rosenbaum, 1972, p. 83. Copyright 1972. Adapted with permission.

• Pancer and Eiser (1977) gave subjects anagrams to perform and also fictitious causal attributions of others. If others succeeded, then subjects expected to perform best when that success was described as due to the ease of the task, whereas if others failed, they anticipated performing the worst when that failure was ascribed to the difficulty of the task.

• Heilman and Guzzo (1978) examined the relationship between the perceived causes of successful job performance and a decision to promote the employee (which can be considered an index of future expectancies). Promotion was most suggested when success was due to ability and hard work, and least advised when the past positive outcome was ascribed to good luck ("simply being in the right place at the right time").

General Summary

There are a few evident characteristics of the correlational and manipulational investigations examining the relations between attributions, causal stability, and expectancy. The studies are relatively similar: Success and failure at some task are manipulated, and causal attributions are either varied or assessed. The experimental

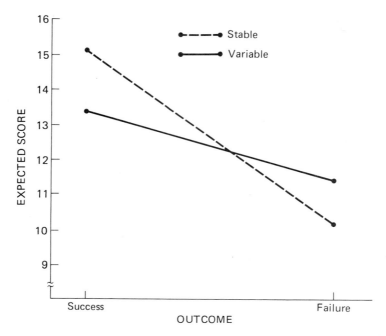

Figure 4-5. Mean expected score as a function of comparison group outcome and comparison group attribution to stable versus variable factors. From "Social Comparison and Some Determinants of Expected Personal Control and Expected Performance in a Novel Task Situation" by G. Fontaine, 1974, *Journal of Personality and Social Psychology, 29*, p. 491. Copyright 1974. Reprinted with permission.

designs are straightforward, and the pattern of results in the studies also is virtually identical. It also is apparent that both the correlational and the manipulational investigations were conducted primarily during the short interval between 1972 and 1978. I am not aware of all the investigations conducted during that period and do not pretend that a definitive search has been conducted. A few additional investigations completed after this period are presented in the methodology section of this chapter, for they highlight procedural issues. It is reasonable to conclude that research using these paradigms is for the most part a thing of the past (albeit the recent past). And such studies should be part of history, because the empirical question is no longer whether attributions and causal stability relate to expectancy change and expectancy. This has been determined both logically and empirically.

One might nevertheless look upon the theoretical analysis and the data thus far reviewed with something less than enthusiasm. It is true that typical and atypical shifts in skill and chance settings can be accounted for, and that a wealth of laboratory studies support an attribution-expectancy linkage. Yet the attributional position merely repeats the logic of what is meant by a cause-effect relationship. If a particular effect is perceived as determined by a particular cause, and if that cause is anticipated to remain, then the effect should be expected to reoccur. On the other hand, if the cause might change, then the effect also is subject to change. These statements surely do not reveal anything new, or anything other than what common sense or shared knowledge would provide. Why, then, all the fuss?

As already discussed, this position is important because it is at variance with social learning theory, which had instigated many pertinent, and perhaps fruitless, investigations (see, for example, Graybill, 1978). Additionally, and of more significance, the simple cause-effect rules outlined here have enormous implications for diverse areas in the field of motivation, they have resulted in new interpretations of established phenomena in psychology, and a general law for human and perhaps infrahuman behavior has been provided. These three topics are examined in turn.

Implications of the Stability-Expectancy Relation

The research concerning expectancy change in skill and chance situations as well as the attribution-expectancy research reviewed above took place in laboratory settings. This may lead to questions as to whether the relations under study are exhibited in the real world (see Phares, 1978, p. 270). However, field research has documented that the stability-expectancy relationship does extend beyond the laboratory and to domains other than achievement. As with most field research, the majority of the data obtained are correlational and thus do not permit one to determine the direction of causality. However, additional "fieldlike" research is also included in this section because real-life intentions or behaviors were assessed, even though causal variables were experimentally manipulated. This research thus allows a more definitive statement regarding the direction of influence.

Crime and Perceptions of the Criminal

A criminal act is certainly negative from the standpoint of society and is at variance with normative behavior. Thus, it should elicit an attributional search to determine why the crime was committed. The results of this attributional decision have far-reaching consequence for the length of the criminal sentence, the treatment during incarceration, and the decision to release or not release the prisoner early (parole).

Saulnier and Perlman (1981) asked criminal inmates as well as the prison staff acquainted with the prisoners about the causes of their crimes. The participants then responded to the following causal dimension questions (which were slightly varied for each population):

1. Overall, think about the causes of the crime. Did it occur mainly because of something about you (such as your personality or habits), or was it due to something about the situation or another person or persons?
2. Did the crime occur because of something that changes easily (such as luck, fate, person's mood)—or because of something pretty unchanging (such as long-term lack of a job, or other unchanging qualities of a person or situation)? (p. 560)

Table 4-5. Attribution and Recidivism Ratings by Inmates and Staff[a]

Rated Variable	Inmates	Staff
Externality	2.87	2.12
Stability	2.72	3.54
Recidivism	1.70	3.49

[a] Higher scores reflect more external (less internal) attributions, more stable attributions, and a greater perceived likelihood of recidivism.
Note: From "The Actor-Observer Bias Is Alive and Well in Prison: A Sequel to Wells" by K. Saulnier and D. Perlman, 1981, *Personality and Social Psychology Bulletin*, *1*, p. 561. Copyright 1981. Reprinted by permission.

In addition to the locus and stability ratings, both groups were asked about the possibility of the criminal taking part in a similar crime again (recidivism).

The results of this study are given in Table 4-5. The staff rated the cause of the crime as less external (more internal) and more stable than did the inmates. Thus, they tended to attribute criminal behavior to traits. The staff also had a higher expectancy of recidivism than did the prisoners. Within both groups there was a positive correlation between causal stability and expectancy of another crime.

Inasmuch as the expectancy of future criminal behavior appears to be in part determined by the perceived stability of the cause of the prior crime, the decision to release or not release a prisoner early should be guided by perceptions of causality. After all, one of the main concerns of a parole board is whether the criminal is a risk to society, where risk implies a reasonable probability that a crime might be repeated.

According to Carroll and Payne (1976), a parole decision is a complex judgment in which causal attributions play a major role. Figure 4-6 in part depicts the parole decision process as conceptualized by Carroll and Payne (1976, 1977a). Figure 4-6 indicates that the decision maker is provided with information about the criminal, the crime, and other pertinent facts. This information is combined and synthesized, yielding attributions about the causes of the crime and their stability. The causal perceptions, in turn, influence judgments about social risk, which is believed to be the main determinant of the final parole decision (see Carroll, 1978).

Carroll and Payne (1976, 1977a) and Carroll (1978) have furnished support for this line of reasoning, examining professional parole decision makers as well as the judgments of college students when given simulated criminal cases. In the research most closely approximating a field (i.e., nonintervention) study, Carroll (1978) designed a two-page questionnaire to be completed by members of a parole board immediately following a parole hearing. The questionnaire included the recommendation decision, 22 possible factors influencing this decision, and an open-ended assessment of the causal attribution for the crime. The attributions were coded on the three causal dimensions by the experimenter. Carroll (1978) reported that:

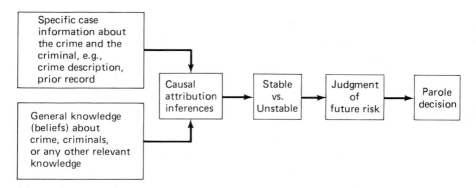

Figure 4-6. An attribution framework for the parole decision process for parole board members. From "Judgments About Crime and the Criminal: A Model and a Method for Investigating Parole Decisions" by J. S. Carroll and J. W. Payne, 1977a, in B. D. Sales (Ed.), *Perspectives in Law and Psychology* (Vol. 1), New York: Plenum, p. 200. Copyright 1977. Adapted with permission.

> Parole recommendations did not depend upon sentence, crime type, or record, but did depend on the individual decision maker and upon the stability of the offense cause. More stability is associated with less favorable recommendations. (p. 1506)

He then went on to conclude:

> The Board seems to take the viewpoint that the judge *evaluates* the seriousness of the crime and assigns punishment, whereas the parole board predicts the benefits to the client and the risks to the community in deciding upon release. As we have previously shown, the stability of causal attributions regarding the offense appears to affect recommendations by mediating predictions of the risk of future crime. (pp. 1507–1508)

Depression and Reactions to Rape

Janoff-Bulman (1979) examined perceptions of personal causality among depressed and nondepressed persons and among rape victims. She distinguished between two types of self-blame, "one representing an adaptive, control-oriented response, the other a maladaptive, self-deprecating response" (p. 1799). The former places blame on a particular behavior (e.g., walking down the wrong street as the cause of the rape), whereas the latter faults personal character (e.g., inability to stay out of trouble). Janoff-Bulman (1979) related the distinction between behavioral and characterological blame to the differentiation in the achievement domain between effort and ability attributions. Behavioral blame, like effort, is unstable and controllable, whereas characterological blame, like ability, is perceived as stable and uncontrollable.

In two investigations, Janoff-Bulman examined the correlates and the potential consequences of these attributional tendencies. One investigation included participants who differed in their level of depression. These subjects were presented with hypothetical personal events, such as a car accident or the ending of a love affair. They then revealed whether the cause of the event would be characterological (due to the kind of person you are) or behavioral (due to what you did) had the event actually happened to them. The participants also rated whether such "failures" could be prevented in the future. Depressed individuals scored higher in characterological blame than nondepressed ones, and behavioral blame was related to a lower expectancy of these negative outcomes occurring in the future.

In a second preliminary study of rape victims, self-blame again could clearly be differentiated into those victims blaming their character and those blaming their behavior. Janoff-Bulman (1979) contends that the women who blamed their character will have more difficulty in coping with their experience than the behavioral blamers, in part because different future expectancies are generated by the disparate perceptions of causal stability.

Academic Intents

It is known that behavioral intentions are to a large degree determined by expectations of future success (Fishbein & Ajzen, 1975). If anticipation of a reward for a particular activity is low, then the actor will probably not intend to engage in that action. Conversely, high expectancies of a reward increase the intention to perform a particular behavior. It therefore also follows that causal ascriptions, which influence expectancy of success, should also affect behavioral intents. More specifically, an ascription of failure to stable factors ought to reduce the intention to engage in the failed activity in the future. This also should hold relatively true if success is attributed to unstable causes. On the other hand, failure ascribed to unstable causes or success to stable causes should relatively augment the intention to engage in the outcome-linked activity in the future.

The relation between attributions and intentions has been directly examined in three field studies, all conducted in achievement-related contexts. In perhaps the most straightforward of these, Day (1982) asked students who were prematurely withdrawing from college what caused them to drop out. The students' intentions of returning to school were also ascertained. Students indicating that the causes of dropping out were unstable (e.g., "Need a break from academic work") were more likely to state an intention to return to the university.

Pancer (1978) addressed the issue of intentions to enroll in particular courses in school. Three weeks before the end of the school term, Pancer (1978) asked students enrolled in an introductory psychology course how many future psychology courses they intended to take. In addition, he assessed their perceptions of the contributions of ability and effort to their current performances. The correlations between attributions and intentions as a function of success or failure in the course are shown in Table 4-6. Table 4-6 reveals that, given success, attributions to high ability related positively with the number of course intended to be taken, whereas the more that failure was attributed to (low) ability, the more likely the intention not to enroll in

Table 4-6. Correlations of Estimated Number of Future Courses and Attribution Measures

Measure	Final grade	
	A	C or lower
Attribution to ability	.199	−.435
Attribution to effort	.207	.276

Note. From "Causal Attributions and Anticipated Future Performance" by S. M. Pancer, 1978, *Personality and Social Psychology Bulletin, 4,* p. 602. Copyright 1978. Adapted by permission.

other psychology courses. One interpretation of these findings is that causal stability plays a key mediating role, increasing subsequent expectancy and intent given a positive outcome and decreasing these factors given a negative outcome.

The data for the effort attributions also confirm theoretical predictions. As already revealed, effort tends to be perceived as relatively stable in situations of success. Thus, as in the case of ability attributions, the correlation between ascription of success to effort and behavioral intentions is positive. In the case of failure, however, effort is an unstable ascription. One anticipates trying harder in the future given an attribution of failure to lack of effort. Hence, ascription of failure to insufficient trying also correlates positively with the intention to enroll in more psychology courses. This illustrates the positive consequences of ascribing all achievement-related outcomes to effort expenditure.

Finally, Crittended and Wiley (1980) examined a decision closer to the hearts of many readers: the intention to resubmit a manuscript that has been rejected for publication. These investigators first identified stable (e.g., author's training and ability) as well as unstable (e.g., editorial judgment, choice of reviewers) causes of rejection (see Wiley, Crittended, & Birg, 1979). In accordance with attributional thinking, it was predicted that ascription of rejection to stable causes would result in a cessation of intention to publish the manuscript, whereas attributions to unstable causes would foster a decision to resubmit. This hypothesis was confirmed, but only for the female authors. None of the independent variables, including prior success history or professional status, contributed to an understanding of publication persistence among the males.

In sum, three studies have related causal attributions to intentions in real-life achievement situations. There is a consistant data pattern: The intent to return to school, to take more psychology classes, and (among females) to resubmit a rejected manuscript is increased by ascriptions of "failure" to unstable causes and/or attributions of success to stable causes.

Consumer Behavior

What do consumers do, or intend to do, after purchasing a product that is defective? According to Folkes (1984), this depends on the perceived cause of the deficiency.

Folkes manipulated the causes of product deficiency in an experimental setting, thus departing from a nonintervention strategy. Folkes supplied eight causes of product failure, each cause fitting within a cell of a 2 (Locus) × 2 (Stability) × 2 (Controllability) matrix (see Table 3-2). For example, among the situations and causes used by Folkes (1984) were the following:

> A student bought a new type of weight-loss breakfast drink. After a week, he had not lost any weight. This was because:

1. The student never follows a constant menu and avoided the prescribed diet [internal, stable, controllable]
2. The student is allergic to the ingredients [internal, stable, uncontrollable]
3. The manufacturer knows that the product does not work [external, stable, controllable]
4. Unknown by the manufacturer, a freak heat wave damaged the product [external, unstable, uncontrollable].

The respondents rated expectations, emotions, and the actions of the students in this situation for each of the reasons provided. Among the rated scales were:

1. If the manufacturer gave the student another container of the weight-loss drink, do you think the student would expect to lose weight?
2. Would the person prefer a product exchange or a refund?

Folkes (1984) reported that if the cause of product failure was perceived as unstable, then the consumer was thought to have relatively high future expectations and would express the desire to exchange the product. On the other hand, if the cause was perceived as stable, then subjects inferred low expectations and that a refund would be preferred (see Table 4-7). These findings are entirely consistent with attributional predictions.

Table 4-7. Mean of Expectancies and Preferred Redress Ratings

Type of Cause	Expectancies for Future[a]	Refund vs. Exchange[b]
Consumer-related, unstable	7.1	6.2
Consumer-related, stable	3.9	3.8
Manufacturer-related, unstable	6.3	4.1
Manufacturer-related, stable	2.4	1.7

[a] The higher the number, the more failure is not expected.
[b] The higher the number, the more an exchange is preferred.
Note. From "Consumer Reactions to Product Failure: An Attributional Approach" by V. S. Folkes, 1984, *Journal of Consumer Research, 11*, p. 405. Copyright 1984. Adapted by permission.

Soliciting Blood Donations

Two experiments regarding the solicitation of blood donations also depart from the nonintervention strategy of field research by manipulating causal attributions. As previously indicated, I somewhat arbitrarily include them here because of the real-life context that was contrived by the experimenters.

Anderson and Jennings (1980) told subjects that the Red Cross was examining persuasion techniques used by telephone solicitors when asking others to donate blood. The subjects were tricked into believing that they would be phoning individuals for blood donations and were asked to prepare a sales pitch. In fact, the calls were made to a confederate who refused to donate.

To manipulate causal ascriptions, another confederate (thought to be a subject by the real research participants) commented on his or her perceptions of the causes of success and failure in this situation. Two attributions were manipulated: task strategy (unstable) and ability (stable). In the strategy condition the confederate remarked:

> It seems to me that we could do all right if we approach this thing in the right way. I have a friend in Oakland who is a salesman for Bristol-Meyers. At first he didn't do too well. Then, he started using different tactics until he found one that worked. He's developed a strategy that's pretty successful. I think we should try the same type of thing. What do you say? (p. 397)

On the other hand, in the ability condition the confederate said:

> I think that the problem is exactly what that guy [the experimenter] said it was: some people do well, others do poorly. I had some friends calling for the Cancer Research Foundation. One guy was really good. He could talk just about everybody into contributing. The other guy couldn't get anybody to contribute. It is sort of like either you've got it or you don't. What do you say? (p. 397)

The key dependent variable was a judgment, after initial failure, of how many donations would be solicited in the next 50 calls. Success expectancies were stated in terms of five blocks of 10 calls each and are shown in Figure 4-7. The figure unambiguously reveals that persons in the strategy condition expected continual improvement, whereas those in the ability condition did not anticipate increments in volunteer rates. A control group of subjects not given any feedback following their failure fell in between these extremes.

This experiment was subsequently replicated and extended by Anderson (1983c). Anderson demonstrated that both a general attributional bias (characterological versus behavioral blame) as well as an experimental treatment influences expectations and behaviors. Participants first reponded to a general questionnaire assessing ascriptions of interpersonal failure to characterological deficits versus behavioral mistakes. A typical item on this scale, along with the possible responses, was:

> You were recently unsuccessful at trying to cheer up your roommate, who was having personal problems. [The reason was]
>
> 1. I did not use the right strategy to cheer him/her up

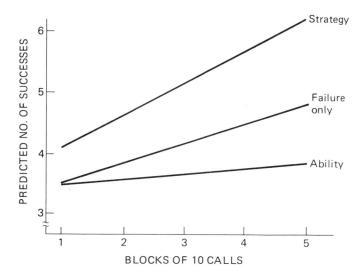

Figure 4-7. Predicted number of successes as a function of anticipated number of calls, for the experimental and control (failure) conditions, following an initial failure. From "When Experiences of Failure Promote Expectations of Success: The Impact of Attributing Failure to Ineffective Strategies" by C. A. Anderson and D. L. Jennings, 1980, *Journal of Personality*, *48*, p. 403. Copyright 1980. Adapted by permission.

2. I am not good at cheering other people up
3. I did not try very hard to cheer him/her up
4. I do not have the right personality traits necessary for cheering people up
5. I was not in the right mood to cheer him/her up
6. Other circumstances (people, situations, etc.) produced the outcome

Ascriptions to ability and personality traits (answers 2 and 4) indicated a general bias toward characterological blame, whereas attributions to strategy and effort (answers 1 and 3) were presumed to be indicators of behavioral blame.

Anderson (1983c) then used the same general experimental treatment as Anderson and Jennings (1980), examining expectancies of blood donations and varying strategy-effort (an expansion of the strategy instructions) versus ability-personality trait attributions. In addition, subjects were asked to actually make soliciting calls during the following week and indicated whether they would be willing to volunteer to help during a blood drive.

Figure 4-8 shows the expectancy estimates. Given no attributional manipulation, subjects making characterological attributions for interpersonal failure had lower estimates of success than those making behavioral ascriptions. The experimental manipulation, however, takes precedence over these tendencies, with strategy-effort ascriptions resulting in higher expectancies after initial failure than ascriptions to ability-personality traits. In addition, those making strategy-effort attributions, whether they did so naturally or were induced to by the manipulation, exhibited

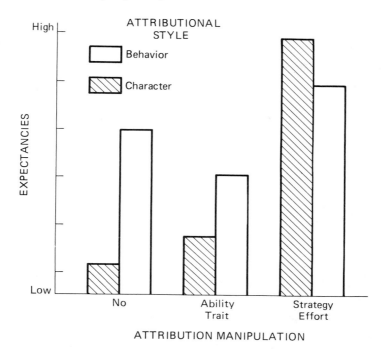

Figure 4-8. Expectancy of soliciting among individuals differing in attributional style, as a function of the experimental intervention. From "Motivational and Performance Deficits in Interpersonal Settings: The Effects of Attributional Style" by C. A. Anderson, 1983, *Journal of Personality and Social Psychology*, *45*, p. 1142. Copyright 1983. Reprinted by permission.

greater subsequent motivation, as evidenced by making more phone calls and being more willing to volunteer for help.

Hyperactivity and Drug Treatment

Whalen and Henker (1976) outlined an attributional analysis of drug treatment for hyperactivity. They contended that when hyperactivity is combated with a drug, the belief is inadvertently conveyed to both the child and his or her parents that the cause of hyperactivity is a physiological dysfunction. Furthermore, Whalen and Henker (1976) stated, "the reputed physiological dysfunctions used to explain the failures of hyperactive children are frequently viewed as stable and relatively unresponsive to behavior change effects" (p. 1123). The perception of fixed causality, in turn, might lead to "demoralization about problem solutions . . . and interferes with effective coping" (Whalen & Henker, 1976, p. 1124).

In sum, again there is an analysis of a psychological phenomenon from the perspective that is shown in Figures 1-4 and 4-6. Individuals are presumed to utilize information (treatment technique) to infer causation about a negative "event" (hyperactivity). The perceived cause generated by the treatment information (a genetic deficit) is perceived as stable. This is thought to weaken the perceived possibility of recovery (a harmful consequence). This intriguing causal sequence regarding beliefs about hyperactivity remains to be tested, but it illustrates yet another context in which causal attribution-expectancy linkages may be operative.

Summary

Perceived causal stability has been either demonstrated or proposed to influence:

1. The perceived likelihood of a future crime and parole decisions
2. The anticipation of future negative events among depressives and perhaps rape victims
3. The intention to return to school or enroll in particular courses
4. The intention to resubmit a manuscript for publication
5. Beliefs about future weight loss and requests for product exchange versus product refund
6. Beliefs about the responses of potential blood donors
7. Perceptions of possible improvements of hyperactives.

These are just a few of many possible applications. Later in this book a number of studies are reviewed demonstrating that a stability-expectancy principle also is of use in therapeutic settings and has provided the foundation for an attributional therapy. Who can doubt that a negative reply to a dating request accompanied by such stable causes as, "I am not allowed to go out with someone of a different religion," "I am moving to Alaska," "I do not date during the school year," or "You are too short (tall, intelligent, dumb)," would lower the future hopes and aspirations of the suitor? On the other hand, responses such as, "I have a terrible headache tonight," "My parents are visiting," "I already have an engagement this evening," or "I have to study for an exam tomorrow," should at least maintain a spark of hope in the heart of the caller. Only the stability of the attributions differentiates these two causal groupings. Although the stability-expectancy linkages proposed in this chapter might at first glance seem obvious, its ramifications extend far beyond what is immediately evident, to many facets of everyday life.

Reinforcement Schedules and Experimental Extinction

It was indicated earlier that the stability-expectancy union has resulted in a reinterpretation of some established fields in psychology. One familiar phenomenon to which this relation has been extended is experimental extinction. Two rules pertaining to this area of study, derived from the prior discussion, may be phrased as follows:

1. When persistence (resistance to extinction) is observed in the face of nonattainment of a goal, one should be alert to find an attribution to an unstable factor.

2. When quitting (extinction) is observed in the face of nonattainment of a goal, one should be alert to find an attribution to a stable cause.

The vast majority of research probing issues of experimental extinction has used infrahuman subjects. In addition, the percentage of reinforced trials (the reinforcement schedule) during the training or learning period has been the parameter most often demonstrated to influence resistance to extinction. Animal psychologists typically account for the data with mechanistic, often Skinnerian, explanations, but attributional accounts of the effects of reinforcement schedules on resistance to extinction also have been offered (see Rest, 1976).

An attributional interpretation of the association between schedules of reinforcement and extinction assumes that instrumental behavior in humans, as well as in some infrahuman species, can be understood in terms of rules, principles, and strategies. One such rule might be, "If I work hard, I will receive a reward." Another could be, "Reward will be forthcoming regardless of what I do." The contingency of reinforcement, which is preprogrammed by the experimenter, is assumed to provide the information needed to formulate such a rule (Wong, 1977). Thus, attributionists view stimuli as sources of information that are given meaning by the responding organism.

More specifically, consider the situation in which reward is presented randomly to the responding organism, provided that a response has been made. Investigations have established that this schedule during training results in greater resistance to extinction than a 100% reward schedule (an exception to this rule will be examined later). One interpretation of this finding is that random reward signals to the organism that reinforcement is in part a matter of good or bad luck or some other varying factor. Indeed, with human subjects it has been found that variability in a series of outcomes elicits luck attributions (Weiner et al., 1971). It is therefore suggested that extinction is impeded given a partial reinforcement schedule because nonreward is ascribed to an unstable cause. Unstable attributions during the extinction period maintain goal expectancies, and the organism continues to make the perceived instrumental response. A random schedule of reinforcement during the training period of an experiment using infrahuman subjects is conceptually equivalent to telling human subjects that the outcome of the task, or the reception of the reward, is determined by luck or some other variable cause. This process is depicted in Figure 4-9.

Similarly, Wong (1977) has contended that certain schedules elicit a "try" strategy. For example, consider the distinction between interval and ratio schedules. In a fixed-interval schedule, reinforcement is externally determined. There are no behaviors an organism can make that increase the frequency of reward. Therefore, there is no "reason" to respond, nor to increase responding, as the interval between the rewards lengthens. In accordance with this analysis, it has been observed that the rate of response per unit of time decreases as the reward interval increases.

On the other hand, given a ratio schedule, the number of rewards is increased by engaging in appropriate instrumental activities. Furthermore, the greater the difficulty of the task (the greater the number of responses required to receive the

Figure 4-9. An attributional explanation of reinforcement schedules.

reward), the more effort may be perceived as necessary to attain the desired rewards. In accordance with this analysis, it has been documented that response rate is augmented as the number of responses required for a reward increases. In sum, it can be argued that the differential response rates exhibited given interval versus ratio reinforcement schedules are mediated by attributions of causality (see Rest, 1976).

It is, of course, difficult to demonstrate directly that perceptions of a "try" rule increase resistance to extinction, particularly for an infrahuman sample. Research that might be considered as supporting this argument was reported by Lawrence and Festinger (1962). They found that resistance to extinction is postively related to the effortfulness of a response. In one confirming experiment, rats were required to climb up inclines differing in steepness to receive a food reward. The group expending greater effort required more nonreinforced trials prior to extinction than did the group that expended less effort during the learning period. The effortfulness of the response during training may have made a "try" principle for the receipt of a reward highly salient. According to attributional beliefs, ascriptions to lack of effort expenditure for goal nonattainment would retard extinction.

Social Learning and Extinction

Rotter and his colleagues conducted a series of investigations with human participants in which schedules of reinforcement were combined with skill and chance instructions to determine their joint efforts on resistance to extinction (Holden & Rotter, 1962; James & Rotter, 1958; Rotter, Liverant, & Crowne, 1961). It might be anticipated that these investigations with human subjects would yield more definitive data regarding the linkages between causal perceptions and experimental extinction. Unfortunately, interpretation of this research is equivocal, although data pertinent to the present discussion were generated.

Consider, for example, the research of James and Rotter (1958), who examined resistance to extinction at a "perceptual-acuity" task. The subjects reported whether an X or an O was flashed during a supposed tachistoscopic presentation. False feedback enabled the experimenter to control the reinforcement schedule (percentage of "correct" responses). Two schedules were employed: 100% and 50% success. Further, half of the subjects within each reinforcement condition were told that "successful guessing is purely a matter of luck," whereas the remaining half of the subjects were informed that "there is evidence that some people are considerably skilled at this."

Following 10 reinforcement trials, extinction procedures were initiated, with all subjects receiving 0% reinforcement. To assess resistance to extinction, the subjects estimated their expectancy of success before each trial. Extinction was assumed when the subjective expectancy of a correct response was .10 or less.

The mean number of trials to extinction and standard deviations are shown in Table 4-8. It can be seen that, given skill instructions, there was a greater number of trials to extinction in the 100% than in the 50% reinforcement condition. This is a reversal of the usual partial reinforcement effect. On the other hand, in the chance situation there was a greater number of trials to extinction in the 50% than in the 100% reinforcement condition, thus replicating the pattern of results in most extinction investigations employing infrahuman subjects.

The data of James and Rotter (1958) are interpretable within the attributional framework advanced here. Consider the results when the task is introduced as skill determined. The instructions in that condition connote that performance is a function of ability. Following acquisition, subjects in one condition (100% reinforcement) are likely to infer that they have considerable ability at the task, whereas the performance of the subjects in the 50% condition indicates that they have relatively intermediate ability. When the attributions generated by the 0% schedule are established, that is, when the subjects believe that they have insufficient ability to perform the task (or that the task was altered so that it is now too difficult), extinction should occur. The change in self-perception from high to low ability in the 100% reward condition should take longer than the change in self-perception from intermediate to low ability in the 50% reward condition. Another way of stating this is that it requires more time for subjects in the 100% reinforcement condition to ascribe failure to the fixed factors of low ability or task difficulty.

The results in the chance condition are less readily interpretable. Within the chance condition, one subgroup received random 50% reinforcement. Hence, two sources of information (instructions and outcome) combined to produce ascriptions that performance is completely determined by good or bad luck. But during extinction the 0% schedule now intimates that chance alone cannot account for the outcome. Causal elements in addition to luck must be recruited to explain consistently poor performance. Indeed, were luck the only perceived causal attribute, then

Table 4-8. Mean Trials to Extinction and Standard Deviations Between Groups Differing in Percentage of Reinforcement During Acquisition and Task Instructions

Group	Percentage of Reinforcement	Instructions	Trials to Extinction	Standard Deviation
A	100	Skill	22.90	4.84
B	50	Skill	19.75	7.27
C	100	Chance	15.55	9.86
D	50	Chance	29.05	9.41

Note. From "Partial and 100% Reinforcement Under Chance and Skill Conditions" by W. H. James and J. B. Rotter, 1958, Journal of Experimental Psychology, 55, p. 401. Copyright 1958. Adapted by permission.

extinction might not occur. James and Rotter did report that only in the 50% chance condition were there subjects who never extinguished. These persistent subjects were poor "scientists," for they apparently ignored the new source of outcome evidence and continued to make unstable attributions in the face of a stable outcome.

The second group within the chance condition received 100% reinforcement. Hence, the pattern of actual performance contradicts the luck ascription induced by the instructions, for repeated success indicates that luck is not the sole outcome determinant. A stable outcome contradicts the belief in an unstable cause. Further, during the extinction phase of the 100% chance condition the subjects must become even more confused. They were first instructed to believe that the outcome was determined by luck; they then find out that they are skilled performers; and the final pattern of reinforcement conveys that they have little skill at the task.

Given the above phenomenological analysis, it would be difficult for the notion of causal stability to predict relative trials to extinction (subjective expectancy estimates) in the chance conditions. However, the analysis does suggest that greater variability should be displayed in the chance than in the skill conditions. This expectation is borne out (see Table 4-8). In the 100% chance condition, which theoretically generates the greatest attributional confusion, the most variability is displayed.

The intent of this rather extended discussion is not to prove that extinction, or resistance to extinction, is mediated solely by attributional thoughts and perceptions of the stability of the perceived cause of nonreinforcement. That is not realistically possible given the complexity of the phenomena, the little research conducted on this issue from an attributional viewpoint, and the great differences in cognitive competence among the species that have been tested. Rather, my goal has been to show that the attribution-stability-expectancy sequence can be applied fruitfully to an established area of psychology with somewhat surprising ease and yields heuristic interpretations of old data.

Finally, it should be noted that the analysis of resistance to extinction following nonattainment of a reward is conceptually identical to the explanation of the effects of failure in achievement situations on expectancy of future success and task persistence. These two distinct empirical areas are integrated in Figure 4-10.

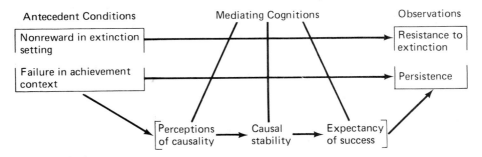

Figure 4-10. Integration of research on experimental extinction and achievement strivings. (Expectancy of success is sometimes referred to as a mediating cognition and sometimes assessed.)

Theoretical and Empirical Issues

Before the formal stating of a general law relating attribution to expectancy, some theoretical and empirical issues that have been raised throughout this chapter require further attention. These concern the prediction of expectancy change versus expectancy, possible alternative explanations of the determinants of future anticipations, and methodological inadequacies in some of the research investigations.

Does Causal Stability Relate to Expectancy, Expectancy Change, or Both?

At the outset of this chapter a recommendation was made to attempt initially to relate causal attributions to shifts in the expectancy of success. This was accomplished by examining expectancy change in level of aspiration contexts and at games of chance. But then stability was somewhat suddenly hypothesized to relate to expectancy of success, in addition to expectancy change. The question therefore arises as to which index, expectancy shifts or expectancy, is theoretically and empirically related to causal stability?

To predict actual expectancy of success, much more information is required than just causal ascriptions. Indeed, expectancy of success might be very low on subsequent tasks even though prior failure is ascribed to unstable factors such as bad luck. This is quite evident when reseeking to win a lottery after a loss. As already documented, there are an unbelievably large number of antecedents that influence actual expectancy level. Researchers therefore examine expectancy of success nomothetically across groups of individuals, with relative comparisons made between the subject groupings. Absolute comparisons or predictions are not made.

On the other hand, predictions about expectancy change can be made for any individual at any task, if one knows only the perceived causal stability of the outcome attribution and whether the outcome was a success or a failure. Between-individual comparisons are not needed. Hence, expectancy change is the more appropriate of the two indexes, from both a theoretical and an empirical perspective.

Alternative Explanations of Goal Expectancies

The main alternative to the attributional interpretation of expectancy shifts has been supplied by Rotter and other social learning theorists. As documented throughout this chapter, the evidence warrants discarding the hypothesis that an internal-external distinction relates to expectancy shifts.

Another well-known approach to the expectancy of success is based on the concepts of perceived control and learned helplessness (Seligman, 1975). Although individuals with this theoretical perspective do accept a stability-expectancy linkage (e.g., Abramson, Seligman, & Teasdale, 1978), they also advance the argument that personal control is a determinant of expectancy of success. In addition, it is hypothesized that if the probability of success is not perceived as changeable through instrumental responding, then a state of helplessness ensues.

It first should be noted that whether a syndrome labeled "learned helplessness" is or is not determined by perceived personal control is quite independent of the issue of the determinants of expectancy. For example, failure ascribed to an external, unstable source may not decrease expectancies, but may promote feelings of personal helplessness—an unreliable uncle who usually does but sometimes does not send money may make one feel helpless, yet expectancies could remain reasonably high. Thus, it is important to distinguish the antecedents of helplessness from the determinants of expectancy of success. Investigators such as Seligman at times blur these issues.

In addition, it is necessary to distinguish beliefs about helplessness ("Nothing I do matters") from feelings of hopelessness ("Things will not get better"). One may feel totally helpless yet have great hopes. For example, one might be unable to earn money while attending school, yet have great confidence that an uncle will send the necessary money. Helplessness therefore is but one determinant or contributor to hopelessness (see Weiner & Litman-Adizes, 1980). The concepts of helplessness and hopelessness have not been sufficiently distinguished in the literature.

When the determinants of helplessness are distinguished from the determinants of expectancy, and when helplessness is differentiated from hopelessness, it becomes evident that causal stability, and not perceived control, influences expectancy of success. As intimated above, an uncontrollable cause for nonattainment of a goal might or might not reduce subsequent expectancy of success. An unusual summer rain forcing cancellation of a picnic is not likely to reduce future beliefs about a successful picnic, although the rain was uncontrollable. This is the case whether the cause is internal or external. Thus, failure ascribed to a bad cold, which typically is considered a personal and uncontrollable cause, also need not result in a lowering of future expectancy of success.

It is evident, however, that at times expectancy of success appears to be maintained by the belief that future outcomes are subject to personal control. The implication of this statement is that the person can do something to influence the course of events or change the past. The cause of the outcome is therefore not only controllable, but also amenable to change (unstable). The concept of personal control merges the dimensions of locus (internal), stability (unstable), and controllability (controllable). But locus need not be linked to hopelessness (one can feel hopeless because of internal or external barriers), nor need uncontrollable causes give rise to hopelessness, as they may either aid or hinder goal attainment. On the other hand, stable causes for failure always promote feelings of both helplessness and hopelessness. It therefore appears that concepts other than causal stability do not explain expectancy shifts and relative expectancy of success.

Methodological Issues

A number of experiments examining the stability-expectancy linkage have been methodologically flawed. These investigations are not normative representations of work in this area, for the vast majority of studies are without experimental shortcomings. Nonetheless, it is instructive to examine some of these studies, for they also shed light on the attributional principle that is being advocated relating causal stability to expectancy of success.

The overriding flaw in the empirical research has been a failure to conceptualize the situation as perceived by the respondent (see Weiner, 1983). That is, phenomenal causality has not guided the investigation; rather, an a priori classification of causes on the stability dimension has been accepted. This has resulted in a misclassification of causes from the subject's perspective, thereby rendering experimental conclusions invalid. Consider, for example, the following oft-cited experiment by Riemer (1975):

> The experimenters recruited subjects who had no previous experience with piano music for a "music practicum." The subjects individually received 15 minutes of instruction on piano with the "correspondence of notes technique." When finished, all subjects were given a written evaluation . . . and . . . the feeback "you were successful." In order to manipulate the subjects' causal attributions of this success, subjects were handed one of four instruction sheets before they began playing. One-fourth of the subjects were instructed that their successful performance was entirely due to ability, one-fourth were told that their success was entirely due to effort, one-fourth were told that their success was entirely due to the simplicity of the task, and one-fourth were told that their success was entirely due to chance. (p. 1164)

Among other questions, the subjects were asked, "How well do you think you would do with a subsequent more difficult set of pieces?" Causal stability was then related to the expectancy of success at this next task.

To predict the relation between causal stability and task expectancy, Riemer classified ability and task ease a priori as stable, and effort and luck as unstable, as Weiner et al. (1971) had earlier specified. Considering only the task ease manipulation, recall that Riemer informed some subjects that success at the piano task was "entirely due to the simplicity of the task." But task ease or difficulty would be judged as stable only if the same or similar tasks were again confronted or anticipated to be confronted. If the task situation is perceived as changing, then the ease or the difficulty of the task would be perceived as altered and, therefore, unstable. Note that in this particular experiment the future task was designated as one of greater difficulty ("How will you do with a subsequent more difficult set of pieces?"). It contradicts cause-effect logic to predict that the attribution "I succeeded because of the simplicity of the task" will be positively related to future expectancy (certainty) of success given that the future task is designated as one of greater difficulty. And Riemer found no relation between her classification of causal stability and future expectancy of success. She then incorrectly concluded that this hypothesized association was disconfirmed. Because this research was so flagrantly flawed, I did not include it among the previously cited studies.

Field research examining expectancy of success at subsequent school examinations, which also was not previously reviewed, frequently suffers from a similar problem (see, for example, Bernstein, Stephan, & Davis, 1979; Halperin & Abrams, 1978). Students often have implicit theories regarding the sequence of exam difficulty throughout a course, believing that the final exam, or its grading curve, will be more (or less) difficult than the midterm exam and assignment of grades. Thus, success at a midterm exam attributed to task ease, or failure because of perceived task difficulty, need not intimate that there is a respectively higher subjective certainty of success or failure on the final exam.

Ability also has at times been misclassified as stable and then incorrectly related to expectancy of future success. Often ability is perceived as unstable, particularly when it connotes skill or knowledge rather than aptitude, for an increase in skill or knowledge may be foreseen. This possibility typically requires that there be some time period between an initial outcome and a subsequent performance, and that skill be perceived as below asymptote at the initial performance.

Consider this issue in the light of an investigation by Covington and Omelich (1979a). Students who completed an exam were allowed to retake an equivalent examination 2 days later if they perceived their performance to be below their personal standards of success. After the initial exam feedback, the subjects rated a variety of causes of their "failure," and indicated as well their expectancy of success on the subsequent test. Among the attributions rated for the initial exam failure was, "I lack the skill and ability." In this situation, an attribution to lack of skill and ability might be perceived as an unstable cause of failure that can be overcome through effort (see Porac, 1981). However, Covington and Omelich (1979a) classified the cause as stable. Then they reported that causal stability was unrelated to expectancy of success. Of course, this relation will not emerge if causes are incorrectly categorized.

A changing situation also may result in the conceptualization of ability as unstable. Foersterling and Engelken (1981), for example, specified that a student did well in a physics course because of either high ability or high effort. They then asked their college subjects whether this student would do well in the dissimilar subject of German. It was reported that significantly higher expectancies were anticipated in the effort (typically classified as unstable) than in the ability (typically classified as stable) attribution conditions.

At first glance, the above results appear to contradict the hypothesized relation between causal stability and expectancy. However, given this changing task situation, ability might be perceived as unstable (or, as Foersterling and Engelken state, ability in physics provides no information about ability in German). On the other hand, effort may be perceived as stable (that is, trying in physics is predictive of trying in German). Research I conducted (reported in Weiner, 1983) indeed has confirmed that the effort required for success in physics and language is more similar than the ability required for success at these two subjects. (Note that in this analysis the generality of ability is included within the stability dimension.)

In sum, the primary error in the pertinent research has been the unquestioned acceptance of a priori categorization schemes, without ascertaining the subjective perceptions of the respondents. To facilitate capturing the phenomenology of the experimental subjects, Russell (1982) has developed a Causal Dimension Scale. This scale, shown in Table 4-9, contains nine items, three of which are pertinent to each of the causal dimensions. This scale has been demonstrated by Russell (1982) to have the properties of an acceptable psychometric instrument.

Ronis, Hansen, and O'Leary (1983) examined the predictive validity of assessing perceptions of causal stability in research concerning expectancy of success. Ronis

Table 4-9. Causal Dimension Scale

Instructions: Think about the reason or reasons you have written above. The items below concern your impressions or opinions of this cause or causes of your outcome. Circle one number for each of the following scales.

1. Is the cause(s) something that:

| Reflects an aspect of yourself | 9 | 8 | 7 | 6 | 5 | 4 | 3 | 2 | 1 | Reflects an aspect of the situation |

2. Is the cause(s):

| Controllable by you or other people | 9 | 8 | 7 | 6 | 5 | 4 | 3 | 2 | 1 | Uncontrollable by you or other people |

3. Is the cause(s) something that is:

| Permanent | 9 | 8 | 7 | 6 | 5 | 4 | 3 | 2 | 1 | Temporary |

4. Is the cause(s) something:

| Intended by you or other people | 9 | 8 | 7 | 6 | 5 | 4 | 3 | 2 | 1 | Unintended by you or other people |

5. Is the cause(s) something that is:

| Outside of you | 1 | 2 | 3 | 4 | 5 | 6 | 7 | 8 | 9 | Inside of you |

6. Is the cause(s) something that is:

| Variable over time | 1 | 2 | 3 | 4 | 5 | 6 | 7 | 8 | 9 | Stable over time |

7. Is the cause(s):

| Something about you | 9 | 8 | 7 | 6 | 5 | 4 | 3 | 2 | 1 | Something about others |

8. Is the cause(s) something that is:

| Changeable | 1 | 2 | 3 | 4 | 5 | 6 | 7 | 8 | 9 | Unchanging |

9. Is the cause(s) something for which:

| No one is responsible | 1 | 2 | 3 | 4 | 5 | 6 | 7 | 8 | 9 | Someone is responsible |

Note. A total score for each of the three subscales is arrived at by summing the responses to the individual items as follows: (1) locus of causality—Items 1, 5, and 7; (2) stability—Items 3, 6, and 8; (3) controllability—Items 2, 4, and 9. High scores on these subscales indicate that the cause is perceived as internal, stable, and controllable.

From "The Causal Dimension Scale: A Measure of How Individuals Perceive Causes" by D. Russell, 1982, *Journal of Personality and Social Psychology, 42*, p. 1143. Copyright 1982. Reprinted by permission.

et al. (1983) first noted that many investigators (e.g., Arkin & Maruyama, 1979; Bernstein et al., 1979; Luginbuhl, Crowe, & Kahan, 1975; Rosenfield & Stephan, 1978; Stephan, Rosenfield, & Stephan, 1976; Zuckerman, Larrance, Porac, & Blanck, 1980) have obtained ratings of ability, effort, task difficulty, and luck following success or failure, and then derived a stability index by adding the ratings of the a priori-specified stable attributions and subtracting from this total the sum of the ratings of the unstable attributions:

$$\text{stability} = (\text{ability} + \text{task difficulty}) - (\text{effort} + \text{luck}).$$

Thus, for example, if a subject judged the cause of success in the following manner: ability, a rating of 5, say, on a 6-point scale; effort, a rating of 3; task ease, 6; and luck, 1, then the stability score for this subject would be $[(5 + 6) - (3 + 1)] = 7$. But, as Ronis et al. (1983) pointed out, "These practices apparently represent the assumption that the original taxonomy [of causes proposed by Weiner et al., 1971] was intended to describe the meanings of commonsense explanations across all settings. The assumption may well be unwarranted" (p. 703).

The shortcoming of an a priori classification procedure, and the advantages of assessing subjective perceptions of causal stability, was then demonstrated by Ronis et al. (1983). These investigators had subjects read scenarios that involved success and failure at a variety of activities, including games and lotteries. The respondents indicated the extent to which these outcomes were perceived as influenced by ability, effort, task difficulty, and luck. The subjects were then asked, "How likely is it that this person's future level of performance at the task will be about the same as his recent performance?" Finally, subjective perceptions of the stability of the cause of the outcome were directly assessed. Subjects rated items asking if the cause were "something unchanging and stable over time" and whether it were "something changing and unstable over time." These questions were very similar to items 6 and 8 on the Russell (1982) inventory.

The expectancy rating was then related to two indexes of causal stability. One index was derived from the a priori method of adding ascriptions to ability and task difficulty and subtracting attributions to effort and luck. A second index was based on scores from the two questions directly assessing causal stability. The data from this investigation revealed that the subjective, but not the a priori, index significantly predicted expectancy of success.

In sum, given sound methodology, the stability-expectancy linkage is found consistently. Hence, it is now appropriate to propose a general principle to account for goal anticipations.

A General Law

Individuals classify their thoughts into broad categories. Hence, phenotypic disparities might be connotatively, or genotypically, similar. Failure at athletics because of lack of height, failure in math because of low aptitude, and failure in politics because of poor charisma are phenotypically different events with diverse causes. Yet the causes are likely to be similarly categorized as stable or enduring. Hence, future hopes in these heterogeneous contexts will be minimized. On the other hand, failure in athletics because of insufficient practice, failure at math because of temporary illness, and failure in politics because of a current economic recession are diverse events that will likely be categorized as due to unstable causes. Hopes for the future therefore are likely to be maintained.

The amount, extensity, and consistency of the empirical findings documents a fundamental psychological law relating perceived causal stability to expectancy change:

Expectancy Principle: Changes in expectancy of success following an outcome are influenced by the perceived stability of the cause of the event.

This principle has three corollaries:

Corollary 1: If the outcome of an event is ascribed to a stable cause, then that outcome will be anticipated with increased certainty, or with an increased expectancy, in the future.

Corollary 2: If the outcome of an event is ascribed to an unstable cause, then the certainy or expectancy of that outcome may be unchanged, or the future will be anticipated to be different from the past.

Corollary 3: Outcomes ascribed to stable causes will be anticipated to be repeated in the future with a greater degree of certainty than outcomes ascribed to unstable causes.

A conservative scientist might qualify the principle and its corollaries as applicable only to adults in the Western world, following our system of cause-effect logic. A bolder scientist might maintain that this principle and its corollaries are pancultural, suitable across historical time periods, most age groups, and to infrahuman species with the necessary cognitive capabilities. One goal for the conservative scientist might be to identify the diversity of settings to which this belief system is being naively applied. The goal for the bolder scientist is to gather the necessary data to document the generality of the principle and its corollaries.

Summary

The question first raised in this chapter was what might be the psychological consequences of causal thinking, and particularly the significance of the three main causal properties. One suggestion was that they should relate to expectancies (goal anticipation), as this is a key variable in cognitive approaches to motivation. It was then indicated that the prediction of expectancy change, rather than the absolute magnitude of expectancy, might provide a good starting point. Research on level of aspiration in skill settings and examination of subjective probabilities at games of chance revealed different directions of expectancy change following positive and negative outcomes. Typical shifts were more often exhibited at skill tasks, and atypical shifts were more often observed in chance settings, although reversals of these patterns were sometimes noted. Social learning theorists hypothesized that these changes are mediated by perceptions of the locus of causality, with internal attributions related to typical shifts and external ascriptions associated with atypical shifts. On the other hand, an attributional analysis proposed that the direction of expectancy change following an outcome is determined by perceptions of causal stability, with stable causes producing typical shifts whereas unstable causes generate atypical shifts. Research directly comparing the social learning versus the attributional approach unequivocally supported the attributional predictions. A large number of laboratory investigations, some correlational and other manipulating causal ascriptions, also provided positive evidence for the attributional position. In addition, an array of real-life phenomena, including the perceived likelihood of a criminal act; parole decisions; beliefs about future negative events among individuals differing in styles of self-blame; the intent to return to school, enroll in classes, or resubmit a manuscript for publication; expectancies of product failure; anticipated blood donations from others; and thoughts about recovery from hyperactivity have been related to perceptions of causal stability.

It was then suggested that the reinforcement literature might be reinterpreted, with reinforcement schedules considered sources of information used to infer the causes of reward or nonreward. It was proposed that nonattainment of a reward in an extinction paradigm and failure at an achievement-related task be considered conceptually or genotypically similar. Both resistance to extinction and persistence at an achievement-related task appear to be mediated, in part, by causal perceptions.

On the basis of the great amount of empirical support, a general law and three corollaries were then proposed linking causal stability and expectancy of success. I perceive this association to be a fundamental psychological principle.

Chapter 5
Perceived Causality and Emotional Reactions

In which the author reveals his feelings about feelings. It is documented that causal ascriptions are linked with emotional reactions, and again general laws are established. The foundation for a social psychology of emotions is proposed.

Causal ascriptions influence expectancy change and the expectancy of success. This is a necessary linkage for the development of an attributional theory of motivation, inasmuch as goal anticipations certainly affect other thoughts and actions. As Rotter and Hochreich (1975) stated when criticizing psychoanalytic theory:

> Simply knowing how much an individual wants to reach a certain goal is not sufficient information for predicting his behavior. A student may want very badly to finish school and qualify himself for a well-paying job. But his past experiences may have led him to believe that no amount of studying will result in passing grades. ... If his expectancy for success in the situation is low ... he is unlikely to study, despite his strong desire to graduate. A fellow student may share the same strong goals, and as a result of a different set of past experiences in school, have a high expectancy that studying will lead to academic success. In this instance, one could safely predict that the second student would be likely to study in order to obtain his goals. As you can see, the goals in these two cases are identical, but the expectancies differ, and as a result, the behavior of the two students is likely to differ. (p. 95)

But goal expectancies also are not, in and of themselves, sufficient determinants of action. After all, an infinite number of actions are not undertaken although goal attainment is absolutely certain. I can surely beat my 5-year-old neighbor at tennis, yet I infrequently challenge her to a match in spite of my love of winning. Additional factors obviously must play a motivational role.

Both cognitive and mechanistic conceptions have identified another class of variables with motivational impact. They are called "goal incentives" and may be considered the "fit" between one's needs and the properties of the goal object. I may know that if I walk one block I will find a nickel on the street corner, yet I will not perform that activity because the reward is insufficient to instigate the action. Conversely, given monetary desires and an assurance of finding 5 dollars, the necessary steps will be taken. Motivation is determined by what one can "get," as well as by the likelihood of getting it. This is the essence of the Expectancy × Value position expressed by theorists such as Tolman, Lewin, Atkinson, and Rotter.

How, then, should attribution theorists conceptualize value, or the incentive of the goal? There seems to be no reason to believe that value (i.e., the intrinsic properties of the goal object) is determined by perceived causality—the subjective reason why the goal was reached. For example, assuming a given level of hunger, the identical meal should have the identical value when ordered at a restaurant, cooked at home, or discovered on the doorstep. The cause of the presence of food does not seem to determine its incentive value or inherent quality. In a similar manner, one might contend that a dollar has the "value" of 1 dollar when attained because of good fortune, hard work, or as a gift from another. Perhaps it must be accepted that goal incentive will not have as direct a connection with causal ascriptions as has goal expectancy.

However, rather than conceiving incentive value in terms of the objective properties of the goal interacting with the needs of the person, consider instead the meaning and the consequences of goal attainment for the actor. We prefer a dollar to a nickel, or gourmet to ordinary food, because the anticipated consequences will make us happier, give greater satisfaction and pleasure, and the like. That is, the subjective value of the goal has an isomorphism, or a one-to-one correspondence, with its emotional impact. If something has positive value for a person, then attainment of that object will have positive affective consequences; the greater the subjective value, the greater the anticipated satisfaction if it is attained.

Although causal ascriptions do not influence the objective properties of the goal, they do guide its emotional impact. This influence is both in terms of the magnitude of feeling as well as the quality of affect that is experienced. For example, 5 dollars attained because of good luck (finding it at the corner) is likely to elicit surprise; 5 dollars earned by hard work might produce pride; and 5 dollars received from a friend could beget gratitude. In a similar manner, Heider (1958) noted that a gift from someone beloved is likely to have different affective significance than the same gift from an enemy.

Perceptions of causality, then, do influence the affective consequences of goal attainment. This is particularly evident in the achievement and affiliative domains, where the affects associated with success at an exam or being accepted for a date are very much determined by the perceived causes of these positive outcomes. Surely receiving an "A" because of hard work will have different affective consequences than an "A" received because of a computer error. And an affiliative acceptance perceived as owing to the partner being bored has a different subjective value than an acceptance due to the requester being perceived as charming.

In this chapter, emotional states are integrated into an attributional theory of motivation, and the linkages between causal thinking and feeling are detailed. As I stated in the initial chapter, prior theories of motivation have been remiss in ignoring the emotions, save for an acceptance of the pleasure-pain principle. I will not be guilty of this sin of omission; the relations between causal ascriptions and affects, like the linkage between causal ascriptions and expectancy, form powerful and general laws.

The Approach to Emotions

The field of emotion is vast and complex; the formulation of a "compleat" theory of emotion is not my goal. Rather, the aims of this chapter are to document the relations between causal ascriptions and emotion, show the significance of these postulates in everyday life, and propose general laws linking thinking and feeling. To do this, some basic issues in the field of emotion must be addressed, even if only briefly.

The most embracing presumption guiding this chapter is that how we think influences how we feel. This clearly is a cognitive approach to emotion. Cognitive emotion theory assumes that emotions are guided by the construal or appraisal of a situation (Arnold, 1960; Ellis, 1975; Lazarus, 1966). Cognitions are believed to give rise to qualitative distinctions between feelings and therefore are responsible for the richness and diversity of emotional life. The cognitive perspective adopted here does not deny that some emotions may be elicited without intervening thought processes. For example, conditioned fear and hormonally induced depression may not be preceded by higher level thinking. Nor does this perspective deny that emotional states influence cognitive processes. For example, a person in a depressed mood may be prone to recall unpleasant memories and to perceive the world as a hostile or demanding place. Rather, it is simply postulated that cognitions quite typically precede and determine affective reactions. To an attributionist, this means that perceptions of what caused a positive or a negative outcome in part determine the affective reactions to that outcome.

A second assumption guiding this chapter is that there is no fixed demarcation point between a "hot" affect and a "cold" cognition. At times, research participants have reported feeling "dumb" or "incompetent" when failure is ascribed to lack of ability. But feeling "dumb" certainly sounds like a cognition. On the other hand, it is also evident that the hot emotion of anger can be clearly differentiated from a cold thought such as "This is a chair." The differentiation between emotion and cognition is in part based upon the definition of emotion that I follow. Along with many others (e.g., Averill, 1982), I define emotion as a complex syndrome or composite of many interacting factors. Emotions are presumed to have 1) positive or negative qualities of 2) a certain intensity that 3) frequently are preceded by an appraisal of a situation and 4) give rise to a variety of actions. Affects therefore come at a juncture between behavioral events, summarizing reactions to the past and instigating future actions. This combination of features (hedonic direction, intensity, antedating cognition, and subsequent action) does not characterize cold cognitions. In the present discussion, no position is taken regarding other possible correlates or parts of the emotion syndrome, including nonspecific or specific physiological arousal and facial or postural involvement. Whereas these components are central to some approaches to emotion, they are not relevant to the concerns expressed here.

A third assumption guiding this chapter is that a theory of emotion should be able to address common or everyday affective states. This contrasts, for example, with the dominant emotion theory proposed by Schachter and Singer (1962), which does not address *any* specific emotions. There have been a number of attempts to identify the most common emotional experiences. Davitz (1969) identified 14 emotions of high-frequency written usage on the basis of an established word-count procedure. In a totally different attempt to ascertain the predominant emotions, Bottenburg (1975) found the 30 emotions reported as most frequently experienced by a large sample of college students. Combining the research endeavors of Davitz and Bottenburg, five emotions have been identified that are both high in word-count frequency and reported as often experienced. These emotions are anger, happiness, love, pity, and pride. I believe that a theory of emotion must address at least some of these prevalent emotional experiences. In accord with this belief, later in the chapter I will show that anger, happiness, pity, and pride can be accounted for from an attributional perspective. To determine how these emotions are explained, the issue of the general emotion process must first be addressed.

The Cognition-Emotion Process

Most emotion theorists of a cognitive persuasion conceive of emotional experience as a temporal sequence involving cognitions of increasing psychological complexity. Arnold (1960) and Lazarus (1966), for example, contend that the perception of a distal stimulus gives rise to a primary appraisal and a rather primitive emotional reaction. As an illustration, one might perceive a large dog on the street (primary appraisal) and experience fear (although a great deal of cognitive work already is involved in the labeling of "dog" and the recognition of its potential harm). This primary appraisal is believed to be followed by a secondary appraisal. The secondary appraisal often involves "ego-related" or more advanced psychological mechanisms such as ego defenses. The elicitation of these processes can intensify or modulate the emotional experience or alter the quality of the emotion. For example, if defenses such as denial or intellectualization are aroused, then the perceiver may deny any danger, concluding, "That is a large, *playful* dog." This defensive reaction, in turn, alters the fear response, perhaps to the positive effect of excitement or joy.

    Another possible emotional sequence has been proposed by Scherer (1982), who contended that emotion should be conceptualized "as a process rather than a steady state . . . characterized by sequential intraorganismic information processing" (pp. 555–556). He went on to postulate that "The evaluation of the relevance of any external stimulus which is registered by an organism's sensorium is established by a sequence of specific checks in terms of relevant dimensions of its meaning for the organism" (Scherer, 1982, p. 558). The first check hypothesized by Scherer involves an evaluation of the novelty of the stimulus. This is followed by appraisal of its inherent pleasantness or unpleasantness, goal relevance, and the organism's ability to cope with it. Each of these checks results in particular affective reactions. Thus, again increasing cognitive involvement in the emotion process is postulated, with greater problem-solving capacity and increasing emotional differentiation involved in the latter parts of the sequence.

Schachter (1964) proposed the most often cited emotion sequence. He hypothesized that the initial step in this sequence is the experience and recognition of non-differentiated internal arousal. Then the source of the arousal is determined on the basis of situational cues, and this cognitive labeling plus the arousal give rise to emotional states (although the cognition of the arousal and the cognition of the source of the arousal typically take place simultaneously). To illustrate the former sequence, which has been the one most examined experimentally, the unwitting ingestion of a drug or residual arousal from exercise can produce unlabeled arousal. A cause is then sought, and the arousal may be ascribed, for example, to an attractive person who happens to be in the aroused person's visual field. The arousal in conjunction with this perceived arousal source is anticipated to produce an "appropriate" emotional experience that, in this case, may subjectively be considered "lust" or "longing."

The attributional framework advanced here also assumes a sequence in which cognitions of increasing complexity enter into the emotion process to further refine and differentiate experience. Following the outcome of an event, there is initially a general positive or negative reaction (a "primitive" emotion) based on the perceived success or failure of that outcome (the "primary" appraisal). For example, after receiving an "A" in a course, hitting a home run in a baseball game, or being accepted for a date an individual will feel happy. In a similar manner, after receiving an "F" in a course, failing to get a hit in a baseball game, or being rejected for a date the person will experience frustration or sadness. These emotions are labeled as "outcome dependent-attribution independent," for they are determined by the attainment or nonattainment of a desired goal, and not by the cause of that outcome.

Following the appraisal of the outcome, a causal ascription will be sought if that outcome was negative, unexpected, and/or important. A different set of emotions is then generated by the chosen attribution(s). For example, success perceived as due to good luck produces surprise. Emotions such as surprise are labeled as "attribution-dependent," inasmuch as they are determined by the perceived cause of the prior outcome. Note that increasing cognitive complexity generates more differentiated emotional experience.

Additionally, causal dimensions play a key role in the emotion process. Each causal dimension is uniquely related to a set of feelings. For example, success and failure perceived as due to internal causes such as personality or effort respectively raise or lower self-esteem or self-worth. That is, feelings related to self-esteem are influenced by causal properties (dimensions) rather than by a specific cause.

The cognition-emotion sequence suggested in the above paragraphs is depicted in Figure 5-1. It is evident from Figure 5-1 that this approach to emotions assumes that feelings arise from how an outcome is evaluated or construed. More specifically, imagine a situation in which a student has just been informed that she received the highest grade in the class on the final exam. Upon learning of her grade, the student experiences great happiness. Because this is an important course, and the grade was better than anticipated, a cause for the outcome is sought. On the basis of social comparison information, past history, and so on, the student ascribes the outcome

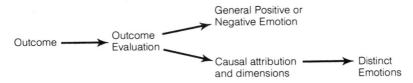

Figure 5-1. The cognition-emotion process.

to ability. This elicits feelings of competence. Because ability is an internal ascription, self-esteem and personal worth are also enhanced. Hence, the student feels happiness, competence, and positive self-esteem, respectively associated with outcome, the specific attribution, and the dimensional location of the attribution.

The cognition-emotion process that has been proposed provides the focus and the outline for the remainder of this chapter. I will first examine outcome-related affects, and then consider dimension-linked emotions. The associations between causal dimensions (the structure of thought) and affects are emphasized, for these linkages have the most extensive empirical support.

Outcome-Dependent Affects

A few years ago an enigmatic article appeared in the sports pages. A championship soccer match was being held, and the visiting team spent the night at a local hotel. During the evening, the townspeople walked around the hotel making as much noise as possible, in an attempt to keep the visiting team from sleeping. Of course, this would impede their play the next afternoon. I naively wondered why one would want to win in this manner? Could positive affect be experienced (rather than, say, guilt) if this unseemly behavior were the cause of success?

An answer to this question was provided in studies I subsequently conducted with my associates (Weiner, Russell, & Lerman, 1978, 1979). In an initial investigation, we compiled a dictionary list of approximately 250 potential affective reactions to success and failure. This list began with the emotions of amazed, amused, and appreciative and ended with wonderment, worried, and wretched. Then a cause for success or failure was given within a brief story format, and participants reported the intensity of the affective responses that they thought would be experienced in this situation. Intensity was indicated by marking rating scales for each of the positive affects given a success outcome and each of the negative affects given a failure. For example, one story read:

> It was extremely important for Pat to receive a high score on an exam about to be taken. Pat has very high ability. Pat received a high score on the test and felt that score was received because of ability. After receiving the score, what do you think the feelings were?

Ten attributions were supplied for success and 11 for failure, including ability, stable

Table 5-1. Success: The Top Five Affective Intensity Ratings by Attribution for Success

Ability	Unstable Effort	Stable Effort	Task Difficulty	Mood
Pleased	Good	Satisfied	Pleased	Cheerful
Satisfied	Happy	Good	Contented	Good
Confident	Satisfied	Pleased	Happy	Delighted
Competent	Delighted	Secure	Secure	Happy
Happy	Gratified	Comfortable	Satisfied	Pleasant

Personality	Other's Effort	Other's Motivation and Personality	Luck	Intrinsic Motivation
Pleased	Pleased	Good	Happy	Pleased
Happy	Happy	Happy	Thankful	Happy
Contented	Appreciative	Delighted	Delighted	Satisfied
Proud	Satisfied	Satisfied	Pleased	Proud
Satisfied	Proud	Cheerful	Relieved	Confident

Note. Data from "Affective Consequences of Causal Ascriptions" by B. Weiner et al., 1978, in J. H. Harvey et al. (Eds.), *New Directions in Attribution Research* (Vol. 2). Hillsdale, NJ: Erlbaum. Copyright 1978. Reprinted by permission.

and unstable effort, task difficulty, luck, mood, and help or hindrance from others (see Table 5-1).

Table 5-1 shows the most intensely rated affects as a function of the causal attribution for success. It is evident that, regardless of the ascription, feelings of good, happy, pleased, and satisfied were reported. For failure, dissatisfied, unhappy, and uncheerful were the dominant affects not linked with causal ascriptions, although many negative affects were expressed in more than one attributional condition (see Table 5-2).

In a follow-up investigation (Weiner et al., 1979), participants reported a critical incident in their lives when they actually succeeded or failed an exam because of a specified cause. Six causes were supplied: ability, stable and unstable effort, personality, others, and luck. The respondents recalled the event and their three most dominant affects at that time. The data for this study for successful outcomes are shown in Table 5-3. The most dominant affect reported was "happy"; about 45% of the subjects reported experiencing this affect in all the causal conditions. For failure (Table 5-4), anger, depression, fear, and frustration were the dominant affects in the causal conditions. Thus, failure again generated a greater array of affects than success, and the findings for failure were not as consistent across the two studies as were the data for a successful outcome. I will return to the issue of affective differences in success versus failure situations at other points in the chapter.

Why, then, did the townspeople attempt to keep the opposing players from sleeping, and how would they feel if their soccer team won because the opposition was fatigued? I now suspect that following a victory they would describe their feelings

Table 5-2. Failure: The Top Five Affective Intensity Ratings by Attribution for Failure

Ability	Unstable Effort	Stable Effort	Task Difficulty	Mood
Concerned	Sorry	Troubled	Displeasure	Uncheerful
Uncheerful	Lousy	Displeasure	Uncheerful	Unhappy
Dissatisfied	Unhappy	Unsatisfied	Unhappy	Disgust
Upset	Regretful	Uncheerful	Sad	Disturbed
Discontent	Troubled	Depressed	Upset	Lousy

Personality	Other's Effort	Other's Motivation and Personality	Luck	Intrinsic Motivation	Fatigue-Illness
Displeasure	Uncheerful	Disturbed	Frustrated	Unhappy	Dissatisfied
Unsatisfied	Discontent	Concerned	Concerned	Sad	Unhappy
Upset	Dissatisfied	Dissatisfied	Dissatisfied	Depressed	Sorry
Unhappy	Bitter	Upset	Irritated	Uncheerful	Lousy
Joyless	Miserable	Dismayed	Perturbed	Displeasure	Sad

Note. Data from "Affective Consequences of Causal Ascriptions" by B. Weiner et al. 1978, in J. H. Harvey et al. (Eds.), *New Directions in Attribution Research* (Vol. 2). Hillsdale, NJ: Erlbaum. Copyright 1978. Reprinted by permission.

Table 5-3. Percentage of Emotional Recollection as a Function of the Causal Attribution for Success

Affect	Ability	Unstable Effort	Stable Effort	Personality	Others	Luck
Competence	30	12	20	19	5	2
Confidence	20	19	18	19	14	4
Contentment	4	4	12	0	7	2
Excitement	3	9	8	11	16	6
Gratitude	9	1	4	8	43	14
Guilt	1	3	0	3	2	18
Happiness	44	43	43	38	46	48
Pride	39	28	39	43	21	8
Relief	4	28	16	11	13	26
Satisfaction	19	24	16	14	9	0
Surprise	7	16	4	14	4	52
Thankfulness	0	1	0	0	18	4

Note. From "The Cognition-Emotion Process in Achievement-Related Contexts" by B. Weiner et al., 1979, *Journal of Personality and Social Psychology, 37*, p. 1214. Copyright 1979. Reprinted by permission.

Table 5-4. Percentage of Emotional Recollection as a Function of the Causal Attribution of Failure

Affect	Ability	Unstable Effort	Stable Effort	Personality	Others	Luck
Anger	16	38	33	25	53	36
Depression	22	20	21	34	10	29
Disappointment	12	17	17	13	20	12
Disgust	2	10	4	3	8	5
Fear	7	25	21	13	18	12
Frustration	22	18	4	13	20	19
Guilt	9	15	29	9	3	5
Incompetence	14	7	8	0	10	0
Mad	7	3	0	3	10	7
Resignation	16	0	4	9	2	0
Sadness	9	10	0	6	0	14
Stupidity	14	10	13	9	0	19
Surprise	2	3	4	0	7	14
Unhappiness	14	3	4	9	2	14
Upset	9	10	8	0	8	10

Note. From "The Cognition-Emotion Process in Achievement-Related Contexts" by B. Weiner et al., 1979, *Journal of Personality and Social Psychology, 37,* p. 1215. Copyright 1979. Reprinted by permission.

as happy. The affect linked with failure is less evident, but would perhaps be labeled "dissatisfied" or "frustrated." These reactions are hypothesized to be experienced whether the team succeeded because of the actions of the townspeople, good team performance, the poor performance of the opposition, good luck, and so on, or failed because the opposition slept soundly, poor team performance, the good performance of the opposition, or bad luck. Affects such as happiness for success, and perhaps dissatisfaction and frustration for failure, hence are labeled as "outcome dependent-attribution independent," for their elicitation depends on attainment or nonattainment of a goal and not on the cause of those outcomes.

The investigations by Weiner et al. (1978, 1979) provide the main source of empirical evidence to support the notion of outcome-linked affects. But other theorizing and data also buttress the existence of this affective category. For example, in his analysis of interpersonal relationships, Kelley (1983) reasoned that there are two sources of emotion. He stated:

I am pleased or displeased by the more specific or concrete things I experience. . . . So when my wife prepares a picnic lunch for our afternoon's outing, my pleasure-displeasure comes partly from the quality of the lunch itself, but also (as a partly separate matter) from the quality of the love and thoughtfulness I attribute to her for the effort. In general, then, people evaluate interaction on a dual basis, partly in terms of the concrete outcome . . . and partly in terms of the interpersonal tendencies . . . that they and their partners manage to express. (Kelley, 1983, p. 15)

Kelley (1983) went on to conclude that, "The dual basis for evaluation in interpersonal relations is identical to [that in] . . . person-task interaction" (p. 52).

Although Kelley (1983) did not provide empirical evidence to support this line of reasoning, other findings confirming the existence of outcome-dependent affects have been presented by Bryant and Veroff (1982). These investigators explored the broad and complex domains of self-evaluation and subjective well-being. In a large survey study, respondents were interviewed regarding their happiness, distress, inadequacy, and coping in many areas of their lives, including marriage, parenthood, and work. The questionnaire data were then factor analyzed, with a three-factor solution emerging for both men and women. The factors were labeled unhappiness (defined as the absence of positive affect), strain (defined as the presence of negative affect), and personal inadequacy (the perceived shortcomings of the self). Bryant and Veroff (1982) suggested that these three dimensions may be "fundamental aspects of well-being reliably found in American populations" (p. 661). They went on to conclude:

> The overall positive or negative values of outcomes in peoples' lives dominate their affective evaluation of experience independent of causal attributions [whether their personal adequacy or inadequacy or other ascriptions influences these outcomes]. (Bryant & Veroff, 1982, p. 662)

In another investigation making use of a survey methodology, Smith and Kluegel (1982) also examined the relations between outcome and emotion. The participants in this national survey first evaluated their financial standing (from poor to prosperous), for this was stipulated by the investigators to be the most relevant determinant of success and failure in life. The respondents also rated a number of affects said to describe their life as a whole. Satisfaction ratings were positively associated with outcome ($r = .44$), whereas frustration was rated as negatively associated with the global outcome indicator ($r = -.16$). Thus, the data are consistent with the findings reported by Weiner et al. (1978, 1979).

Another source of evidence for the conceptualization of happiness and frustration or dissatisfaction as primitive emotions stems from research on emotional development. Many investigators have reported that facial expressions of "happy" and "sad" are recognized and discriminated earliest by children, followed later by the recognition of other affects such as surprise and anger (e.g., Deutsch, 1974; Izard, 1971). In addition, research concerning the spontaneous generation of emotional labels has identified happy, sad, and mad as those first consistently used and understood (Harter, 1982). Finally, when asked to characterize emotional experience in a variety of hypothetical achievement-related situations, young children primarily use the labels of happy and sad, whereas older children describe the emotions with more differentiated terms such as proud, thankful, and surprised (Weiner, Kun, & Benesh-Weiner, 1980). These data do not demonstrate that, among adults, happy and sad (or one of their many synonyms) are the initial emotional reactions to achievement-related outcomes. This would be confusing the course of emotional development with the emotional sequence expressed by an adult. However, the data do suggest that happy and sad do not require a great deal of cognitive work for their elicitation and do not vary as a function of causal ascriptions.

Cognitions and Outcome-Dependent Affects

Although it has been proposed that happiness and displeasure derive from concrete outcomes and are independent of perceptions regarding the causes of these outcomes, this does not imply that these affects are free from cognitive determination. Success and failure are subjective states, in part dependent on one's level of aspiration, or a comparison between the perceived and the desired outcome. Different determinants of aspiration level have been proposed to generate disparate affects. For example, Higgins, Strauman, and Klein (1985) distinguish between "ideal" standards (the performance one would ideally like to attain) and "ought" standards (the performance one "should" attain according to moral or ethical values). Disparities between ideal and actual performance are hypothesized to produce disappointment and dissatisfaction, whereas discrepancies between "ought" and actual performance are hypothesized to generate guilt. Although these hypotheses remain to be verified, one of the messages of the approach of Higgins et al. is that success and failure might produce differential outcome-linked affects as a function of nonattributional cognitions. Thus, greater differentiation between the outcome-related affects is required (particularly given nonattainment of a goal; see de Rivera, 1977). This remains a task for future research.

Attribution-Linked Affects

It has thus far been suggested that the emotion process begins with the interpretation of an event as a success or a failure (that is, the environment is evaluated as "good" or "bad"). This results in a general positive (happy) or negative (sad? frustrated?) affective reaction. If the outcome is negative, unexpected, or important, then attributional processes are elicited to determine the cause of that outcome. Causal attributions and their underlying properties of locus, stability, and controllability in turn generate differentiated affective reactions that are presumed to coexist with the initial broad emotional response.

A logical next step in this analysis therefore might be to determine the dominant affective reaction linked with each specific attribution, and in so doing to generate a list of thinking-feeling relations. This potential mapping is important to ascertain and should be pursued in the future. Yet there also appear to be many difficulties associated with such an endeavor. Within any motivational domain the list of causal ascriptions is enormous, and these causes show little overlap with causes in other motivational domains (as documented in Chapter 2). One greatly doubts that there will be so many differentiated emotional states; that is, the number of causal ascriptions may be greater than the number of differentiated emotions. In addition, the search for all cause-affect associations is very unparsimonious, remindful of the mere listing of causal ascriptions for outcomes.

In Chapter 3 it was documented that phenomenal causality might be meaningfully studied by reducing causes to their basic properties, or common denominators. Chapter 4 buttressed this position by documenting that one of the properties of causes, namely, stability, relates to expectancy of success. Might it also be the case that the study of emotion is facilitated by linking feelings with causal properties? It is intuitively reasonable to speculate that the most prevalent emotions will be associated with general properties of perceived causes, inasmuch as causal properties are represented across idiosyncratic causal situations.

In the following sections the above ideas are examined, and causal dimensions are related to emotions. I will document that the very prevalent human emotions of anger, pity, and pride are related to causal dimensions. Pride is linked with the perceived locus of causality, whereas pity and anger are related to causal controllability. It is also demonstrated that perceptions of control relate to the emotions of gratitude, guilt, and shame. In brief, some of the most common emotional experiences have activated structures of causality as their antecedents.

Causal Locus and Self-Esteem (Pride)

The first hypothesis to be examined is that perceived locus of causality influences self-esteem or self-worth. More specifically, successful outcomes that are ascribed to the self (e.g., personality, ability, effort) are anticipated to result in greater self-esteem (pride) than success that is externally attributed (e.g., task ease, good luck). Thus, self-esteem should be enhanced when an A in an exam is ascribed to high ability or hard work, when compared to the situation in which the high grade is ascribed to a teacher who gives all students As. In a similar manner, failure ascribed to the self is hypothesized to result in lower self-esteem than failure that is externally attributed. Thus, failure ascribed to lack of ability produces lower self-esteem than failure that is attributed to bad luck or to interference from others. Humans thus at times seem to define themselves as "commodities" having high or low "value," and this value is in part determined by causal perceptions.

The hypothesis of a relation between causal locus and self-esteem (pride) has been long entertained and recognized by philosophers. Hume, for example, believed that what a person is proud of must belong to the person. Spinoza reasoned that pride consists of knowing one's merits or power, and Kant nicely captured the locus-pride union by noting that everyone at a meal might enjoy the food, but only the cook could experience pride.

Contemporary philosophers and psychologists also have postulated a locus-pride relation. Isenberg (1980), for example, stated, "The definition of pride, then, has three parts. There is (1) a quality which (2) is approved (or considered desirable) and (3) is judged to belong to oneself" (p. 357). And Stipek (1983) added:

> A . . . quality of pride . . . is self-reflection. . . . Furthermore, the object of pride . . . must be perceived by the individual to have some value; the possession or accomplishment must result in confirming or increasing the individual's merit. Thus, pride . . . is intimately related to individuals' perceptions of their self-worth. (p. 43)

What, then, might an attributional approach add to this long-examined topic? First, the attributional literature can be brought to bear on the presumed linkage between locus and pride, shedding light on the association and pointing out related empirical consistencies or inconsistencies. Second, topics such as the development of the relation and its usage in everyday social interaction have been experimentally examined from an attributional perspective. Finally, the locus-pride linkage can be placed within a larger conceptual framework. In so doing, it will be shown that the linkage between locus and pride is conceptually similar to the relation between controllability and anger, or uncontrollability and pity, in that attributional dimensions are influencing emotion. Thus, the locus-pride relation is not anomalous in the emotion field, but rather is an integral part of a more coherent picture.

Pertinent Attributional Research

The initial investigations to ascertain the effects of causal properties, including locus of causality, on affective reactions were conducted by Weiner et al. (1978, 1979). As a reminder to the reader, in two investigations causal ascriptions were specified for success and failure, and the participants either indicated on rating scales the intensity of affect that they thought would be experienced or recalled the emotions that they did experience in these situations. To determine if causal locus influences affect, the combined responses for internal causes (e.g., ability, effort, personality) were compared with the combined data given the external causes (e.g., task difficulty, luck, others). The differences for successful outcomes in Weiner et al. (1978) and Weiner et al. (1979) are shown in Table 5-5, which reveals that in both investigations internal ascriptions for success augment reports of pride, confidence, competence, and satisfaction. Pride, competence, confidence, and perhaps satisfaction can be subsumed within the rubric of self-worth or self-esteem; the affective labels connote pride in oneself, belief that one is competent, self-confidence, and self-satisfaction (although satisfaction was found by Weiner et al., 1978, and Smith and Kluegel, 1982, to be an outcome-dependent affect).

In a subsequent study using children as subjects, Graham, Doubleday, and Guarino (1984) asked children to recall an incident in their lives in which they expe-

Table 5-5. Discriminated Affects for Success as a Function of Locus of Causality

Weiner, Russell, & Lerman (1979)	Weiner, Russell, & Lerman (1978)
pride	pride
competence	competence
confidence	confidence
satisfaction	satisfaction
	zest

rienced pride. The causes of the reported events were classified as internal (e.g., "I felt proud that I passed the test of swimming around the pool because I kept trying and believing I could do it"), external (e.g., "I felt proud when my uncle got married and had a baby"), and intermediate (e.g., "We beat another basketball team that was really good; I tried hard but everyone else did too so I really didn't do it all"). The classification of the causal antecedents of pride as a function of the age of the respondents is shown in Table 5-6. There is a growing association between internal causality and feelings of pride, although this relation is evident even among the 6-year-olds.

A much vaster literature that is germane to a locus-pride association is included under the general category of attributional biasing, or what is more specifically known as the "hedonic" or "self-serving" bias (see Weary, 1978). This bias has been one of the most extensively examined topics in the field of attribution. Substantial research has revealed that individuals are more likely to make self-attributions for positive than for negative outcomes. For example, in the achievement domain there is a tendency to attribute success to ability and effort (internal factors), and to ascribe failure to task difficulty and luck (external factors). Although there has been controversy over the interpretation of these data, and alternative nonmotivational explanations have been offered, the operation of ego-enhancing and ego-defensive biases generally has been accepted as explaining the experimental findings. As Harvey and Weary (1981) noted, "By taking credit for good acts and denying blame for bad outcomes, the individual presumably may be able to enhance or protect his or her self-esteem" (p. 33).

This huge body of literature is directly relevant to the postulated association between locus and pride (self-esteem). Indeed, the basic premise of the hedonic bias research is that internal attributions for goal attainment, and external attributions for nonattainment of a goal, enhance and protect self-esteem. It seems rather surprising that individuals working in the hedonic bias area have not called attention to the underlying presumption that attributions or thinking influence feeling. In any case, the documentation of self-serving attributional biases can be considered strong evidence supporting the hypothesized locus-esteem relation.

Table 5-6. Causes of Pride Classified as Internal, Intermediate, and External, as a Function of Age

	Percent Classified		
Locus	Age 6 (N = 35)	Age 9 (N = 37)	Age 11 (N = 37)
Internal	48	76	82
Intermediate	26	11	16
External	26	13	02

Note. From "The Development of Relations Between Perceived Controllability and the Emotions of Pity, Anger, and Guilt" by S. Graham et al., 1984, Child Development, 55. Copyright 1984. Reprinted by permission.

Use in Everyday Life

The bias toward ascribing success rather than failure to the self, and failure rather than success to external factors, demonstrates that individuals may bias attributions and, in so doing, alter or manage feelings toward the self. Additionally, the linkage between locus and self-esteem is consciously used to influence the emotional lives of others and, in turn, their interpersonal behaviors. That is, the association between internal ascriptions for outcomes and self-esteem is not only recognized by philosophers and social psychologists—it is an integral part of everyday interpersonal interaction and the basis of a naive theory of emotion.

Perhaps the most evident conscious or calculated use of the locus-esteem association occurs in affiliative contexts. Frequently, individuals are asked to take part in a social engagement, such as a date or a party. The recipient of this request may prefer to refuse and will communicate a rejection. Because a rejection is a negative (and perhaps unexpected) outcome for the requester, he or she is likely to ask "why" to determine the cause of the refusal. Most readers have surely heard the query, "Why can't you come to the party?" or "Why won't you go out with me?" The rejector may then tell or not tell the truth. One question that arises is, Under what conditions will the rejector withhold the truth and communicate a false cause (i.e., tell a lie)?

Folkes (1982) examined this issue in a simulational study. Participants in her experiment were asked to imagine that they had turned down a request for a date. Sixteen reasons for rejection were provided, equally representing causes within the three-dimensional matrix. For example, rejection was specified as due to a lack of physical attractiveness (internal to the requester, stable, and uncontrollable), religious restrictions (external, stable, and uncontrollable), and so on. The female subjects were asked to reveal what cause they publicly would give to the requester. In addition, the participants indicated the extent to which the public and private (real) causes would "hurt the feelings" of the individual asking for a date, if those causes were known to him. It was assumed that "hurt feelings" captures the general meaning of personal esteem.

The relations between anticipated hurt feelings and the three causal dimensions are shown in Figure 5-2, which reveals that internal causes for rejection maximize the belief that the other's feelings will be hurt. In addition, Figure 5-2 shows that an internal cause for rejection that is stable (e.g., "His face and body type are not attractive") exacerbates these perceived reactions more than does public rejection because of an internal, unstable cause. In this context, causal stability functions as a scalar variable, magnifying the anticipated affective response to rejection.

Other data revealed that the communications from the rejectors were guided by their beliefs about thinking-feeling associations. When the true cause of rejection was external to the requester, the participants stated that reason 99% of the time. But when the real cause of rejection was internal to the requester, the female subjects stated an external reason (withheld the truth) over two thirds of the time. Hence, the behavior of the rejecting females was apparently benevolent, guided in part by an attempt to protect the self-esteem of others and mediated by the "naive" assumption

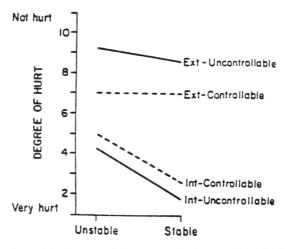

Figure 5-2. The rejector's judgments of the requester's degree of hurt feelings as a function of the dimensional classification of the reason for rejection. From "Communicating the Causes of Social Rejection" by V. S. Folkes, 1982, *Journal of Experimental Social Psychology*, *18*, p. 245. Copyright 1982. Reprinted by permission.

of a causal locus-self-esteem relation. We therefore attempt to control or influence the emotional lives of others by communicating false reasons for rejection, providing "excuses" (*ex* = other; *causa* = cause) for their "failure." In achievement contexts the same type of attribution-affect manipulation also may be observed, although this has not been experimentally examined. For example, in athletic competition teammates often attempt to cheer up a disheartened player after a fumbled ball, offering external causes such as, "The sun is very strong today," or "That was a really difficult play." There is an implicit belief that these communications, by maintaining the self-esteem and confidence of the player, will aid future performance. We are also likely to embrace such excuses from others when making our own attributions for a "fumbled ball," thus maintaining personal esteem. Hence, a hedonic bias may be fostered by false communications from others.

However, costs are also attached to untruthful ascriptions. If a false external attribution for a dating request is communicated and accepted, then the recipient of the communication is misled and may continue to pursue a friendship that the other party does not desire. Many of the letter writers to the advice column of "Dear Abby," for example, state that they prefer to hear the truth, even though it may hurt their self-esteem. They contend that if the truth were known, then they would not waste time pursuing the other person. However, as some of the correspondents also note, there is an optimal solution to this dilemma, namely, to provide an external but stable attribution for rejection (e.g., "My fiancé wouldn't like it if I went out with you"). In this manner, the cause will not result in hurt feelings, but the relationship should be less actively sought inasmuch as expectancy of success is minimized. Such communications are impressive in that two attributional dimensions and their linked consequences (locus-self-esteem and stability-expectancy) are simultaneously used, and often without apparent difficulty or response hesitation. This strongly implies that the attribution-consequence linkages are deeply ingrained and quite salient.

An empirical investigation examining the naive use of a locus-esteem association has also been conducted with children. Weiner and Handel (1985), guided by the methodology of Folkes (1982), asked children 5-12 years of age to "Pretend that a boy (girl) from your class asks if you would like to go out and play with him (her). You decide not to go out and play because. . . ." This was followed by eight causes, four internal to the requester (e.g., "Your classmate always cheats at games," "Your classmate is never good at games") and four external to him or her (e.g., "You are sick with a bad cold," "You can't get to his or her house"). Following each cause of rejection, the experimenter asked how much the classmate's feelings would be hurt if that cause were conveyed.

The data revealed that hurt feelings were anticipated to be greater given communication of internal rather than external causes (Figure 5-3). This finding was equally evident across the age groups; a developmental trend was not displayed. In addition, children in all age groups indicated that they would be more likely to lie and withhold internal rather than external causes. Thus, the data were entirely consistent with the findings reported by Folkes (1982).

A Genetic Component?

The data reported thus far indicate that children label the same situations as enhancing or deflating pride and self-esteem as do adults. It certainly must be the case that the specific label of pride and its adult meaning are learned. Nonetheless, one might speculate that very young children experience the same emotional reactions to

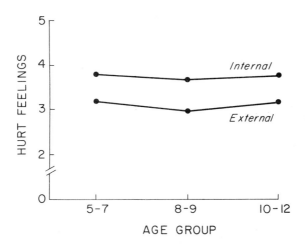

Figure 5-3. Anticipated degree of hurt feelings as a function of age of the subjects. Data from "Anticipated Emotional Consequences of Causal Communications and Reported Communication Strategy" by B. Weiner and S. Handel, 1985, *Developmental Psychology, 21*. Copyright 1985. Reprinted by permission.

personally caused events as do adults, even though the specific label of pride might not be attached to their reactions.

Watson and Ramey (1972) have presented very preliminary evidence that infants as young as 6 *weeks* of age exhibit augmented positive reactions when they have effected a change in their environment. Watson and Ramey placed a mobile over infants' cribs. For some infants, the movement of the mobile was caused by very small head rotations. Thus, a response contingency was established such that the infant was able to cause a change in the external world. Data revealed that these infants did engage in increased head turning over time, thus substantiating that mobile movement is a positive reinforcer. In a control condition, the mobile was moved by an adult. For these children, head movements remained stable over time.

Watson and Ramey questioned mothers about the emotional reactions of their infants in these two conditions. They write:

> We now inserted a causal inquiry as to whether the infant ever displayed any smiling or cooing behavior toward our mobile. The average response of experimental mothers can be summarized by an emphatic yes with answers of the following kind: "It was hysterical," and "Oh yes, a great deal." The response of the control mothers can be summarized by a passive yes as exemplified by answers such as "Yes, I think so," and "Yes, now and then.". . . With further inquiry it appeared that the experimental babies blossomed into smiling and cooing after a few days of exposure to the contingency mobile. . . . (Watson & Ramey, 1972, pp. 224–225)

Although Watson and Ramey presented only anecdotal data, they did raise a number of very basic issues in the study of emotion. One question is whether children this young can indeed experience "pride." According to the prior analysis, for this to occur the infant would have to have an idea of a "self." But is this structure likely to have developed at the age of 6 weeks?

An alternative to the presumption that these infants are displaying pride is to assume that what is being experienced is "joy" or "happiness." Recall that these are less complex affects linked to positive outcomes, and not to attributions. In support of this position, Stipek (1983) has proposed that there is an inherent association between mastery and feelings of joy. She reasoned:

> There is a difference between the obvious pleasure experienced by infants as a result of early accomplishments [mastery] and the emotion described by philosophers and psychologists as pride. Lacking symbolic thought, infants' delight is noncognitive, automatic, and is intrinsically derived. This pleasure lacks the reflective quality of pride discussed earlier. . . . The infant's affective response is not "esteem-enhancing" because it is 'momentary;' esteem requires a more stable concept of self than infants possess. . . . (Stipek, 1983, pp. 44–45)

The question remaining to be resolved is, How should the observation that children smile when they make a mobile turn (or, as more commonly observed, laugh when they take their first steps) be interpreted? Is this outcome-linked joy, or attribution-linked pride? This remains a very difficult task for the future.

Causal Controllability and Social Emotions

It has thus far been contended that outcome evaluations influence general affects such as happy and sad, whereas the antecedent of pride and self-esteem is the locus of the cause of the outcome. I will now examine the causal dimension of controllability and its linkage to emotions.

It is hypothesized that if personal failure is due to causes perceived as controllable by others, that is, "if one could have done otherwise" (Hamilton, 1980), then anger is elicited. For example, when failure is caused by an inconsiderate neighbor who kept one awake the night before an exam, one reacts with anger. On the other hand, uncontrollable causes of negative outcomes of others elicit pity. Thus, if it is discovered that the neighbor was violently ill, or was being attacked by thieves and was making noise to attract attention, then pity rather than anger is likely to be experienced. The causal dimension of controllability also is associated with the affects of gratitude and guilt. Thus, for example, one is grateful when one receives a gift freely given, while when one does not freely provide help to needy others, guilt may be experienced. Uncontrollable causes, on the other hand, are linked with shame (embarrassment, humiliation). One is embarrassed, for example, when one fails at sports because of being shorter or less coordinated than others. Inasmuch as the perceived degree of controllability is thought to influence the very prevalent emotions of anger, pity, gratitude, guilt, and shame, this causal dimension plays an important role in the maintenance of social relationships and social order.

In addition to the rational approach of attribution theory, the biological conception proposed by the sociobiologists, with its link to altruism, also has addressed the emotions of anger, pity, gratitude, and guilt. The sociobiological conception is so different from the attributional viewpoint that it deserves some very brief attention here.

Sociobiologists contend that altruism is a genetically programmed behavior in service of the preservation of one's gene pool. However, it can also be survival relevant to cheat; cheaters take unfair advantage of the general altruistic system and increase their survival fitness at the expense of others. This temptation, sociobiologists argue, has resulted in the evolution of mechanisms to protect against cheating. They point out that anger, sympathy (pity), gratitude, and guilt are in service of the maintenance and regulation of the altruistic system and aid in preventing cheating (Trivers, 1971). Specifically:

Anger (and the aggression that it instigates) "counteracts the tendency of the altruist in the absence of reciprocity to continue to perform altruistic acts, . . . educates the unreciprocating individual by frightening him with immediate harm or with the future harm of no more aid; and . . . select[s] directly against the unreciprocating individual by injuring, killing, or exiling him" (Trivers, 1971, p. 49).

Sympathy (pity) "has been selected to motivate altruistic behavior as a function of the plight of the recipient of such behavior; crudely put, the greater the potential benefit to the recipient, the greater the sympathy and the more likely the altruistic gesture" (Trivers, 1971, p. 49).

Gratitude "has been selected to regulate human response to altruistic acts . . . that emotion is sensitive to the cost/benefit ratio of such acts" (Trivers, 1971, p. 49).

Guilt "has been selected for in humans partly in order to motivate the cheater to compensate for his misdeed and to behave reciprocally in the future, and thus to prevent the rupture of reciprocal relationships" (Trivers, 1971, p. 50).

The convergence of two quite different theoretical systems on the same set of emotions certainly encourages one to think that fundamental issues and important affective states are under consideration. I now turn to the specific emotions of anger, pity, gratitude, and guilt, as well as shame, and examine in detail how attribution theory accounts for their elicitation.

Anger and Pity

A large survey study by Averill (1982, 1983) illustrates the attributional antecedents of anger. Averill asked his respondents to describe a situation in which they were made angry, and then examined the characteristics of these situations. He concluded:

> The major issue for the person in the street is not the specific nature of the instigating event; it is the perceived *justification* for the instigator's behavior. Anger, for the person in the street, is an accusation. . . . Over 85% of the episodes described by angry persons involved either an act that they considered voluntary and unjustified (59%) or else a potentially avoidable accident (e.g., due to negligence or lack of foresight, 28%). . . . To summarize, the typical instigation to anger is a value judgment. More than anything else, anger is an attribution of blame. (Averill, 1983, p. 1150)

Averill (1983) noted that others "have pointed out that anger involves a normative judgment, an attribution of blame" (p. 1150). For example, in one of the very first of the pertinent investigations, Pastore (1952) demonstrated that blame attributions influence the relation between frustration and aggression. He found that aggression (and, by implication, anger) is not merely the result of nonattainment of a desired goal, but rather follows when a barrier imposed by others is "arbitrary" rather than "nonarbitrary." Among the arbitrary, aggression-instigating conditions identified by Pastore (1952) was, "Your date phones at the last minute and breaks an appointment without an adequate explanation." The so-called nonarbitrary equivalent situation was, "Your date phones at the last minute and breaks an appointment because he (she) had suddenly become ill." Blame and aggression are therefore linked with perceptions of causal controllability.

In contrast to the linkage between controllability and anger, uncontrollable causes are associated with pity. (In this context, emotions such as compassion and sympathy are not distinguished from pity, although they might indeed be discriminable). Another's loss of a loved one because of an accident or illness (a cause external to the target of the pity, and uncontrollable by that person), or failure of another because of a physical handicap (internal to the target of pity and uncontrollable) are prevalent situations that elicit pity. Uncontrollability, however, is not likely to be a sufficient condition for the generation of pity. After all, we may not pity a child who is not tall enough to reach a toy on the shelf. It appears that objects of pity must be suffering a severe distress, one that is perhaps central to their lives. In addition, the other person might have to be defined as "fundamentally different" to be the target of a full-blown pity reaction.

Inasmuch as pity is associated with perceptions of uncontrollability and a fundamental (and adverse) difference, communicated pity could serve as a cue promoting the self-perception of difference, deficiency, and inadequacy (see Graham, 1984; Weiner, Graham, Stern, & Lawson, 1982). For this reason, when the teacher of Helen Keller began her training, it is reported that she stated to Ms. Keller's family, "We do not want your pity!" Similarly, a contemporary author, Robertson Davies, wrote, "I will not expose myself to the pity of my inferiors," thus conveying that a target of pity is associated with some deficiency.

There has been little research examining the emotion of pity, and what research there has been typically involves comparisons with anger. In one investigation conducted by Weiner, Graham, and Chandler (1982), college students were asked to describe instances in their lives in which anger or pity was experienced. After recounting two experiences for each emotion, the concept of causal dimensions was introduced and defined. The subjects then rated the cause of the event in question, if applicable, on each of the three dimensions.

Concerning pity, 71% of the causes were rated as stable and uncontrollable, with equal apportionment between the internal and external alternatives. Two quite typical instances were:

1. A guy on campus is terribly deformed. I pity him because it would be so hard to look so different and have people stare at you.
2. My great-grandmother lives in a rest home, and everytime I go there I see these poor old half-senile men and women wandering aimlessly down the halls . . . I feel pity every time I go down there. (Weiner, Graham, & Chandler, 1982, p. 228)

For the affect of anger, 86% of the situations involved an external and controllable cause, as Averill (1982) and others also have documented. Two typical anger-arousing situations were:

1. My roommate brought her dog into our no-pets apartment without asking me first. When I got home she wasn't there, but the barking dog was. . . . As well, the dog had relieved itself in the middle of the entry.
2. I felt angry toward my boyfriend for lying to me about something he did. All he had to do was tell me the truth. (Weiner, Graham, & Chandler, 1982, p. 228)

Weiner, Graham, and Chandler (1982) additionally ascertained reactions of pity and anger in a variety of manipulated situations. Four story themes were created that involved failing to repay a debt, committing a crime, failing an exam, and needing class notes. Within each of these themes, eight situations were generated providing disparate causes of these outcomes. Each of the eight causes represented one cell within the usual Locus × Stability × Controllability matrix. For example, two of the external, stable, and uncontrollable causes were, "The person cannot repay because a computer breakthrough suddenly made his job unnecessary," and "He committed the crime because he lived in a depressed area where there were no opportunities for employment and adequate schooling." For each of the 32 conditions (4 themes × 8 causes), the subjects rated the degree to which they would feel anger and pity toward the story character. It should be noted that in these examples the actor may not have been in "severe" distress and may not have been "fundamentally" different; thus, more moderate pity was anticipated to be elicited given the uncontrollable causes.

The findings across the four story themes were quite similar and are combined in Figure 5-4, which shows that when the cause is classified as controllable, reports of anger exceed those of pity, whereas when the cause is classified as uncontrollable, reports of pity are greater than those of anger. These relations are particularly true given internal causes. Furthermore, stable causes maximize feelings of pity given uncontrollable causes, and feelings of anger given controllable causes. For example, more pity is expressed when the individual has permanently, rather than temporarily, lost a job. Stability again therefore appears to be an effective magnifier.

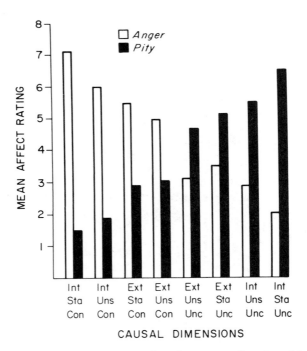

Figure 5-4. Ratings of pity and anger, across four themes, as a function of the dimensional classification of the cause. *Int*, internal; *Ext*, external; *Sta*, stable; *Uns*, unstable; *Con*, controllable; *Unc*, uncontrollable. From "Pity, Anger, and Guilt: An Attributional Analysis" by B. Weiner et al., 1982, *Personality and Social Psychology Bulletin*, *8*, p. 231. Copyright 1982. Reprinted by permission.

The linkages between perceived causal controllability-anger and uncontrollability-pity also have been examined in children. In one pertinent study, Graham, et al., (1984) asked children to "tell me about a time when you felt pity for (anger toward) another." The children also indicated whether the cause of the negative outcome was "mostly something that (the target) of the emotion made happen, or mostly something that (the target) could not stop from happening" (Graham et al., 1984, p. 563). A special scale tailored for a younger population was created to assess the degree of perceived controllability. The data from this investigation, shown in Table 5-7, reveal that anger is elicited by perceived controllable causes and pity by uncontrollable causes. There is no developmental trend between the age groups.

Of course, the data in Table 5-7 do not reveal the source of these attribution-affect relations. This void in knowledge also characterizes the union between locus and pride (although some developmental hypotheses have been offered; see Stipek, 1983). Sociobiologists propose that genetics influence the basis for anger and pity experiences. In the case of anger, this may not seem surprising inasmuch as many emotion theorists consider anger to be a primary emotion, exhibited by animals as well as humans (see Izard, 1977). However, the early comprehension of pity and its pairing with uncontrollability were unexpected. I would like to call attention to some "data" that might be considered supportive of a genetic hypothesis, although it will be evident that what is being proposed is highly speculative. Some animals are known to engage in appeasement gestures, which then inhibit the victor from imposing harm. The mechanism that accounts for the inhibition of aggression given an appeasement gesture stimulus is unknown. The gestures, such as exposing one's neck, place the loser in a vulnerable and completely uncontrollable position. Might it be that some primitive form of pity is aroused by the uncontrollable plight, which then elicits prosocial (nonaggressive) behavior? Pleading for mercy while on one's knees, also a perilous position, is a similar gesture among humans that is also thought to inhibit aggression or increase the likelihood of forgiveness. The position and accompanying words convey, "Have (take) pity on me." In addition, it has often been reported that animals, just as humans, bring food to the sick and injured

Table 5-7. Mean Controllability Ratings as a Function of Emotion and Age

Emotion	Controllability Rating		
	Age 6–7	Age 9	Age 11
Anger	6.1	6.9	7.1
Pity	2.9	2.4	2.8

Note. $N = 40$ in each age group. High ratings indicate high perceived controllability.
From "The Development of Relations Between Perceived Controllability and the Emotions of Pity, Anger, and Guilt" by S. Graham et al., 1984, *Child Development*, *55*, p. 563. Copyright 1984. Adapted by permission.

members of their pack or group. Could these phenotypically similar observations in humans and animals be mediated by similar pity reactions? If there is a phylogenetic representation of an uncontrollability-pity association, then this relation would probably have a genetic basis. I am unsure how seriously to take this hypothesis, but I do think that a biological underpinning for an uncontrollability-pity linkage should not be summarily rejected (see also Hoffman's, 1982 contention that empathy is genetically transmitted).

Use in Everyday Life. In a previous section it was documented that individuals use a perceived association between locus of causality and self-esteem to manipulate or control the emotions of others. This is accomplished by giving "excuses" when rejecting others for a social engagement. This is an important empirical finding because it documents that attribution-affect understanding is prevalent in everyday life and that social interactions are guided by these perceived psychological laws.

In a similar manner, the use of excuses also demonstrates that the relations between controllability-anger and uncontrollability-pity are part of naive psychology (i.e., the average person's understanding of psychological principles). Picture a scenario in which you are waiting for someone to arrive for an appointment of either a social or business nature. You wait 10, 30, and finally 60 minutes until the person finally appears. During the waiting period you might experience many emotional reactions, ranging from worry (Did something happen?) and self-doubt (Is this the right place?) to frustration and anger (Where the hell is he?). When the person does appear, it is likely that an explanation will be immediately offered or asked for (because unexpected, negative events elicit attributional search). Imagine that the tardy person states, "It was so nice out that I took my time getting here," or "I decided to first watch a program on television." These responses probably evoke laughter from the reader, who intuitively recognizes that they are not "good" excuses. A good excuse lessens personal responsibility. In so doing, it is anticipated that anger will be mitigated, one's positive image will be maintained, and the interpersonal relationship will not be weakened. Thus, a better strategy would be to say, "My car broke down," or "There was a tie-up on the freeway," or "I temporarily became dizzy." These are good excuses because the perception of the cause of lateness is changed from uncertain, or controllable, to uncontrollable. Of course, there are other ways of dealing with a broken social contract, including acceptance of responsibility and retributions, offering an apology, providing a justification, and so on. The functions of these alternative strategies are not examined in this context. In addition, excuses need not be given only for broken social contracts. A cartoon I recently read showed a little boy saying to his parents: "I have joined a religion whose dietary laws forbid the eating of broccoli." As the cartoon caption intimates, a simple rule is followed. Deny personal reponsibility and negative intents, thus lessening anger.

To explore these ideas, my colleagues and I (Weiner, Amirkhan, Folkes, & Verette, in press) asked college students to recall recent occasions in which social contracts were broken and to provide the true and false reasons that were communicated, as well as any uncommunicated (withheld) reasons. The participants also

Table 5-8. Categories of Explanation and Percentage Frequencies as a Function of Type of Reason

Category of Explanation	Type of Reason (Percentage Frequency)[a]		
	True (Communicated)	False (Communicated)	Withheld
Transportation	24	15	2
Work/school	14	25	4
Prior commitment	13	22	4
Physical ailment	12	16	4
Negligence	17	6	28
Preference	9	1	53
Miscellaneous	10	15	4

[a]$N = 116$ within each type.

were asked how angry the recipient of the communication would feel if given the real reason and if given the false communication (assuming that a lie were told).

Table 5-8 describes the type of reason that was given when a social contract was not fulfilled, including situations in which a true reason was communicated as well as situations in which a false reason was given. The majority of the communicated explanations involved transportation problems ("My car broke down"), work or school requirements ("I had to study"), other commitments ("My friend needed a ride to the airport"), and physical ailments ("I came down with the flu"). Table 5-8 also reveals that the reasons that were withheld predominantly involved a preference (desire) not to engage in the contracted activity (53%), or negligence (28%). These categories of explanations were withheld significantly more often than they were offered as true or false reasons.

The causes were next reliably rated according to their placement on the locus, controllability, and intentionality dimensions. The withheld reasons were primarily internal, controllable, and intentional ("I did not want to go"). Internal, controllable, and unintentional causes ("I forgot") are the only other category of withheld reasons, although they often were truly (but not falsely) communicated. Conversely, true and false communicated reasons tended to be external, uncontrollable, and unintentional ("My car broke down").

Table 5-9 moves from an analysis of the explanations given or withheld to the consequences, or perceived consequences, of the true and false communications. It is evident from Table 5-9 that the recipient of the communication is rated highest on anger when assuming that the withheld explanation was known. Thus, the true and false communications were significantly less likely to provoke anger.

In sum, the investigation tells a simple but meaningful story. There is a naive belief that anger is in part influenced by causal ascriptions concerning why a social contract has not been fulfilled. To ward off these consequences, individuals may withhold the truth (lie), substituting instead explanations that are anticipated to result in positive consequences. The causal configuration of the "good" excuses is

Table 5-9. Perceived Emotional Consequences of Excuse
Related to Excuse Clasification

Type of Reason	Anger Reaction
True	2.03
False	2.26
Withheld	4.39

external, uncontrollable, and unintentional; the suppressed causes of transgression are internal, controllable, and intentional.

The function of excuse giving as a moderator of anger also was documented by Weiner and Handel (1985). We gave children ranging in age from 5 to 12 the following scenario: "You promised to play with a friend after school, but then did not show up. The real reason was. . . ." Four controllable causes (e.g., "You decided to watch TV") and four uncontrollable causes (e.g., "Your bike had a flat tire") were then provided. The subjects were asked how angry their friend would be if that reason were communicated. The data, depicted in Figure 5-5, reveal that among all age groupings controllable causes for nonappearance are believed to elicit more anger than uncontrollable causes. In addition, children of all age groups indicated that they would be more likely to communicate uncontrollable than controllable causes. That is, if they would be perceived as personally responsible, then there was an inclination to lie. It is thus again evident that 5-year-olds already have learned the art of excuse making and perceive the relation between controllable causes for a social "failure" and anger from others.

Anger, Pity, and the Stigmatized. Individuals with so-called social "marks," including obesity, alcoholism, physical disability, mental illness, and mental retardation, suffer from many debilitating social consequences not inherently associated with these marks (see Jones et al., 1984). In our culture, these persons are perceptually salient and monitored, they elicit unusual reactions from others, and often they are socially rejected and isolated. To be stigmatized is in many ways similar to being a "failure," although this may be neither a self-perception of the stigmatized individual nor an objective fact. As "failures," stigmatized persons elicit causal search and attributions from others. Why is individual X an alcoholic? or How did individual Y become crippled? are frequent questions that others either overtly raise or covertly think (see Wright, 1983).

Obesity. A survey at Kent State University asked 630 students to rate two statements concerning the causes of the marks of stigmatized groups. Included in the questionnaire were statements about four such groups (obese, alcoholics, mentally ill, and homosexuals). The rated statements regarding causality were:

a. A mentally ill (obese, alcoholic, etc.) person is responsible for his or her condition.

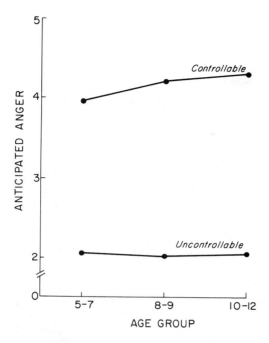

Figure 5-5. Anticipated anger as a function of the controllability of the breaking of a social contract, as a function of the age of the subjects. Data from "Anticipated Emotional Consequences of Causal Communications and Reported Communication Strategy" by B. Weiner and S. Handel, 1985, *Developmental Psychology, 21.* Copyright 1985. Reprinted by permission.

b. Mental illness (obesity, alcoholism, etc.) is most always the result of forces
   beyond the person's control.

Respondents rated a 9-point scale ranging from *strongly disagree* (given a score of 1) to *strongly agree* (given a score of 9).

The results of this survey are given in Table 5-10. The resultant difference scores (responsible [controllable] minus nonresponsible [uncontrollable]) indicate that alcoholism and obesity particularly are believed to be under volitional control, so that individuals with these marks are held responsible for their states. Other research has revealed that obese males are believed to exercise too little, whereas obese females are believed to eat too much. Both energy output and energy intake are thought of as personally controllable.

It has been contended that the union between obesity and personal control "goes right to the roots of our social customs" (Mackenzie, 1984). Mackenzie stated that fat and thin people alike share the opinion that fatness indicates a loss of personal control, which is "considered the ultimate moral failure in our culture." Because they are fat, obese individuals are considered not in control of their lives. Mackenzie

Table 5-10. Judgments of Personal Causality Concerning Four Stigmatized Groups (data from Kent State University Survey, 1981)

	Judgment		
Group	Personal Responsibility[a]	Nonresponsibility[b]	Difference
Mentally ill	2.7	5.3	−2.6
Homosexuals	5.7	3.8	1.9
Alcoholics	6.4	3.5	2.9
Obese	5.8	3.4	2.4

[a] Low numbers indicate not responsible.
[b] High numbers indicate not responsible.

reasoned that overweight people exhibit self-deprecation and self-hatred because lack of perceived control is often also a self-perception as the cause of obesity.

From the principles documented in the preceding sections, the obese individual should elicit anger rather than pity from others. This negative reaction has been indirectly documented in a number of investigations (indirectly in that anger or pity are not assessed, but have to be inferred from other evaluative judgments). In one series of studies (Richardson, Hastorf, Goodman, & Dornbusch, 1961), 10- and 11-year-olds rank-ordered drawings of children according to how much they would like them. The drawing of an obese child was almost always ranked last or next to last, below that of other stigmatized groups such as those with physical handicaps or facial disfigurement. Obese persons also have been shown to be least often chosen in sociometric studies of friendship (see Staffieri, 1967).

The relation between controllability (responsibility) and initial impressions of obese individuals has been examined by DeJong (1980). Subjects believed that they were participating in a "getting acquainted" experiment. They were given folders describing another person before they were to meet. The folders portrayed either a normal-weight or an obese individual. Furthermore, the person's obesity was attributed either to a thyroid condition (uncontrollable) or a liking for food (controllable). DeJong (1980) found that when obesity could be attributed to a physical source, the overweight individual initially was liked more and was less likely to be derogated, in comparison to the condition in which obesity was perceived as controllable. As already indicated, this does not necessarily mean that the respondents were angry at the obese person who "liked to eat." Nonetheless, the data are consistent with that position.

Alcoholism. As documented in the Kent State University survey, alcoholics also are perceived as responsible for their state. This finding has been corroborated by Beckman (1979). Beckman asked a large sample of both alcoholic and nonalcoholic respondents to rate a number of statements concerning the causes of excessive drinking. Among both alcoholics and nonalcoholics, the finding was that one is held personally responsible for drunkenness.

Given a perception of controllability, it should be anticipated according to the attributional perspective that others will feel angry toward the alcoholic. In one test of this hypothesis, Weiner (1980a) described a person falling down in a subway who "apparently is drunk. He is carrying a liquor bottle wrapped in a brown paper bag and smells of liquor" (p. 190). The subjects were asked to imagine that they were in the subway at that time and to report what their three most dominant affects would be. In addition, a person described as ill was also presented as falling down in a subway, and affective reactions again were elicited. More than 25% of the respondents directed negative affect, such as anger, toward the drunk, whereas this characterized feelings toward the ill individual in fewer than 3% of the respondents.

Physical disability. In contrast to alcoholism and obesity, physical disability is perceived as an uncontrollable cause of personal "failure." As such, pity is anticipated to be elicited. In the study by Weiner (1980a), nearly 50% of the respondents indicated that they would experience sympathy and concern when an ill person falls down in a subway.

Hastorf, Northcraft, and Picciotto (1979) examined evaluative reactions toward disabled persons in a laboratory setting. An experimental stooge either wearing or not wearing leg braces attempted to complete a maze task. This task should not necessarily have been more difficult for someone wearing leg braces. After each attempt, subjects gave the confederate feedback, ranging from "You did very well" to "You did poorly." The data indicated that more praise was given to the handicapped than to the nonhandicapped performer, although their performances were identical. Hastorf et al. (1979) suggested that there is a "norm to be kind" to the handicapped (but see Russell et al., 1985). The origin of this norm, or its current practice, could be mediated by the sight of handicapped persons eliciting pity and thus generating prosocial behavior (positive evaluations). The question of whether the positive behavior is "cooly" guided by a norm or "hotly" mediated by aroused affect is impossible to disentangle in this research. However, other investigations presented in the next chapter lend strong support to the hypothesis that affects are involved as mediating processes.

In a follow-up investigation, Strenta and Kleck (1982) had subjects view videotapes of an apparently handicapped or nonhandicapped person receiving praise or other feedback from another. The subjects rated the degree to which the evaluation was perceived as corresponding with the actual task performance, as opposed to being based on "other facts." The data revealed that positive feedback was considered more contingent on actual behavior given an able-bodied rather than a handicapped person. Thus, part of lay psychology is the belief that positive evaluation of a handicapped person is due to nonoutcome determinants (which are likely to include inferred pity).

Summary of stigma research. There are many psychological issues that must receive attention before we can understand stigmatization and its consequences (see Jones et al., 1984). One psychological factor to be considered, however, is the perceived controllability of both the origin of the problem and its solution. Perceptions of controllability in part dictate affective reactions of anger and pity toward others. More specifically, anger and derogation are communicated toward obese and alcoholic individuals because their problems are perceived as controllable, whereas pity is directed toward physically disabled persons because their plight is uncontrollable. Difficulty has even been reported in collecting charity for alcoholics and the obese. It follows that if perceptions of perceived responsibility of these stigmatized groups could be changed, then the social reactions they elicit would also be altered. Thus, for example, if the public were more aware of the demonstrated genetic influence on obesity and alcoholism, then perhaps reactions would be more of concern toward members of these groups, rather than ridicule or derogation.

Anger, Pity, and Achievement Evaluation. A voluminous literature concerning the evaluation of "normals" in achievement contexts (at school, during sporting competition, on the job) has some of the same characteristics as research on the stigmatized. Perceptions of the perceived controllability of failure have been varied, and the influence of this causal property on evaluation has been assessed. A series of studies by Weiner and Kukla (1970) provided the prototypical evaluation methodology. Pupils were described as succeeding at or failing an exam. This outcome information was factorially combined with descriptions of the ability level and effort expenditure of each pupil. Thus, for example, in one condition a student was described as high in ability, low in effort, and failing an exam, whereas in a contrasting condition another student was characterized as low in ability, high in effort and succeeding. The subjects were to assume that they were teachers and had to provide positive (reward) or negative (punishment) feedback to the students.

The data from one investigation reported by Weiner and Kukla are shown in Figure 5-6, which reveals, as one would expect, that positive outcomes are rewarded more (punished less) than negative outcomes. Of greater importance in the present context, high effort is rewarded more given success and punished less given failure than is low effort. Lack of effort accompanied by high ability when failing is particularly punished. That is, when the student can be held personally responsible for failure, dispensed punishment is maximal. Lack of effort activates thoughts of responsibility inasmuch as not trying is carried out "knowingly and recklessly." This pattern of data suggests that the teacher (or responding subject) would be angry at the student.

In addition, low ability is rewarded more than high ability given success, and punished less given failure. This intimates that there might be a "norm to be kind" toward the "disabled," and again this rule could be associated with feelings of pity and sympathy. Indeed, it has been found that when a person who is low in ability fails, supervisors distort their feedback to make it seem that the performance was more positive than it had been (Ilgen & Knowlton, 1980).

The pattern of data reported by Weiner and Kukla (1970), especially the documented reward for trying and punishment for not trying, has been replicated many times and can be considered an established truth. These replications span numerous cultures including Brazil (Rodrigues, 1980), England (Rogers, 1980), Germany (Rest, Nierenberg, Weiner, & Heckhausen, 1973), India (Esware, 1972),

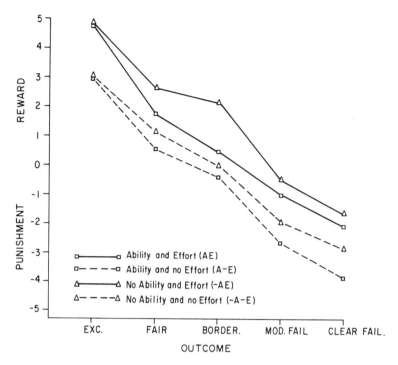

Figure 5-6. Evaluation as a function of pupil outcome, effort, and ability. (From "An Attribu-tional Analysis of Achievement Motivation" by B. Weiner and A. Kukla, 1970, *Journal of Personality and Social Psychology, 15*, p. 3. Copyright 1970. Reprinted by permission.)

and Iran (Salili, Maehr, & Gilmore, 1976). In addition, children as young as 5 years of age exhibit the same pattern of data (Rogers, 1980; Salili et al., 1976; Weiner & Peter, 1973). The situations explored include hypothetical settings where only out-come, ability, and/or effort information are provided (e.g., Covington, Spratt, & Omelich, 1980; Nicholls, 1976; Weiner & Kukla, 1970), as well as more complex classroom contexts (e.g., Medway, 1979). This is far from an exhaustive list of sup-porting studies and parameters along which the investigations vary. In addition, this same general pattern of data has been reported in work environments (e.g., Knowlton & Mitchell, 1980; Pence, Pendleton, Dobbins, & Sgro, 1982), labora-tory-test settings (e.g., Wittig, Marks, & Jones, 1981), and athletic contexts (e.g., Iso-Ahola, 1977). Even in affiliative contexts, complimenting is increased if "suc-cess" (attractiveness) is due to a controllable cause such as dieting (Folkes & Mar-coux, 1984).

If it is indeed appropriate to infer emotional states from the evaluation data, then the relations between perceived controllability of failure and anger, uncon-trollability of failure and pity, and controllability of success and positive affect span cultures, age groups, and situational contexts. In support of this claim,

| IIO | *The Holy State.* | Book II. |

He studieth his scholars natures as carefully as they their books; and ranks their difpofitions into feverall forms. And though it may feem difficult for him in a great fchool to defcend to all particulars, yet experienced Schoolmafters may quickly make a Grammar of boyes natures, and reduce them all (faving fome few exceptions) to thefe generall rules.

1 Thofe that are ingenious and induftrious. The conjunction of two fuch Planets in a youth prefage much good unto him. To fuch a lad a frown may be a whipping, and a whipping a death ; yea where their Mafter whips them once, fhame whips them all the week after. Such natures he ufeth with all gentleneffe.

2 Thofe that are ingenious and idle. Thefe think with the hare in the fable, that running with fnails (fo they count the reft of their fchool-fellows) they fhall come foon enough to the Poft, though fleeping a good while before their ftarting.Oh, a good rod would finely take them napping.

3 Thofe that are dull and diligent. Wines the ftronger they be the more lees they have when they are new. Many boyes are muddy-headed till they be clarified with age,and fuch afterwards prove the beft. Briftoll diamonds are both bright, and fquared and pointed by Nature, and yet are foft and worthleffe ; whereas orient ones in India are rough and rugged naturally. Hard rugged and dull natures of youth acquit themfelves afterwards the jewells of the countrey, and therefore their dulneffe at firft is to be born with, if they be diligent. That Schoolmafter deferves to be beaten himfelf, who beats Nature in a boy for a fault. And I queftion whether all the whipping in the world can make their parts, which are naturally fluggifh, rife one minute before the houre Nature hath appointed.

Figure 5-7. Attributional analysis from Thomas Fuller (1642).

read the following passage from Thomas Fuller, written in 1642 (see also Figure 5-7).

> *He studieth his scholars natures as carefully as their books*; and ranks their dispositions into severall forms. And though it may seem difficult for him in a great school to descend to all particulars, yet experienced Schoolmasters may quickly make a Grammar of boyes natures, and reduce them all (saving some few exceptions) to these generall rules.

1 Those that are ingenious and industrious. The conjunction of two such Planets in a youth presage much good unto him. To such a lad a frown may be a whipping, and a whipping a death; yea where their Master whips them once, shame whips them all the week after. Such natures he useth with all gentlenesse.

2 Those that are ingenious and idle. These think with the hare in the fable, that running with snails (so they count the rest of their school-fellows) they shall come soon enough to the Post, though sleeping a good while before their starting. Oh, a good rod would finely take them napping.

3 Those that are dull and diligent. Wines the stronger they be the more lees they have when they are new. Many boyes are muddy-headed till they be clarified with age, and such afterwards prove the best. Bristoll diamonds are both bright, and squared and pointed by Nature, and yet are soft and worthlesse; whereas orient ones in India are rough and rugged naturally. Hard rugged and dull natures of youth acquit themselves afterwards the jewells of the countrey, and therefore their dulnesse at first is to be born with, if they be diligent. That Schoolmaster deserves to be beaten himself, who beats Nature in a boy for a fault. And I question whether all the whipping in the world can make their parts, which are naturally sluggish, rise one minute before the houre Nature hath appointed.

4 Those that are invincibly dull and negligent also. Correction may reform the latter, not amend the former. All the whetting in the world can never set a rasours edge on that which hath no steel in it. Such boys he consigneth over to other professions. Shipwrights and boatmakers will choose those crooked pieces of timber, which other carpenters refuse. Those may make excellent merchants and mechanics which will not serve for Scholars. (Fuller, 1642, pp. 110-111).

Summary. A variety of observations, experimental data, and intuitions have been offered related to the hypotheses that personal failure (nonattainment of a goal) caused by the controllable actions of others elicits anger, whereas failure of others due to uncontrollable causes tends to elicit pity. Additional empirical support for these associations is presented in subsequent chapters. Indeed, confirmation of the controllability-anger and uncontrollability-pity associations is unequivocal. This is not to imply that there are not a myriad of other factors influencing the amount of anger or pity that is experienced. Nor is it presumed that finer distinctions between, say, pity and compassion, do not remain to be made. It is not even contended that one invariably feels anger given controllable interference from others, or pity given an uncontrollable cause of another's "failure." After all, we might not be angry at the noisy neighbor nor pity the blind. And self-directed anger and pity have yet to be examined. Nonetheless, the amount that remains unknown and unexplored does not detract from the basic psychological principles that have been documented.

Gratitude

Gratitude, like pride and pity, has been the focus of little experimental research. It is, however, an emotion of great apparent prevalence. Gratitude has been considered the moral memory of mankind and is a means of social cohesion that, as the sociobiologists point out, helps maintain the social order.

It is hypothesized that gratitude toward another is elicited if and only if the act of a benefactor was voluntary and intentional. Thus, for example, if it is known that I was forced to give a gift to another, or gave that gift only so others would think highly of me, then the recipient of the gift would feel relatively little gratitude (and I would not be perceived as "kind"; see Baldwin & Baldwin, 1970). In one of the few empirical studies assessing gratitude (or, more accurately, thoughts about gratitude), Tesser, Gatewood, and Driver (1968) gave subjects scenarios that involved a benefactor and asked the subjects how they would feel in the various circumstances that were portrayed. The benefactor's gift varied in cost to the giver and value, and was given either to benefit the recipient or to indirectly benefit the giver (enhance his reputation). Tesser et al. (1968) found that reported gratitude was maximized when the gift was intended to benefit only the receiver and when the cost to the giver and the value were high. Increased cost and value also might indicate a strong intent to help the receiver.

Other pertinent research has assessed reciprocity rather than gratitude. Reciprocity might or might not be mediated by gratitude—it could be undertaken out of indebtedness or obligation, without accompanying feelings of gratitude. Nonetheless, consistent with the Tesser et al. (1968) data, it has been reported that reciprocity is more likely when a gift was deliberately rather than accidentally given (Greenberg & Frisch, 1972). In a similar manner, the return of help is more likely when an individual was previously aided voluntarily rather than compulsorily (Goranson & Berkowitz, 1966).

In sum, intuition, philosophical analysis, and very scant empirical evidence do support the hypothesis of a relation between causal controllability (and intentionality) and feelings of gratitude. It would almost seem banal to point out that much more empirical study of this emotion is needed.

Guilt

In great contrast to the study of gratitude, philosophers and social scientists have devoted considerable attention to the experience of guilt, its antecedents, and its consequences. In this brief discussion, my concerns are limited to the attributional determinants of guilt and the general fit of this affect with the analysis that has been proposed. As in the discussion of causes (Chapter 2), my aspiration certainly is not to make fundamental contributions to the understanding of a topic that already has a long history of careful analysis.

Reviewing the guilt literature, Wicker, Payne, and Morgan (1983) concluded, "In general, guilt is said to follow from acts that violate ethical norms, principles of justice . . . religious codes, or moral values. Guilt is [accompanied by] feelings of personal responsibility" (p. 26). In a similar manner, Izard (1977) concluded:

> Guilt results from wrongdoing. The behavior that evokes guilt violates a moral, ethical, or religious code. . . . Guilt occurs in situations in which one feels personally responsible. There is a strong relationship between one's sense of personal responsibility and one's threshold for guilt. (pp. 423–424)

In sum, there is general agreement that guilt is produced when one perceives himself or herself as personally responsible for a negative outcome. Of course, one may perceive a negative outcome as personally controllable and yet not experience guilt. But if guilt is experienced, then *perceived* self-responsibility seems to be a necessary antecedent (see Hoffman, 1975, 1982).

There have been a number of empirical verifications of these descriptions of guilt. For example, Davitz (1969) gave individuals a list of emotions and 556 potentially associated descriptive statements. The subjects indicated which descriptors were pertinent to each of the emotions. The three statements selected as most linked with feelings of guilt were: 1) There is a sense of regret, 2) I get mad at myself for feelings or thoughts or for what I've done, and 3) I keep blaming myself for the situation (Davitz, 1969, p. 62).

Weiner, Graham, and Chandler (1982) asked college students to describe a time they felt guilty and to rate the cause of the outcome on the three causal dimensions. The most frequent guilt-related situations involved lying to parents, cheating on an exam, and being disloyal to a dating partner. Typical stories were:

1. One situation in which I felt guilt was in lying to my mother about having a certain guest over in my apartment. She thought he was staying somewhere else, but he was really staying with me. . . .
2. When I got caught cheating on a math final in high school, I had extreme guilt feelings.

Ninety-four percent of these occurrences were rated as personally controllable by the guilty person. Similar findings among children aged 9 to 12 have been reported by Graham et al. (1984). Among 6 and 7-year-olds, on the other hand, there are frequent reports of guilt even though the outcome was accidental (Graham et al., 1984). This is consistent with the moral judgment literature, for children judge others as having transgressed even when the outcome is accidental.

Guilt versus Shame. The emotion of shame has been neglected thus far in this chapter, although among philosophers and social scientists it has been one of the most often discussed feelings. Thus, it certainly deserves attention, particularly when examining the affective reactions to failure.

In both the philosophical and the social science literature, shame sometimes is discussed along with guilt, and these two emotions are not distinguished. Davitz (1969) and Wicker, Payne, and Morgan (1983) noted that these emotions have much in common. As Wicker et al. (1983) summarized, both "involve negative self-evaluations and are painful, tense, agitating, real, present, and depressing" (p. 33). On the basis of the prior discussion of locus of causality, some similarity between these emotions is anticipated in that both result from internal ascriptions and hence lower self-esteem. In addition, both follow from undesired outcomes and should therefore coexist with negative, outcome-related feelings.

Yet differences between the two affects are frequently reported. For example, anthropologists tend to contrast guilt and shame cultures. It is hypothesized here that shame results from an attribution to failure that is self-related and uncontrollable (although it will be seen that this is not a sufficient antecedent to elicit shame). Thus, for example, shame is experienced when one fails at an achievement-related task because of low ability, or loses at a sporting event because of being too slow (or short, uncoordinated, etc.). This contrasts with the antecedents of guilt, which already have been documented to be self-related causes of failure that are controllable, such as lack of effort.

A few empirical studies in the achievement domain have examined the proposed ability-shame linkage. Covington and Omelich (1979b) found that most public shame is reported following failure and high effort. They suggest that failure in the face of high effort strongly intimates that lack of ability was the cause. In a more direct test of the low ability-shame as well as low effort-guilt associations, Brown and Weiner (1984) had subjects rate the extent to which 10 emotions would be experienced as a result of failure due to lack of ability, as well as when failure was caused by lack of effort. Included among the emotions were three that were considered a priori to be shame-related (humiliation, disgrace, embarrassment) and three that were considered guilt-related (guilt, regret, remorse). The data revealed higher ratings of the guilt-related affects when lack of effort was specified as the cause of failure, and higher ratings of the shame-related affects when low ability was the cause of failure. Furthermore, in related investigations Brown and Weiner (1984) found that ratings of guilt-related emotions were uncorrelated with ratings of shame-related emotions. Similar findings have been reported by Jagacinski and Nicholls (1984) and Covington and Omelich (1984).

Numerous studies outside of the achievement domain also have revealed various differences between shame and guilt reactions. Wicker et al. (1983), summarizing both their own findings and the pertinent literature, concluded:

> Shame causes one to lose control, to feel powerless and externally controlled; . . . the way one appears in the eyes of others is . . . basic to shame; . . . with shame, one expects abandonment and attempts to change the self, to hide, or to run away . . . [there is] a general picture of greater helplessness in the shame situation. (p. 27)

Table 5-11 contrasts guilt with shame on some relevant antecedents and experiential and consequence parameters. To summarize Table 5-11, guilt arises from a particular act that is under volitional control and produces a desire to make amends (see Brewin, 1984a; Carlsmith & Gross, 1969). Shame, on the other hand, is elicited as

Table 5-11. Comparison of Guilt and Shame

	Guilt	Shame
Antecedents		
Audience	Not necessary	Necessary
Sanctions	Internal	External
Source	Action of self	Action or characteristic of self
Cause	Controllable	Uncontrollable
Experience and consequence	Seek control, make amends	Submission, feel inferior, helpless, withdrawal
Achievement attribution	Lack of effort	Lack of ability
Affect from other	Anger	Pity

Attribution

Lack of Effort   Lack of Ability

	Lack of Effort	Lack of Ability
Self-generated emotion	Guilt	Shame
Other-generated emotion	Anger	Pity

Figure 5-8. Self- and other-affected consequences of failure due to lack of effort versus lack of ability.

a result of an act or a characteristic of the self that is not under volitional control and produces a desire to withdraw. Relating these differences to the dominant attributions for success and failure, Table 5-11 indicates that guilt follows when failure is ascribed to lack of effort, whereas shame is produced when failure is ascribed to lack of ability.

It is also of interest to point out that, given success, ability and effort generate common affects including pride, whereas given failure they produce partially differentiating experiences. That is, pride results whether an attribution for success is to an internal, uncontrollable or an internal, controllable factor, whereas for failure these ascriptions generate different affective reactions. This more generally intimates that the affects associated with failure might be more distinct from one another than those associated with success. The greater diversity of outcome-related affects given failure than given success tends to support this hypothesis. In addition, it has often been documented that there are more negative than positive affective labels (see, for example, Weiner et al., 1978). We know from Chapter 2 that attributional search is more likely to be instigated by failure than by success. Perhaps the differential cognitive activity given nonattainment versus attainment of a goal is responsible for the differential affective discriminations as a function of outcome.

Guilt, Anger, Pity, and Shame. Recall that prior research demonstrated that anger is elicited given controllable causes of failure, whereas pity is aroused given uncontrollable causes. In a similar manner, guilt is linked with controllable causes, whereas shame is associated with uncontrollable causes. Lack of effort, anger, and guilt should then covary, as will lack of ability, pity, and shame. Figure 5-8 shows that an individual (e.g., a student) who fails because of lack of effort is prone to experience guilt, and an observer (e.g., the teacher) will then direct anger toward the student. On the other hand, a student who fails because of lack of ability is prone to experience shame, and the teacher will then direct pity toward the student.

Causal Stability and Time-Related Emotions

Thus far I have examined the outcome-dependent emotions, such as happiness and frustration, and dimension-linked emotions including pride, anger, pity, gratitude, guilt, and shame. The one dimension remaining to be discussed is stability.

Although causal stability might be a very important influence on emotional reactions, very little pertinent research can be reported.

Chapter 4 documented rather convincingly that causal stability in part determines expectancies regarding future success and failure, and particularly the direction of expectancy shifts. Thus, any emotion involving anticipations of goal attainment or nonattainment will likely be influenced by perceptions of causal stability. Mowrer (1960) identified two such emotions: hope and fear. Hope, he stated, is the continued anticipation of a positive reinforcer; fear is the continued anticipation of a negative reinforcer. In attributional language, hope should be experienced given success and an attribution to a stable cause, whereas fear should arise given failure and an attribution to a stable cause.

In another time-related analysis of emotion, Weiner and Litman-Adizes (1980) suggested that, when failure is ascribed to stable causes, hopelessness follows. This is anticipated to be the case regardless of the locus of the causal ascription. Thus, failure attributed to low aptitude (internal) and failure because the teacher constructs exams that are too difficult for everyone (external) are both hypothesized to elicit feelings of hopelessness. In one pertinent investigation related to this hypothesis, Weiner et al. (1978) found that affective reports of aimlessness, depression, helplessness, hopelessness, and resignation appear given stable and internal ascriptions for failure (e.g., lack of ability, low stable, effort, poor personality). Thus, two dimensions of causality are implicated as necessary to produce this set of future-related emotions. In sum, the hypothesis set forth by Mowrer in 1960 and by Weiner and Litman-Adizes 20 years later, namely, that hope, fear, and hopelessness are related to future anticipations, certainly seems plausible. This area is therefore ripe for a concerted research effort.

Summary and Conclusion

When psychologists study emotion, they are most often concerned with the emotion process. The search for the emotion process is understandable, inasmuch as the research psychologist typically is interested in laws that transcend any particular emotional experience. The process proposed here is that emotions are instigated following a positive or negative event, such as achievement-related success or failure. These outcomes are evaluated as good or bad and give rise to outcome-related affects. Then an attribution for the outcome may be sought, and the attribution selected in turn elicits more differentiated affects based on the specific cause of the outcome and the more general properties of that cause.

However, while many theorists have addressed the emotion process, few have been concerned with specific emotions. This issue most often is left to philosophers or is merely neglected by postulating, for example, that the emotional experience is a function of whatever environmental stimulus happens to be present (Schachter & Singer, 1962). Indeed, when reading psychological accounts of emotion, one rarely encounters an emotion! Rather, one reads about concepts such as arousal or other emotional mechanisms such as facial expressions. On the other hand, the present conception is concerned not only with the nature of the emotion process, but also with specific feelings and their meanings.

The prevalent human emotions incorporated within this attributional approach include happiness and frustration (which are outcome dependent), and pride, anger, pity, gratitude, shame, hope, and fear (which are dimension linked). Thus, although a complete theory of emotion has not been offered, I do think that some of the most common emotional experiences can be accounted for within this attributional approach.

The very cognitive and logical viewpoint presented here has other virtues. The conception implies that people can be "reasoned" out of their anger, guilt, pride, pity, and so on, inasmuch as these are appropriate emotions only when particular causal attributions are made. Hence, causal thoughts might be communicated in social contexts, such as when rejecting another for a date or coming late for an appointment, to change the feelings or anticipated feelings of the other person involved. Documenting social "lies" provides evidence of the strength of attribution-emotion linkages.

The associations between causal thinking and feeling form well-established and robust laws. Linkages between, for example, internal ascriptions and pride and self-esteem; causal controllability and anger, guilt, and gratitude; causal uncontrollability and pity and shame; and success and happiness are, in my opinion, unequivocal. In addition associations between causal stability and hope or fear, and failure and frustration, displeasure, and/or sadness could be established as empirical facts in subsequent research. Competing theories of motivation cannot make such claims in the emotion area.

Part II
The Structure of the Theory

Chapter 6
An Attributional Theory of Achievement Motivation and Emotion

In which the author proposes a theory of motivation based on causal perceptions. The empirical support for the theoretical network within the area of achievement strivings is discussed. Achievement-change programs are examined from this perspective.

In this chapter a theory of motivation and emotion developed from an attributional perspective is presented. Before undertaking this central task, it might be beneficial to review the progression of the book. In Chapter 1 it was suggested that causal attributions have been prevalent throughout history and in disparate cultures. Studies reviewed in Chapter 2 revealed a large number of causal ascriptions within motivational domains, and different ascriptions in disparate domains. Yet some attributions, particularly ability and effort in the achievement area, dominate causal thinking. To compare and contrast causes such as ability and effort, their common denominators or shared properties were identified. Three causal dimensions, examined in Chapter 3, are locus, stability, and controllability, with intentionality and globality as other possible causal properties. As documented in Chapter 4, the perceived stability of a cause influences the subjective probability of success following a previous success or failure; causes perceived as enduring increase the certainty that the prior outcome will be repeated in the future. And all the causal dimensions, as well as the outcome of an activity and specific causes, influence the emotions experienced after attainment or nonattainment of a goal. The affects linked to causal dimensions include pride (with locus), hopelessness and resignation (with stability), and anger, gratitude, guilt, pity, and shame (with controllability). These emotions, in addition to happiness and sadness (which are outcome dependent) and, for example, surprise (specific attribution-linked), were considered in Chapter 5. Now, in Chapters 6 and 7, my goal is to integrate these extensive, self-contained fields of study within a broad theory of motivation and emotion. First I will examine the value of the theory within achievement-related contexts. Then, in Chapter 7, this analysis is extended to helping behavior and a wide variety of other motivational concerns.

As George Kelly so well articulated (Kelly, 1955), a theory has a focus and a range of convenience; both are of importance when attempting to determine the value of any construct system. Hence, the reader is asked to judge the value of this theory with both Chapters 6 and 7 in mind. The questions to be addressed are: 1) Is this theory better able than others to explain (account for, predict) behavior in achievement-related contexts? and 2) Is this theory more readily extended to other motivational domains than alternative conceptions of achievement strivings? I think the answer to both questions is yes.

The Mind-Body Problem

The form that a theory of motivation takes depends fundamentally on the relations between thinking (central processes) and acting (peripheral processes) assumed by the theorist. Many hypotheses or presumptions relating central and peripheral processes have been entertained. Here I will consider only those views that accept the existence of both the mind and the body ("dualistic" positions). One dualistic supposition is that the mind and the body are completely independent, with distinct and parallel functions that do not interact (see Figure 6-1). The processes of the mind and the body, however, may be correlated. For example, deprivation may lead one to think about food, to experience an intention to obtain food, and to produce approach behavior toward food. The thoughts and the intentions, however, do not affect the action; the central representations are epiphenomena (*epi*, "upon").

In contrast to the independence theory depicted in Figure 6-1, it has been proposed that mind and body interact. There are various interactionist positions. One group has contended that thoughts are the product of action (see Figure 6-2). Sequences of molar events illustrating this position are, "I am eating a great deal; I must be hungry," or "I argued for the passage of a controversial bill; I must strongly favor it," or "I am running; I must be afraid." In these examples, thoughts are

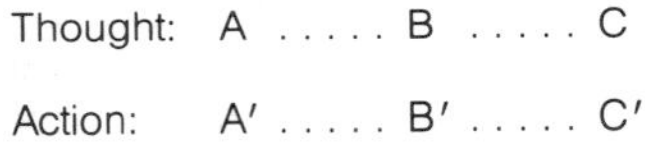

Thought: A . . . . . B C

Action: A' . . . . . B' . . . . . C'

Figure 6-1. Mind and body as independent organizations. From *Human Motivation* by B. Weiner. New York: Holt, Rinehart, & Winston, 1980, p. 88.

Thought: A . . . . . B C

Action: A' . . . . . B' . . . . . C'

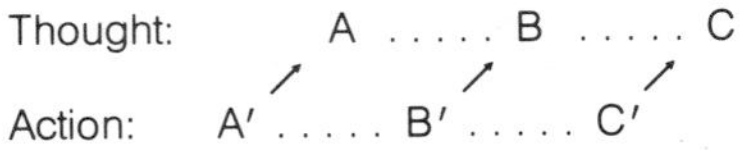

Figure 6-2. Mind and body as interacting organizations: Thought follows action. From *Human Motivation* by B. Weiner. New York: Holt, Rinehart, & Winston, 1980, p. 88.

Thought: A . . . . . B C

Action: A' . . . . . B' . . . . . C'

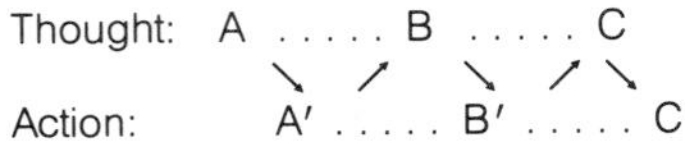

Figure 6-3. Mind and body as interacting organizations: Action influenced by thought. From *Human Motivation* by B. Weiner. New York: Holt, Rinehart, & Winston, 1980, p. 88.

behavioral by-products rather than causes. Once more, they might be considered epiphenomena, for they do not influence action. Among psychologists associated with attributional concerns, Bem (1972) is the one most closely allied with this position.

Figure 6-3 depicts a contrasting interactionist position. In Figure 6-3 thoughts are causes; in part, they determine action (e.g., "I am in favor of this bill; I will argue for it"). This is the belief I will follow. Although thoughts are presumed to influence action, it is acknowledged that not all behaviors must be mediated by thoughts (e.g., reflex actions may not). In addition, I accept that not all of the determinants of behavior need to have a conscious or a cognitive representation (e.g., hormonal influences may not). Furthermore, behaviors may have informational value that in turn affects thought processes (as shown in the A'-B and B'-C linkages in Figure 6-3). Finally, thoughts will be proposed to influence action in part via intervening emotional reactions, which in turn have both cognitive and bodily components. Thus, the general theory to be presented might be considered "flexibly cognitive."

It is not known whether thoughts are preceded by some mechanical actions, such as specific physiological activity in the brain. Thus, at the molecular level it is moot whether Figure 6-2 or Figure 6-3 is correct. My acceptance of interactionism and a mind-body sequence reflects a theoretical preference for how one should proceed with motivational analyses at the molar (i.e., action) level.

The Complete Theory

It is now possible to present an attributional theory of motivation and emotion based on the earlier discussions of the theoretical components. The theory was cursorily offered in Chapter 1 and is repeated here in Figure 6-4. This conception captures a historical or a temporal sequence; motivation is not conceived as an "ahistorical problem" (Atkinson, 1964, p. 146). The sequence depicted in Figure 6-4 is first used to discuss the following contrived (but surely extant) achievement-related scenario:

1. Johnny plays Little League baseball. In a recent important game Johnny struck out when batting, and his team lost. Johnny missed practice the next day, did not appear at the game that night, and quit the team.

Other scenarios, including Johnny reacting to failure by taking extra batting practice and coming early for the next game, and a depiction of enhanced motivation after success, are subsequently also used to illustrate how the theory depicted in Figure 6-4 conceptualizes an achievement-related motivational episode. But let us first turn to the failure-motivational decrement scenario.

Figure 6-4 indicates that a motivational sequence is initiated by an outcome that the person interprets as positive (goal attainment) or negative (nonattainment). Inasmuch as some affects are directly linked with outcome perceptions, or the primary appraisal, Figure 6-4 includes a connection between subjective outcomes and the reactions of happiness (if the outcome was perceived as positive) and frustration or sadness (if the outcome was perceived as negative). These associations are

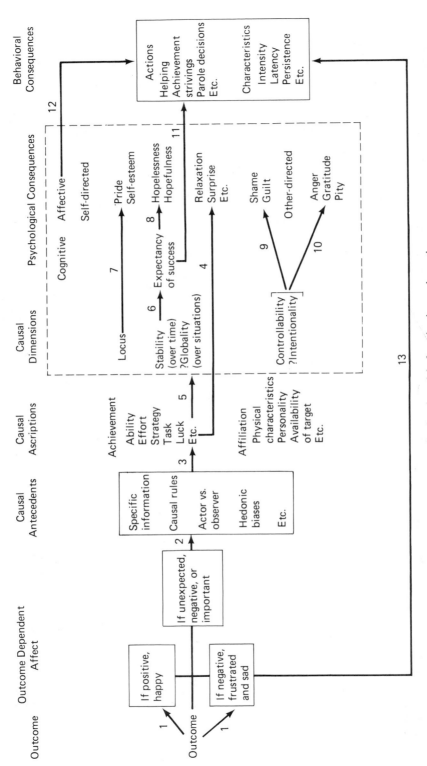

Figure 6-4. An attributional model of motivation and emotion.

designated with a "1" in Figure 6-4. In the baseball vignette, Johnny performed poorly in the game, and this failure will elicit general negative reactions.

Then, as documented in Table 2-1, if the outcome was unexpected or negative, a causal search is undertaken to determine why the outcome occurred (Linkage 2). This search also is likely if the outcome was important. In the example, Johnny perceived the performance as an important failure, and attributional activity therefore is instigated. That is, he should overtly ask or covertly wonder, "Why did I perform so poorly?"

A large number of antecedents influence the causal ascription(s) reached. This topic has not been discussed in this book. Some of the known attributional antecedents are included in Figure 6-4, such as specific information (e.g., past personal history, performance of others). The "et cetera" at the bottom of the antecedents conveys that there is a multitude of unlisted determinants of the selected attribution.

The causal decision reached is biased toward a relatively small number of causes such as ability and effort in the achievement domain (see Table 2-3). Again Figure 6-4 is incomplete, as denoted by the "et cetera" at the bottom of the causal lists. In our example, let us assume that Johnny played quite poorly in the past and that other children on the team are playing well. He also practiced many hours. On the basis of past outcome history, social comparison, and effort expenditure, Johnny thinks that he is low in baseball-playing ability. That is, he decides, "I failed because I am not any good at baseball" (Linkage 3).

The causal decision reached may elicit a unique affective reaction (Linkage 4). In the case of our Little Leaguer, his attribution to low ability tends to evoke feelings of incompetence (although the status of "incompetence" as an affect is subject to debate).

The cause is then located in dimensional space. This dimensional categorization is depicted in Linkage 5. As documented in Table 3-5, the three main properties of causes are locus, stability, and controllability. Further analyses also suggested that globality and intentionality may be causal properties; they are preceded by question marks in Figure 6-4. Johnny ascribed his performance to lack of ability, which is likely to be perceived by him as internal, stable, and uncontrollable. The reader should recall from Chapter 4 that this placement must be analyzed from the phenomenology of the perceiver (see Table 3-2). The attribution might also be global ("I am poor at sports").

Causal dimensions have psychological consequences, being related to expectancy and affect. The stability of a cause influences the relative expectancy of future success (Linkage 6). This association is documented in Tables 4-2, 4-3, and 4-4. In the baseball vignette, Johnny will anticipate repeated failure inasmuch as low ability is perceived as a stable cause. He also might have increased expectancy of failure in other sporting activities if the cause is perceived as global. That is, stability influences temporal aspects of expectancy, whereas globality influences cross-situational expectancies.

Turning to affective consequences, the locus of a cause influences self-esteem and pride—internal ascriptions elicit greater self-esteem for success and lower self-esteem for failure than do external attributions (Linkage 7). Johnny failed because of a cause considered internal and therefore should be experiencing low self-esteem. The stability of the cause, by affecting expectancy of success, also fosters feelings of hopelessness or hopefulness; this is indicated in Linkage 8. The Little Leaguer, with a history of failure and ascription of the current failure to the perceived stable cause of low ability, should be experiencing hopelessness. Finally, causal controllability impacts on social emotions: internal, controllable causes of personal failure promote feelings of guilt, whereas internal, uncontrollable causes generate shame (Linkage 9). These are represented in Figure 6-4 as self-directed affects, as are other specific attribution-linked emotions including surprise and relaxation. Among the affects directed toward others are anger (given a cause of failure that is controllable by others), pity (given an uncontrollable cause of failure), and gratitude (given volitional benefit from others). These are captured in Linkage 10. Johnny therefore is likely to be feeling ashamed of himself and humiliated, but not guilty, whereas his mother or his coach feels pity and "sorry for him," but not anger.

Finally, expectancy and affect are presumed to determine action (Linkages 11, 12, and 13). The actions might be in any motivational domain and can be described according to their intensity, latency, and so on. In the baseball scenario Johnny has a low expectancy of future success and is feeling sad (outcome-related affect), incompetent (ability-related affect), low in self-worth (locus-related affect), ashamed (controllability-related affect), and hopeless (stability-related affect). Others express pity toward him. These conditions are anticipated to decrease achievement strivings and behaviors instrumental to the attainment of the desired goal. Johnny then stays home from practice as well as from the next game, and finally quits the team.

Other Motivational Sequences

The theory illustrated in Figure 6-4 has been used thus far to explain or account for a decrement in achievement strivings after failure. I now want to explore very briefly two other vignettes that involve motivational enhancement in the achievement domain, one following failure and the other after success:

2. Bill plays Little League baseball. In a recent important game, Bill struck out when batting and his team lost. The next morning, he went to the baseball field before all the other players and took extra batting practice. Bill looked forward to the game that night, arriving early to better prepare himself.
3. Susan is undecided about her career goals. She enrolls in a math class and attains a very high mark on the final exam. She then decides to pursue a career in math.

How might the attributional theory be applied to these rather common types of occurrences?

Motivational Enhancement Following Failure. In Scenario 2, Bill performed poorly during a baseball game. This should generate the outcome-related negative affects of frustration and/or sadness (Linkage 1). Negative outcomes also elicit causal search (Linkage 2). Bill performed well in the past, whereas in this game he performed poorly while his teammates played well. He therefore ascribes his failure to lack of adequate preparation before the game and to poor concentration while at bat (Linkage 3). These causes are perceived as internal, unstable, and controllable (Linkage 5). Because they are unstable, Bill maintains a reasonable expectation of success in future games (Linkage 6); he is also hopeful about the future (Linkage 8). Because the causes are internal, his self-esteem decreases (Linkage 7), and because lack of preparation and poor concentration are controllable by Bill, he experiences guilt (Linkage 9), while his coach and teammates are angry at him (Linkage 10). High expectation of success, along with hopefulness and guilt, is able to overcome his feelings of sadness and weakened self-esteem and result in renewed goal strivings and an increase in motivation to perform well at the next game. He therefore takes extra practice and arrives early for the game to be better prepared.

Motivational Enhancement after Success. In Scenario 3, Susan's success at math results in her experiencing happiness. Because this outcome is important to her, she thinks about the causes. Susan realizes that she has performed well in other math classes, better than her classmates. She therefore attributes the high score to her mathematical abilities. This gives Susan a feeling of competence and increases her self-esteem. She anticipates future success in math, feels hopeful about her future in this area, and is proud of herself. Happiness, high expectations of success, high self-esteem, pride, and hopefulness increase her achievement interests in a career in mathematics.

Theoretical Comparisons

Some of the theoretical advantages of the prior analyses can be realized by comparing Figure 6-4 with other conceptions that might address achievement-related behavior. According to Skinnerian psychologists, after failure at baseball a player would be expected to be less likely to appear for the next game. After all, failure to most of us is aversive, and punishment decreases the probability that the antedating behavior will be repeated. This explanation very parsimoniously explains Johnny's behavior in the first vignette. But all the emotional reactions and all the cognitive processes known to play such a major part in human behavior, as well as all the potential reactions from others, fall beyond the range of Skinnerian conception. Hence, this approach just does not capture the well-documented richness of life. In addition, although Skinnerians can provide an explanation for the decreased achievement strivings in this situation, they cannot readily account for an increase in goal-directed activity following failure, as is illustrated and explained with attributional concepts in the second vignette.

Atkinson's (1964) theory of achievement motivation also might be able to predict when a baseball player will be more or less likely to show up for the next game. For these predictions to be made, there must be knowledge of the direction of expectancy change and its relation to intermediate task difficulty, as well as information about the person's level of achievement needs. For the person high in achievement needs, motivation is enhanced when failure is at an easy task and decreases when failure is at a difficult task. The reverse is anticipated for persons low in achievement needs.

Note again, however, that this conceptual framework cannot address the complexities of emotional reactions of the self and others. Furthermore, the limiting assumptions regarding motives and perceived likelihoods must be imposed; most damaging, prior research has not clearly substantiated the predicted consequences when these conditions are met (see review in Weiner, 1980c).

Finally, Bandura's (1977) conception of self-efficacy also might be applied to explain Johnny's behavior in Scenario 1. This theory stresses that failure lowers one's perception of personal competence. That is, following failure Johnny would conclude "I cannot" and therefore would not attempt the task again. Here also it can be pointed out that the complexities of human behavior are overlooked, particularly affective reactions. It is also the case that the self-efficacy approach, just like the Skinnerian position, has difficulty in accounting for increments in motivation after nonattainment of a goal.

In sum, the attributional conception proposed here seems richer than current alternative conceptions and seems better able to capture the complications of human motivation. I use the words "seems to," although my deep belief is stronger than this.

Experimental Tests of the Theory Within Achievement Contexts

The achievement-related situations discussed above were crafted to be without ambiguity. There was no uncertainty regarding the perceptions of the outcome, nor were there conflicting attributions or doubts about the dimensional classification of the causes. Most problematic, the explanations offered were not accompanied by any experimental evidence. They were merely logical explanations of the behavior, given the framework of the theory. Observations of boys quitting baseball teams after failure, or of women motivated by achievement success, certainly exist; documentation of such events is not really necessary. What is necessary is to provide supporting evidence pertinent to the motivational significance of the factors postulated to mediate the behaviors in these scenarios; that is, evidence about the role of causal ascriptions, expectancy, and emotion in motivational sequences must be furnished.

Unfortunately, the achievement literature does not yield unambiguous proof in support of the complete attributional theory, in part because the conception has only recently been fully developed, in part because even recent investigations have not included all the pertinent variables, and in part because some of the findings have been disconfirmatory. What an overview of the research does reveal, however, is a history of studies that can be increasingly incorporated within the theory, that is, a history documenting more and more of the processes hypothesized to mediate between the task stimulus and performance. This history documents that individual differences in achievement needs and anxiety, which were the early focus for studies on achievement strivings, more and more have given way to a concentration on causal ascriptions.

In the following sections, the research history in the achievement performance area is reviewed from an attributional perspective. This is a selective review in which prototypical investigations are highlighted to capture the historical changes. However, the reader should not be lulled into thinking that each study discussed is merely one from a huge sample; quite the contrary, investigations that include measures of expectancy and affect and that also gauge some indicator of motivation are limited in number. I also include in this very circumscribed summary an extensive examination of achievement-change programs, for these therapeutic attempts shed light on the intervening attribution-related processes that contribute to achievement strivings. Indeed, change programs perhaps provide the most extensive evidence for the value of an attributional conception in the achievement domain. In addition, achievement change programs are reviewed in detail because these investigations indicate one important direction of applied attributional work.

Individual Difference Research

The early experimental research in the area of achievement strivings quite typically included an individual difference variable, especially the need for achievement and/or anxiety, along with some experimental manipulation. Hundreds of investigations followed this paradigm (see Atkinson, 1964; Weiner, 1972, for reviews). A common manipulation was to provide false information that the subject was performing well or poorly. Speed or quality of performance was monitored as the subject received these outcome reports. In a somewhat different procedure, the subjects were given success or failure feedback during a preliminary series of trials. Then an index of motivation was measured during a subsequent test series.

As an example of this type of research, an investigation by Lucas (1952) examined the effects of anxiety and failure on immediate memory. Six series of consonants were presented to subjects for immediate memorization. The degree of failure was varied between experimental conditions, with failure feedback after 0, 2, 4, or all 6 of the trials. Then a test series was administered in which the subjects were asked to remember three lists of consonants. In addition to manipulating the number of prior failures, the experimenter also classified the subjects as high or low in anxiety, as determined by their score on an anxiety scale.

The results of this investigation are depicted in Figure 6-5. For highly anxious subjects, performance decreased as a function of the degree of prior failure. Conversely, memory performance increased as a function of the number of past failures for subjects low in anxiety. It has been concluded that the interaction between anxiety and failure is a reasonably reliable finding, supported by a large research literature (see Weiner, 1972; Wine, 1971).

An Attributional Interpretation. This research apparently has little relevance to the study of attributional processes and their influence on achievement strivings. However, one might raise the possibility that individuals differing in anxiety also

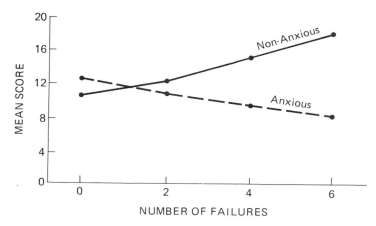

Figure 6-5. Mean recall scores in four experimental conditions varying in the number of failures, with subjects classified as high or low in anxiety. From "The Interactive Effects of Anxiety Failure and Interserial Duplications" by J. D. Lucas, 1952, *American Journal of Psychology*, *65*, p. 64. Copyright 1952. Reprinted by permission.

differ in their causal biases or their attributional tendencies. In the case of anxiety, there is a very reliable association between anxiety and intelligence: Persons scoring high in anxiety are comparatively low in intelligence. This correlation tends to be in the magnitude of $r = -.25$. Hence, it is suggested that individuals high in anxiety are more likely to make an attribution for failure to lack of ability than persons low in anxiety. Low-ability attributions, in turn, impede motivation because of their negative effects on expectancy and because they elicit shame and humiliation. Those low in anxiety, on the other hand, would then be presumed to ascribe their failure primarily to other factors such as lack of effort. A lack of effort ascription enhances motivation because of its positive influence on expectancy and the elicitation of guilt.

Some evidence is available in support of these speculations (see Arkin, Detchon, & Maruyama, 1981, 1982; Arkin & Maruyama, 1979), although these data were gathered one or two decades after much of the individual difference research. For example, Arkin et al. (1981, 1982) reported that in situations of failure persons low in anxiety tend to ascribe achievement outcomes more to lack of effort, and perceive themselves as having more ability, than persons high in anxiety. This research primarily has taken place in classrooms following an actual examination, thus lending ecological validity to the research findings. None of the reported investigations relating anxiety to causal tendencies provides definitive results, and the data often include complex interactions. Nonetheless, the direction of the findings does support an attributional (cognitive) interpretation of the debilitating effects of high anxiety on performance, as well as the facilitating effects of low anxiety on performance, when persons are faced with failure.

A similar argument can be offered regarding research classifying persons according to their level of achievement needs. It appears that failure augments the performance of persons high in achievement needs, while decreasing the performance of persons low in achievement needs. One can make the argument that persons high in achievement needs, like those low in anxiety, ascribe failure to lack of effort. On the other hand, persons low in achievement needs, like persons high in anxiety, may perceive failure as due to lack of ability. These attributional differences then mediate the observed performance discrepancies between the two motive groups in situations of failure. Again a smattering of evidence supports this analysis (e.g., Covington & Omelich, 1979a; Kukla, 1972; Weiner & Kukla, 1970; Weiner & Potepan, 1970), although none of the studies is at all conclusive. For example, Weiner and Potepan reported a correlation of $r = -.33$ ($N = 107$) between resultant achievement needs and ascription of failure to a lack of ability. They also found a very modest positive correlation ($r = .08$) between achievement needs and ascription of failure to lack of effort.

Individual Difference Research Within an Attributional Context

The research relating anxiety and achievement needs to performance might be considered one of the precursors of attributional analyses, for if these individual differences do relate to achievement performance (as has been reported), then one must search for the mediating mechanisms responsible for the performance effects. Meyer (1970) was one of the first researchers to look toward causal attributions as the mediating mechanism; he provided a bridge between the traditional focus of achievement researchers on individual differences and the developing interest in causal ascriptions and the consequences of these ascriptions. In his research, Meyer examined the associations between achievement needs, causal ascriptions for failure, expectancy of success, and performance speed. Hence, here we see the rudiments of an attributional theory of achievement strivings. Few experiments have included all four of these variables (see also Covington & Omelich, 1979a).

In Meyer's research, male high-school students were first classified according to their level of achievement needs. They were then given five failures at a digit-symbol substitution task. In this activity, an appropriate digit must be inserted under (substituted for) its corresponding symbol. After each trial the research participants attributed their failure to low ability, bad luck, low effort, or task difficulty. Recall that, at the time, these four were thought to be the dominant causes of achievement outcomes. In addition, the subjects estimated their probability of successfully completing the next trial (a fixed number of digit substitutions within a given time period). While they were working, performance intensity was assessed as the indicator of motivation.

I will examine each of the hypothesized associations in turn (at the time of this investigation, causal modeling techniques were not yet developed and/or rarely used in psychological research). Figures 6-6 and 6-7 show the relations between individual differences in achievement needs and causal ascriptions to effort and

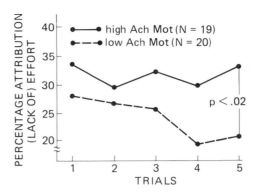

Figure 6-6. Percentage attribution to lack of effort following failure as a function of motive classification and trials. From *Selbstverantwortlichkeit und Leitungsmotivation* by W. U. Meyer, 1970. Copyright 1970. Reprinted by permission.

ability. The figures clearly illustrate that persons high in achievement needs ascribe their failure to lack of effort more than those low in achievement needs, whereas persons in the low motive group tend more to ascribe failures to lack of ability. These differences are most evident as failure continues. The data were in accord with predictions and consistent with other research in the early 1970s (e.g., Weiner & Kukla, 1970; Weiner & Potepan, 1970) documenting associations between achievement dispositions and causal preferences.

Next, causal ascriptions were related to expectancy of success. Figure 6-8 combines the ascriptions of the stable factors (ability and task difficulty) and of the unstable factors (effort and luck). It is quite evident from Figure 6-8 that attributions to stable factors particularly lower expectation of success, with the drop increas-

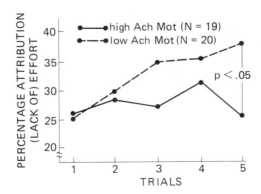

Figure 6-7. Percentage attribution to lack of ability following failure as a function of motive classifications and trials. From *Selbstverantwortlichkeit und Leitungsmotivation* by W. U. Meyer, 1970. Copyright 1970. Reprinted by permission.

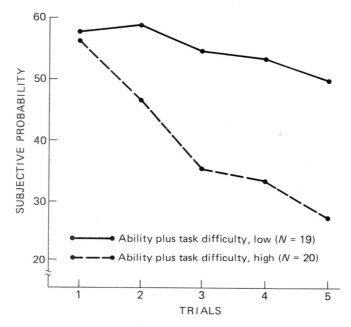

Figure 6-8. Subjective probabilities given repeated failure for groups high or low in ascription to stable factors (lack of ability plus task difficulty). From *Selbstverantwortlichkeit und Leitungsmotivation* by W. U. Meyer, 1970. Copyright 1970. Reprinted by permission.

ingly great as failure mounts. The relation between causal ascriptions and expectancy is consistent with the vast array of literature documented in Chapter 4.

The final step in the motivational sequence outlined in Figure 6-4 is to relate expectancy of success to performance intensity. Unfortunately, I do not have these data. What is available is the relation between causal ascriptions and performance speed. Meyer reported a correlation of $r = -.43$ between causal ascriptions to stable factors and performance. That is, the more one ascribes failure to ability and task difficulty (and, by implication from Figure 6-8, the lower the expectancy of future success), the worse the relative speed of performance.

In sum, the general pattern of data is quite supportive of an attributional approach. Although all of the desired correlations are not reported here, and although current statistical techniques would provide more subtle information about the sequence of associations, the analyses that were possible are certainly consistent with Figure 6-4. Individual differences relate to causal ascriptions, causal ascriptions are linked with expectancy, and causal ascriptions (and therefore expectancies) are associated with performance intensity.

The next step in the attributional evolution was the application of attributional *methodologies* dominant at the time to the study of achievement strivings, while still keeping individual differences in achievement needs as an integral component of the research. The attributional literature that emerged in the late 1960s and early 1970s made much use of a so-called "misattribution" paradigm. In this research procedure, subjects were provided with "false" reasons for an event; these events ranged from internal autonomic arousal to task failure (see review in Weiner, 1980c). The research most pertinent to the present review was guided by the presumed causal biases of individuals differing in their levels of achievement needs. Recall that persons low in achievement needs were thought to ascribe failure to low ability, which theoretically would result in expectancy decrements, shame, and, in turn, performance inhibition. On the other hand, persons high in achievement needs were thought to ascribe failure to lack of effort, which theoretically would result in expectancy maintenance, guilt, and, in turn, performance increments. It was therefore reasoned that if failure could be "misattributed," that is, if different causes could be substituted for the causes most used by those high and low in achievement needs, then expectancy and affect, as well as performance, should be altered.

Attributions for failure among individuals differing in achievement needs were experimentally manipulated by Weiner and Sierad (1975). Subjects were given four trials of repeated failure at a digit-symbol substitution task. Before the failure, one half of the participants were assigned to a drug-attribution condition; the remaining subjects were in a control condition. The subjects in the drug condition were given a placebo pill that allegedly interfered with hand-eye coordination, a skill described as needed for good performance at the substitution task. This type of placebo manipulation was popular in the misattribution research procedures used at that time. In the control condition, no attempt was made to alter attributions.

Now consider how attribution theory leads to predictions in this rather complex experiment. First let us examine the predictions for subjects low in achievement needs. In the experimental condition, their bias toward ascribing personal failure to low ability is altered so that failure is ascribed to the presumed action of the drug. Unlike ability, which is perceived as internal, uncontrollable, and stable, the drug is an external, uncontrollable, stable cause (it was described as lasting through the entire time of the experiment). Hence, the affective reactions of shame and humiliation, which require internal, uncontrollable ascriptions, should be minimized. Because these affects are presumed to impede motivation, the theory specifies that the affective change will produce comparative performance increments.

Next consider the hypotheses for persons high in achievement needs. Their bias toward ascribing failure to insufficient effort also is altered in the experimental condition. Effort is perceived as an internal, controllable, unstable cause, whereas, as just indicated, the pill is external to the actor, uncontrollable, and stable. Hence, expectancy of success should no longer be maintained and guilt should be minimized. The reductions in expectancy of success and guilt were anticipated to produce comparative performance decrements.

The results of two identical experiments were combined and are depicted in Figure 6-9. The index of motivation in Figure 6-9 is the improvement in speed of performance (number of digit substitutions per unit of time) over trials, relative to pretest performance. The data for the control condition reveal that subjects high in achievement needs improve more over failure trials than do subjects low in achievement

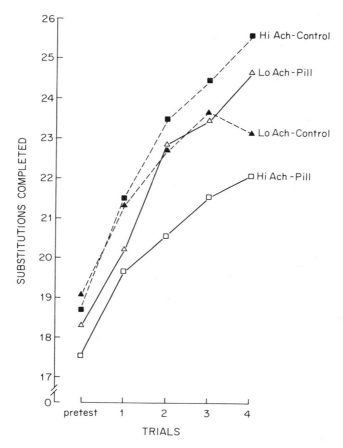

Figure 6-9. Mean increments in speed of performance (number of digit-symbol substitutions) relative to pretest performance on four trials as a function of level of achievement needs and the experimental condition. From "Misattribution for Failure and Enhancement of Achievement Strivings" by B. Weiner and J. Sierad, 1975, *Journal of Personality and Social Psychology, 31*, p. 419. Copyright 1975. Reprinted by permission.

needs. This is consistent with other research in the achievement area when failure is manipulated. On the other hand, in the experimental condition persons low in achievement needs exhibit greater improvement in their speed of performance than do persons in the high motive group. As predicted, the change in attributions improved the performance of those low in achievement needs, while reducing the intensity of substitution activity for persons in the high motive group. These data provide strong support for an attributional analysis of achievement strivings. The experimental rather than correlational design also permitted the conclusion that causal attributions affect performance intensity.

Away From Individual Differences in Achievement Needs

In the individual difference-based research of Meyer (1970) and Weiner and Sierad (1975), hypotheses were derived from attributional principles, and in the latter study a methodology unique to attribution theory was used. These studies and others therefore seemed to promise a rapprochement between the traditional achievement concern with individual differences and an attributional conception of achievement strivings. The mediating bridge was that individuals with contrasting achievement and/or anxiety dispositions exhibit differential biases in their causal ascriptions for success and failure. However, subsequent research shied away from this marriage. The reason was straightforward, as indicated in this quote from an earlier work of mine:

> It is to be expected that there are individual differences in causal preferences that influence attributional decision making. Everyday observations suggest, for example, that some individuals readily invoke luck explanations when they interpret events, while others perceive ability, or hard work, as the primary determinant of achievement-related success.
>
> There has been extensive work investigating achievement needs . . . that apparently demonstrates the effects of predispositions on causal ascriptions. Although some of these investigations have yielded promising results (see optimistic statements in Weiner, 1972), the prior enthusiasm must now be tempered inasmuch as many other investigations . . . fail to replicate prior findings. (Weiner, 1980c, p. 38)

The conclusion expressed above was in part based on my own unpublished work, letters of dismay from others, and inconsistent correlations frequently reported in the literature (see, for example, Arkin et al., 1981, 1982; Covington & Omelich, 1979a; Weiner & Potepan, 1970). The underlying problems, which cannot be discussed in this context, are partially traceable to the lack of reliability in measurement of achievement needs by the Thematic Apperception Test and to uncertainties about the generality of the trait concept of need achievement.

Subsequent attribution-based research with the goal of developing a theory of achievement strivings therefore moved away from the achievement tradition of including individual differences in need strength in their studies. Two different research paths or paradigms were pursued. One approach still took individual differences into account, but now the personality characteristic examined was attributional style, or the tendency (cognitive trait) to bias attributions in a particular direction (see Cutrona, Russell, & Jones, 1985; Peterson et al., 1982). Much of this research did not originate from an achievement tradition, but rather was guided by the learned-helplessness orientation and focused on the analysis of depression. However, the research investigations typically took place in achievement-related contexts.

There is a huge experimental literature representing this point of view. Here I will present one illustrative study (discussed previously in Chapter 4) that was concerned with achievement performance rather than with depression (Anderson, 1983c). This study nicely illustrates how attributional tendencies as well as situational manipulations were used in a way that now appears to support an attributional theory of motivation. Anderson first administered an "Attributional Styles Assessment Test" to his subjects. This instrument consisted of 20 hypothetical situations of interpersonal success and failure. A sample vignette is:

> You were recently unsuccessful at trying to cheer up your roommate, who was having personal problems.

Each vignette was followed by six possible causes, including ability and personality (character deficits) and effort and strategy (behavioral mistakes). Character deficits were considered stable or unchangeable causes of failure, whereas behavioral mistakes were believed to be unstable or changeable causes. Subjects indicated which of the six possible causes would best explain why they would have failed in this situation.

The participants were then asked to help in the collection of blood for a blood bank. Specifically, they were to contact potential student donors, calling a random list of students on the phone. Before the solicitation, attributions were manipulated by communicating that success was primarily due to the stable factors of traits and abilities ("Some people just have persuasive abilities") or was due to proper strategy and effort, which are unstable causes. The subjects then made a practice call, which actually reached an experimental confederate who refused to donate. Following this failure, the subjects indicated their expectancy of success on future calls and left the laboratory.

During the 1 week prior to their return, the subjects kept a record of their calls and their rates of success. Upon returning, they again indicated their expectancy of future success as well as whether they would be willing to continue as a Red Cross volunteer. The number of calls made during the week, their success rate, and their willingness to volunteer provided motivational indexes. In sum, Anderson (1983c) included two attributional sources (individual differences and an experimental manipulation), measures of expectancy of success, and a variety of performance indicators.

Figure 6-10 (which repeats Figure 4-8) reveals that attributional styles and the attributional manipulation influenced success expectancies. In the no-attribution or control condition, persons who tended to ascribe failure to behavioral mistakes had a higher expectancy of future success following the initial failure than did subjects who ascribed failure to characterological deficits. However, when there was an attributional manipulation, it took precedence over (masked) these general biases. Figure 6-10 indicates that unstable attributions for failure (effort and strategy instructions) resulted in higher expectancies of success after the initial failure than did stable attributions, regardless of the individual-difference classification of the subjects. The associations between attributional stability and expectancy of success in both the control and the manipulation conditions again are in agreement with the conclusions reached in Chapter 4.

Turning next to the relations between attributions and the motivational indexes, Anderson (1983c) reported that subjects receiving unstable attributions for their initial failure exhibited significantly higher motivation (number of calls made plus willingness to volunteer) than did subjects given a stable attributional manipulation.

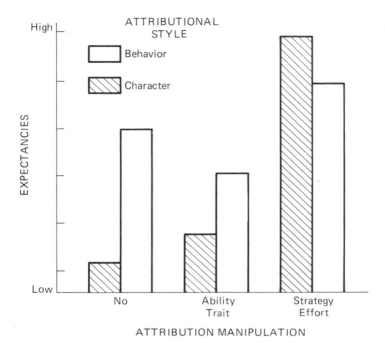

Figure 6-10. Composite index of success expectancies as a function of attributional style and attribution manipulation. From "Motivational and Performance Deficits in Interpersonal Settings: The Effects of Attributional Style" by C. A. Anderson, 1983a, *Journal of Personality and Social Psychology, 45*, p. 1142. Copyright 1983. Reprinted by permission.

The best predictor of motivation was how much the person expected to improve, or the difference between the initial and the final expectancy. Anderson (1983c) suggested that, "viewing one's failures as a result of poor strategy should lead one to attend to strategic features of a task, to expect improvement as one learns effective strategies, and to actually perform better" (p. 1144). Thus, Anderson's data and thinking suggest a temporal sequence of attribution-expectancy-motivation.

Centering on Process and Temporal Sequence

A separate path of achievement-related research shifted to the search for general laws, away from interactions with need for achievement, anxiety about failure, and/or attributional styles. This procedure is consistent with my views (see Chapter 1). Most of this research documented one of the specific associations shown in Figure 6-4, as reviewed in the prior chapters. Hence, there remained a dearth of investigations including the full sequence of relations specified by attribution theory and culminating with some performance indicator (but see Covington & Omelich, 1979a; Bernstein, Stephan, & Davis, 1979).

One pertinent investigation incorporating many (but not all) of the linkages was conducted by Graham (1984). In her study, children about 12 years of age were given a block-design puzzle to complete. There were four consecutive failure trials, and after each failure, ratings of causal attributions, expectancy of future success, and perceived competence were made. Graham manipulated causal attributions by means of experimenter affective feedback (documenting the effects of this feedback was one of the major goals of the experiment and will be discussed in a subsequent chapter). On the final puzzle attempt, the subjects were permitted to work for as long as they liked at an insoluble puzzle; persistence of behavior in the face of failure provided an index of strength of motivation.

Table 6-1 shows the relations between the attributions for failure to ability and effort and the expectancy, competence, and persistence measures. The table reveals that the correlations with effort ascriptions are weak, but ability attributions for failure correlate negatively with expectancy of success, perceived competence, and persistence of behavior. That is, the more one ascribes failure to low ability, the lower the expectancy, perceived competence, and persistence. Figure 6-11 shows the path-analytic representation of these data and reveals that causal ascriptions to ability minus effort, which indicate the relative stability of the perceived cause of failure, are negatively related to expectancy of success. Again this replicates the large number of research studies showing that the stability dimension is related to hopes for the future. As suggested in Chapter 4, this should be considered a basic psychological law. Figure 6-11 also indicates that causal attributions relate to perceived competence, with attributions to low ability associated with low perceived competence. However, only competence, and not expectancy, significantly predicted motivated behavior. In sum, the attributional theory depicted in Figure 6-4 is only partially supported in this investigation. The sequence from attributions to expectancy is supported, but in opposition to the findings of Meyer (1970) and Anderson (1983c), expectancy of success is not linked with behavior.

The investigation by Graham (1984) did not include affective reactions to failure, including shame and guilt. It therefore was not possible to test fully the attribution

Table 6-1. Correlations Between Attributions to Ability and Effort, Expectancy, Perceived Competence, and Persistence

	Ability Ascription	Effort Ascription
Expectancy	−.28**	−.04
Competence	−.39**	−.01
Persistence	−.21*	−.07

*p < .01. **p < .001.

Note. From "Communicated Sympathy and Anger to Black and White Children: The Cognitive (Attributional) Consequences of Affective Cues" by S. Graham, 1984, Journal of Personality and Social Psychology, 47, p. 47. Copyright 1984. Adapted by permission.

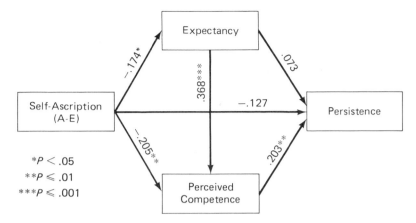

Figure 6-11. Path diagram of causal relations between attributions, expectancy, perceived competence, and persistence. From "Communicated Sympathy and Anger to Black and White Children: The Cognitive (Attributional) Consequences of Affective Cues" by S. Graham, 1984, *Journal of Personality and Social Psychology*, 47, p. 48. Copyright 1984. Adapted by permission.

theory that is being put forward. (Previously I did suggest that persons might "feel" competent, so that competence might be considered an affect. However, in the study by Graham the competence measure indicated a self-perception of ability relative to others, rather than an affective reaction). In a later study, Covington and Omelich (1984) did include affects, as well as expectancy, in an achievement-related investigation. In addition, their research was conducted directly in the classroom, thus contrasting with the laboratory approach of the prior investigations discussed in this chapter.

Covington and Omelich (1984) gave students who considered their midterm exam a failure (regardless of the objective grade) the opportunity to retake an equivalent exam 3 weeks later. After the initial exam feedback, the students made attributions for their subjectively unsatisfactory performance to low ability and lack of effort; they reported their feelings of humiliation, shame, and guilt; and their expectancy of success on the next exam also was revealed. The index of motivation in this classroom context was actual retake exam performance.

Figure 6-12 shows the path-analytic representation of these data, retaining only the significant paths. The figure reveals that both effort and ability attributions are related to all of the affects (perhaps indicating some response bias), but low effort is more highly related to guilt, whereas lack of ability is more highly related to shame and humiliation. These patterns are in agreement with the discussion in Chapter 5. Humiliation (but not shame) negatively relates to performance, whereas guilt is positively associated with exam score. Turning next to the expectancy variable, only lack of effort is related to expectancy, and in a direction opposite to that predicted since attribution of failure to low effort results in low expectation of success. Expectancy, however, is related to exam score—the higher the expectancy, the

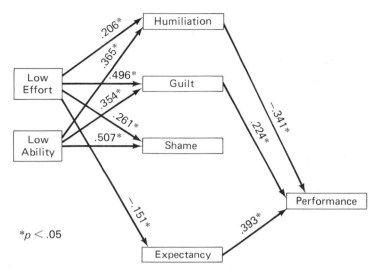

Figure 6-12. Path diagram of the effects of causal attributions, affective reactions, and expectancy on subsequent performance following failure. From "An Empirical Examination of Weiner's Critique of Attributional Research" by M. V. Covington and C. L. Omelich, 1984, *Journal of Educational Psychology*, 76, p. 1217. Copyright 1984. Reprinted by permission.

better the performance. In sum, in this investigation many of the key unions in Figure 6-4 were documented (attribution-affect; affect-action; expectancy-action), save for the relations between attributions and expectancy.

General Summary

What, then, can be concluded regarding the viability in the achievement domain of the attributional theory shown in Figure 6-4? Are the constructed analyses of the Little League baseball players supported by the empirical evidence? The most evident conclusion is that the jury is still out and, in this case, is far from returning to the courtroom. There is a historical interpretation of achievement research when perceived from an attributional perspective that sees it coming closer and closer into contact with the theory in Figure 6-4. First, the research in this area included individual differences in need for achievement and/or anxiety, along with some experimental manipulation (see Lucas, 1952); then causal attributions and their correlates, such as expectancy of success, were added (see Meyer, 1970; Weiner & Sierad, 1975); next individual differences in need strength were replaced with a measurement of attributional tendencies (e.g., Anderson, 1983c); and last, individual differences were totally discarded (e.g., Graham, 1984; Covington & Omelich, 1984).

Although promising from an attributional perspective, the picture is not as bright as one would hope. On the negative side, only one study included direct affective reports (Covington & Omelich, 1984), and this same investigation did not find relations between attributions and expectancy; another study found no relation between expectancy and action (Graham, 1984), and the majority did not include most of the mediating factors depicted in Figure 6-4. On the other hand, the weight of the total evidence reviewed thus far is quite promising. Altering attributions does produce performance change (Weiner & Sierad, 1975), attributions do relate to expectancy and/or performance (Anderson, 1983c; Graham, 1984; Meyer, 1970), and affect also influences performance (Covington & Omelich, 1984). And, of course, there is the vast supporting literature reviewed earlier that examines the individual linkages within the theory. Hence, although the jury is still out, there is reason for optimism and the expectation of a favorable decision for the attributional litigant.

Attributional Therapy

As already stated, a good deal of research supporting the hypothesized linkage between causal attributions and achievement-related behavior has been conducted in applied, as opposed to theoretical, contexts. These application-oriented investigations have been carried out by psychologists and educators concerned with personal adjustment and improving the lives of others. To effect these positive changes, therapeutic programs have been developed that attempt to replace maladaptive or dysfunctional causal ascriptions with other attributions that better aid coping and increase the likelihood of the attainment of desired goals. The underlying principle guiding such intervention attempts is that if causal attributions do influence achievement strivings, then a change in attributions should produce a change in behavior (see Foersterling, 1980b, 1985).

The investigations by Weiner and Sierad (1975), Anderson (1983b), and Graham (1984) also induced causal attributions, respectively communicating that a pill, strategy or ability, or effort or ability was the cause of prior failure. However, change program research differs from these studies in fundamental ways. First, the participants in change program research are typically selected because of maladaptive behaviors: They are doing poorly in school, exhibit low frustration tolerance, quit in the face of failure, and the like. Second, the intervention procedures, like clinical methods, often involve repetitions of the attributional change attempt, rather than merely "one-shot" instructions. Finally, the investigator hopes that long-term, generalized changes take place as a result of the treatment (although this is rarely assessed).

But what "bad" attributions have these programs attempted to replace, and what "good" attributions do they attempt to induce? The answers to these questions are somewhat complex, for different theoretical approaches have given rise to attribution-change attempts, and these conceptions do not fully agree on what are the functional and dysfunctional ascriptions. However, there are important areas of consensus, and the great majority of the attribution-change attempts, in spite of theoretical disagreement, have focused on the identical causal ascriptions. (This reminds one of the findings in the general area of psychotherapy, for therapists with quite different theoretical orientations apparently engage in the same behaviors during clinical treatment.)

One of the theoretical perspectives guiding attributional intervention techniques is called "learned helplessness." The basic supposition of this approach is that if one's responses are perceived as not increasing the probability of goal attainment, then a state of helplessness is produced (see Seligman, 1975). That is, helplessness results when outcomes are not under personal control. In the learned-helplessness formulation, controllability is of prime importance because it affects expectancy of success: Failure due to uncontrollable factors is linked with low expectancy, whereas failure ascribed to controllable factors maintains hope for the future, inasmuch as one can "do something about it." Low expectancy of success, in turn, is proposed to cause a cessation in instrumental responding and, therefore, learning and performance deficits.

This theoretical perspective therefore suggests that attributions indicating that failure is due to factors beyond the personal control of the actor are maladaptive; such ascriptions are hypothesized to produce helplessness, low expectancy of success, and motivational decrements. Ascriptions of failure to low ability (aptitude), bad luck, external hindrance, and so on are therefore dysfunctional (see Diener & Dweck, 1978). On the other hand, attributions of failure to lack of effort or to poor strategy are functional, for these causes can be volitionally changed.

The actual change programs guided by a learned-helplessness perspective have attempted to alter attributions of failure toward insufficient effort. The "bad" attribution has been lack of ability, although as intimated above, any of a number of causal ascriptions for failure are equally dysfunctional. Given the dominance of ability and effort as the causes of achievement performance, however, it is not surprising that lack of ability has been the target ascription to be replaced (see Chapin & Dyck, 1976; Dweck, 1975; Dweck & Repucci, 1973). Learned helplessness was associated with the first attribution-change attempts, but there has been a void in follow-up investigations for over a decade.

A second conception providing direction for intervention programs was formulated by Bandura (1977) and is labeled "self-efficacy theory." As already indicated, this conception focuses attention on the debilitating effects of "I cannot" self-statements, which inhibit motivation. Motivational inhibition is presumed because expectancy of success is minimized by "I cannot" beliefs. Hence, attribution of failure to lack of ability is dysfunctional, whereas attributions that imply "I can," such as insufficient effort or poor strategy, are adaptive. Research investigations in the achievement domain guided by Bandura's thinking therefore have also concentrated on changing causal ascriptions from lack of ability to lack of effort (Schunk, 1981, 1982, 1983). Although this research literature is contemporary, it has been the product of primarily one investigator.

Finally, attribution theory also has given rise to intervention research. These investigations were conducted before attributional analyses of affect were completely formulated, and therefore the full theory shown in Figure 6-4 has not been utilized. Attribution theory specifies that an attribution of failure to a stable factor is dysfunctional inasmuch as hopes about future success are minimized. On the other

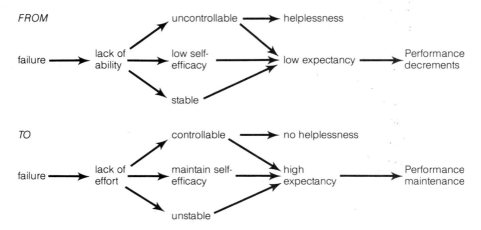

Figure 6-13. Assumed attribution-consequent linkages in achievement-change programs.

hand, ascriptions of failure to unstable causes would then be functional. These principles lead attributional researchers to alter attributions from stable factors (again low ability) to unstable factors (primarily lack of effort) (Andrews & Debus, 1978; Fowler & Peterson, 1981; Gatting-Stiller, Gerling, Stiller, Voss, & Wender, 1979; Zoeller, Mahoney, & Weiner, 1983). Other researchers have broken from the lack-of-effort mode and manipulated causal attributions by providing information regarding the increasing ease of college success as one progresses past the freshman year (Wilson & Linville, 1982, 1985).

To summarize, all three theoretical approaches (assuming preaffect attribution theory) agree that ascription of failure to lack of ability, which is uncontrollable, an antecedent of "I cannot," and stable, is maladaptive. Similarly, all agree that ascriptions of failure to insufficient effort, which is controllable, maintains "I can" beliefs, and is unstable, is an adaptive ascription. This consensus is due to a shared belief that expectancy of success is a (or *the*) key determinant of motivation (see Figure 6-13).

Because the vast majority of research studies attempt to change attributions of failure from low ability to insufficient effort, the research findings do not provide a critical test of the differential predictive validity of the theories (see the final section of this chapter). But the data do provide evidence regarding the more basic issue of the effectiveness of attributional change for the alteration of achievement-related behavior.

The Experimental Findings

The achievement-change programs that have been conducted follow a rather similar format. Subjects are chosen for training on the basis of some maladaptive cognition or behavior. The maladaptive cognition is merely assumed to be the tendency to ascribe failure to lack of ability, or the tendency not to ascribe achievement outcomes to effort. The maladaptive behaviors include little persistence in the face of failure, poor school performance, and judgments of helplessness by teachers. Then these selected individuals participate in a change program designed to influence their attributions. Most often the experimenter informs participants that induced failure at a laboratory task was caused by insufficient effort. But models voicing that they failed because they did not try, reinforcement when the participants communicate that failure was due to lack of effort, and false attribution-relevant information also have been used. These programs often last for 2 or 3 weeks. Then the retrained subjects are tested for persistence in the face of failure or task performance relative to a control group of subjects who did not undergo the training manipulation.

A review of the findings of the attributional-change research in the achievement domain fortunately has already been undertaken. Foersterling (1985) stated, "It can be concluded from the present review that attributional retraining methods have been consistently successful in increasing persistence and performance." (p. 509) Table 6-2 summarizes the attribution-change literature, listing for each investigation the guiding theoretical framework (helplessness, self-efficacy, attribution theory), the particular problem area of the participants, how the subjects were selected (cognitive or behavioral index), the type and duration of the training technique, and the type of dependent variable and results. The great variety in the specific experimental techniques, in spite of similar goals of changing attributions from ability to effort, and the consistency in the published data add to one's confidence in the general findings.

Special attention should be directed to the studies by Wilson and Linville (1982, 1985), who induced task difficulty rather than the more typical lack-of-effort ascriptions. Wilson and Linville identified students who felt that their first-year performance in college was a failure. The researchers then merely presented an experimental group of subjects with information indicating that the school grading policy becomes more lenient as the students progress through school. This was conveyed by means of video interviews with students sharing their experiences about the increasing ease of school.

The data indicated that the students receiving the unstable task difficulty manipulation were less likely to drop out of school (although the absolute number of comparison students was quite small) and attained better grades than students not exposed to the manipulation. In spite of subsequent partial replications by Wilson and Linville (1985), these findings must be considered promising rather than definitive (see Block & Lanning, 1984), and replication attempts are badly needed.

An Alternative Interpretation

The change program research assumes that performance enhancement is due to relative increments in the expectancy of success, mediated by either unstable attributions, perceived controllability, or self-efficacy. However, these conceptions completely neglect the role of affect as a behavioral determinant. As stated earlier, the attribution-based therapeutic attempts neglect emotion in part because of their later introduction into this theory.

Table 6-2. Attributional Retraining (adapted from Foersterling, 1985, pp. 498–500)

Study	Theoretical Position/ Direction of Change	Problem Area/ Subject Selection	Reattribution Techniques/ Training Duration	Dependent Variables/ Results
Andrews & Debus (1978)	Attributional: Change to effort attributions for success and failure	Circle design, anagrams: Selection according to cognitions	Operant reinforcement (verbal and plus token): Up to 6 blocks (1 block containing 5 success and 5 failure trials)	Increase of effort attributions, immediately, 1 week, and 4 months after the training at similar and dissimilar tasks; increased persistence at all different times and tasks; no changes were found in the IAR or the Effort-Ability-Attribution Scale; both methods of reattribution showed similar results
Chapin & Dyck (1976)	Learned helplessness, Attributional: Change to effort for success and failure	Reading performance: Selection according to performance (below grade level)	Persuasion (the experimenter verbalized the desired attributions following each outcome): 3 days (with 15 trials each)	Increased persistence (number of sentences with a difficult word voluntarily read aloud)
Dweck (1975)	Learned helplessness, Attributional: Change to lack of effort for failure	Arithmetic: Selection according to behaviors (children who were judged to be helpless by their teachers)	Persuasion (the experimenter attributed failure to lack of effort): 15 trials	Increased effort attributions, improved performance (less decrease of correct math problems after failure); IAR scores, test anxiety, and repetition choice tasks were not influenced

Author	Goal	Sample/task	Intervention	Results
Fowler & Peterson (1981)	Learned helplessness: Change to effort for success and failure	Reading performance: Selection according to performance (low reading skills) and cognitions (intellectual achievement responsibility) as well as teachers' judgments	Persuasion (the experimenter stated the desired attribution to the subject) or the subject listened to (recorded) attributions: 3 sessions	Persistence (number of sentences read aloud) increased; no differences were found concerning overall IAR score, but the training influenced effort attributions
Gatting-Stiller, Gerling, Stiller, Voss, & Wender (1979)	Attributional: Change to lack of effort for failure	Academic (intelligence test tasks): Pupils (5th and 6th grade of a German high school) low in achievement motivation	Modeling (A videotaped stimulus person attributed failure to lack of effort, and persisted following failure): One-shot intervention	Persistence at a similar and dissimilar task and generalized attributions were uninfluenced; increased effort attributions at the training task, but not at a dissimilar one
Medway & Venino (1982)	Attributional: Change to effort for success and failure	Visual discrimination tasks: Selection according to cognitions (elementary school students with a tendency not to perceive effort as a cause for performance)	Persuasion (the experimenter stated the desired attributions to the subject): 8 blocks with 6 trials each	Persistence (time spent on discrimination tasks and number of tasks completed) improved; attributions were not influenced
Schunk (1981)	Self-efficacy: Change to effort for success and failure	Arithmetic: Selection according to performance (children with low arithmetic performance)	Persuasion (experimenter stated the desired attribution every 5 to 6 min to the subject): 3 sessions (each lasting about 50 min)	Persistence (time spent on division tasks), accuracy, general mathematical abilities, and perceived efficacy were not significantly influenced

Table 6-2. (continued)

Study	Theoretical Position/ Direction of Change	Problem Area/ Subject Selection	Reattribution Techniques/ Training Duration	Dependent Variables/ Results
Schunk (1982)	Self-efficacy: Change to effort for success at past and future performances	Arithmetic: Selection according to behavior (teachers identified children with low subtraction skills)	Persuasion (experimenter told the subjects that their past performance was due to high effort, or indicated that high effort will be necessary for future success): 3 sessions (each lasting 40 min)	Only linking past outcomes to effort increased performance (subtraction skills) and self-efficacy; persistence (time spent at similar and dissimilar tasks) was not influenced
Schunk (1983)	Self-efficacy: Change to ability, effort, or ability + effort for success	Arithmetic: Selection according to behaviors (teachers identified children with low subtraction performance)	Persuasion (experimenter stated the desired attribution to the subject): 3 sessions (each lasting 40 min)	Performance as well as self-efficacy (at subtraction task) improved in all attributional conditions; persistence did not increase
Shunk (1984)	Self-efficacy: Change to ability or effort	Arithmetic: Selection according to behaviors (teachers identified children with low subtraction performance)	Persuasion (the experimenter stated the desired attribution to the subject): 4 sessions (each lasting 40 min)	Performance, self-efficacy, and ability attributions increased as a function of the training; ability feedback yielded superior results to effort attribution training

Study	Attributional change	Setting	Method	Results
Wilson & Linville (1982; replicated by Wilson & Linville, 1985)	Attributional: Change to variable attributions (informational antecedents rather than specific causes were provided)	Academic (college grades and GRE tasks): Selection according to self-reported dissatisfaction with college, low performance, and worry about performance	Informational (statistical information and fake videotaped interviews indicated that GPAs and general college problems improve over time): One-shot intervention	Improved performance (better GRE task performance immediately and 1 week after training, improved GPA after 1 year); increased persistence (college dropout rate); expectations of better GPAs (in the long run but not in the short run); subjects who were asked to think about attributions reported better mood during the first week after training
Zoeller, Mahoney, & Weiner (1983)	Attributional: Change to effort and ability for success, and to lack of effort for failure	Psychomotor coordination: Subjects (mentally retarded adults) who were rated to have motivational difficulties and who had performance decrements following failure were selected	Modeling (subjects watched on a video a peer working on the criterion task; a commentator made attributions) and persuasion (subjects worked on the criterion task and received in vivo attributional feedback); 3 sessions (each lasting about 15 min)	Both methods increased performance (time needed to complete the psychomotor task)

Note. IAR = Intellectual Achievement Responsibility Scale. GRE = Graduate Record Exam. GPA = grade point average.

Figure 6-13 and the hypothetical vignettes earlier in this chapter revealed that lack-of-ability attributions are presumed to retard performance, whereas lack-of-effort ascriptions are hypothesized to enhance performance. Recall from our earlier analyses in this chapter and from chapter 5 that ascriptions of failure to lack of ability elicit feelings of incompetence, shame, and humiliation. On the other hand, lack-of-effort attributions give rise to guilt. Indeed, the experimenter feedback in some of the change programs following induced failure is that "You should have gotten this correct," indicating the moral imperative evoked when failure is due to insufficient effort.

It has been suggested that feelings of incompetence, shame, and humiliation impede achievement strivings, whereas guilt generates renewed motivation (even in the face of lowered self-worth). Hence, the observed effects of the achievement-change procedures, which have been ascribed to altered cognitions (expectancy of success), could be explained as due to the unintended manipulation of affect (see Figure 6-14).

This emotion-based interpretation of the change data is of special interest when examining the task difficulty induction by Wilson & Linville (1982, 1985). Altering attributions from ability to unstable task difficulty not only changes the stability of the ascription for failure, but also alters the locus of causality: Task difficulty is external, whereas ability is internal. Hence, rather than (theoretically) changing affects from shame to guilt, as in the lack-of-effort induction, the procedure of Wilson and Linville maintains the self-worth of the participants while reducing shame and not arousing guilt.

If the data in all the change studies were "true," and if expectancy of success had been partialed from the analysis, then it would be possible to argue that the differences in performance between the ability and the effort induction conditions demonstrates the motivating effects of guilt relative to shame, whereas the difference in performance given ability versus task difficulty ascriptions is attributable to the effects of self-esteem maintenance. Clearly, an experimental design using all three attributions (ability, effort, task difficulty) is needed. It is also possible to include inductions to stable task difficulty so that expectancy would experimentally be held stable. An infinite number of attributional variations are possible; the concentration of research on ability versus effort attributions has not aided comparative theoretical growth, although it might be too early in this line of research to make the more subtle, between-theory comparisons.

FROM

　　　　　Failure—Lack of Ability—Feelings of Shame—Performance Decrements

TO

　　　　　Failure—Lack of Effort—Feelings of Guilt—Performance Increments

Figure 6-14. Suggested attribution-affect-behavior sequence in achievement-change programs.

Related Issues

A number of pertinent issues can be raised with regard to achievement-change pro-grams. One related issue of importance concerns the concentration of research on attributions for failure rather than success (but see Andrews & Debus, 1978; Diener & Dweck, 1980). Theoretically, attributions of success to, for example, good luck, which minimize pride in accomplishment and expectancy of success, might be just as dysfunctional as ascription of failure to low ability. The message being conveyed is that maladaptive ascriptions for positive outcomes are in need of exploration; the research thus far has concentrated too heavily on attributions for failure.

Another neglected topic in change-research programs involves continued persis-tence at an unobtainable goal. In the romantic literature this flaw characterized Anna Karenina and Emma Bovary, ultimately resulting in their destruction. Persis-tence in the face of repeated failure can be just as maladaptive as premature quitting (see Janoff-Bulman & Brickman, 1982). Given maladaptive persistence, training programs should perhaps attempt to alter unstable attributions to stable ones. It seems to be assumed by the training procedures that unstable ascriptions for failure must be adaptive. This rather complex issue implicates some unsolvable philosophi-cal issues, including the pitting of social reality versus social construction positions (is there really, really a true cause?). In addition, who should decide, and at what point should it be decided, that one indeed cannot complete a task or reach a goal? After all, we have often heard about the accomplishment of "impossible" feats that perhaps would have been abandoned had stable attributions been made. But these philosophical issues are best addressed elsewhere, and by others. What is again apparent is that the achievement training programs have been too constrained. But perhaps this is not unexpected, given that the published investigations number only around one dozen.

A final suggestion to consider is the pursuit of investigations that permit a disen-tangling of helplessness, self-efficacy, and attributional explanations. Close inspec-tion of the theories reveals that differential theoretical predictions are possible. For example, according to learned-helplessness theory, an attribution for failure to bad luck is maladaptive inasmuch as luck is not subject to volitional control. On the other hand, luck certainly is unstable, so that from an attributional perspective this is an adaptive ascription. And luck neither enhances nor diminishes the belief that "I cannot," so that self-efficacy theorists would consider it a good causal ascription in comparison with an ascription to low ability, but perhaps bad in comparison with lack of effort expenditure.

Another causal ascription that can separate the validity of the different conceptual frameworks is task difficulty. According to learned-helplessness theory, this again is a poor ascription for failure because the imposed objective difficulty of a task is beyond personal control. From an attributional point of view, the difficulty of the task would be a dysfunctional attribution if it were construed as stable, but a positive coping attribution if task difficulty were considered unstable. From the perspective of self-efficacy theory, the "goodness" of this ascription is somewhat unclear, depending on whether task attributions have implications for self-perceptions of ability. Two publications already reviewed include inductions of failure to unstable task difficulty (Wilson & Linville, 1982, 1985). Both reported motivational enhancement, thus supporting attributional predictions and disconfirming predictions from the helplessness perspective. More "crucial" change program inductions that result in differential theoretical predictions would greatly benefit both researchers and practitioners.

General Conclusion

A theory of motivation and emotion has been offered, with its theoretical focus in achievement settings. The component associations of this theory—the existence and antecedents of attributional search, the determinants of attributional decisions, and the effects of causal thinking on expectancy and emotion—have been definitively documented. It is also quite clear that the theory can be completely utilized to construct scenarios that explain the approach to and avoidance of achievement strivings. Yet experimental testing of the value of the entire conception to explain achievement-related performance has been relatively ignored. I would be remiss in burying my head in the sand in the face of the insufficient evidence; it also would be foolish to follow the lead of Pangloss in *Candide* and express unwarranted optimism. But neither is this the proper place for undue modesty: The paucity of research is to be expected given the recent evolution of the theory and the number and complexity of the intervening processes. Furthermore, the evidence that has been gathered is promising: The achievement literature is assuming more and more of an attributional perspective, and change programs based on attributional principles are developing. Perhaps this will help meet Kurt Lewin's definition of a good theory—it is practical. From the evidence in basic research and applied investigations it can be concluded that attributions are without doubt linked to achievement performance. The ferreting out of the contributions of expectancy as well as qualitatively different emotions to achievement performance—in other words, the full utilization of the theory—remains the difficult and more subtle task for the future.

Chapter 7

Beyond Achievement Motivation: The Generality of Attribution Theory

In which the author discusses the range or generality
of the theory, extending the analysis to helping
behavior and a variety of other phenomena. It
appears that a general theory of motivation and
emotion is under development.

Achievement strivings have been the focus of convenience of the attributional approach advanced in this book. The conception illustrated in Figure 6-4 grew as an alternative to Atkinson's theory of achievement motivation, and achievement-related contexts provided the research sites for many of the supporting empirical investigations. But a theory must have range or generality if it is to have lasting significance and influence. In this chapter I explore the breadth of the conception, examining a variety of phenomena that the theory is able to address.

The foundation for theoretical generality is provided by two conceptual mechanisms. First, it is proposed that a motivational episode is initiated following any outcome that can be construed as attainment or nonattainment of a goal. Achievement success and failure clearly capture this requirement and, in part for this reason, have been the subject of much study. In addition to achievement performance, the conception has been used to examine a number of broadly conceived personal "failures" including, for example, alcoholism (McHugh, Beckman, & Frieze, 1979), crime and the related topic of parole decisions (Carroll, 1978), depression (Abramson, Seligman, & Teasdale, 1978); deprivation (Mark, 1985), loneliness (Cutrona, 1982; Peplau, Miceli, & Morasch, 1982; Peplau, Russell, & Heim, 1979), need of help (Betancourt, 1983; Reisenzein, 1986; Weiner, 1980a, 1980b), maladaptive reactions to rape and pregnancy (Janoff-Bulman, 1979; Major, Mueller, & Hilderbrandt, 1985), cigarette smoking (Eiser, Van der Pligt, Raw, & Sutton, in press; Goldstein, Gordon, & Marlatt, 1984; Marlatt, 1985; Schoeneman, Cheek, Fischer, Hollis, & Stevens, 1985), and wife battering (Frieze, 1979).

In all these arenas of study, after identifying the negative outcome, the authors determined the perceived cause of that outcome, such as the perceived cause of a need for help, of a crime, or of failure to quit smoking. Although the specific causes reported vary greatly, both within and between the topics under consideration, they can be described according to their structural properties of locus, stability, and controllability (and perhaps intentionality and globality). The dimensional analysis then furnishes the second mechanism for theoretical generality, for once the structure of the cause is ascertained, its impact on expectancy, affect, and action can be determined. Hence, causal dimensions emerge as the key concept fostering theoretical range.

I begin this chapter with an extended discussion of helping behavior. Except for the achievement area, helping has received the most attention from attribution theorists. Additionally, research regarding helping has clearly shown the role of emotion in motivated behavior, and also has been associated with the most sophisticated path-analytic techniques to test the temporal sequence depicted in Figure 6-4.

This discussion is followed by an examination of three topics: criminal parole decisions, smoking cessation, and the rather unusual subject of reactions to airline delays. These areas have not been the focus of many empirical investigations. However, they have been examined from path-analytical perspectives, centering on the temporal sequence between an instigating event and the final response. Other topics examined from an attributional perspective, such as alcoholism and wife battering, have not been sufficiently considered from a historical or sequential viewpoint to be included here.

Lastly, attributional analyses of depression and reactions to rape and unwanted pregnancy are considered, for some very popular and heuristic approaches to these problems are directly based upon the attributional theory advocated in this book. It will be seen, however, that the application of attributional principles to these topics which are pertinent to clinical psychology, has been either incomplete or faulty, thereby creating a number of unresolved theoretical and empirical difficulties.

Helping Behavior

A huge array of factors influence the decision to help or not to help another person in need. Among the documented determinants of help giving are the perceived cost and benefit to the help giver as well as to the recipient of the aid, the number of people available to help (i.e., the amount of responsibility that the potential help giver must take), the values and norms of the culture, the behavior of models, and on and on. But most important in the present context, it also has been documented that the perceived cause of a need is one of the major determinants of the decision to help or to neglect a person requiring aid. In a manner quite similar to the study of achievement motivation, attributional concepts have slowly played a greater and greater role in the explanation of help giving.

The Effects of Perceived Causality on Helping

An often-cited investigation by Piliavin, Rodin, and Piliavin (1969) demonstrated that the perceived reason why help is needed influences the decision to help or to neglect another. However, attributional thinking did not guide this research. In the methodology employed by Piliavin et al. (1969), a person either obviously drunk or obviously ill falls down while riding a subway. Observations of the behavior of the passengers revealed that help was more likely to be offered to the ill person than to the drunk person. Piliavin et al. reasoned that there are great potential costs when helping a drunk: The person might resist aid, be aggressive, and so on. These costs, in turn, were presumed to hinder the likelihood of helping.

A study published in the same year by Berkowitz (1969) was among the first to explicitly demonstrate an effect of causal ascriptions on help giving. Subjects in this experiment requested aid from another subject. The reason for the need was manipulated and was due to an experimenter error or to the subject "taking it easy." These were respectively conceived as differing on the locus dimension of causality, with experimenter error being external to the subject, whereas "taking it easy" is an internal ascription. The data clearly revealed that more aid was extended when the cause of the need was attributed to the experimenter rather than to the subject. A similar finding was previously reported by Schopler and Matthews (1965), although these investigators did not specify what subject shortcoming produced the need state.

Helping From an Attributional Perspective

It was not until a decade later that Barnes, Ickes, and Kidd (1979) recognized that helping behavior is amenable to a more complete attributional analysis than the locus-only approach suggested by Berkowitz. In the study by Barnes et al., students were telephoned by an alleged classmate, who asked to borrow their class notes. The classmate indicated that the reason for his need was either low ability (uncontrollable) or lack of effort (controllable). In addition, it was reported that this was either a stable or an unstable condition. Hence, two dimensions of causality were independently varied to determine their influence on help giving. Inasmuch as ability and effort are internal ascriptions, the locus dimension was held constant. Barnes et al. found that more helping requests were granted when low ability rather than lack of effort was given as the cause of needing notes, and help was increased given a stable rather than an unstable causal ascription.

These data suggested a reinterpretation of the findings reported by Berkowitz (1969) and Piliavin et al. (1969). In the experiment by Berkowitz, two causes of a need were compared: the experimenter (external and not controllable by the subject) and lack of effort (internal and controllable by the subject). Berkowitz contended that aid giving was a function of the locus of the cause, with external causes generating more help giving than internal causes. But locus and control were inseparable and thereby confounded in his experiment. Thus, the differential helping might have been due to the controllability, rather than (or in addition to) the locus of the cause. The data reported by Barnes et al. (1979), which held the locus dimension constant by manipulating only the internal causes of ability and effort, strongly suggest that the disparate effects found by Berkowitz were due to differences in the perceived controllability of the cause of the need. The reader may recall from Chapter 4 that studies of expectancy of success manipulating skill versus luck perceptions confounded causal locus with causal stability: It was first thought that locus influenced expectancy shifts, when in fact stability was the key determining causal dimension. It is now being proposed (following Barnes et al.) that Berkowitz also incorrectly inferred causal locus as a determinant of a particular behavior; in this case,

However, it was confounded with causal controllability rather than with causal stability.

The controllability explanation first offered by Barnes et al. also may be applied to the data reported by Piliavin et al. (1969). Drinking is perceived as a controllable cause of a need—people typically are held responsible for their alcohol consumption. There is a wealth of data supporting this conclusion (see Reisenzein, 1986; Weiner, 1980a). For example, in the unpublished survey (discussed in Chapter 5) conducted at Kent State University, college students' ratings of a variety of stigmatized groups, including the mentally ill, homosexuals, and the obese, revealed that alcoholics were perceived as the group most responsible for their plight. Beckman (1979) also reported that female alcoholics are held responsible by others as well as by themselves for their drinking behavior. And the recent attacks by Mothers Against Drunk Drivers (MADD) quite clearly hold drunk individuals responsible for any untoward events that happen when they are under the influence of alcohol. To the contrary, one usually is not held responsible or blamed for being ill (see Reisenzein, 1986; Weiner, 1980a), although one can create special situations in which this could be the case.

It is therefore apparent that a controllability explanation can be applied to the data reported by Berkowitz (1969), Piliavin et al. (1969), and Barnes et al. (1979). On the other hand, the cost-benefit analysis advanced by Piliavin et al. does not seem applicable to the other two studies. In the investigation by Berkowitz, it is not readily apparent that there is less "cost" involved in providing help to a student hindered by the experimenter, as opposed to one who is self-hindered because of lack of effort. Nor is there clearly less cost involved in helping a "dumb" as opposed to a "lazy" student (although again it might be possible to create a scenario in which this would be the case). Pursuing this line of reasoning, the locus argument offered by Berkowitz also does not generalize to the other experiments, inasmuch as illness and drunkenness, as well as lack of ability and insufficient effort, are all likely to be conceived as internal causes.

Because of the robustness of only the controllability explanation first suggested by Barnes et al., I continued with this line of thought (Weiner, 1980a). Hypothetical situations were created in which students again were asked about their likelihood of lending another student their class notes. In this investigation, a more complete sampling of causes was employed, and three (rather than two) dimensions of causality were varied. This resulted in eight experimental conditions corresponding to the eight cells of a 2 (Locus) × 2 (Stability) × 2 (Controllability) matrix. For example, it was indicated that the notes were needed because of low ability (internal, stable, uncontrollable), because the teacher was unable to give clear lectures (external, stable, uncontrollable), and so on. The effects of locus and controllability on judgments of help giving are shown in Table 7-1. Table 7-1 reveals that help was reported as unlikely only when the cause was internal to the subject and controllable (lack of effort); in all other conditions in which the person in need was described as unable to control the reason for the need, help was stated as likely to be offered. Hence, the central prediction regarding the importance of perceived personal control was replicated. In this investigation, stability did not influence the helping judgments.

Table 7-1. Mean Likelihood of Helping as a Function of
Locus and Control of the Cause

Locus	Controllable	Uncontrollable
Internal	3.13	6.74
External	7.35	6.98

Note. The higher the number, the greater the likelihood of help-
giving.
From *Human Motivation* (p. 189) by B. Weiner, 1980, New York:
Holt, Rinehart & Winston. Copyright 1980. Reprinted by permission.

Brophy and Rohrkemper (1981) subsequently applied attributional principles in
another school-related context (see also Rohrkemper, 1985). They presented
teachers with 12 vignettes portraying students with classroom problems. In some,
the behavior of the students interfered with general classroom learning. These
problems were labeled as "teacher-owned" (this does not represent a locus attribution, but rather implicates who experiences the problem). Defiance and hyperactivity exemplified two such teacher-owned problems. Other vignettes portrayed
pupils with "student-owned" problems; these difficulties blocked student performance but did not interfere with the learning of others. Shyness and perfectionism
exemplify two maladaptive obstacles experienced by students.

Brophy and Rohrkemper found that teacher-owned problems were perceived by
teachers as controllable by the pupils; defiant and hyperactive children were held
responsible for their disruptive actions. On the other hand, pupil-owned problems
such as shyness were perceived by teachers as not controllable. To cope with these
two types of adversities, the teachers selected different strategies. Teacher-related
(controllable) problems were treated with punishment and threatening actions. In
contrast, given student-owned difficulties:

teachers' responses... featured extensive talk designed to provide support, nurtur-
ance, and instruction... The teachers frequently mentioned working on long term
goals with these students... teaching them coping techniques that would allow
them to succeed in situations in which they were now failing. (Brophy & Rohrkemper, 1981, pp. 306–307)

That is, uncontrollable problems "apparently translated into teaching commitments
to help these students" (Brophy & Rohrkemper, 1981, p. 306).

A rather evident conclusion emerges from the disparate investigations conducted
by Piliavin et al. (1969), Berkowitz (1969), Barnes et al. (1979), Weiner (1980a),
and Brophy and Rohrkemper (1981): Causes perceived as subject to personal control
by the individual in need give rise to neglect, whereas causes perceived as uncontrollable by that person generate help. Hence, there is an association between a
dimension of causality (controllability) and a behavioral consequence (help versus neglect).

This linkage is quite prevalent in everyday affairs and even guides governmental actions with regard to financial aid. Consider the following analysis of President Reagan's social policy:

> One cannot avoid the impression that the cuts in social spending the Reagan Administration is proposing are not simply the means toward the end of economic recovery, *they are the ends themselves.* What Reagan proposes to do, by his own admission, is to get the federal government out of the social-welfare business.
>
> The Administration has attempted to soften this position by promising to retain the "social safety net of programs" that benefit the "truly needy." In his address to Congress, Reagan defines the "truly needy" as "those *who through no fault of their own* must depend on the rest of us." That definition implies a moral distinction between those whose poverty is unavoidable and those whose poverty is "their own fault." Thus presidential counselor Edwin Meese III has spoken in terms of the "deserving" and the "undeserving" poor. (*Los Angeles Times*, Dec. 8, 1982)

It is evident from this quote that the government is offering to help those with uncontrollable causes of their problems (the "truly" needy) but not those with causes of need that the administration perceives as controllable.

The relation between perceived controllability and help giving is so pervasive that it also apparently has an influence on medical decisions. Brewin (1984b) gave a group of medical students a list of some stressful life events, such as divorce or illness, and ascertained how controllable these events were perceived to be. He then asked whether the students would be willing to prescribe tranquilizers or antidepressants to help in coping. Independent of the perceived severity of the event (the amount of readjustment required), medical students were more willing to prescribe tranquilizers for perceived uncontrollable than for perceived controllable stress.

The Focus on Process and Temporal Sequence

But why should we not want to aid those with needs that are contingent upon personal actions, and why should we want to help those whose needs are due to uncontrollable factors? Common sense dictates that individuals with needs due to controllable factors are responsible (able-to-respond) and thus must take personal blame, or be accountable, for their plight. Figure 6-4 and the discussion in Chapter 5 indicated that we do not feel sorry for those who fail and are in control of their own destiny. On the contrary, their failures tend to generate anger. But we do feel pity and sympathy for those who fail and are unable to help themselves. Thus, the reason we neglect those with controllable needs may be that this causal perception elicits anger, which in turn evokes neglect. Conversely, we may help those with uncontrollable needs because this perception elicits pity (sympathy), which in turn evokes approach behavior and help. These motivational sequences can be depicted as:

Personal control over the cause of the need → anger → neglect

Lack of personal control over the cause of the need → sympathy → help

A more general depiction of the sequences outlined above is:

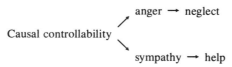

This, of course, is a subset of the even more general sequence of:

Causal attribution → emotion → action

Five investigations have been conducted that not only document the associations between controllability and help giving, but also analyze the affective reactions that intervene between causal thinking and action. These studies permit a fuller examination and test of the attributional conception.

To examine directly to role of affect in helping behavior, I repeated the experiments conducted by Piliavin et al. (1969) and Barnes et al. (1969) in a simulational rather than a real context (Weiner, 1980a, 1980b). In one research investigation, the subjects were presented with the following scenario:

> At about 1:00 in the afternoon you are riding a subway car. There are a number of other individuals in the car and one person is standing, holding on to the center pole. Suddenly, this person staggers forward and collapses. The person is carrying a black cane and apparently is ill. (Alternate form: The person apparently is drunk. He is carrying a liquor bottle wrapped in a brown paper bag and smells of liquor.) (Weiner, 1980a, p. 190)

Subjects then rated the degree to which the cause was perceived as personally controllable, their feelings of sympathy and disgust, and their judged likelihood of helping.

Table 7-2 shows the correlations between the causal, affective, and behavioral judgments. It is evident that there are linkages between control, disgust (anger), and neglect and between lack of control, sympathy, and help. In general, the drunk is reacted to with disgust and neglect, and the ill person with sympathy and help, and drunkenness, but not illness, is considered to be subject to personal control. The helping judgments therefore are in agreement with the helping observed in a real

Table 7-2. Correlations Between the Judgments of Control, Affect, and Help, Including Both the Drunk and Ill Conditions

Variable	2	3	4
1. Control	−.77***	.55**	−.37*
2. Sympathy	—	−.64***	.46**
3. Disgust		—	−.71**
4. Help			—

$*p < .05.$ $**p < .01.$ $***p < .001.$
Note. From *Human Motivation* (p. 194) by B. Weiner, 1980, New York: Holt, Rinehart & Winston. Copyright 1980. Reprinted by permission.

situation, as documented by Piliavin et al. (1969). This lends credibility to the role-playing methodology used in this research.

Further analyses were then conducted relating controllability to help giving with affective reactions partialed out, and relating affect to help giving with the effects of perceived controllability partialed from the analysis. The logic of this procedure is that if the relation between controllability and helping reports is mediated by affective reactions, then taking affect from this relation by means of partial correlation techniques should greatly reduce the magnitude of that association. On the other hand, partialing control from the association between affect and help should minimally reduce that relation if perceived causality is not a mediating variable.

Table 7-3 shows this partial correlation analysis. The first row of Table 7-3 repeats the last column of Table 7-2, showing the relations between control and help, and affects and help, with nothing partialed from these associations. In Row 2, control is taken from the affect-helping linkages. Table 7-3 shows that the correlations are somewhat reduced in magnitude, but remain substantial. In Column 2 of Table 7-3, affects are partialed from the association between control and helping. The data indicate that the magnitude of that relation is reduced to near zero. Hence, the pattern of data suggests a controllability-affective reaction-help (neglect) temporal order in the motivational sequence.

I next undertook a conceptual replication of this study (Weiner, 1980b). Subjects were presented with the following scenario:

> At about 1:00 in the afternoon you are walking through campus and a student comes up to you. He says that you do not know him, but that you are both enrolled in the same class and he has happened to notice you. He asks if you would lend him the class notes from the meetings last week. He indicates that he needs the notes because he was having difficulty with his eyes, a change in type of glasses was required, and during the week he had difficulty seeing because of eye-drops and other treatments. You notice that he is wearing especially dark glasses and has a

Table 7-3. Correlation of Variables with Judgments of Helping, Including Both Drunk and Ill Conditions, With Individual Variables Statistically Partialed From the Analysis

Partialed Variable	2	3	4
1. None	−.37*	.46**	−.71***
2. Control	—	.30	−.66***
3. Sympathy	−.02[a]	—	−.61***
4. Disgust	.04	.01	—

[a] Indicates the correlation between perceptions of control and helping ratings, with sympathy ratings partialed out.

*$p < .05$. **$p < .01$. ***$p < .001$.

Note. From *Human Motivation* (p. 194) by B. Weiner, 1980, New York: Holt, Rinehart & Winston. Copyright 1980. Reprinted by permission.

Table 7-4. Correlations Between the Dependent Variables

Variable	2	3.	4
1. Control	− .54*	.36*	− .40*
2. Sympathy		− .50*	.59*
3. Anger			− .49*
4. Lend			

*p < .001.
Note. From "May I Borrow Your Class Notes? An Attributional Analysis of Judgments of Help-Giving in an Achievement-Related Context" by B. Weiner, 1980, *Journal of Educational Psychology*, 75, p. 679. Copyright 1980. Reprinted by permission.

patch covering one eye. (Alternate form: He needs the notes because, instead of going to class, he went to the beach.) (Weiner, 1980b, p. 677)

The subjects were asked to rate the degree to which the causes were perceived as personally controllable, their feelings of sympathy and anger, and their judged likelihood of helping.

Table 7-4 gives the correlations between the causal, affective, and behavioral judgments. We see the familiar pattern of linkages between control, anger, and neglect (all mean judgments are elevated in the beach condition) and between lack of control, sympathy, and help (all mean judgments elevated in the eye condition).

Again partial correlational analyses were computed, with both perceptions of control and presumed affective reactions held constant. These data are shown in Table 7-5. Across the top row are the correlations between helping and the attributional and affective judgments. In the second row it can be observed that the associations between affect and action are scarcely reduced when perceptions of control are held constant. Conversely, as shown in Column 2 of Table 7-5, the relation between controllability and help is greatly weakened when affect, and sympathy in particular, is

Table 7-5. Correlations Between Lending and Other Dependent Variables, Holding Control or Affect Constant

Partialed Variable	Dependent variable correlated with lending		
	Control	Sympathy	Anger
None	− .40*	.59*	− .49*
Control	—	.48*	− .41*
Sympathy	− .12	—	—
Anger	− .28*	—	—

*p < .001.
Note. From "May I Borrow Your Class Notes? An Attributional Analysis of Judgments of Help-Giving in an Achievement-Related Context" by B. Weiner, 1980, *Journal of Educational Psychology*, 75, p. 680. Copyright 1980. Reprinted by permission.

held constant. In sum, there is a conceptual replication of the Weiner (1980a) study. Going to the beach and getting drunk are genotypically similar, as are illness and eye problems, inasmuch as these causes have identical dimensional representation and therefore relate in an identical manner to affect and behavior.

Among the potential mediating factors not included in the research of Weiner (1980a, 1980b) is the stability of the perceived cause and the effects of future expectancy on help giving. Thus, the complete expectancy-affect analysis in Figure 6-4 was not examined. Meyer and Mulherin (1980), on the other hand, did include expectancy as well as affective variables in their investigation of helping. Their research closely resembles the procedures used by Weiner (1980a, 1980b), but was independently conceived and simultaneously conducted.

Meyer and Mulherin (1980) described hypothetical situations in which an acquaintance was portrayed as asking for financial aid. The reasons for the need of money were manipulated and fit within the eight classifications created by varying the three dimensions of causality. For example, financial aid was said to be required because the acquaintance never liked to work (internal, stable, controllable), or because of conditions of high unemployment (external, unstable, uncontrollable), and so on. Subjects then rated the degree to which they would experience each of 25 affects in these situations, their beliefs about how much the person would require aid in the future, and their likelihood of offering financial assistance.

The affective ratings could be described by two distinct dimensions, labeled anger versus concern (a bipolar dimension) and empathy (sympathy). A path analysis was then constructed to account for the helping judgments (see Figure 7-1). Figure 7-1 indicates that perceived causal control relates positively to anger, negatively to empathy, and negatively with help. Anger, in turn, relates negatively to helping

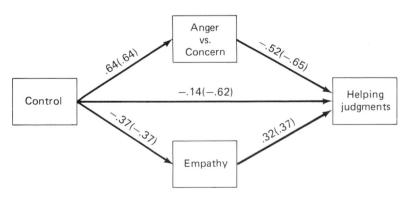

Figure 7-1. Simplified attributional model of helping behavior with results of path analysis. The correlations (in parentheses) and path coefficients were obtained with the variables scored in the controllable, anger, empathy, and high likelihood of helping directions. (From "From Attribution to Helping: An Analysis of the Mediating Effects of Affect on Expectancy" by J. P. Meyer and A. Mulherin, 1980, *Journal of Personality and Social Psychology*, *39*, p. 209. Copyright 1980. Reprinted by permission.

judgments, whereas empathy correlates positively with these judgments. Expectancy had no influence on the behavioral ratings. In sum, the data closely conform to the findings reported by Weiner (1980a, 1980b).

In a follow-up investigation, Betancourt (1983) reached similar conclusions. He demonstrated that empathy and attributional approaches to helping could be integrated within one theoretical framework. Empathy theorists contend that empathy increases emotions such as pity and sympathy, and these affective reactions then promote altruistic behaviors (see, for example, Batson et al., 1981; Coke, Batson, & McDavis, 1978; Hoffman, 1975; Krebs, 1975). Hence, their predictions and findings are entirely consistent with the present approach.

In the tradition of empathy researchers, Betancourt (1983) manipulated the instructional sets given to subjects reading a plea for help. The empathic set instruction asked subjects to "imagine how the person feels about what happened and how it affects his or her life" (Betancourt, 1983, p. 32). On the other hand, an objective set included instructions to attend to the facts and the details of the request. It has been demonstrated by empathy researchers that the former instruction increases empathic reactions (sympathy).

Subjects given these two sets then read a story apparently written by a fellow student. The story explained why he or she recently failed at school. The stories varied the attribution of the cause of the failure and ranged from "going out of town and having fun" (extreme controllability) to "having an accident that required hospitalization" (extreme uncontrollability). After reading one of five vignettes under one of the two empathic set conditions, the perceived controllability of the cause of the failure, affective reactions, and the likelihood of helping were assessed.

The correlations between the control, affect, and behavioral judgments are shown in Table 7-6. The bottom row of Table 7-6 reveals that the pertinent variables were associated with reported willingness to help: An empathic set, uncontrollable causes, and sympathetic emotions all enhanced the stated likelihood of help giving. Figure 7-2 shows the path-analytic model constructed for these data. The model reveals that the manipulated attributions relate to perceived controllability; for example, an accident is perceived as less controllable than a planned vacation. In

Table 7-6. Correlations Among Relevant Variables

Variable	1	2	3
1. Perspective (empathetic set)			
2. Uncontrollability	.19*		
3. Empathic emotion (sympathy)	.41**	.40**	
4. Helping	.31**	.43**	.45**

$*p < .01. **p < .001. N = 150.$
Note. From *Causal Attributions, Empathy, and Emotions as Determinants of Helping Behavior: An Integrative Approach* by H. Betancourt, p. 38. Copyright 1983. Adapted by permission.

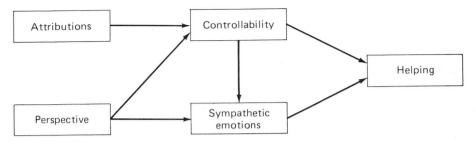

Figure 7-2. Helping behavior as a function of causal attributions for a person's need, a potential helper's psychological perspective, perceived controllability of attributions, and sympathetic emotions. From *Causal Attributions, Empathy, and Emotions as Determinants of
Helping Behavior: An Integrative Approach* by H. Betancourt, 1983, p. 31. Copyright 1983.
Adapted by permission.

addition, an empathic set perspective increases the perceived uncontrollability of
the situation; for example, subjects instructed to think about the feelings of the
needy person perceived the accident situation as more uncontrollable than did subjects instructed merely to collect the facts. Both perceived controllability and
empathic set then influenced empathic reactions (sympathy). Sympathetic reactions, as well as the direct influence of perceived controllability, determined helping
judgments. Note, then, that Weiner (1980b), Meyer and Mulherin (1980), and
Betancourt (1983) all found that controllability does have a direct influence on helping. However, the indirect association between controllability and help, which is
affect mediated, is of far greater importance than is the direct relation between controllability and help.

The final studies in this rather extended section on the attributional determinants
of helping were conducted by Reisenzein (1986). He differentiated five possible
attributional models of helping and then used path-analytic techniques to test these
disparate models. The five are:

1. Eliciting stimuli → perceived controllability ⟨ anger ⟩ help
                                                    ⟨ sympathy ⟩

This is the model most explicitly tested in the prior investigations.

2. Eliciting stimuli → perceived controllability ⟨ anger ⟩———→ help
                                                    ⟨ sympathy ⟩

In this model, there is a direct as well as an indirect path between controllability and
help. This model has received the best support in the prior research studies.

This model adds a path between anger and sympathy. It may be that these affects are mutually inhibitory or hedonically incompatible.

Here the additional paths in Models 2 and 3 are combined.

This final model includes a direct path from the eliciting stimuli to help giving. For example, it may be that falling down in a subway elicits more help than a request for class notes because less "cost" is involved, it is more dramatic, physical needs are associated with stronger cultural norms to help, and so forth.

To test these models of helping, Reisenzein (1986) again made use of a role-playing methodology. The two most prevalent situations examined in past attribution research—a person falling down in a subway and someone requesting class notes— again were presented in vignette form. The reasons for the need were varied in the usual manner (drunk versus ill, and went to the beach versus eye problems), and again the subjects were queried regarding their perceptions of causal controllability, feelings of sympathy and anger, and likelihood of help giving.

The data in the subway scenario displayed the quite reliable drunk-controllable-anger-neglect and ill-uncontrollable-sympathy-help relations. Model 1 significantly fit these data; the added paths depicted in Models 2-4 did not enhance the effectiveness of the model. Thus, a direct path between controllability and help was not supported, nor were the two affects mutually inhibitory. Model 5, however, which added a path between the situation and helping, did slightly improve the fit of the model to the data. This pattern of findings also characterized the class notes scenario, although the inclusion of the path between the eliciting situation and help added relatively little in accounting for the behavioral judgments.

Summary and Conclusion

The research on helping tells a story of increasing sophistication and increasing progression toward the theory shown in Figure 6-4. Studies first manipulated the reason why help was needed but were not guided by attributional concepts. It was documented that different reasons for need, such as drunkenness versus illness, indeed influenced help giving (e.g., Piliavin et al., 1969). Early investigators who did consider causal attributions (Berkowitz, 1969) thought that locus of control was the essential mediating variable. But it was later contended that locus of causality had been confounded with controllability (Barnes et al., 1969); causal controllability was then documented to be a central determinant of helping (Barnes et al., 1969; Weiner, 1980a, 1980b). Next, it was found that the manipulated causes also differentially influence affective reactions of sympathy and anger and that these affective responses directly relate to help giving (Meyer & Mulherin, 1980; Weiner, 1980a, 1980b). Finally, complex path-analytic models were created that more precisely determined the influence of both attributions of control and affective reactions on help (Meyer & Mulherin, 1980; Betancourt, 1983; Reisenzein, 1986).

The reader should recall that the progression of investigations in the achievement domain followed a similar course: The initial investigations were not guided by attributional concepts, whereas in the more recent research the full theory in Figure 6-4 is being examined. The research in the helping domain *perhaps* provides an even better test of the attributional theory than studies in the achievement area, for more of the investigations have been undertaken with path-analytic tools in mind for theoretical testing. As indicated in Chapter 1, this technique permits the investigator to uncover the temporal sequence of a motivational episode. On the other hand, the pertinent research literature is still relatively sparse.

The total body of data that has been reported is inescapably consistent. Controllable causes give rise to neglect, whereas uncontrollable causes of need promote help-giving. Furthermore, controllable causes elicit anger, whereas uncontrollable causes generate sympathy, and affects exert a direct influence on helping. An attributional model of helping therefore takes the following form:

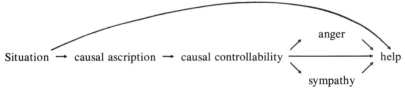

In this model, perceived controllability indirectly influences helping through the mediating affective variables, and a direct path between control and help is included. However, some investigators find that a direct path is not warranted. I suggest that the amount of variance in helping behavior (and helping judgments) that is directly accounted for by thought (attributions) as opposed to emotions will in part depend on the emotion-arousing properties of the situation. It is hypothesized that, as one becomes increasingly involved in a situation, perceptions of controllability will have a lessening direct influence on the decision to help or neglect. On the other hand, as situations become increasingly remote or trivial to an actor, "cold" thoughts will play a large, direct part in helping, with emotions relegated to a less important role.

In addition, it appears quite likely that a direct path from the situation to helping is needed. This path captures the many nonattributional determinants of help giving and embraces concerns such as costs and benefits. This path is included even though it falls beyond the range of attribution theory. It surely is not being argued here that there are only attributional determinants of help giving; helping, like all other behaviors, is overdetermined. Attributions will only account for some part of the pie (albeit an important slice).

Finally, the role that expectancy plays in help-giving (as opposed to help seeking; see Ames & Lau, 1982) remains to be determined (but see Meyer & Mulherin, 1980). It is intuitively reasonable to believe that if there is a very low expectancy that an instrumental action will have an effect, or a low expectancy that the person will require help in the near future, then it is likely that help will be minimized. It is of interest to note that, in the achievement area, expectancy has received great attention, whereas few investigations have directly taken affect into account. On the other hand, in the helping domain affects have been quite prominent, whereas expectancy has been relatively ignored. These asymmetries need correction—one must consider the passion in achievement striving and reason in moral behavior, as Kant initially proposed (see Chapter 1).

Exploring Other Domains for Attributional Paths

Achievement striving and helping behavior stand out because they are characterized by systematic literatures guided by attributional concepts. Other areas of study also have been guided by Figure 6-4, but the pertinent research literature is relatively sparse and the theory has been less fully utilized. Nonetheless, these topics of study offer important evidence for the generality of attributional analyses and provide avenues for future researchers. I now turn to three research domains demonstrating the efficacy of attributional thinking: parole decisions, smoking cessation, and reactions to airline flight delays. These areas have been selected for discussion because the research has been guided by the attribution-affect-action and attribution-expectancy-action sequences at the heart of Figure 6-4.

Parole Decisions

A recent case of a positive parole decision for a killer has attained much publicity. A graduate student in mathematics at Stanford murdered his dissertation chairman. The graduate student stated that for 19 years he had tried to obtain his Ph.D. and was prevented from reaching this goal by his chairman. After serving time in jail, the offender was offered parole on the grounds that he had been a model prisoner. But one of the conditions of parole was that the prisoner agree that he intends to lead a crime-free life and that he "would not kill again." Instead, the prisoner would only confirm that it was "unlikely" he would kill again, but he could not be certain given the prior wrongdoings of the math faculty. One can imagine the reactions of the other math professors at Stanford when reading this statement. Following a great university as well as public outcry, the offer of parole was revoked and the criminal had to serve the remainder of his sentence. He has now been released, and the public and the Department of Mathematics at Stanford are waiting with much anxiety, hoping that nothing untoward will happen.

Parole decisions and the related issue of criminal sentencing have been the subject of much philosophical discussion and psychological research. There appear to be two major rationales or motivations for criminal punishment: behavioral control and retribution (see Miller & Vidmar, 1981). Behavioral control is present and forward-looking and is concerned with elimination of the antisocial behavior; retribution is more backward-looking, concerned with redressing a previously committed injustice. Often punishment for a crime serves both these functions, inasmuch as it can inhibit future antisocial actions as well as provide retribution for the past wrongdoings. However, this double function need not be intended by the punisher, who might merely be interested in behavioral control and indeed is against an "eye-for-an-eye" philosophy, or conversely, may be solely interested in revenge without concern for future actions.

Criminal sentencing and parole judgments are complex decisions, determined by a wide array of factors ranging from social and economic conditions to individual differences in the personalities of the judges. Psychologists working in this area, particularly Carroll and Payne (1976, 1977a, 1977b) have documented that causal ascriptions, or the perceived reasons why a crime was committed, have an important impact on criminal justice. The effect of attributions is complex and is dependent on a variety of factors, such as the subject population being examined and the intended purpose of the punishment. Nonetheless, a role of attributions is unmistakably evident and can be best understood from the theoretical position presented in Figure 6-4.

Table 7-7. Causes of Criminal Offenses as Perceived by Parole Officers

Cause	Frequency
Alcohol abuse problem	19
Drug abuse problem	15
Long-term greed for money	9
Sudden desire for money	7
Precipitated by victim	7
Influence of associates	6
Domestic problems	4
Lack of control	4
Mental problems	4
Criminal easily influenced	3
Environment	2
Immaturity	2
Aimlessness	1

Note. From "Cognitive Social Psychology in Court and Beyond" by J. S. Carroll and R. L. Wiener, 1982, in A. H. Hastorf and A. M. Isen (Eds.), *Cognitive Social Psychology*, p. 227. New York: Elsevier/North Holland. Copyright 1982. Reprinted by permission.

Table 7-8. Total Number of Statements by Type and Position in Protocol

Statement Type	Position in Protocol				
	First	Second	Third	Fourth	Total
Severity of crime	8	6	9	10	33
Risk of future	15	13	22	46	96
Institutional adjustment	10	32	25	28	95
Parole decision	5	13	18	41	77
Treatment	5	16	33	92	146
Questions	26	43	41	52	162
Attributions	6	43	66	58	173
Total	75	156	214	327	782

Note. From "Judgments About Crime and the Criminal: A Model and a Method for Investigating Parole Decisions" by J. S. Carroll and J. W. Payne, 1977a, in B. D. Sales (Ed.), *Perspectives in Law and Psychology* (Vol. 1), p. 234. New York: Plenum. Copyright 1977. Reprinted by permission.

Attributions in Parole Decision Processes. For many years, public opinion polls have inquired about the causes of crime. These polls typically elicit a diversity of causes, including parental upbringing and the breakdown of family life, bad environments, the leniency of laws, drugs, mental illness, and poverty and unemployment. Carroll and Wiener (1982) noted that:

> Sociopolitical ideologies provide different ideas about crime drawn from markedly different viewpoints on society and individuals. The conservative political right proposes that the bulk of serious crime is produced by people who have had defective upbringing, inadequate moral and religious training. . . . As a result, they lack self-control and care little about society or other people. . . . In contrast, the liberal political left proposes that inequities in wealth, power, and privilege lead the victims of society to commit crimes out of need or frustration . . . Those individuals who commit crimes without adequate justification are usually disturbed or sick people who need help rather than punishment. (pp. 226–227)

The perceived causes of crime have been studied not only among laypeople but also among parole board members. Immediately following parole board meetings, Carroll (1978; see also Carroll & Wiener, 1982) asked the members of the board their opinions about the "underlying cause for the offense committed." The reasons given are shown in Table 7-7. It is evident from the table that substance abuse (drugs and alcohol), monetary lust, and other environmental and personality factors are perceived as the major causes of crime.

Opinion polls and questions directed toward parole board members are reactive attributional methodologies—causes are elicited in response to direct questions. To document spontaneous attributional search in parole procedures, Carroll and Payne (1977a, 1977b) asked expert parole decision makers to "think out loud" as they were reaching a parole decision. Their statements were then coded into categories, which are shown in Table 7-8. Table 7-8 reveals that attributions were the largest category describing thought content, representing 22% (173 statements) of all coded thoughts.

Figure 7-3. Temporal sequence of the parole decision process.

In sum, it has been established that laypeople as well as parole experts seek to know the causes of crime and can provide all kinds of plausible accounts. In the case of the parole decision maker, attributions appear to be of vital importance when making a decision regarding the fate of the criminal. But how specifically does a causal attribution influence parole judgments?

Attributions in Parole Decisions. Carroll and Wiener (1982), guided by the prior thinking of Carroll and Payne (1977a, 1977b), conceived of the parole decision process in the manner shown in Figure 7-3, which indicates that case information, such as past criminal record and the severity of the crime, results in an attribution regarding the cause of the crime. This attribution is then placed within a three-dimensional scheme differentiating causes according to their locus, intentionality, and stability. The locus and the intentionality of the cause result in judgments about blame and deserved punishment. This is the backward-looking, retribution function of a criminal sentence. The stability of the cause of the crime determines the risk of the criminal to society, for a stable cause connotes that the criminal is likely to engage in the same antisocial behavior in the future, necessitating continued incarceration. This is the forward-looking, behavioral control function of a criminal sentence. Blame and risk, in turn, or "deserved" punishment and social protection, are postulated to determine the judgment of the parole officer. It is evident that this scheme is entirely compatible with the more complete attributional theory that I have been advocating in this book.

To test whether Figure 7-3 captures the thinking of laypeople and parole decision officers, Carroll and Payne (1977b) constructed eight scenarios that varied the causes of crimes according to their locus, stability, and intentionality (see Table 7-9). Then subjects, including both college students and members of parole boards, made judgments about these crimes, including the risk of the person to society, the deserved punishment, and the criminal sentence they would recommend. The data regarding criminal sentence length, determined by students and parole officials, (Table 7-10) reveal both substantial agreement and important disagreement between the students and the parole officers. For the students, the locus and stability dimensions of causality contributed to the sentence decision, and their effects were additive. Crimes with an internal rather than external locus and perceived stable rather than unstable causes increased sentence length (see also Barnett, 1981). This was in accord with expectations and strongly support the parole process as conceived in Figure 7-3. The pattern of results for the parole officers was similar, but greater complexity was exhibited. Table 7-10 reveals that the effects of the causal dimen-

Table 7-9. Cause Manipulations

Locus	Stability	
	Stable	Unstable
Intentional		
Internal	Interviews indicated that he had thought about this situation for some time and had developed several plans.	Interviews indicated that he had made a momentary decision to do it and had deliberately ignored the consequences.
External	Interviews indicated that he had been under constant intense pressure from his elderly mother and his family to do things for them, make more money, and give up his free time.	Interview indicated that his wife had told him without warning that she had decided to divorce him.
Unintentional		
Internal	Interviews indicated that he had an aggressive nature and exhibits many hostile feelings toward society in general. He had difficulty following social rules.	Interviews indicated that he was in a depressed mood, had been drinking, and was overcome by impulse.
External	Interviews indicated that he could not find a good job because his skill had been replaced by mechanization. The circumstances around the crime had been acting on him for some time.	Interviews indicated that he had been temporarily laid off work due to economic situations. At the time of the act, circumstances seemed to come together to make it happen.

Note. From "Judgments About Crime and the Criminal: A Model and a Method for Investigating Parole Decisions" by J. S. Carroll and J. W. Payne, 1977a, in B. D. Sales (Ed.), *Perspectives in Law and Psychology* (Vol. 1), p. 201. New York: Plenum. Copyright 1977. Reprinted by permission.

Table 7-10. Effects of Causal Locus and Causal Stability on Sentencing, for College Students and Parole Board Members

Causal Classification	Subjects	
	Students	Parole Board Members
Internal-stable	9.1	5.9
Internal-unstable	6.6	3.1
External-stable	5.2	3.7
External-unstable	3.6	4.0

Note. From "Crime Seriousness, Recidivism Risk, and Causal Attributions in Judgments of Prison Term by Students and Experts" by J. S. Carroll and J. W. Payne, 1977b, *Journal of Applied Psychology, 62,* p. 600. Copyright 1977. Adapted by permission.

sions on sentence decision were interactive rather than additive: Internal and stable causes exacerbated the sentence; the judgments in the other three conditions did not significantly differ.

Parole experts also use information ignored by college students. For example, they know that murderers tend not to recommit murder when released from prison and therefore are less severe in their reactions to this crime than are college students. In addition, subsequent research revealed that parole officials primarily are interested in social risk, leaving the issue of punishment to the judges. Thus, the actual parole decision process is less well captured in Figure 7-3 than are the naive judgments of college students. Nonetheless, parole processes, and perceptions of what the parole decision should be by the lay public, clearly fall within the range of attributional analyses and again demonstrate the generality and the heurism of an attributional approach to motivation. What remain to be incorporated in the study of parole decisions are emotional processes, particularly the anger and the pity reactions to the crime. Then the full expectancy-affect theory can be tested in criminal-sentencing as well as in parole-granting contexts.

Smoking Cessation

The search for attributional homes can lead to some unanticipated neighborhoods. Helping behavior has been one of these unexpected communities, and parole decisions also seemed, at least at first glance, to be beyond the range of convenience of attributional analyses. Another of these apparently strange places where one finds attribution theory is the topic of smoking or, more specifically, the cessation of smoking. When an intention to quit smoking has been established and then has not been fulfilled, a "failure" is experienced. Goldstein et al. (1984) nicely elaborated this point:

> Being a nonsmoker requires repeated practice, and it is likely that the learning process will include some mistakes. In this sense, we are defining smoking cessation (and addictive behavior in general) as an "achievement task." I am making the point of defining smoking cessation as an achievement task because such an approach opens up a rich body of social psychological theory and research on attributional processes and achievement motivation which we can use to try to better understand and prevent our most persistent problem with behavioral change—relapse. (p. 1)

According to Marlatt (1985), an abstinence violation effect (AVE) follows an initial slip when attempting to refrain from some substance. The greater the AVE, the greater the probability of a relapse into substance abuse. The magnitude of the AVE, in turn, is hypothesized to be determined by causal attributions. Marlatt (1985) reasoned as follows:

> An increased AVE is postulated to occur when the individual attributes the cause of a relapse to internal, stable, and global factors ... the intensity of the AVE is decreased, however, when the individual attributes the cause of the lapse to external, unchangeable, and specific factors. (pp. 179–180)

Note that again causal dimensions play the key role in providing for theoretical generality.

To test this hypothesis, 36 smokers indicated their attributions of causality following initial relapse when attempting to quit (Goldstein et al., 1984). They specified the major cause of their relapse and then answered questions regarding the dimensional placement of the cause on the locus, stability, and globality dimensions. A single AVE score was determined by adding the three attribution dimension ratings. It was found that relapsers had significantly higher AVEs than "slippers" (those who had temporary relapses but then continued with their abstinence). Further analyses revealed significant differences on all three causal dimensions, with relapsers making more internal, stable, and global attributions than "slippers."

From the perspective of Figure 6-4, stable and global attributions result in lower expectancies of future success than do unstable and specific ascriptions. This, in turn, should result in a greater likelihood of a relapse. Internal attributions reduce the self-esteem of the failing person; this reduced self-esteem would also interfere with the difficult task of remaining free from the undesired substance. Hence, the findings reported by Goldstein et al. (1984) are entirely consistent with attributional thinking, although the reported investigation clearly does not fully utilize the attributional conception.

A related yet distinguishable attributional approach to smoking cessation has been suggested by Eiser et al. (in press). These investigators contend that the decision facing a would-be quitter is not whether to smoke or quit, but whether to smoke or *try* to quit. This focuses attention on peoples' predictions of their own success at the difficult task of quitting.

Guided by these ideas, Eiser et al. (in press) asked a national sample of 20,000 respondents, "Why do you think so many smokers fail when they try to give up smoking?" The response alternatives were classified according to their locus and stability and were used to create internality and stability indexes. The respondents also were asked how confident they personally felt about giving up smoking and if they intended to try to quit. The correlational results revealed that respondents attributing the failure of others to stable factors had a lower expectancy of personal success at giving up smoking and a weaker intention to make such an attempt.

About 1 year later these respondents again were contacted and asked if they had tried to stop smoking and if they had succeeded. It was found that persons reporting that they tried to stop had a higher expectancy of success (confidence) 1 year earlier than did those who had not tried, and also a stronger intention to stop smoking. A simplified path analysis of these data (Figure 7-4) shows that stable (but not internal) attributions influence confidence; confidence, in turn, relates to the intention to try to stop and to actual behavior (smoking cessation).

In concluding, Eiser et al. noted that, "The concepts of self-perception, attribution and expectancy are of central importance within the literature on social cognition, but what has often been lacking has been a demonstration that these can have long-term behavioral consequences." In their investigation, long-term consequences were indeed demonstrated.

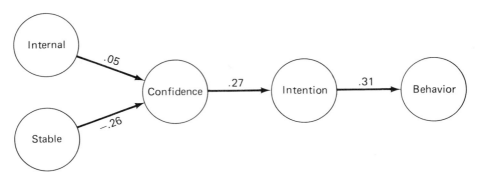

Figure 7-4. Path analysis for the determinants of smoking cessation. From "Trying to Stop Smoking: Effects of Perceived Addiction, Attributions for Failure and Expectancy of Success" by J. R. Eiser et al., in press, *Journal of Behavioral Medicine*. (In press). Adapted by permission.

In sum, data on smoking cessation (and presumably other addictions as well) lend themselves nicely to our attributional analysis. It can be seen that the theory therefore has the potentiality of great practical importance. It is also evident that achievement failure, helping behavior, parole decisions, and smoking cessation can be subject to the same genotypic analysis. Recognition of this similarity, it is hoped, will lead to fuller use of this conception, so that the analyses of smoking cessation will be broadened to include important affective reactions such as shame and guilt.

Reactions to Flight Delays

The topics thus far examined when considering the theoretical focus and the range of attribution theory—achievement strivings, helping behavior, parole decisions, and smoking cessation—are quite important to the self and to society. But attributional analyses also can be of value in understanding more trivial issues; indeed such theoretical excursions greatly increase the credibility of a theory. (The reader may recall that dissonance theory in part developed from an attempt to explain the increased certainty in their beliefs expressed by members of a cult group after a significant prediction had been disconfirmed.) One such relatively inconsequential topic that has been examined from an attributional perspective is reactions to airline delays (see Folkes, 1985b). Folkes (1985b) noted:

> Anyone doubting the diversity in consumers' reactions to the same product problem should go to an airport and watch passengers waiting for a delayed flight. A glance around the departure gate reveals considerable variation in how consumers react to problems—some fume, others are unperturbed. The reader may even be struck by the diversity in his or her own responses to flight delays—sometimes grousing at the gate agent, other times being quite complaisant. (p. 1)

To explain this response variation, Folkes called upon attribution theory. A delayed flight represents a negative outcome. It also might be unexpected, and often it is important to arrive punctually at one's destination. Hence, the delay of one's flight should elicit attributional search to determine why the takeoff has been postponed.

At times the reasons for a flight delay are evident, as when there is a terrible storm or a labor strike. On other occasions, information about less evident causes might be provided to passengers, as when an attendant announces over a loudspeaker that there has been a mechanical failure, or that some connecting flight has been held up. On many other occasions, however, the delayed person is left uncertain and reaches his or her own conclusion regarding the source of the delay.

In her research, Folkes (1985b) asked passengers who were delayed at least 15 minutes why their plane was late in taking off. The responses to the query, shown in Table 7-11, reveal that mechanical failure is perceived as the most prevalent cause of delay. Other important attributions for the temporary postponement included actions or inactions by airline personnel (e.g., poor management, carelessness, lateness in reporting for work, etc.), the late arrival of other planes or passengers, and bad weather.

Folkes also asked these delayed passengers to dimensionalize the cause of the problem on the stability and controllability dimensions (locus was irrelevant in this context, as passengers do not blame themselves for the delay). She also gathered information about the importance of the flight, anger reactions, whether the waiting people would fly again with this particular airline, and if they planned to initiate a complaint.

On the basis of studies already reviewed, it was hypothesized that important outcomes perceived as caused by controllable factors would exacerbate anger. Furthermore, causes perceived as stable were also expected to increase anger (recall from Chapter 5 that stability magnifies particular affective reactions). Anger, in turn, was predicted to result in an intention not to fly again with that carrier and the instigation of complaint actions. These linkages are shown in Figure 7-5. The results of this investigation, based on questionnaires given to nearly 100 persons, are also shown

Table 7-11. Attributions for Flight Delay

Reason	Percentage Reporting Reason
Airline personnel	17
Other passengers	10
Previous flight departure delayed	14
Mechanical problems	33
Weather	7
Don't know	19

Note. From *Predicting Reactions to Service Problems: The View From the Departure Lounge* by V. S. Folkes. Copyright 1985. Reprinted by permission.

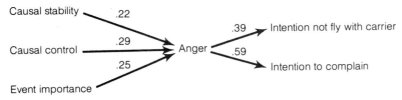

Figure 7-5. Antecedents and consequences of anger in a delayed-flight context.

in Figure 7-5. As predicted, stable and controllable causes (e.g., poor management) of an important event resulted in greater anger than did perceived unstable, uncontrollable causes (e.g., bad weather) of an unimportant delay. The strength of the path coefficients between these three predictors and reports of anger are included in Figure 7-5. In addition, anger influenced both the intention not to purchase tickets again with the responsible airline and the intention to initiate a complaint. The correlations between reported emotion and anticipated action average to about $r =$ .50. As was also found in the helping literature, there were direct but less significant relations between causal controllability and both anticipated actions, as well as between causal stability and future purchase intention (see Table 7-12). It is consistent with attributional thinking to presume that the future purchase intention is related to causal stability because of the mediating influence of the expectancy of future delays. Unfortunately, as is also true in most helping studies, expectancy was not assessed in this investigation.

In sum, the picture is very consistent with the findings in the helping domain and with the general attributional theory being proposed (although this study does not have the path-analytic sophistication of the more recent help-related research). Causal ascriptions concerning why a flight is held up impact on anger as a function of perceived controllability, and anger influences subsequent reports about action.

Table 7-12. Path-Analytic Results

Dependent Variable	Explanatory Variable	Path Coefficient[a]	R²%
Anger	Control	.29	32%
	Importance	.25	
	Stability	.22	
Repurchase intentions	Anger	.39	46%
	Stability	.28	
	Control	.19	
Propensity to complain	Anger	.59	48%
	Control	.18	

[a] All paths are significant at $p < .01$.

Note. From *Predicting Reactions to Service Problems: The View From the Departure Lounge* by V. S. Folkes. Copyright 1985. Reprinted by permission.

This is the usual thinking-feeling-acting sequence at the very heart of the attributional approach.

As summarized by Folkes (1985b):

> The attributional model accounted for almost half of the repurchase and complaining variance. This is substantial . . . considering that only attributions for delays were examined . . . The amount of variance accounted for . . . is also encouraging considering that a non-laboratory setting's reduced control generally produces lower quality of data. (p. 17)

Of course, one might counter that behavior was not assessed, as in the Eiser et al. investigation. Nevertheless, Eiser did show (as have many others) that intentions do relate to actual behavior.

Folkes (1985b) went on to give some advice to the airlines:

> Attributions' effect is important for firms because many determinants of consumer reactions are not amenable to marketers' interventions. For example, firms can do little to change personality variables such as assertiveness or aggressiveness, which influence complaining. Firms can, however, provide explanations for why products fail, excusing their actions. For example . . . an airline can explain that bad weather forced the late departure, emphasizing the lack of control and unstable occurrence. (p. 19)

This is very close to the naive psychology used by individuals when they offer excuses for why they have come late for an appointment (see Chapter 5).

Extensions Into Clinical Psychology

Inasmuch as attribution theory in part addresses reactions to failure, or nonattainment of a goal, it comes as no surprise that it is directly relevant to some issues shared by clinical psychologists. This was documented in the previous chapter when examining attribution-change programs for individuals making maladaptive ascriptions for achievement failure. Two very popular clinical applications of attribution theory involve reactions to rape and the determinants of depression. But there is controversy and uncertainty in these areas regarding the usefulness of the attributional approach. Critics of attributional analyses are especially to be found in the depression literature. In addition, the theory has been neither fully nor correctly utilized in these research areas, in part because the pertinent studies have also been guided by other conceptual systems.

Coping With Rape

It has been documented that although self-blame is a positive predictor of coping with a severe accident, it also is a precursor of low self-esteem and perhaps depression. Janoff-Bulman (1979) seems to have successfully resolved this paradox by pointing out that two types of self-blame need to be distinguished: behavioral self-blame and characterological self-blame (see also Chapter 4). She stated:

> In the case of rape, for example, a woman can blame herself for having walked down a street alone at night or for having let a particular man into her apartment (behavioral blame), or she can blame herself for being "too trusting and unable to say no" or a "careless person who is unable to stay out of trouble" [characterological blame]. (Janoff-Bulman, 1979, p. 1799)

Janoff-Bulman (1979) went on to explain how this distinction relates to the conception of motivation being advocated in this book:

> This . . . corresponds to the distinctions drawn by Weiner and his colleagues in their scheme of attributions in the area of achievement. In attributing failure to oneself (internal attribution) one can point to his/her own lack of ability or effort, attributions that have very different implications for perceived control. Individuals who make an attribution to poor ability believe that there is little they can do to control the situation and succeed, for ability is stable and relatively unchangeable. Effort attributions, on the other hand, will lead one to believe that as long as he/she tries harder, he/she will be able to control outcomes in a positive manner. (p. 1799)

The differentiation between characterological and behavioral self-blame has been applied to the study of such central life events as reactions to rape (Janoff-Bulman, 1979), depression (Peterson, Schwartz, & Seligman, 1981), and unwanted pregnancy (Major et al., 1985). Research investigators studying these experiences report evidence substantiating the two types of self-blaming tendencies. For example, Janoff-Bulman was able to gather attributional data from 38 rape victims. She found that 74% of these women partially blamed themselves for the rape. Of these, nearly 70% blamed their behavior (e.g., "I shouldn't have let someone I didn't know into the house," "I shouldn't have been out that late"). Conversely, about 20% blamed themselves characterologically (e.g., "I'm a weak person," "I'm too naive and gullible"). There is very little evidence, however, concerning the differential consequences of these divergent blaming tendencies. In one study involving self-ratings of depression, Janoff-Bulman (1979) reported that negative outcomes, such as interpersonal rejection, were believed to be more avoidable in the future by people classified as high, as opposed to low, in behavioral self-blame.

In related research using a population of women about to undergo an abortion, Major et al. (1985) found evidence of self-blame for the pregnancy. Of these women, 96% blamed some aspect of their behavior (which seems more reasonable for pregnancy than for rape), whereas 57% made some attributions to their character. This replicated the preponderance of behavioral self-blame also reported by Janoff-Bulman. Furthermore, women who were classified as high in characterological self-blame for their pregnancy coped significantly less well immediately following the abortion (i.e., had more physical complaints, were in a worse mood, expected greater negative consequences, and were more depressed) than women who were low in characterological self-blame. The differences between the self-blaming groups were also reported 3 weeks after the abortion, although they were much less evident.

In sum, the distinction between characterological and behavioral self-blame is logical and quite consistent with attributional thinking. It is an important differentiation to make among those who do self-blame, surely as critical as the separation of ability and effort in the achievement domain. However, from my perspective, and this was not unrecognized by Janoff-Bulman (1979), the typology contrasting characterological and behavioral self-blame blurs or ignores the dimensions of causality. Characterological blame, just as an ability or a trait attribution, is internal, stable, and uncontrollable. Behavioral blame, on the other hand, corresponds to an effort attribution and is internal, unstable, and controllable. The lack of separation of these three dimensions weakens the value of the overly encompassing blaming classification. In addition, the dependent variables in the research investigations have, for the most part, not been theoretically derived, thus making predictions less certain or meaningful. Hypotheses regarding reactions to rape or unwanted pregnancy should include expectations of future negative occurrences in the sexual domain and affective reactions, such as shame versus guilt or anger versus sympathy from others, because the blaming classification includes differences on both the stability and the controllability dimensions. These aspects of reaction to rape or pregnancy have not been examined. I believe that studies in these areas from an attributional perspective could benefit by closer adherence to their attributional roots.

Depression

I have great trepidation about writing this section, for the relevant attributional literature is abundant, and the general investigations and theoretical discussions of depression are legion. Hence, my goal is merely to introduce the best known attributional approach to depression, indicate in what ways it is similar to and differs from the theory shown in Figure 6-4, and point out some theoretical shortcomings as well as some criticisms voiced by depression theorists. I will conclude that one cannot expect to explain or predict depression using attributional concepts alone, so that nonconfirmation of predictions does not make a negative statement about attribution theory per se. However, I do think that attributional analysis can add to the understanding of some depressive disorders and could be particularly useful in shedding light on demoralization and despondency among those not clinically depressed.

The Attributional Analysis of Learned Helplessness. Three quite similar and apparently independently formulated attributional theories of depression were published in the late 1970s (Abramson et al., 1978; Litman-Adizes, 1978; Miller & Norman, 1979). Thus, an attributional approach was in the air during this period; it might be said that its time had come. Of these conceptions, the one formulated by Abramson et al. (1978) has attracted the most attention. Hence, I will restrict my discussion to this theory.

The Abramson et al. conception was presented as a reformulation of a theory of "learned helplessness" introduced by Seligman (1975; see also Chapter 6). That theory conceived of helplessness as a consequence of perceptions of a noncontingency between one's responses and desired outcomes. More specifically, it was argued that if the probability of a desired outcome is conceived as not increased by one's actions, then helplessness results. A high expectancy of noncontingency (help-lessness), in turn, was postulated to result in cognitive, motivational, and behavioral deficits, which are the components of a general syndrome labeled "depression." The theory therefore can be represented as:

$$\text{Noncontingency} \rightarrow \begin{array}{c} \text{expectations of} \\ \text{future noncontingency} \end{array} \rightarrow \begin{array}{c} \text{symptoms of} \\ \text{helplessness (depression)} \end{array}$$

The so-called reformulated theory of helplessness gave causal attributions a central place. It was contended:

> We argue that when a person finds that he is helpless, he asks *why* he is helpless. The causal attribution he makes then determines the generality and chronicity of help-lessness deficits as well as his later self-esteem. (Abramson et al., 1978, p. 50)

The theory therefore was expanded to:

$$\text{Noncontingency} \rightarrow \begin{array}{c} \text{attributions for} \\ \text{noncontingency} \end{array} \rightarrow \begin{array}{c} \text{expectations} \\ \text{of future} \\ \text{noncontingency} \end{array} \rightarrow \begin{array}{c} \text{symptoms of} \\ \text{helplessness} \\ \text{(depression)} \end{array}$$

Both Seligman's (1975) original conception and the reformulated theory "hold the expectation of noncontingency to be the crucial determinant of the symptoms of learned helplessness" (Abramson et al., 1978, p. 52). However, the attribution-enriched conception spells out in greater detail the determinants of expectancy. In addition, the reformulated theory is able to suggest distinctions that were beyond the capability of the earlier helplessness conception.

According to Abramson et al., the attribution for a response-outcome noncontingency can be classified on three dimensions of causality: locus, stability, and globality. The consequences of these attributions have been discussed throughout this book and are linked respectively with esteem-related affects and the temporal and situational generality of expectancy.

Abramson et al. used the locus dimension of causality to distinguish personal from universal helplessness. Personal helplessness corresponds to an internal attribution for perceived noncontingency and lowers self-esteem (as noted in Chapter 5). This is an important relation because many theorists regard low self-esteem as a major symptom of depression. Universal helplessness, on the other hand, corresponds to an external perception of causality and is based on the presumption that other persons in this situation also would not enhance their likelihood of goal attainment through personal responses. For example, Abramson et al. suggested that parents of a child with leukemia often experience universal, rather than personal, helplessness. Both types of perceived noncontingency, however, will result in passivity, negative beliefs about the future, and general negative effect.

The stability and globality dimensions of causality influence the expectancy of future noncontingency and therefore have implications for the chronicity and the generality of helplessness. The more stable and global the perceived cause of non-contingency, the more likely it is that the noncontingency will be expected in the future, and the greater the variety of situational cues that also will elicit perceptions of noncontingency. Inasmuch as expectations of a lack of covariation between responses and outcomes determines helplessness (depression), the linkages between causal dimensions and expectancy play key parts in this theory.

Abramson et al. (1978) summarize their attributional approach to depression as follows:

1. Depression consists of four classes of deficits: motivational, cognitive, self-esteem, and affective.
2. When highly desired outcomes are believed improbable or highly aversive outcomes are believed probable, and the individual expects that no response in his repertoire will change their likelihood, (helplessness) depression results.
3. The generality of the depressive deficits will depend on the globality of the attribution for helplessness, the chronicity of the depression deficits will depend on the stability of the attribution for helplessness, and whether self-esteem is lowered will depend on the internality of the attribution for helplessness. (p. 68)

Comparison with Other Attributional Conceptions. It is immediately evident that the theory formulated by Abramson et al. has much in common with the earlier conceptions of motivation I proposed (Weiner et al., 1971, Weiner; 1972), although some differences with prior theories as well as with the current conception in Figure 6-4 are also evident. The most obvious similarity is the postulation of an attribution-expectancy-behavior sequence. That is, the structures of the theories are identical. Second, Abramson et al. agree that it is not the specific attribution that is of importance, but rather its dimensional representation. Third, causal dimensions are linked with both expectancy and esteem-related affects. These very basic similarities exceed in importance any differences between the Abramson et al. conception and the one I had constructed.

As indicated above, however, there are theoretical differences, and some are rather major. Concerning causal dimensions, Abramson et al. introduced the dimension of globality into the psychological literature. I have yet to fully accept this as a basic property of causes (see Chapter 3), although it must be seriously considered. Globality may prove especially important in the understanding of depression, for in this disorder cross-situational generality of expectancies could be of special concern.

On the other hand, Abramson et al. did not posit a controllability dimension, although they stated such a dimension is "logically orthogonal to the Internal × Global × Stability dimensions. . . and as such is a candidate for a 2 × 2 × 2 × 2 table of attributions" (p. 62). However, this treatment of controllability would be inconsistent with their theory. Perceived noncontingency implies uncontrollability; that is, uncontrollability is treated in the same way that I treat failure or a negative outcome. Individuals make attributions for uncontrollability in the Abramson et al. conception (see Cutrona, Russell, & Jones, 1985).

Yet from the summary by Abramson et al. reproduced above it can be concluded that noncontingency is not a sufficient condition for helplessness—there must be a failure to obtain a desired goal or a failure to avoid an undesired goal. Hence, again there appears to be a confusion between noncontingency and failure. As currently conceived, helplessness theory presumes that if one fails because of a lack of effort (that is, there is perceived contingency between responses and outcomes but nonattainment of a goal), then helplessness (and therefore depression) cannot follow.

Finally, the reformulated theory, just like the original theory proposed by Seligman (1975), is remiss in not addressing the full variety of affects. Inasmuch as controllability is a determinant of guilt, and guilt is often considered an essential characteristic of depression, the addition of a controllability dimension might prove quite beneficial (providing that attributions were made for outcomes rather than for noncontingencies—the latter imply noncontrollability and therefore exclude the possibility of guilt). Other affects central to various theories of depression, such as shame and anger, cannot be incorporated into the reformulated theory. And it is unclear what causes sadness, a major characteristic of depression. In Figure 6-4 sadness is explicitly linked to a negative outcome. Abramson et al. seem to relate sadness to perceptions of noncontingency, but this is empirically (and introspectively) invalid, for the reception of a noncontingent reward (e.g., my rich uncle leaving me $1 million in his will) does not produce negative affect.

Is Depression Amenable to an Attributional Analysis? In the previous paragraph I noted that the reformulated theory implies that lack-of-effort ascriptions for failure cannot result in helplessness and, therefore, depression. This raises the broader issue of whether helplessness is a necessary condition for depression. Might one feel depressed following a stressful event that was controlled, such as a divorce? The answer to this question appears to be yes. The depression literature documents a myriad of antecedents to the onset of depression, with the main determinants being major life stresses, accompanied by so-called vulnerability factors such as lack of social support (see review in Oatley & Bolton, 1985). Hence, it can be concluded that causal perceptions are not necessary antecedents for the experience of depression. It would therefore seem unreasonable to attempt to predict onset of depression given only data regarding perceptions of noncontingencies and expectancies of future noncontingencies.

Given that one cannot confidently predict depression from attributional data alone, the next question to ask is whether causal beliefs add anything to knowledge about, and predictions of, depression. This has proven to be a very difficult query to answer. First, even if so-called maladaptive attributions (internal, stable, and global) for either failure or noncontingency are associated with depression, it then must be demonstrated that these beliefs precede the onset of depression rather than being caused by it (see Brewin, 1985). And one must ask the degree to which the perceived noncontingency (failure) has to be present and for what events, how many maladaptive attributions are needed to induce the onset of depression, and what attributional dimensions are of crucial importance (see Anderson & Arnoult, 1985). Finally, research in this area is difficult to conduct; most frequently college populations are used for testing hypotheses, but college students are rarely clinically depressed, thus making generalizations from this sample to full-blown clinical depression problematic.

The data that are available regarding the contribution of causal beliefs to predictions of depression are not definitive. Perhaps the most extensive studies have been conducted by Hammen and her colleagues (e.g., Cochran & Hammen, 1985). They find little support for an attribution-depression linkage, a conclusion shared by others (see Coyne & Gotlib, 1983). Many, however, believe that causal attributions do explain some of the variance in predictions of depression (see Anderson & Arnoult, 1985; Cochran & Hammen, 1985). That is, stable, internal, and/or global attributions for stressful events do correlate with some indexes of depression, albeit weakly. This accomplishment, even if weak, should not be dismissed.

In part because of the correlational nature of much of this research, which then does not unambiguously permit conclusions about the direction of an attribution-depression relation, an Attributional Style Questionnaire has been developed (Metalsky, Abramson, Seligman, Semmel, & Peterson, 1982; Peterson & Seligman, 1984; see Chapter 6). This scale presents hypothetical positive and negative outcomes, and respondents indicate their attributions for these events (note that attributions are assessed for outcomes, rather than for noncontingencies, which is inconsistent with the theory). Internal, global, and stable attributions for failure (and external, specific, and unstable attributions for success?) are believed to be precursors of depression. The development of such a scale gives rise to the hope that individuals can be identified who later will develop depressive symptoms. However, development of the scale has been marred by psychometric inadequacies (see Cutrona et al., 1985), and there is little evidence that attributions have cross-situational generality. For example, attributions for failure in achievement settings do not relate to attributions for rejection in affiliative contexts. Similar problems have been faced and not overcome in locus-of-control research, which resulted in the development of specific locus-of-control scales (Lefcourt, Von Baeyer, Ware, & Cox, 1979). Indeed, internal attributions for success in achievement contexts do not even correlate with internal attributions for failure (see review in Weiner, 1980c). It therefore appears that the role of individual differences as determinants of attributional responses is relatively small (see Cutrona et al., 1985), and it is unlikely that an attributional trait will be identified.

Summary. Attribution theory has not been particularly successful in understanding and predicting depression. Part of my attribution for this has been a lack of theoretical clarity, demonstrated in a confusion of noncontingency with failure and causal stability with uncontrollability, lack of specification of key sources of affect including sadness and guilt, and indecision about the effects of success ascriptions. In addition, there are many antecedents of depressive episodes, some mediated by cognitions and others not. Furthermore, some of these cognitions are attributions, whereas others are not (see Coyne & Gotlib, 1983). And there seem to be many types of depression, some with clear genetic loadings. Given this complexity, along with the theoretical looseness, it is impressive that causal ascriptions for stress and/or failure do have some relation with depression. One might speculate that attributions, or a particular dimension of causality, relate to only a particular type of depression, which would be an important theoretical and empirical contribution.

In light of the above discussion, I suggest that it will prove useful to move away from clinical depression and consider what might be called discouragement, demoralization, or despondency from an attribution perspective. Because most subjects in depression studies are college students, this already captures the direction of research. Our theory suggests that failure leads to sadness, lack-of-effort attributions produce guilt, lack-of-ability ascriptions result in shame, stable attributions for failure generate hopelessness, and so on. These lawful relations could provide the foundation for an understanding of nonclinical depression. I believe, for example, that the Little Leaguer discussed in Chapter 5 might be quite demoralized by his baseball experience and refuse to leave his darkened room. In my opinion, this is a more promising direction for future research than are the attributional attempts to predict clinical depression.

Summary and Conclusion

A promising theory should have a range as well as a focus on convenience, breadth as well as depth, generalizability as well as a specific target of investigation. The focus of this theory, presented in Chapter 6, is achievement strivings; the breadth of the theory, examined in the current chapter, includes helping behavior, parole decisions, smoking cessation, response to flight delay, reactions to rape, and depression. This strange array of topics share a common characteristic that makes them amenable to attributional analyses: There is a negative "outcome" for which attributions can be made. The vast number of attributions for these diverse outcomes can be subsumed within the same few dimensions of locus, stability, controllability, and perhaps intentionality and globality. The dimensions are then linked to expectancy and affect, which influence the decision to help or to neglect others in need, to grant or not to grant early release from prison, to smoke or to try to give up smoking, to complain or not to complain about an airline delay. In addition, reactions to rape and proneness to depression also may be influenced. I think it is neither unfair nor immodest to assert that no other contemporary theory of motivation can lay claim to such breadth. And I have chosen not to discuss other topics that have been examined from this theoretical perspective, including wife battering, response to deprivation, and alcoholism, to name just a few.

In Chapter 1 it was warned that, in psychology, theoretical breadth and precision seem to be inversely related. The relative downfall of the Freudian approach to motivation was in part attributed to its ability to address too great an array of topics, ranging from war to wit. It is hoped that the range of attributional analyses presented here has not resulted in a sacrifice of precision. The topics addressed are firmly tied to an empirical literature, and predictions often have been tested with path-analytic techniques that permit examination of the full temporal sequence of a motivational episode. The fundamental associations in the theory between attribution-expectancy-action, and attribution-affect-action, cannot be doubted. Controllable attributions are linked to anger, which gives rise to neglect of the needy and to airline complaints; uncontrollable attributions are linked to pity, which produces help for the needy and patient waiting for a delayed flight; stable attributions for failure result in expectancy of future failure, which gives rise to a "no parole" vote, a decision not to try to give up smoking, and maladaptive reactions to rape. The theory suggests the genotypic similarity or phenotypically dissimilar situations.

The theoretical breadth certainly has not been exhausted, inasmuch as any "failure" is fair game for attribution theory. Careful examination of the affiliative domain, which embraces social success (acceptance) and social failure (rejection) is a natural direction for the theory (see Sobel, Earn, Bennett & Humphries, 1983). This is especially important because affiliation has not received sufficient attention from motivational psychologists. Power motivation, described by gain or loss of personal impact, also provides a ready avenue for study from an attributional perspective, as do other "success" and "failure" experiences ranging from addiction to zombie-like behavior.

It must be recognized that attributional analyses are not readily applicable to hunger or thirst motivation (except when one wonders why dinner has not been served, or why the meal tastes so bad). Hence, traditional topics in the study of motivation as studied from a Hullian perspective, which frequently have involved viscerogenic needs, fall beyond the range of the theory. In addition, attribution theory does not easily incorporate unconscious motivation and the Freudian concerns with love and hate. Recall that Hullian and Freudian psychology dominated the field of motivation until about 1950. I do not have the chutzpah even to suggest that this is a watershed for the psychology of motivation. But I do deeply believe that the proposed theory provides an awfully good explanation for some phenomena, and furnishes a strong foundation for further scientific growth.

Chapter 8
Elaborating the Theory: Transactional Associations and Added Relations

In which the author finally acknowledges that life is transactional and that any conceptual system must include feedback loops and bidirectional cause-effect linkages. This is a theoretical nuisance.

The temporal sequence moving from left to right in Figure 6-4 captures the historical approach to motivation from an attributional perspective. There is a pleasing simplicity to this conception; it is without complication when compared with, say, interactional or transactional theoretical perspectives. Unfortunately, although the theory is uncluttered, motivated behavior is not as neat. For example, it is often the case that postulated relations in the field of motivation have bidirectional cause-effect linkages: Attitudes influence behavior, and behavior affects attitudes; needs influence perception, but perceptions also generate needs; and desires can alter subjective expectancies, just as expectancy can modify desire.

Hence, it must be acknowledged that the relations between thinking, feeling, and acting are not fixed within the orderly sequence that has been advocated—the linkages are bidirectional and include recurrent feedback loops. Just as how we feel depends on what we think, what we think in part depends on how we feel, which in turn influences those feelings. And just as what we think affects what we do, behavior can exert an influence on thought processes, which again guide action. This additional complexity is depicted in Figure 8.1. For ease of discussion, I will label bidirectional cause-effect associations and repeated feedback loops as indicators of transactionality. In the present context, a transactional theory of motivation is one that accepts the continuous interplay of cognition, emotion, and behavior on one another.

In this chapter I examine five transactional associations that to this point in the book have not been considered:

1. Linkage 1 in Figure 6-4. Outcome perceptions (success and failure) give rise to general positive and negative affective reactions; conversely, general positive and negative states influence outcome perceptions. Hence, there is a continuous outcome-mood-outcome sequence.
2. General affective states influence causal ascriptions. More specifically, reactions of happiness and sadness in part influence the stability, controllability, and locus of perceived causality.

Figure 8-1. Relations between thought, emotion, and action.

3. Linkage 6 in Figure 6-4. Causal ascriptions (causal stability) influence expectancy of success; conversely, expectancy of success influences causal ascriptions. This results in a recurring expectancy-attribution-expectancy flow.
4. Linkage 10 in Figure 6-4. Causal ascriptions determine affects directed toward others; conversely, affective communications from others influence the attributions of the target person.
5. Linkage 5 in Figure 6-4. An attribution for an outcome is determined and then is located in causal dimension space; conversely, there is a focal point in causal dimension space, and then a specific attribution is selected.

The Influence of Affective States on Cognitive Processes

The growing interest in the study of emotion has recently been extended to the influence of affective states on cognitive processes. In reviewing this body of literature, Bower and Cohen (1982) concluded:

> We find powerful effects of people's feelings upon their cognitive processes . . . a person's feelings act like a selective filter that is tuned to incoming material that supports or justifies those feelings; the filter admits material congruent with the perceiver's mood but casts aside incongruent material. Feelings cause congruent material to become more salient, to stand out more, arouse more interest, cause deeper processing and greater learning of the congruent material. . . . People's social perceptions as well as their imaginative fantasies are subjective; they are easily influenced by their feelings at the moment. These influences occur when people evaluate their friends, themselves, their possessions, and their future. (p. 291)

If these conclusions have validity, and they apparently do, then I have been remiss in assigning merely a response role to affect in relation to outcome perceptions and attributional cognitions. Rather, affects also are likely to influence perceived outcomes and causes, just as they shape behavior.

Affective States and Outcome Perceptions

As Bower and Cohen (1982) stated, the general literature in this area documents what might be called a "congruency principle"; that is, positive feelings selectively enhance the perception and processing of positively evaluated information, whereas negative feelings selectively enhance the perception and processing of negatively evaluated information. It therefore follows that individuals in a positive mood

should be more likely to attend to positive events and interpret them more positively, whereas those in a negative mood should be more likely to perceive negative
events and interpret them more negatively, than persons not in these affective states.
A number of studies provide evidence intimating that this is the case (e.g., Isen &
Shalker, 1982; Mischel, Ebbesen, & Zeiss, 1973; Postman & Brown, 1952).
However, only one investigation, conducted by Wright and Mischel (1982), examined the hypothesis specific to Figure 6-4 that general affective states influence
perceptions of success (goal attainment) and failure (nonattainment of a goal).

Wright and Mischel (1982) manipulated mood by having each subject imagine a
situation that would create a happy, sad, or neutral state. The subjects then undertook a series of achievement tasks. Subsequently, perception of performance at those
tasks, as well as expectations of future success, were assessed. It was found that
positive affective induction resulted in higher estimates of both past and future success, whereas negative mood induction produced lower estimates of past and future
success, as compared with a neutral mood condition. Hence, this study documents
a causal connection between affective states and outcome perceptions.

In general, persons in a positive mood selectively filter and interpret the world
positively, whereas those in a negative mood selectively filter and interpret the
world negatively. Given the wealth of data supporting this general relation, I feel
some confidence in suggesting a transactional recurrent connection between outcome perceptions-affect-outcome perceptions.

Affective States as Attributional Determinants

Given the extensive impact of affect on cognitions, it is reasonable to anticipate that
emotional states also will have an influence over what attribution is perceived as the
cause of an outcome. If this is indeed the case, then yet another linkage needs to be
incorporated into the theory. The evidence that general affective states are attributional antecedents is not unequivocal, but it seems sufficient to accept this additional connection.

Affective Influence on Causal Stability. In the experiment conducted by Wright and
Mischel (1982), positive affect induction increased the perceived likelihood of
future success, whereas a negative mood state lowered that expectancy estimate. As
indicated throughout this book and documented in Chapter 4, expectancy of success
is mediated by causal attributions and, more specifically, by causal stability. It therefore logically follows that, in the Wright and Mischel study, individuals in the positive mood state must have particularly ascribed success to stable factors, whereas
those in the negative mood condition must have ascribed their failure to stable
factors. That is, the mood induction influenced causal perceptions along the stability dimension.

To test this hypothesis, Brown (1984) repeated the investigation of Wright and
Mischel, again arousing a positive or a negative mood state by means of direct mood
induction and then giving subjects success or failure feedback at an achievement
task. In addition to assessing future expectations of success, subjects rated the

perceived stability of the cause of their achievement performance. The predicted pattern of results was found, but only in the success condition. That is, happy subjects had higher posttask expectancies, and attributed the outcome more to stable causes, than did the momentarily depressed subjects. Hence, this is a very promising initial experiment demonstrating an affect-attributional stability connection.

Affective Influence on Causal Controllability. In the previous chapter, the theory of learned helplessness was reviewed. That theory postulates perceived uncontrollability as a necessary antecedent of depression. Even if there is an association between uncontrollability and depression (which was questioned in the earlier discussion), the direction of such a relation would be uncertain. It may be that perceived uncontrollability causes depression, or that depression produces perceptions of uncontrollability. If the latter is correct, then evidence would be provided that a negative affective state influences causal perceptions, in this case along the controllability dimension. An association between negative mood and biased causal perceptions regarding controllability could exist without implications for the determinants of depression or the viability of the learned-helplessness theory of depression.

To test an affect-perceived controllability relation, Alloy, Abramson, and Viscusi (1981) aroused a positive, negative, or no-mood state among depressed and nondepressed college students. Subjects were then given a problem in which they did or did not perform a response (pushed or did not push a button) and received one of two outcomes (a light did or did not come on). A reward was received every time this light came on. In fact, the subjects had no control over the light coming on, which was randomly determined. The major dependent variable was the perceived degree of control over this outcome.

Alloy et al. (1981) reported that, given no mood alteration, depressed subjects perceived the outcome as less controllable than did nondepressed subjects (who were described as having an "illusion of control"). However, when made temporarily elated, the perceptions of control among the depressed students were somewhat greater than those of the nondepressed subjects in the no-mood-alteration condition. Further, when the nondepressed were made temporarily depressed, their perceptions of control were somewhat less than those of the depressed persons in the no-mood-alteration condition. Alloy et al. (1981) concluded, "The major finding of the study is that people's current mood states do influence their accuracy in judging the degree of control they exert over events" (p. 1137). As with Brown's (1984) investigation, these data provide intriguing but preliminary evidence that current affective state alters causal perceptions.

Affective Influence on Causal Locus. The hedonic bias has been one of the most investigated effects in the attributional literature (see Chapter 5). It is well documented that success, more than failure, is self-attributed, whereas failure tends to be ascribed to external factors. There also is a good deal of evidence that this bias, or error, is at least in part due to ego-enhancing and ego-defensive motivational factors.

It has been suggested that the affect produced by success and failure alters the magnitude of the hedonic bias. That is, general affective states modify attributions on the locus dimension. Experimental research has been undertaken attempting to provide evidence for an affect-locus-of-attribution connection (Gollwitzer, Earle, & Stephan, 1982; Stephan & Gollwitzer, 1981). The general procedure in this program of research is first to induce success and failure. Then the perception of the affective reaction to these outcomes is manipulated by means of false feedback, use of a placebo pill, or introduction of an irrelevant source of arousal (an exercise task). The authors reported that if the perceived affective reaction to success and failure is minimized, or if these reactions are ascribed to a non-achievement-related source, then the tendency to attribute success to the self and failure externally is weakened. For example, if before an achievement performance subjects are given a placebo pill and told that it will make them feel very good, then following success their ascription of this outcome to internal causes is reduced.

Why might there be this affect-locus linkage? According to Gollwitzer and Stephan, if the perceived reaction to the achievement-related outcome is mild, then the actor will assume that that event was unimportant. For example, if pleasant feelings following success are ascribed to the actions of a pill, then the affective experience will not be perceived as due to the achievement. Ego-related processes, in turn, will then not be elicited, thereby reducing the hedonic bias. Note, therefore, that affect does not directly influence locus attributions. Rather, affect (internal arousal) is a cue used by the actor to judge event importance, and this cognition influences causal ascriptions. Given this theoretical perspective, not only is the attribution-affect linkage reversed to affect-attribution, but still another mediating variable is introduced. The theory therefore takes the following form:

$$\text{Outcome} \rightarrow \begin{array}{c} \text{outcome-related} \\ \text{affect} \end{array} \rightarrow \begin{array}{c} \text{perceived event} \\ \text{importance} \end{array} \rightarrow \begin{array}{c} \text{locus} \\ \text{attribution} \end{array}$$

In conclusion, it has been contended that outcome-generated affects influence perceived stability, controllability, and locus of causality. At present, these associations must be considered equivocal; additional studies of all the presumed affect-causal dimension linkages await undertaking.

The Influence of Expectancy on Attributions

Expectancy, like affect, also exerts an influence on causal ascriptions. Recall that it was previously documented that an attribution of success to a stable factor produces a high expectancy of future success, and that an attribution of failure to a stable factor produces a high expectancy of future failure. Bidirectionality connotes that a high expectancy of success, when followed by a success, will result in attributions to stable factors such as aptitude and traits, and that a high expectancy of failure, when followed by a failure, also results in attributions to stable factors. In sum, congruency between expectancy and outcome, or confirmation of an expectancy, elicits stable attributions (see Table 8-1).

It then can be logically deduced that inconsistencies between expectancies and outcomes generate ascriptions to unstable causes. That is, high expectancy of success accompanied by failure, and low expectancy of success accompanied by success, give rise to ascriptions to unstable causes such as luck and effort. The stability or instability of causes, in turn, has an influence over the expectancy of future success, so that there is a continuous cycle or feedback loop between expectancy of success-attribution-expectancy of success, just as was noted previously between outcome perceptions-affect-outcome perceptions (see Table 8-1).

There have been a large number of investigations demonstrating that performance expectancies indeed are a determinant of causal ascriptions. Feather and Simon have been particularly early and active contributors in this area (Feather & Simon, 1971, 1972; Simon & Feather, 1973), but compatible findings have been reported by many other researchers (e.g., Ames, Ames, & Felker, 1976; Etaugh & Hadley, 1977; Frieze & Weiner, 1971; Hayashi & Yamauchi, 1974; Kepka & Brickman, 1971). It is evident that most of this research was published more than a decade ago; the empirical question certainly was decided at that time, and demonstration experiments are no longer needed.

The general procedure in these research investigations was to manipulate or measure prior expectancies, either by giving false initial success or failure feedback or by

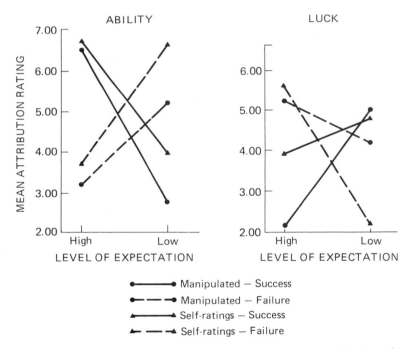

Figure 8-2. Mean attributions to ability and luck given manipulated and self-ratings of expectation of success as a function of outcome and level of expectation of success. From "Causal Attributions for Success and Failure in Relation to Expectations of Success Based Upon Selective or Manipulative Control" by N. T. Feather and J. G. Simon, 1971, *Journal of Personality*, *39*, p. 534. Copyright 1971. Adapted by permission.

Table 8-1. Hypothesized Relations Between Outcomes, Expectancy, Attributions, and the Subsequent Expectancy, Based on Attributional Principles

Independent Variables		Dependent Variables	
Outcome	Expectancy 1	Attribution	Expectancy 2
Success	High	Stable	High
Success	Low	Unstable	Low
Failure	High	Unstable	High
Failure	Low	Stable	Low

having subjects rate their abilities and confidence without false initial feedback. These correspond respectively to experimental and correlational methodologies (see also Chapter 4). Then success and/or failure at a pertinent task was manipulated, and attributional ratings were made. Quite often ability, effort, task difficulty, and luck were the only causes rated, because the research was conducted before the expansion of causal lists.

Figure 8-2 illustrates rather typical data for ability and luck ascriptions after expected or unexpected success and failure. In this study by Feather and Simon (1971), initial expectancy was manipulated in one condition and determined by self-ratings in a second condition. It is evident from Figure 8-2 that expected outcomes (success given high initial expectancy and failure given low initial expectancy) are ascribed to the stable cause of ability. On the other hand, inconsistent outcomes of failure given high expectancy or success given low expectancy are ascribed to luck, an unstable cause.

Some Unfortunate Consequences

The preceding analysis leads to some surprising as well as unfortunate practical consequences. Table 8-1 shows the predicted relations between initial expectancies and achievement outcomes (the independent variables) on subsequent attributions and expectancies (the dependent variables). It is evident from Table 8-1 that expectancies tend to be perpetuated: High expectancies remain high given either success or failure, and low expectancies remain low. This inertia to change is mediated by attributions of causality and their perceived stability.

Table 8-1 has serious and negative implications for individuals in society who might be described as "at risk"—persons who have had a history of negative outcomes either at achievement tasks (the unable and underachievers), at affiliative activities (the lonely and social isolates), or in general adaptation to life (criminals, the demoralized, the mentally ill, the needy, and so forth). These persons are likely to have key areas in their lives in which failure is expected. That is, they anticipate a low grade on an exam, being rejected when asking for a date, getting turned down for a job. According to the preceding analysis, when failure is in fact experienced, it is ascribed to stable factors (e.g., low ability) so that future failure again is anticipated. Low expectancy of success evokes feelings of hopelessness and still further withdrawal and reluctance to engage in appropriate instrumental activities, such as taking other courses or asking out other people for dates. On the other hand, occasional success, when experienced, will tend to be ascribed to unstable causes (e.g., good luck). In this manner, expectancy of success is minimally, if at all, increased and could even decrease. This pattern of attributions therefore maintains a maladaptive belief system and the behavior fostered by such beliefs.

Self-maintaining, dysfunctional belief systems have been identified for many groups and vulnerable individuals, including psychiatric rehabilitees (Menapace & Doby, 1976), lonely and depressed persons (Anderson, Horowitz, & French, 1983), retarded persons (Chan & Keogh, 1974; MacMillan & Keogh, 1971), persons with low general self-esteem (Burke, 1978; Shrauger & Osberg, 1980), and those with more specific areas of low esteem such as self-perceptions of low reading ability (Nicholls, 1979). This listing represents only a small sampling of the pertinent literature. Not all of this research was undertaken from an attributional perspective, and some may be interpreted without postulating an expectancy-attribution-expectancy cycle. However, all the investigations may be explained from this theoretical perspective.

• Menapace and Doby (1976) had psychiatric rehabilitees and a control group of college students perform a manual task. Success and failure were manipulated, and causal ascriptions were rated. Rehabilitees ascribed their failure to stable causes, whereas students attributed failure to unstable causes. The data given success were not systematic.

• Anderson et al. (1983) identified students who were lonely and/or depressed. The students were presented with typical interpersonal and achievement situations they might confront, each having either a positive or a negative outcome (e.g., "You just attended a party for new students and failed to make any new friends"). The lonely and depressed subjects tended to ascribe failure in the interpersonal situations to personal characterological deficits, such as lack of ability or some aversive trait. This is remindful of the data reported by Janoff-Bulman (1979) documenting a subset of characterological blamers.

• Burke (1978) manipulated success and failure at an achievement task, with subjects categorized as high or low in self-esteem. Attributions to ability and task ease were greater for success among high self-esteem participants, whereas ascriptions to stable factors following failure were relatively low among these high-self-esteem persons. Nicholls (1979) reported similar findings among children 8 to 12 years old who were classified according to self-perceptions of reading ability. Outcome was not manipulated; rather, the children in this research were asked to recall a time of actual success or failure in reading and then revealed their causal ascriptions for that outcome. As already indicated, the typical pattern of data emerged for this "vulnerable" group with failure, but not success, attributed to stable factors.

Females as an "At-Risk" Group? Deaux (1984) and Frieze and her colleagues (Frieze, Whitley, Hanusa, & McHugh, 1982; McHugh, Frieze, & Hanusa, 1982) have extensively investigated the relation between sex differences and attributions, examining both self-perceptions and stereotypic thinking about others. Figure 8-3 depicts one common set of beliefs about the perceived determinants of success and

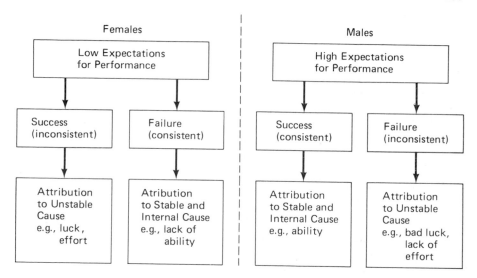

Figure 8-3. Expectancy model of attributions for male and female actors. From "From Individual Differences to Social Categories: Analysis of a Decade's Research on Gender" by K. Deaux, 1984, *American Psychologist*, *39*, p. 106. Copyright 1984. Reprinted by permission.

failure among females and males. Figure 8-3 reveals that, for females, success tends to be ascribed to unstable causes and failure to stable causes, whereas the reverse is the case for males. These attributional differences are presumed to be mediated by inequalities in initial expectancies of success and failure. Research by Deaux, Frieze, and others has revealed, however, that this is too simplified a representation, for attributions depend greatly on the kind of task that is undertaken and the situational context. The analysis shown in Figure 8-3 may apply when stereotypically male tasks (e.g., mechanical puzzles) are attempted. In addition, such patterns are more likely in the perception of others than in self-perception. That is, whereas females might not be less likely to have low expectancy of success and therefore ascribe personal success to unstable factors more than do males, observers of females do exhibit such a pattern of beliefs. This, of course, has grave implications for such actions as job promotions, where gender bias has been documented. Hence, the proposed linkages between attribution-expectancy-attribution are not merely esoteric academic issues, of interest only to attribution theorists, but have important social implications as well.

Altering Self-Concept and Expectancy of Success

How, then, is it possible to progress from low to high expectancy of success at a task, given the reasoning that has been outlined? That is, can self-esteem and future expectancies ever be altered? McMahan (1973) and Valle and Frieze (1976) addressed this issue and developed formal models of expectancy shifts based on the concept of causal stability. Valle and Frieze postulated that personal predictions of expectancies (P) are a function of the initial expectancy (E) plus the degree to which outcomes (O) are attributed to stable causes (S):

$$P = f[E + O[f(S)]]$$

In addition, Valle and Frieze (1976) also noted that the perceived stability of causes of success and failure is related to initial expectancy of success. Hence, they concluded that:

> There is some value for the difference between the initial expectations and the actual outcome that will maximally change a person's predictions for the future. If the difference is greater than this point, the outcome will be attributed to unstable factors to such a great extent that it will have less influence on the person's future predictions (p. 581)

According to the above logic, a change in self-esteem or expectancy of success would have to involve a gradual process. For example, assume that an individual with low self-esteem believes that he or she has a low probability of success at a task. Success would then be ascribed to unstable factors such as good luck, which minimizes increments in expectancy of later success and self-esteem, even though a positive outcome was attained. However, if that outcome was only slightly above expectation, so that attributions to unstable causes were not dominant, then stable factors would be perceived as playing some causal role, and subsequent expectancy would rise slightly to approximate the degree of success. This process of moderate growth is the only possible course to permanent change, given this attributional position (also see Ames, 1978; Fitch, 1970; Gilmore & Minton, 1974; Ickes & Layden, 1978).

Summary

There are some evident parallels between the psychological literature examining the attribution-expectancy linkage and the investigations concerned with the expectancy-attribution union. Both hypothesized directional associations have generated a vast array of both experimental and correlational research, surely embracing more than 50 studies (and this does not include related investigations that might be interpreted from an attributional framework). In addition, both literatures include theory-guided predictions in the laboratory as well as applied problems examined in either laboratory research settings or field contexts. And both literatures are characterized by empirical consistency. As previously concluded, the linkage between attribution and expectancy is a psychological law; this statement also describes the linkage between expectancy and attribution.

The Influence of Communicated Affects on Causal Ascriptions

The effects of attributions on specific affects were thoroughly documented in Chapter 5. There are no doubts concerning the linkages between, for example, internal locus of causality for positive outcomes and pride, stable attributions for failure and hopelessness, and causal controllability and the other-directed emotions of anger and pity. Concerning the latter associations, it was revealed that a perceived controllable cause of a need or of failure, such as alcoholism or lack of effort, evokes anger from observers. On the other hand, uncontrollable causes such as illness or lack of aptitude give rise to pity.

A union going from specific affect to attribution raises the question of whether self-directed affect influences personal attributions, whereas other-directed emotions influence the attributions of the target person. That is, are affects cues or information that can be used by individuals to infer why they have attained or not attained a goal?

The initial investigation of this question was conducted by Weiner, Russell, and Lerman (1979). This study examined whether individuals can use affective information to infer attributions, and not whether they in fact do make use of such cues. My colleagues and I gave subjects scenarios such as the following:

> A person just received a test back in a course that is very important to him or her. He or she has done very well and feels extremely *surprised*, *astonished*, and *thankful*. Why did this person believe that he or she did so well? (Weiner et al., 1979, p. 1218)

Table 8-2 shows the data for eight emotion triads and the six attributions that were rated as causing the outcome. If the emotion-cognition and the cognition-emotion linkages are bidirectional, then the attributions known to elicit these emotions should contain the highest ratings within the columns. For example, the affects known to be elicited by luck attributions (surprise and astonishment for both success and failure) should, in turn, lead to an inference of a luck attribution when these feelings are given. The third and seventh columns of Table 8-2 document that this is the case. Indeed, there is symmetry for all of the attribution-affect linkages in that the highest ratings are inferred given causes that elicit these emotions.

In a follow-up of this investigation, Weiner, Graham, Stern, & Lawson (1982) used a similar role-playing procedure and again examined whether subjects can infer attributions from affective information. The scenario used was as follows:

> A student failed a test and the teacher got [felt, was] _____.
> Why did the teacher think the student failed?

Five affects were manipulated: anger, pity, guilt, surprise, and sadness. The attributional ratings to which the emotions were related were ability ("The student is low in ability"), effort, the teacher made the test too difficult, and bad luck. These attributions and affects were selected because prior research documented unions between low ability and pity, lack of effort and anger, personal responsibility and guilt, and bad luck and surprise. Sadness, in distinction to the other affects, is known to be unrelated to any specific attribution, but it is elicited by failure.

The data from this study are shown in Table 8-3. These data combine the responses of adults and 11- and 9-year-olds, inasmuch as there were no response differences between these three age groups. Table 8-3 shows that, given an anger reaction, subjects infer the teacher made an attribution to lack of effort, pity is most closely tied to a low-ability inference, guilt to teacher/task, surprise to low effort,

Table 8-2. Mean Magnitude of Attributional Inference Elicited in Response to the Indicated Emotional Description

	Emotional Description								
	Success				Failure				
Attribution Inference	Confident Competent Pleased	Relaxed Secure Calm	Surprised Astonished Thankful	Appreciative Grateful Modest	Incompetent Inadequate Panicked	Guilty Troubled Humble	Astonished Overwhelmed Surprised	Bitter Furious Revengeful
Ability	8.06[a]	6.21	3.10	4.56	7.40	4.56	3.44	3.35
Unstable effort	7.08	7.04	3.60	5.60	4.92	7.40	2.73	3.67
Stable effort	7.02	6.77	3.12	5.08	5.46	7.81	2.90	3.81
Task ease	4.67	5.25	4.65	5.54	6.35	4.94	4.94	6.70
Luck	2.60	4.73	7.31	6.08	3.25	2.85	6.52	4.85
Others	3.54	4.92	5.42	6.69	3.48	3.58	3.85	6.75

Note. From "The Cognition-Emotion Process in Achievement-Related Contexts" by B. Weiner et al., 1979, *Journal of Personality and Social Psychology*, 37, pp. 1218–1219. Copyright 1979. Reprinted with permission.

[a] Underlined value predicted as the dominant attributional inference based on attribution-affect linkages.

Table 8-3. Causal Ratings as a Function of Reported Affect

Cause	Affect				
	Anger	Pity	Guilt	Surprise	Sad
Effort	7.7	3.3	3.0	6.3	4.8
Ability	3.9	6.1	3.8	2.6	5.4
Teacher/ task	2.5	5.3	7.6	3.6	5.1
Luck	2.5	5.0	3.5	4.4	4.4

Note. From "Using Affective Cues to Infer Causal Thoughts" by B. Weiner et al., 1982, *Developmental Psychology, 18,* p. 281. Copyright 1982. Reprinted by permission.

and sadness is unrelated to any specific attribution. Hence, all of the linkages are expected save that of surprise-effort. It is known that the unexpected elicits surprise. Apparently, it is anticipated that students will try on a test; hence, surprise in this context is an effort cue.

In sum, it is again evident that affects can function as cues, or strong hints, concerning the perceived cause of an event. The evidence also documents that children as young as 9 years of age are quite adept at using emotional cues to make causal inferences; that is, they may understand the unexpressed attributional thoughts of others if emotions are expressed (and correctly encoded).

Of course, just because individuals can infer attributions from emotions, this does not mean that they do make such deductions, or even that they are given such opportunities. But there is ample evidence that occasions do arise when affects function as cues. As indicated earlier, when Helen Keller's teacher announced to the parents that "We do not want your pity," she was telling the parents not to communicate cues that imply uncontrollability or lack of capability. I am sure that most readers also have said at one time in their lives, "Why are you mad at me? I couldn't help it." This indicates that expressed anger implies perceived controllability. Or imagine what a student would conclude if a teacher exhibited extreme surprise at his success. Given that surprise is a reaction to the unexpected, the student will infer from this that the teacher believed he would perform poorly. That is, the teacher perceives him as low in ability or lazy.

The communicated affect-attribution process being suggested is shown in Figure 8-4, which indicates that the observer (e.g., the teacher) has a private evaluation of the target person, such as his or her ability or effort expenditure. Success and failure then give rise to an emotional experience and expression as a function of this belief system. Thus, for example, if a perceived smart person fails, the teacher might infer low effort or bad luck as the cause. This gives rise to anger or surprise, which could be communicated in a number of ways. If the communication is received and correctly encoded, the actor (e.g., the student) will be able to infer the teacher's opinion of his or her ability and/or effort. This, in turn, has an impact on self-attributions, affective reactions, expectations, and action.

Figure 8-4. Communicated affect–self-attribution process.

Graham (1984) investigated selected aspects of this process in a controlled laboratory setting (see also Chapter 6). She had "teachers" communicate anger ("I'm really mad at you") or pity ("I feel sorry for you") toward children about 12 years old who had been induced to fail at an achievement-related task. This verbal feedback was accompanied by appropriate voice and postural cues. For example, anger was loudly expressed with hands extended, whereas the pity statement was said softly with hands folded. The children subsequently were asked why the teacher thought they had failed, and why they personally believed they had done poorly.

Figure 8-5 shows the inferred experimenter attributions as a function of the affective feedback. It is evident from Figure 8-5 that when sympathy was expressed, low ability was the inferred cause for failure, lack of effort was linked with experimenter displays of anger, and there was no dominant causal inference when affective feedback was not delivered (control condition). This documents that affective feedback is used to infer what others are thinking.

The next question Graham examined was whether this feedback also influences self-attributions for failure. It does, for self-ascriptions for failure due to low ability were highest in the sympathy feedback condition, whereas self-ascriptions to lack of effort were highest in the anger condition. Finally, as discussed in Chapter 6, Graham also documented that the expectations of success in the two conditions also differed, with those subjects receiving the pity feedback more expectant of failure than those receiving the anger feedback. This is consistent with the classification of low ability as stable and lack of effort as unstable for failure.

Graham (1984) concluded:

> This bidirectional influence from thoughts to emotions *elicited* and from emotions to thoughts *inferred* supports the general belief that specific causal ascriptions influence particular affective states. . . . One consequence of these linkages is that emotional displays of others can guide self-perception and therefore may have important implications for self-esteem. One might speculate, for example, that the failing students who were the targets of sympathy in this investigation progressed through communicated affect-self perception scenarios such as the following: "I haven't solved any of these puzzles so far and the teacher obviously feels sorry for me. She must think I'm not good at puzzles like this. I really did get the puzzles wrong because I wasn't good at puzzle solving and I don't expect to do better in the future" (p. 51)

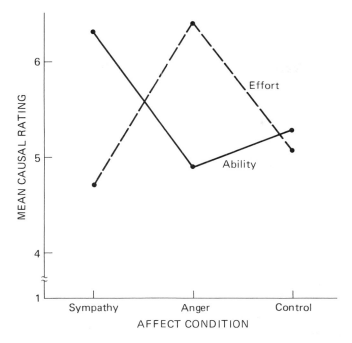

Figure 8-5. Inferred experimenter attributions as a function of the affect condition. From "Communicated Sympathy and Anger to Black and White Children: The Cognitive (Attributional) Consequences of Affective Cues" by S. Graham, 1984, *Journal of Personality and Social Psychology*, *47*, p. 45. Copyright 1984. Reprinted by permission.

The Influence of Attributional Dimensions on Causal Selection

One of the very basic presumptions of this attributional theory is that individuals first select a causal ascription and then locate this attribution in a dimensional space. It is fully documented that there are basic causal dimensions and that causes can be meaningfully classified on these dimensions; that is, the causes can be described according to their placement in dimensional space. But these facts do not confront the presumption that there is a temporal sequence in which a cause is selected and then dimensionalized. Indeed, there are no data presently addressing this assumed logical ordering.

An alternative to this sequence is that there is first a focus or concentration on dimensional space following an outcome, and then a specific attribution is selected. That is, there is a sequential ordering going from causal dimensions to causal attribution. More specifically, for example, a person could fail an exam and conclude, "That was because (or not because) of me." Search is then made among the internal (or external) causes for an appropriate ascription. The specific attributional decision may then be modified as other dimensions also exert an influence on the attributional choice. It is also conceivable that multiple dimensions are initially aroused when searching for causality (e.g., "I am responsible for having failed"). Then

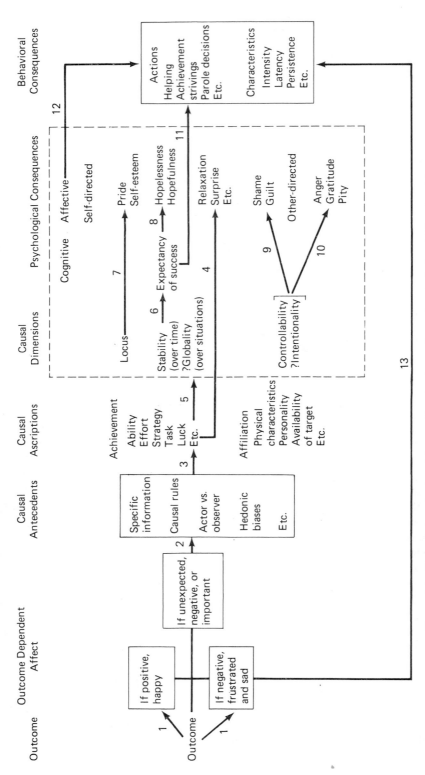

Figure 8-6. Expanded attributional theory of motivation and emotion, including bidirectional linkages.

ERRATUM to *An Attributional Theory of Motivation and Emotion* (SSSP Weiner)
A corrected version of Figure 8-6 on page 240 appears below.

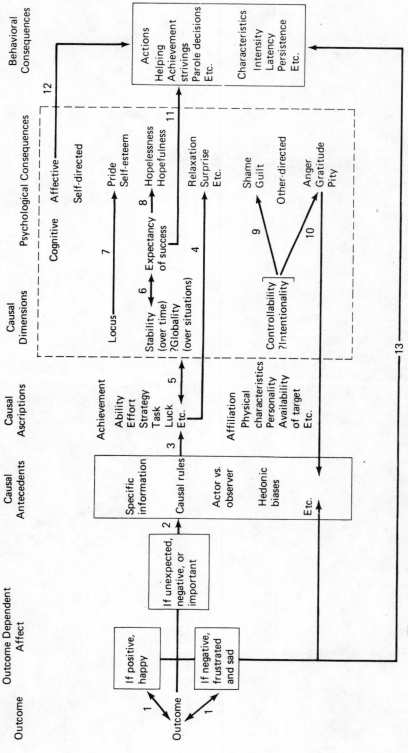

Figure 8-6. Expanded attributional theory of motivation and emotion, including bidirectional linkages.

causes both internal and controllable, such as effort and strategy, are examined as possible explanations. Wong and Weiner (1981) have reported that attributional search is primarily focused on the locus and controllability dimensions.

The above analysis suggests the hypothesis that the dimensional focus guides what causal explanation is reached. It seems reasonable to assume that what we find depends to a great extent on where we look. Hence, if the heuristic used is one of searching for external and uncontrollable causes before considering internal and controllable factors, then it is likely that an acceptable external, uncontrollable cause will be located. But a great void exists regarding the role that causal dimensions play in the attributional search process. One can merely report that research investigations are badly needed to fill this void and to shed light on the suggested bidirectional causal ascription-causal dimension connection.

Summary and Conclusion

It has not been out of ignorance that the complexities in the attributional theory being championed have been shunned. Rather, acceptance of a transactional approach, including bidirectional causality, feedback loops, and recurrent cycles, creates a dilemma, inasmuch as at this point in time overelaboration of the theory might mask its heuristic value and thus would be counterproductive. I believe that overintricacy in part contributed to the downfall of Hullian and contemporary Atkinsonian theory. In addition to the complexities added by a transactional approach, one must decide just how many linkages and loops should be added; more than the five examined in this chapter surely exist. The few associations discussed were selected because they have been the subject of a reasonable amount of thought and research, and/or because they are vital to the theory. But the discussion was not meant to be exhaustive. For example, Folkes and Morgenstern (1981) found that expressed attributions allow a listener to determine if the communicator won or lost an election; Fayans and Maehr (1979) found that people prefer to make certain attributions, and this influences their choice of tasks, and on and on.

What clearly has been documented in this chapter is that there are reversible associations for at least some of the linkages in the theory—outcomes determine general affective states, and general affective states influence outcome perceptions; attributions influence expectancy, and expectancies guide attributions; attributions influence communicated emotions, and communicated emotions provide attributional information; causes are placed in dimensions, and dimensional focus might direct attributional decisions. Some of these symmetrical cause-effect unions will produce recurrent cycles wherein each factor alters the other. In addition, a loop between specific affects and causal inference is required, for affects can function as attributional cues, as well as being responses to attributions.

These additions somewhat clear my conscience, but they do not alter my theoretical modus operandi: The price of complexity may be more than the price of simplicity. Time will have to provide this answer. For now, for those preferring truth to simplicity, an expansion of the theory based on the evidence presented in this chapter is given in Figure 8-6.

Chapter 9

Replicating the Theoretical Associations: A Laboratory Course in Attribution Theory

In which the author shows off his faith in the theory
by contending that the specified associations can be
replicated in front of a classroom. A laboratory
course is designed for that purpose.

Hungry rats typically run faster for food than do satiated rats, and the greater the amount and quality of the incentive, the quicker they run. People tend to resume tasks that they have not completed. In achievement contexts, those high in achievement needs prefer intermediate-difficulty tasks. Success at a chance task produces lesser increments in the subjective expectancy of future success than does success at a skill-related task. These facts provided the needed empirical foundations for the respective theories of Hull (1943), Lewin (1935), Atkinson (1964), and Rotter (1966). This is not to assert that the empirical relations outlined above cannot be interpreted with alternative conceptions: The desire for intermediate risk can be explained without the concepts of expectancy and value used by Atkinson, and expectancy changes in skill and chance settings can be accounted for without recourse to the locus-of-control concept adopted by Rotter and his colleagues. Nonetheless, these facts did provide the building blocks for the respective development of achievement theory and social learning (locus of control) theory.

However, as also indicated many times in the book, motivational theorists have been remiss in not building stronger (i.e., more reliable) empirical foundations to support their conceptual networks. The greater recall of incompleted than completed tasks, a central prediction of Lewinian theory, is uncertain. The differential choice of tasks of intermediate difficulty between persons high and low in achievement needs, the main hypothesis derived from Atkinson's theory, is not replicable. And differential expectancies among persons differing in locus of control, a key supposition of Rotter's social learning theory, have rarely been reported. How often we read about a lack of replication of a hypothesized association in the motivation area, and how often we doubt the reliability of a reported relation! These are the dangers I most want to avoid. A theory can always be modified to fit the empirical facts, but if the empirical facts are incorrect, then the theory accounting for them must also be flawed. The conception that has been put forth here, as all other theories, will ultimately (or even sooner) prove incorrect, incomplete, and inadequate. On the other hand, I hope that the supporting empirical base is incontrovertible, indisputable, and infallible.

Detailed evidence confirming the proposed theoretical linkages has already been reviewed. I have sufficient faith in the certainty of these data to offer in this chapter a laboratory course in which crucial experiments are conducted in front of a classroom of students. Outlining a laboratory course additionally enables me to review the component associations in the theory and to provide concrete exposure to some of the methodologies that have been used to test the theory. It also will prove useful for the reader to join in as an experimental subject; data that one has personally generated are often the most convincing.

I am confident that these demonstrations will replicate the individual theoretical linkages, as well as more complex patterns of associations that have been hypothesized. But because classroom experiments are being proposed, the procedures must be greatly restricted, confined to verbal reports and judgments. This is not to imply that judgments provide the only, or the best, or the weakest testing ground for attribution theory. Rather, they merely provide one avenue of access, and the one most amenable to classroom demonstrations.

A Laboratory Course in Attribution Theory

Linkage 1: Outcome to Affect

The first union in the theory shown in Figure 6-4 and Figure 8-6 specifies that success is followed by the positive affect of happiness, regardless of the perceived cause of that outcome. Failure likewise is accompanied by outcome-related negative affects, but given nonattainment of a goal, the reactions are more varied and are captured by the labels of sad, frustrated, and/or unhappy. These associations have been found by my colleagues and me (Weiner, Russell, & Lerman, 1978, 1979) and also are included in the theory or data reported by Bryant and Veroff (1982), Kelley (1983), and Smith and Kluegel (1982) (see Chapter 5).

Experiment 1 should document these outcome-affect connections. The participants in the study are asked to recall and relive a time when they experienced success or failure and are to report the emotions that were felt at that time (from Weiner et al., 1979). The instructor can then ask each member of the class to relate the story and the three experienced affects; these data can be tabulated in class. Because of the public expression of the stories and the feelings, it is ethically best to restrict the demonstration to successful encounters (it is, of course, just coincidental that outcome-related affects are also clearer given success than failure).

Linkage 2: Outcome to Causal Search

The second linkage in the theory proposes that cognitive as well as affective processes are set in motion by success and failure (attainment or nonattainment of a desired goal). The cognitive process highlighted in Linkage 2 is attributional search: Following outcomes that are unexpected, negative, and/or important, actors seek to identify the cause(s) of those outcomes. In Chapter 2, 20 investigations were reviewed that document the existence of spontaneous causal search. In addition, it was determined that unexpected outcomes and failure particularly provoke attributional concerns.

Experiment 2 is based on the prior research of Wong and Weiner (1981) and the successful extensions of this procedure by Mikula and Schlamberger (1985) and Holtzworth-Munroe and Jacobson (1985). Four hypothetical situations are created; their order can be varied among the participants. In each situation, an event is described and respondents are asked about their thoughts and questions concerning that event. The hypothetical situations vary according to outcome (success or failure) and their expectedness (expected or unexpected). Causal statements can then be identified and tabulated for each condition to determine the extent of causal thinking and also whether failure and an unexpected outcome augment attributional search.

It is evident that Experiment 2 uses a reactive methodology and thus may not capture well what is meant by "spontaneous" attributional activity. This is better represented in archival-type research; perusing the sports pages is recommended as another experimental assignment. On the other hand, Experiment 2 does provide control over the antecedent conditions thought to be related to causal search, and subjects are not "forced" to ask attributional questions.

Linkage 3: Causal Antecedents to Causal Ascriptions

Causal search eventuates in the use of a variety of cues that guide the selection of one or more causal attributions to explain a past event. This topic has been quite consciously avoided in this book, as it is the focus of the attribution theories of Jones and Davis (1965), Kelley (1967), and others who are more concerned with cognitive processes. Another reason for the present neglect is that the process of attribution has been reviewed in many other sources (see Kelley and Michela, 1980, for a metareview). Nonetheless, Experiments 3 and 4 are included to illustrate that cues such as specific information and causal rules can indeed influence attributional decision making in an achievement-related context. Experiments 5 and 6 demonstrate that affective feedback also can function as an attributional cue, a topic more closely related to the contents of this book.

In Experiment 3, participants are given information about social consensus: the percentage of other people succeeding or failing at a task, as well as the outcome of a person undertaking the task (from Weiner & Kukla, 1970; also see Frieze & Weiner, 1971). This is akin to a student examining the grading curve following personal feedback about an exam. The participants then make attributional judgments concerning ability and effort as the cause of the outcome (this also may be interpreted as arriving at attributional judgments about locus of causality). Ability and effort were selected as the attributions to be judged because they are the dominant perceived causes of success and failure (see Chapter 2). This investigation includes 10 judgments (5 levels of social norms × 2 outcomes). The straightforward expectation is that the greater the percentage of others succeeding at the task, the less the likelihood that the success of the actor will be ascribed to the internal causes of high ability and high effort (that is, causality will be perceived as external). Conversely, the greater the percentage of others' successes, the more likely that failure will be attributed to the low ability and lack of effort of the person. As both Jones and Davis (1965) and Kelley (1967) noted, to learn about a person, that person's action must be at variance with social norms. We do not gain knowledge that a person is quiet (quietness as a trait) if he or she is studying noiselessly at the library. But we do infer that this person is talkative if he or she is talking in the library, where the norm is silence.

Experiment 4 demonstrates another antecedent of causal decisions: causal schemata, or rules that relate causes to effects. Two such rules identified by Kelley (1973) concern what are called sufficient and necessary schemata. According to Kelley, if an outcome is expected or typical, such as success at an easy task, then sufficient causality is elicited. That is, the presence of any one cause is sufficient for that successful outcome to occur. On the other hand, if an outcome is unexpected or atypical, such as success at a difficult task, then necessary causality is elicited. That is, the presence of all facilitating causes is necessary to produce the outcome. In Experiment 4 (from Kun & Weiner, 1973), success at a very easy and a very difficult task are specified and one cause (ability) is given. Participants are then asked to infer the presence or absence of a second cause of success (effort). In this investigation, respondents should be uncertain or infer little effort given success at the easy exam (which 90% of others pass), inasmuch as high ability is sufficient to attain success. On the other hand, they should infer the presence of effort given success at the difficult exam (10% pass), even though there is high ability, because a necessary schema is activated. This cursory explanation does not do justice to the attributional theory of Kelley, and I reiterate that the experiment is included here merely to give an illustration of Linkage 3 in the theory.

In the next investigations, which I already indicated are more closely tied to studies examined in this book (see Chapters 5 and 8), it can be demonstrated that communicated affects also are useful cues in the attribution process. The cue function of affects is included only in Figure 8-6, which contains some "right-to-left" linkages (see the arrow emanating from anger, pity, and gratitude and ending in the box of causal antecedents). In Experiment 5, three affective cues are conveyed by a teacher to a failing pupil: guilt, pity (sympathy), and anger (from Weiner, Graham, Stern, & Lawson, 1982; also see Weiner et al., 1979). The participants must then infer why the teacher thought that the student failed. Presumably, a student in such a situation would be engaging in the same inference process and then would use this information to help determine why he or she had failed (see Graham, 1984). It is predicted that guilt will be related to the belief that the teacher self-blames ("the teacher is unclear"); pity will be associated with failure due to an uncontrollable cause, particularly one that is stable ("low ability"); and anger is a cue used to infer that failure is due to a lack of effort ("never studies").

The final study in this grouping (guided by Meyer et al., 1979) differs from the prior investigations in part because even more complex inferences are involved. In this investigation (Experiment 6), a teacher is described as providing feedback to two students who did not perform well on an exam. The teacher conveys performance feedback to one of the students, while to the other this feedback is accompanied by an anger reaction. On the basis of this information, the respondents are asked to infer which student is perceived as *smarter* by the teacher.

The hypotheses regarding the perceptions of the teacher require a two-step derivation. First, as should have been documented in Experiment 5, there is an association between anger and lack of effort. Hence, the recipient of the anger communication will be perceived as not having tried (based on Weiner, Graham, Stern, & Lawson, 1982). In Experiment 6, the student called "Mary" therefore will be perceived as having prepared less than "Jane," who did not receive anger feedback. Second, recall from Experiment 4 (causal schemata as attributional cues) that effort and ability inferences are interrelated and based, in part, on causal rules. Inasmuch as one student (Mary) is perceived as having failed because of lack of effort at a task of unknown difficulty, it will be inferred that she did not fail because of a lack of ability. That is, Mary is considered relatively smart. On the other hand, the second student (Jane) is not perceived as having failed because of lack of effort since anger was not communicated. Hence, she will be perceived as having low ability, inasmuch as a cause of failure must be provided. In sum, Mary, who received the anger feedback, will be perceived as smarter than Jane. One interesting aspect of this experiment is that the judgments can be reached relatively quickly, in spite of the complex cognitive inferences that are involved: from affective feedback to a cause, and then to a conclusion about a second cause.

Linkage 5: Causal Ascriptions to Causal Dimensions

Specific causal ascriptions are linked to both affect (Linkage 4) and to causal dimensions (Linkage 5). Because of the relative empirical uncertainty of Linkage 4, and because of the focus on the affective consequences of causal dimensions, I will progress directly to Linkage 5, involving causal dimensions, and not consider direct attribution-affect associations. Certainly the very heart and soul of the attribution theory I have advocated are causal dimensions, or the basic properties of causes.

Evidence that people think in terms of the broad causal categories of locus, stability, and controllability (and perhaps intentionality and/or globality) was presented in Chapter 3. The 10 investigations cited in that chapter all made use of sophisticated mathematical techniques, primarily factor analyses and multidimensional scaling. Hence, a classroom demonstration of the linkage between specific attributions and causal dimensions (Linkage 5) is quite difficult; one can only provide an imperfect investigation to approximate this classification process.

In Experiment 7, the participants are provided with a list of 16 dominant causes of failure in two achievement domains: sports and school (from Stern, 1983). The instructions direct the respondents to separate the causes into two piles and to identify the principle that they used in this process. They are then asked to do this again, this time using a different principle (concept) to differentiate the causes. This is to be done a maximum of three times, or until the participants cannot think of another classification rule. I expect that locus will emerge as the most dominant classification concept, which is consistent with the role it plays in attributional thinking.

Perhaps stability and controllability also will emerge, although this is questionable given the unsophisticated statistical analyses that are possible in a classroom demonstration.

It is hoped that Experiment 7 documented that people do classify causes into some of the basic categories that have been identified. In Experiment 8, it will be demonstrated that individuals can use the dimensional categories when asked to. This is not a proof of Linkage 5, but it nonetheless does provide evidence consistent with the theory.

In Experiment 8, five dominant causes of achievement outcomes are provided (aptitude, effort, task difficulty, luck, and mood). The three causal dimensions of locus, stability, and controllability are also defined, and the participants rate the causes on these three dimensions. As the studies reviewed in Chapter 3 have documented, aptitude, effort, and mood will tend to be perceived as internal, in contrast to the external classification of task difficulty and luck. As far as stability is concerned, aptitude and task will be perceived as more stable than effort, mood, or luck. There may, however, be greater variability in the stability than in the locus judgments, inasmuch as effort, luck, and mood could be perceived as traitlike rather than statelike causes. Finally, effort and perhaps mood will be rated as controllable, in contrast to aptitude, luck, and objective task difficulty, which will be perceived as uncontrollable.

The fact that respondents can use the dimensions, and the high agreement in the ratings that I believe will be present, are some indication that the dimensions are familiar ways of organizing thoughts. However, it must be repeated that attributions represent phenomenal causality, so even disagreement in the ratings would not invalidate the conception. This experiment therefore cannot falsify the theory and hence cannot be considered a crucial or definitive study.

Linkage 6: Causal Stability to Expectancy of Success

The attributional position regarding the determinants of expectancy change (and, in part, absolute expectancy level) is without complexity: Outcomes ascribed to stable causes will be anticipated to be repeated in the future, whereas there will be uncertainty about future outcomes if the prior causal network is thought of as changing. Nearly 20 studies were considered in Chapter 4 that reported empirical relations between causal stability and expectancy of success. The procedures have included both correlational and experimental studies in the laboratory, as well as field research. Inasmuch as all cognitive motivational theorists include expectancy of success as a component in their theories of motivation, finding attributional antecedents of goal anticipations is a very important goal of this theory.

Experiment 9 follows a typical laboratory experimental approach to the study of goal expectancies. Failure at an exam is specified and four causes are given. Two of the causes (ability and task difficulty) are strongly worded to imply stability, whereas the other two causes (effort and luck) should elicit perceptions of instability. Hence, it is reasonable to assume in this case that the phenomenological interpretations of the stimuli will correspond to the a priori classification that is being imposed. It is predicted that future success will be perceived as less likely given the stable rather than the unstable causes of failure.

It is also possible to use these data to compare the attributional with the locus-of-control position (following Weiner, Nierenberg, & Goldstein, 1976; Inagi, 1977; and Kojima, 1984). According to locus-of-control theorists, internal ascriptions for failure at a school exam result in lesser decrements in expectancy of success than do external attributions. Hence, ability and effort ascriptions (the internal causes) should produce higher expectancies of future success than attributions to task difficulty and luck (the external causes). I believe that this hypothesis will be disconfirmed. In addition, according to the attributional position, effort ascriptions are hypothesized to result in higher anticipations of future success than ability attributions. Similarly, luck ascriptions should elicit higher expectations than attributions to task difficulty. That is, differences in goal expectancies will be exhibited when comparisons are made *within* both the internal and the external causal ascriptions.

Linkage 6: Expectancy of Success to Causal Stability

Here is a second "right-to-left" association that is represented only in Figure 8-6. This linkage, which has been empirically found in over a dozen investigations, specifies that unexpected outcomes (for example, a success when failure is anticipated, or a failure when success is anticipated) will be attributed to unstable causes. This then produces little change in expectancy of future success, thereby perpetuating the initial belief system. Conversely, expected outcomes are ascribed to stable causes, which strengthens the initial belief system. It has been contended that for this reason positive outcomes experienced by depressed persons do little to alter their future hopes—the good outcomes are ascribed to an unstable causal situation. On the other hand, failure or negative outcomes are ascribed to stable causal factors such as low ability, thus strengthening the subjective veridicality of their depression (see Chapter 4).

Experiment 10 is guided by the above principles. High or low expectancy is varied, as well as an outcome that is either congruent or incongruent with the initial expectancy. Then ability (a priori considered to be perceived as stable) and luck (a priori considered to be perceived as unstable) are rated for causal importance. It is predicted that high expectancy accompanied by success, and low expectancy accompanied by failure, will be ascribed to ability rather than to luck. Conversely, low expectancy followed by success, and high expectancy followed by failure, are more likely to elicit luck instead of ability ascriptions. As indicated in Chapter 8, there is a constant interplay involving expectancy-attribution-expectancy sequences.

Linkage 7: Causal Locus to Pride

As so often emphasized in this book, the concept of causal dimensions is of particular importance because dimensions are linked to human emotions as well as with expectancy of success. One of these emotions is pride. It has been contended that for pride to be experienced, there must be self-attribution for success. At times, when others perceived as within one's ego boundaries succeed, such as a spouse or an off-spring, then pride also is felt. Further, success of larger entities with which one identifies, such as a sporting team or even one's country, might also generate pride. But in most instances pride is the direct result of a self-ascription for success. These personal attributions include ability and effort in the achievement domain, and personality and attractiveness in the affiliative domain. The postulated locus-pride relation is consistent with the thinking of many philosophers and is supported by an array of data (see Chapter 5).

Experiment 11 provides a simple demonstration of this connection. Rather than creating a hypothetical or a simulated context, as in the last few experiments, the participants are asked to recall situations in which they did or did not experience pride following a success. They also describe the factors perceived as producing the success. Content analysis of the responses should reveal self-ascriptions only when pride was reported.

Linkage 8: Expectancy of Success to Hopelessness and Hope

There is a dearth of attributional research concerning the linkage between expectancy of success and feelings of hope and hopelessness (see Weiner et al., 1978, for some pertinent data). Some investigations have considered the consequences of helplessness, but these studies primarily have been generated by learned-helplessness theory. The belief that helplessness is a precursor of depression certainly is consistent with the attributional perspective, although, as revealed earlier, there should be a sharp distinction made between hopelessness and helplessness, and there might be many antecedents of depression.

From an attributional perspective, the necessary condition for feelings of hopelessness is failure accompanied by an ascription to a stable cause. That is, if the future is anticipated to be as bad as the present, then hopelessness is elicited. On the other hand, failure ascribed to an unstable cause need not result in hopelessness, for expectancy of success can be maintained and the future can be foreseen as different from the present. Given an unstable ascription, hope rather than hopelessness could be exhibited in the face of failure.

These hypotheses are examined in Experiment 12. The participants are asked to recall a time of failure. One recall is when failure is ascribed to a stable cause; the other recall is when failure is ascribed to an unstable cause. Affective reactions are then recollected. Recall is always problematic as a dependent variable in affect studies for, as Freud suggested, memories are generous. Nonetheless, the investigation does reasonably test the hypothesized linkage between expectancy and affect.

Linkage 9: Causal Controllability to Guilt and Shame

The distinction between guilt and shame has a long history in philosophy and has been the subject of debate among psychologists and anthropologists. I have contended that both of these self-directed affects are connected with the concept of controllability—guilt follows from an attribution for a negative outcome to a controllable cause (e.g., lack of effort), whereas shame and its associated affective network of humiliation and embarrassment require an ascription to an uncontrollable cause (e.g., lack of aptitude). Perceived controllability is not the only antecedent of these affective reactions; for example, guilt antecedents include some foresight of the possible consequences of one's actions, whereas shame probably involves social comparison processes and the assumed judgements of others. Thus, ascriptions to controllable or uncontrollable causes seem to be necessary rather than sufficient antecedents to produce guilt and shame reactions.

There is a great deal of documentation supporting the lack-of-effort-guilt linkage (see Chapter 5), whereas the attributional antecedents of shame remain more controversial and less empirically studied (see Covington & Omelich, 1984; Brown & Weiner, 1984). As part of Experiment 13, participants are asked to report about an occasion in which they experienced guilt and another occasion in which shame was felt. The contents of the reports can then be analyzed for perceived controllability.

Linkage 10: Causal Controllability to Other-Directed Affects: Pity and Anger

The two most experimentally investigated affects from this attributional perspective have been anger and pity (sympathy). Because of a concern by psychologists about aggressive and moral behavior, both anger and empathy (sympathy) also have been the subject of a great deal of thought and study from other theoretical viewpoints. Attribution theory, however, has been able to incorporate these two emotions within the same conceptual network by pointing out that the elicitation of both is in part dependent on causal perceptions along a controllability dimension. It has been hypothesized that anger is evoked when the failure or need of others, or the blocking of a personal goal, is due to a cause controllable by another person, such as lack of effort. Conversely, pity is elicited when the plight of another is due to an uncontrollable cause, such as lack of capability. A great deal of research has confirmed this analysis (see Chapter 5). It also has been documented that gratitude is linked with the controllability dimension, but that will not be pursued further in this section.

Two experiments are included in this section (and more in the next section of the chapter) that should document the controllability-anger and the uncontrollability-pity associations. In Experiment 13, the respondents again are asked to recollect personal experiences of anger and pity. Again these responses can be analyzed for perceptions of controllability. In Experiment 14, a hypothetical situation is created, rather than asking about actual personal experiences. A student is described as failing at an exam, and six causes are provided. Three of these are considered a priori to be controllable (had not done assignments, did not study, did not attend class), whereas the other three are classified a priori as uncontrollable (lack of aptitude, nervousness, and poor tutor). Then the participants are asked how much anger and pity they would feel in these situations. Anger is anticipated to be greater than pity given the controllable causes, and pity greater than anger given the uncontrollable causes.

Linkages 11, 12, and 13: Expectancy and Affect to Action

The last steps in the historical sequence shown in Figures 6-4 and 8-6 are the linkages with a final action or judgment, such as undertaking an achievement-related
task, asking someone for a date, helping another in distress, or reaching a parole
decision. This is presumed to be determined by the subjective likelihood of goal
attainment and one's current affective state. Hence, this attributional approach is
consistent with other Expectancy × Value frameworks. However, there is a departure from the traditional focus on subjective value to an emphasis on present (rather
than future) emotional reactions.

Many prior researchers in the cognitive camp have documented the influence
of expectancy on behavior. Indeed, this has been the empirical center for those using
the theories of Atkinson, Bandura, and Rotter. I will therefore confine my attention
to the more novel role of emotion on action. In addition, the joint influence of
component associations in the theory will be demonstrated. To document a historical sequence involving more than one linkage, complex statistical techniques such
as path analysis are necessary. As these are classroom demonstrations, such
sophisticated analyses are not possible. Rather, correlations between the pertinent
variables are the most than can be shown; the historical sequence must then be logically inferred.

Four experimental studies will be described. The cognitions or actions to be
examined are helping judgments, evaluation of others, excuse giving for breaking a
social contract, and excuses for personal rejection. In three of these investigations,
the critical affects are anger and pity, whereas in the fourth study self-esteem plays
a pivotal role.

In the first of the four studies (Experiment 15), two students are described as
needing to borrow class notes (based on Weiner, 1980a, 1980b; see also Betancourt,
1983; Reisenzein, 1986). One student gives a controllable cause ("went to the
beach"); the other communicates an uncontrollable cause ("eye problems"). Four
questions are then asked: How much anger and how much pity would be felt? What
is the likelihood of help giving? and How controllable is the cause? It is hypothesized
that in the beach condition the cause will be perceived as controllable, feelings of
anger but not pity will be revealed, and help will be withheld. On the other hand,
in the eye problem condition the cause will be perceived as uncontrollable, feelings
of pity but not anger will be expressed, and help will be offered. That is, there will
be correlations between attributions, affects, and action (or, given this simulational
study, judgments of action), with high control-high anger-low pity-low help and low
control-low anger-high pity-high help forming two distinct groupings. As shown in
Figures 6-4 and 8-6, it is believed that there is also a temporal sequence of attribution-affect-action; one first learns why, this generates feelings, and feelings determine what one does.

Experiment 16 shifts to a different context: student evaluation. The participants
are asked to pretend that they are teachers and must give evaluative feedback to eight
students. There are three independent variables: student ability (high or low), effort
(high or low), and exam outcome (success or failure). These three sources of infor-

mation are factorially combined, yielding eight experimental conditions or kinds of pupils (2 levels of ability × 2 levels of effort × 2 levels of outcome). The respondents are asked to evaluate each student, as well as to indicate how much anger toward the pupil they would experience.

It is anticipated that positive outcomes (success) will be evaluated more favorably than negative outcomes (failure), reflecting the fact that outcomes have consequences independent of the attributions for those outcomes (Linkage 13). The main effect of outcome can be determined by summing the evaluations of the succeeding students (Students 1, 3, 5, 7), and then subtracting the sum of the evaluations of the failing students (Students 2, 4, 6, 8). In addition, high effort is predicted to be evaluated more highly than low effort, and *low* ability is hypothesized to be evaluated as favorably as, or even more positively than, high ability. This somewhat surprising result is predicted because high ability accompanied by low effort and failure should be evaluated most negatively, whereas low ability accompanied by high effort and success is hypothesized to be appraised most highly. In our culture (and many others), it is "immoral" not to utilize one's capacity; this will produce maximum punishment. Conversely, overcoming personal handicaps to succeed through hard work is most admired and should result in maximum reward (see Chapter 5). The moral aspects of this situation are expected to be reflected in the anger ratings: More anger is anticipated to be revealed given low than high effort (as also shown in Experiments 13, 14, and 15), with the most anger expected in response to low effort, high ability, and failure.

In sum, in this study complex interactions should be exhibited, with anger and evaluation dependent on patterns of attributions and outcomes. Hence, some additional complexities not shown in the prior studies are introduced. But, as in the prior experiment, it is presumed that there is a temporal sequence going from attributions to affect to evaluation. This sequence will be most clearly revealed in the low effort-high anger-low evaluation pattern, and particularly when low effort is accompanied by high ability and failure.

Now I want to shift to a very different but equally frequent encounter: giving an excuse to another when one has broken a social contract. These "broken contracts" include not appearing for an appointment, coming very late, and so forth. As discussed in Chapters 2 and 5, these negative and unexpected events elicit a causal search from the "wronged" party—he or she is likely to ask the reason for the late arrival or the failure to show up. It is known that controllable causes of negative events will evoke anger. Hence, such explanations should be withheld, replaced instead with excuses that will be perceived as uncontrollable. That is, a lie might be told. Here the assumed sequence of events is: causal controllability→anticipated anger reaction→communication decision.

In Experiment 17, four reasons for breaking a social contract are given. Two seem controllable (visiting a friend, watching TV), whereas the other two appear to be uncontrollable (flat tire, call from mother) (from Weiner & Handel, 1985). On the basis of the earlier analysis it is predicted that controllable causes will be presumed to elicit anger and will be withheld, whereas the uncontrollable causes will not be expected to give rise to anger (indeed, sympathy should be anticipated), and thus the truth will be told. This is a nice place to demonstrate the meaning of a correlation within a lab course!

Experiment 18, the final one in this chapter, reports a very similar situation (from Folkes, 1982; Weiner & Handel, 1985). In this case, a reason must be communicated for the rejection of a date. Two of the reasons are internal to the requester of the date (physical unattractiveness, poor personality), whereas the other two are external to that person (the person asked is not feeling well, has a prior engagement). From Chapter 5 it is known that internal ascriptions for failure result in a loss of self-esteem. Hence, it is predicted that to protect the other from this loss (and, in turn, to maintain the social bond) internal causes will not be communicated, whereas causes external to the requester will be told. That is, there is a sequence that can be represented as: causal locus, anticipated loss of self-esteem, communication decision. This has two component patterns: internal locus, anticipated low self-esteem, response withholding (lie); and external locus, no anticipated loss of self-esteem, truthful communication.

Summing Up

This book began with a set of 12 beliefs about the essential ingredients for a viable theory of motivation. One of these principles was that a theory of motivation must be based upon reliable (replicable) empirical relations. In this chapter, 18 investigations were described that I think fulfill this criterion. I do have some trepidation about the data that will emerge in the outcome-affect investigation (Experiment 1) and am concerned about Experiment 13 involving comparisons between guilt and shame. But I feel confident that 85% to 90% of the proposed studies will yield the anticipated data. I see this as a major feat; the reader might remember that in the initial chapter I challenged the main theoretical rivals, achievement and locus-of- control (social learning) theory, to wager on any *one* theoretically derived hypothesis that includes individual differences in need for achievement or locus of control. It is also important to point out that 11 of the proposed studies include affective reactions. In Chapter 1 it was contended that other theories of motivation have neglected emotions, save for the general pleasure-pain principle. This shortcoming has been overcome by using an attributional framework.

My initial hope when writing this book was that the theory to be formulated would earn its place alongside other major motivational conceptions. For this to occur, I thought that there must be a tightly woven conceptual network, closely tied to the data language. Often conceptions do not have a good theory-data balance, being heavy in one of these two aspects and light on the other. This chapter perhaps will reassure some about the strength of the empirical linkages; almost every postulated association in Figure 6-4 and Figure 8-6 has a substantial empirical basis (the clearest exception to this statement is the linkage between specific attributions and affect).

I also wish to address the "nothing but common sense" criticism at times leveled against attribution theorists, for this comment relates to the clarity and perhaps obviousness of some of the experimental demonstrations. When critics challenge that an attributional approach is "mere" common sense, they are claiming (I think) that the relations predicted by the theory are shared knowledge. That is, for the most part, correct. The lay person associates anger with something that one "should have (or have not) done"; the layperson also is likely to connect hope with "something might change"; and so forth. But what is not realized is that, for example, the determinants of helping behavior (Experiment 15), evaluation (Experiment 16), and communications for breaking social contracts and rejecting others (Experiment 17 and 18) are part of the same system of knowledge. That the component parts of the theory are naively shared underscores their veridicality, thus further supporting the certainty of the empirical foundation that is needed for theory building.

I want to conclude by briefly speculating about what the future might hold for this theory. It was indicated in Chapter 1 that just now the field of motivation is not at the heart of psychology, as it was in the Hull-Tolman era in the 1930s and 1940s. It would lead us too far afield to explore the historical reasons for this descent in importance, but I believe that with the current affective (as opposed to cognitive) revolution, motivation will be restored to its rightful place in psychology. If this happens, then many of the issues examined in this book will be addressed in detail. Regardless of the fate of this particular conception, the empirical findings in part documented in Experiments 1 through 18 will have to be accounted for. I would love to read about how this is conceptually accomplished, from my position on, above, or far below Mount Olympus.

Appendix

Experiment 1: Outcome to Affect

Think of a time that you succeeded (failed) at an achievement-related task, such as doing well (poorly) on an exam, reaching (failing to reach) an occupational goal, winning (losing) at a competitive sporting match, and so on. Write about that event: What was the situation, what caused the outcome, and so on. Try to remember the event vividly.

Use this space to describe the situation and the outcome:

Now try to recall your feelings at that time. Write three emotions that best describe your feelings then.

1. _____

2. _____

3. _____

Experiment 2: Outcome to Causal Search

1. Imagine that you unexpectedly succeeded at a test. For example, you are relatively weak in a particular subject matter or course, yet you received a good mark on the midterm exam, what thoughts, questions, etc., would go through your mind, what might you most likely ask yourself, when this happened? Write those thoughts, questions, etc., below. If there are none, just indicate this.

2. Imagine that you expectedly failed a test. For example, you are relatively weak in a particular subject matter or course, and you received a poor mark on the midterm exam. What thoughts, questions, etc., would go through your mind, what might you most likely ask yourself, when this happened? Write those thoughts, questions, etc., below. If there are none, just indicate this.

3. Imagine that you expectedly succeed at a test. For example, you are relatively strong in a particular subject matter or course, and you received a good mark on the midterm exam. What thoughts, questions, etc., would go through your mind, what might you most likely ask yourself, when this happened. Write those thoughts, questions, etc., below. If there are none, just indicate this.

4. Imagine that you unexpectedly failed a test. For example, you are relatively strong in a particular subject matter or course, yet you received a poor mark on the midterm exam. What thoughts, questions, etc., would go through your mind, what might you most likely ask yourself, when this happened? Write those thoughts, questions, etc., below. If there are none, just indicate this.

Experiment 3: Causal Antecedents (Social Norms) to Causal Ascriptions

You will be given some information about a series of individuals in various situations, and asked to make judgments about certain aspects of their performance. The first column tells that percentage of a group that has succeeded at a certain task. The second column indicates whether the particular person under consideration has succeeded or failed at that task. In the last column you are asked to judge to what extent the person's success or failure was or was not due to his own effort and ability. If the outcome was a success, effort and ability are assumed to be high; if the outcome was a failure, it is assumed that the judgments refer to low effort and to low ability.

Percentage of others succeeding	Outcome of person	Outcome due to person's ability and effort						
		Definitely						Not at all
40%	Success	1	2	3	4	5	6	7
100%	Failure	1	2	3	4	5	6	7
80%	Failure	1	2	3	4	5	6	7
60%	Success	1	2	3	4	5	6	7
20%	Failure	1	2	3	4	5	6	7
80%	Success	1	2	3	4	5	6	7
20%	Success	1	2	3	4	5	6	7
40%	Failure	1	2	3	4	5	6	7
100%	Success	1	2	3	4	5	6	7
60%	Failure	1	2	3	4	5	6	7

Experiment 4: Causal Antecedents (Causal Schemata) to Causal Ascriptions

An exam has been graded with only two possible outcomes, *pass* or *fail*. You will be given information about a student's outcome on the exam. In addition, you will be told what percentage of the other students passed the exam. Finally, you will be told whether the student has ability or not. Your task is to infer whether effort was present or absent, or whether you are uncertain about how hard the student tried.

A student passed the exam. Ninety percent of the other students also passed. The student is able. Do you think he or she also tried hard?

1. Definitely tried hard
2. Probably tried hard
3. Am not certain if the student did or did not try hard
4. Probably did not try hard
5. Definitely did not try hard.

A student passed the exam. Ten percent of the other students also passed (that is, 90% of the other students failed). The student is able. Do you think he or she also tried hard?

1. Definitely tried hard
2. Probably tried hard
3. Am not certain if the student did or did not try hard
4. Probably did not try hard
5. Definitely did not try hard.

Experiment 5: Affects as Antecedents of Causal Ascriptions

In the following examples a student is described as failing, and the emotional reaction of the teacher is given. You are to infer why the teacher thought the student failed. Circle your answers.

1. A student failed a test and the teacher felt guilty. Why did the teacher think the student failed? Because:

The student never studies for tests.

Not at all a cause   1   2   3   4   5   Certainly a cause

The teacher was unclear.

Not at all a cause   1   2   3   4   5   Certainly a cause

The student is low in ability.

Not at all a cause   1   2   3   4   5   Certainly a cause

The student was unlucky on the test.

Not at all a cause   1   2   3   4   5   Certainly a cause

2. A student failed a test and the teacher felt pity and sympathy. Why did the teacher think the student failed? Because:

The student never studies for tests.

Not at all a cause   1   2   3   4   5   Certainly a cause

The teacher was unclear.

Not at all a cause   1   2   3   4   5   Certainly a cause

The student is low in ability.

Not at all a cause   1   2   3   4   5   Certainly a cause

The student was unlucky on the test.

Not at all a cause   1   2   3   4   5   Certainly a cause

3. A student failed a test and the teacher got angry. Why did the teacher think the student failed?

The student never studies for tests.

Not at all a cause   1   2   3   4   5   Certainly a cause

The teacher was unclear.

Not at all a cause   1   2   3   4   5   Certainly a cause

The student is low in ability.

Not at all a cause   1   2   3   4   5   Certainly a cause

The student was unlucky on the test.

Not at all a cause   1   2   3   4   5   Certainly a cause

Experiment 6: From Causal Controllability to Other-Directed Affects

Imagine that there are two students taking a test in a classroom. Both receive the identical grade of C. As feedback to one of the students (call her Jane), the teacher merely says, "You received the grade of C." To the other student (call her Mary), the teacher says, "You received the grade of C. I am very displeased and angry." Answer the following questions about the students.

Jane
How able or smart do you think the teacher regards Jane?

1. Very smart
2. Smart
3. Average
4. Below average
5. Dumb.

How hard do you think the teacher feels that Jane prepared for the exam?

1. Very hard
2. Hard
3. Average
4. Below average
5. Hardly at all.

Mary
How able or smart do you think the teacher regards Mary?

1. Very smart
2. Smart
3. Average
4. Below average
5. Dumb.

How hard do you think the teacher feels that Mary prepared for the exam?

1. Very hard
2. Hard
3. Average
4. Below average
5. Hardly at all.

Both students
Circle the name of the student whom the teacher regards as smarter, Jane or Mary.

Circle the name of the student whom the teacher regards as having worked harder, Jane or Mary.

Experiment 7: Causal Ascriptions to Causal Dimensions

On this page, 16 causes are listed that contribute to failure in school and/or at an athletic competition. You are to consider the 16 causes and sort them into two piles on the basis of some principle or category (concept). For example, you might sort according to the starting letter of the alphabet and put into Pile 1 all causes starting with the letters A to M and in Pile 2 all causes starting with the letter N to Z. (This example was selected because it is unlikely to be used as a psychological category to divide the causes.) All the causes must go into one category or the other, but they do not have to be equally divided into the two piles. After a principle or concept has been selected, put a check on the lines of causes going into Pile 1 and a check on the lines of causes going into Pile 2. Then write the concept that was used to sort the causes. Now go on and try to sort the causes again using a different principle, going through the identical procedure. Do this a maximum of three times, although you should stop whenever you cannot determine a new classification principle.

	Sort 1		Sort 2		Sort 3	
Causes	Pile 1	Pile 2	Pile 1	Pile 2	Pile 1	Pile 2
Arrived tense	___	___	___	___	___	___
Tough opponent	___	___	___	___	___	___
Feeling "down"	___	___	___	___	___	___
Bad coach	___	___	___	___	___	___
Poor concentration	___	___	___	___	___	___
Bad professor	___	___	___	___	___	___
Poor time allotment	___	___	___	___	___	___
Unhealthy	___	___	___	___	___	___
Interference from others	___	___	___	___	___	___
Easy grading curve	___	___	___	___	___	___
Little innate intelligence	___	___	___	___	___	___
Unlucky	___	___	___	___	___	___
Does not practice	___	___	___	___	___	___
Does not study	___	___	___	___	___	___
Poor coordination	___	___	___	___	___	___
Nonsupportive teammates	___	___	___	___	___	___
Explain the principle (concept) used to divide the causes into two piles:	___	___	___	___	___	___
	___	___	___	___	___	___

Experiment 8: Causal Ascriptions to Causal Dimensions

Below are listed five dominant causes of success and failure in achievement-related situations: aptitude, effort, the objective difficulty of the task, luck, and mood. You are asked to judge three characteristics of these causes: 1) whether you think they reside within or outside of the person undertaking a task; 2) whether you think that the causes are stable (constant) over time or whether they change over time; and 3) whether anyone (the actor or others) has control over the causes and can volitionally create change. Please circle your answers.

Cause	Location					Stability					Control				
	In-side				Out-side	Stable				Vari-able	Con-troll-able				Uncon-troll-able
Aptitude	1	2	3	4	5	1	2	3	4	5	1	2	3	4	5
Effort	1	2	3	4	5	1	2	3	4	5	1	2	3	4	5
Objective difficulty of task	1	2	3	4	5	1	2	3	4	5	1	2	3	4	5
Luck	1	2	3	4	5	1	2	3	4	5	1	2	3	4	5
Mood	1	2	3	4	5	1	2	3	4	5	1	2	3	4	5

Experiment 9: From Causal Stability to Expectancy of Success

You have just failed at an exam and think that the failure was due to a certain factor. The responsible cause will be indicated below. You expect to take a similar exam in the near future. Indicate your subjective expectation of succeeding at the next exam.

1. The prior failure occurred because you do not have ability in the subject matter (for example, you think you are poor at math, art, etc.).

Likelihood of future success:

1	2	3	4	5	6	7
Very low			Intermediate			Very high

2. The prior failure occurred because on this occasion you did not study enough.

Likelihood of future success:

1	2	3	4	5	6	7
Very low			Intermediate			Very high

3. The prior failure occurred because this teacher always makes up very difficult exams.

Likelihood of future success:

1	2	3	4	5	6	7
Very low			Intermediate			Very high

4. The prior failure occurred because of bad luck (unlucky guessing, happened to study the wrong material, etc.).

Likelihood of future success:

1	2	3	4	5	6	7
Very low			Intermediate			Very high

Experiment 10: From Expectancy to Causal Stability

Assume that you are about to take an exam and have either a high or low expectancy of success. The exam has many true-false answers, so that luck as well as ability may play some role in the outcome. You then receive feedback that you scored high (success) or low (failure) on the exam. In all the four cases below, you are to indicate the extent that ability and luck are perceived as causes of the outcome. Circle your answers.

Expectancy of success	Outcome	Cause	Causal importance Definitely a cause					Not at all a cause	
High	High (success)	High ability	1	2	3	4	5	6	7
		Good luck	1	2	3	4	5	6	7
Low	High (success)	High ability	1	2	3	4	5	6	7
		Good luck	1	2	3	4	5	6	7
High	Low (failure)	Low ability	1	2	3	4	5	6	7
		Bad luck	1	2	3	4	5	6	7
Low	Low (failure)	Low ability	1	2	3	4	5	6	7
		Bad luck	1	2	3	4	5	6	7

Experiment 11: From Causal Locus to Pride

Think of a situation in which you succeeded and experienced the emotion of pride. Describe what happened. What caused the success?

Think of a situation when you succeeded and did not experience any feelings of pride. Describe what happened. What caused the success?

Experiment 12: From Expectancy of Success to Affect

In this experiment you are asked to think of a time when you failed at something that you considered important at that time. Perhaps it was an exam in school, an athletic competition, or even getting a date with another person you liked. In one situation to be described below, you should discuss a time in which you thought that the cause of the negative outcome was permanent, such as not having the aptitude to pass a math class, or the strength or speed to beat an opponent, or the "charm" or "looks" needed to attract this other person. In the second situation to be described, you are asked to discuss a negative outcome that was due to a cause that you thought might change. For example, you did not study enough for the midterm exam, used poor strategy during an athletic match that later would be played again, or asked the other person for a date when he or she already had plans that evening. In both situations, you are asked to report your feelings at that time.

Situation 1. Describe a time when you failed at something important for what you thought to be a stable cause:

Write three emotions you experienced at that time.

Situation 2. Describe a time when you failed at something important for what you thought to be an unstable cause, or a cause that might change:

Write three emotions you experienced at that time.

Experiment 13: From Causal Controllability to Affects

1. Think of a situation in which you experienced the emotion of *guilt*. Describe the situation in which this happened. If something negative occurred, or there was failure to attain some goal or do something, describe what caused this to happen.

2. Think of a situation in which you experienced the emotion of *shame* (or related feelings such as humiliation). Describe the situation in which this happened. If something negative occurred, or there was failure to attain some goal or do something, describe what caused this to happen.

3. Think of a situation in which you experienced the emotion of *anger* toward another person. Describe the situation in which this happened. What caused this feeling?

4. Think of a situation in which you experienced the emotion of *pity* toward another person. Describe the situation in which this happened. What caused this feeling?

Experiment 14: From Causal Controllability to Other-Directed Affects

Two very prevalent affects are anger and pity. You are presented a number of different situations revolving around a central theme, and are to indicate the degree of anger and pity that you might experience in this situation. Try to visualize the situation and answer as truthfully as possible what you might experience if you were the person involved.

Imagine that you are a college math teacher. You have given the final exam, and one of your students who failed the exam comes to you to explain why he or she failed. The student gives you one of the following eight causes for the failure, which you should assume are true. After each cause for failure, please indicate how much anger and/or pity you might experience toward the student.

1. The student failed the exam because of low math aptitude and couldn't understand most of the material covered in the course.

Anger
A great deal   1   2   3   4   5   6   7   None

Pity
A great deal   1   2   3   4   5   6   7   None

2. The student failed the exam because of lack of sleep the night before and nervousness and tenseness on the day of the exam.

Anger
A great deal   1   2   3   4   5   6   7   None

Pity
A great deal   1   2   3   4   5   6   7   None

3. The student failed the exam because none of the assignments were done during the whole course.

Anger
A great deal   1   2   3   4   5   6   7   None

Pity
A great deal   1   2   3   4   5   6   7   None

4. The student failed because of lack of study.

Anger
A great deal   1   2   3   4   5   6   7   None

Pity
A great deal   1   2   3   4   5   6   7   None

5. The student failed the exam because the math tutor often incorrectly explained answers to problems throughout the quarter.

Anger
A great deal   1   2   3   4   5   6   7   None

Pity
A great deal   1   2   3   4   5   6   7   None

6. The student failed because he or she did not attend most of the classes.

Anger
A great deal   1   2   3   4   5   6   7   None

Pity
A great deal   1   2   3   4   5   6   7   None

Experiment 15: From Attributions and Affect to Action

The following stories concern a student seeking to borrow your class notes. The story will describe this event and indicate why he is seeking help. Afterward, you will be asked to relate you thoughts and feelings about the person involved and what you might do.

> At about 1:00 in the afternoon you are walking through campus and a student comes up to you. He says that you do not know him, but you are both enrolled in the same class and he has happened to notice you. He asks if you would lend him the class notes from the meetings last week. He indicates that he needs the notes because he skipped class to go to the beach and generally "take it easy."

Please answer the following questions about the incident.

1. How much anger and annoyance do you feel toward the person?

A great deal of anger and annoyance	1	2	3	4	5	6	7	No anger and annoyance

2. How much sympathy do you have toward the person?

A great deal of sympathy	1	2	3	4	5	6	7	No sympathy

3. How likely is it that you would lend your class notes to this person?

Definitely *would* lend the notes	1	2	3	4	5	6	7	Definitely would *not* lend the notes

4. How controllable is this reason? That is, is the reason that he does not have the notes subject to personal influence? One might think that one should be able to control the amount that one is influenced by external sources, or that such distractions are not under personal control.

Under personal control	1	2	3	4	5	6	7	Not under personal control

At about 1:00 in the afternoon you are walking through campus and a student comes up to you. He says that you do not know him, but you are both enrolled in the same class and he happened to notice you. He asks if you would lend him the class notes from the meetings last week. He indicates that he needs the notes because he was having difficulty with his eyes, a change in glasses was required, and during the week he had difficulty seeing because of eyedrops and other treatments. You note he has a patch over one eye.

Please answer the following questions about the incident:

1. How much anger and annoyance do you feel toward this person?

| A great deal of anger and annoyance | 1 | 2 | 3 | 4 | 5 | 6 | 7 | No anger and annoyance |

2. How much sympathy do you have toward this person?

| A great deal of sympathy | 1 | 2 | 3 | 4 | 5 | 6 | 7 | No sympathy |

3. How likely is it that you would lend your class notes to this person?

| Definitely *would* lend the notes | 1 | 2 | 3 | 4 | 5 | 6 | 7 | Definitely would *not* lend the notes |

4. How controllable is this reason? That is, the reason that he does not have the notes subject to personal influence? One might think that one should be able to control the amount that one is affected by this problem (for example, he could have brought a tape recorder, etc.), or that such a plight is not under personal control.

| Under personal control | 1 | 2 | 3 | 4 | 5 | 6 | 7 | Not under personal control |

Experiment 16: From Attributions and Affect to Action

In the following study, eight different pupils are described. They have just taken a test and received either a high (success) or low (failure) score. As the teacher of these children, you know each student's ability level and how much effort has been put into the test preparation. You are now to provide evaluative feedback to the children. Pretend this is in the form of stars: gold stars are for a good evaluation and red stars for a bad. You can put anywhere from 10 gold stars (represented by "+") to 10 red stars (represented by "−"), but you cannot put both gold and red stars on a paper, so a single decision must be reached. You are also to indicate how much anger you might experience. This can be from absolutely none (0) to a very great deal (10).

Student	Ability	Effort	Outcome	Anger (0–10)	Student feedback (Evaluative Judgement) (+10 to −10)
1	High	High	Success	_____	_____
2	High	High	Failure	_____	_____
3	High	Low	Success	_____	_____
4	High	Low	Failure	_____	_____
5	Low	High	Success	_____	_____
6	Low	High	Failure	_____	_____
7	Low	Low	Success	_____	_____
8	Low	Low	Failure	_____	_____

Calculations for main effects:	For Anger	For Evaluation
Success (lines 1, 3, 5, 7) =	_____	_____
Failure (lines 2, 4, 6, 8) =	_____	_____
Difference =	_____	_____
High effort (lines 1, 2, 5, 6) =	_____	_____
Low effort (lines 3, 4, 7, 8) =	_____	_____
Difference =	_____	_____
Low ability (lines 5, 6, 7, 8) =	_____	_____
High ability (lines 1, 2, 3, 4) =	_____	_____
Difference =	_____	_____

Experiment 17: From Attributions and Affect to Action

You make an appointment or have a date with a person whom you know (although
not that well) and then arrive one hour late. Below the real reasons are given. You
are to indicate if you would convey this reason and, if so, how angry the recipient
of the communication would be. Circle your answers.

1. Your car had a flat tire.

    a. Would you reveal this cause?

    Definitely yes   1   2   3   4   5   6   7   Definitely no

    b. How angry would the person be if the cause was communicated?

            Very   1   2   3   4   5   6   7   Not at all

2. You decided to first stop and see another friend

    a. Would you reveal this cause?

    Definitely yes   1   2   3   4   5   6   7   Definitely no

    b. How angry would the person be if the cause was communicated?

            Very   1   2   3   4   5   6   7   Not at all

3. You wanted to watch a new program on TV first.

    a. Would you reveal this cause?

    Definitely yes   1   2   3   4   5   6   7   Definitely no

    b. How angry would the person be if the cause was communicated?

            Very   1   2   3   4   5   6   7   Not at all

4. Your mother called long-distance about a serious operation just before you left.

    a. Would you reveal this cause?

    Definitely yes   1   2   3   4   5   6   7   Definitely no

    b. How angry would the person be if the cause was communicated?

            Very   1   2   3   4   5   6   7   Not at all

Experiment 18: From Attributions and Affect to Action

A person who exhibits some interest in you suggests that you have supper together. You answer "no." Below the real reasons for this refusal are given. You are to indicate if you would convey this reason and, if so, how much the feelings (self-esteem) of the other person would be hurt. Circle your answers.

1. You find this person physically unattractive.

    a. Would you reveal this reason?

    Definitely yes   1   2   3   4   5   6   7   Definitely no

    b. If you revealed the reason, how much would his or her feelings be hurt?

    Very much   1   2   3   4   5   6   7   Not at all

2. You have a very bad headache and a cold.

    a. Would you reveal this reason?

    Definitely yes   1   2   3   4   5   6   7   Definitely no

    b. If you revealed the reason, how much would his or her feelings be hurt?

    Very much   1   2   3   4   5   6   7   Not at all

3. You have a prior engagement and tickets to a concert.

    a. Would you reveal this reason?

    Definitely yes   1   2   3   4   5   6   7   Definitely no

    b. If you revealed the reason, how much would his or her feelings be hurt?

    Very much   1   2   3   4   5   6   7   Not at all

4. You find the person very boring.

    a. Would you reveal this reason?

    Definitely yes   1   2   3   4   5   6   7   Definitely no

    b. If you revealed this reason, how much would his or her feelings be hurt?

    Very much   1   2   3   4   5   6   7   Not at all

References

Abramson, L. Y., Seligman, M. E. P., & Teasdale, J. (1978). Learned helplessness in humans: Critique and reformulation. *Journal of Abnormal Psychology, 87*, 49–74.

Allen, B. A., & Potkay, C. R. (1981). On the arbitrary distinction between states and traits. *Journal of Personality and Social Psychology, 41*, 916–928.

Alloy, L. B., Abramson, L. Y., & Viscusi, D. (1981). Induced mood and illusion of control. *Journal of Personality and Social Psychology, 41*, 1129–1140.

Ames, C. (1978). Children's achievement attributions and self-reinforcement: Effects of self-concept and competitive reward structure. *Journal of Educational Psychology, 70*, 345–355.

Ames, C., Ames, R., & Felker, D. W. (1976). Informational and dispositional determinants of children's achievement attributions. *Journal of Educational Psychology, 68*, 63–69.

Ames, R., & Lau, S. (1982). An attributional analysis of student help-seeking in academic settings. *Journal of Educational Psychology, 74*, 414–423.

Amsel, A. (1958). The role of frustrative nonreward in noncontinuous reward situations. *Psychological Bulletin, 55*, 102–119.

Anderson, C. A. (1983a). The causal structure of situations: The generation of plausible causal attributions as a function of the type of event situation. *Journal of Experimental Social Psychology, 19*, 185–203.

Anderson, C. A. (1983b). Abstract and concrete data in the perseverance of social theories: When weak data lead to unshakeable beliefs. *Journal of Experimental Social Psychology, 19*, 93–108.

Anderson, C. A. (1983c). Motivational and performance deficits in interpersonal settings: The effects of attributional style. *Journal of Personality and Social Psychology, 45*, 1136–1147.

Anderson, C. A., & Arnoult, L. H. (1985). Attributional style and everyday problems in living: Depression, loneliness, and shyness. *Social Cognition, 3*, 16–35.

Anderson, C. A., Horowitz, L. M., & French, R. D. (1983). Attributional style of lonely and depressed people. *Journal of Personality and Social Psychology, 45*, 127–136.

Anderson, C. A., & Jennings, D. L. (1980). When experiences of failure promote expectations of success: The impact of attributing failure to ineffective strategies. *Journal of Personality, 48*, 393–407.

Andrews, G. R., & Debus, R. L. (1978). Persistence and the causal perception of failure: Modifying cognitive attributions. *Journal of Educational Psychology, 70*, 154–166.

Arkin, R. M., Detchon, C. S., & Maruyama, G. M. (1981). Causal attributions of high and low achievement college students for performance on examinations. *Motivation and Emotion, 5*, 139–152.

Arkin, R. M., Detchon, C. S., & Maruyama, G. M. (1982). Roles of attribution, affect, and cognitive interference in test anxiety. *Journal of Personality and Social Psychology*, *43*, 1111–1124.

Arkin, R. M., & Maruyama, G. M. (1979). Attribution, affect, and college exam performance. *Journal of Educational Psychology*, *71*, 85–93.

Arnold, M. B. (1960). Perennial problems in the field of emotion. In M. B. Arnold (Ed.), *Feelings and emotions* (pp. 169–203). New York: Academic Press.

Atkinson, J. W. (1964). *An introduction to motivation*. Princeton, NJ: Van Nostrand.

Atkinson, J. W., & Birch, D. (1970). *The dynamics of action*. New York: Wiley.

Averill, J. R. (1982). *Anger and aggression: An essay on emotion*. New York: Springer-Verlag.

Averill, J. R. (1983). Studies on anger and aggression. *American Psychologist*, *38*, 1145–1160.

Baldwin, C., & Baldwin, A. (1970). Children's judgment of kindness. *Child Development*, *41*, 29–47.

Bales, R. F. (1950). *Interaction process analysis: A method for the study of small groups*. Reading, MA: Addison-Wesley.

Bandura, A. (1977). Self-efficacy: Toward a unifying theory of behavioral change. *Psychological Review*, *84*, 191–215.

Barker, R. G. (1965). Explorations in ecological psychology. *American Psychologist*, *20*, 1–13.

Barnes, R. D., Ickes, W. J., & Kidd, R. (1979). Effects of perceived intentionality and stability of another's dependency on helping behavior. *Personality and Social Psychology Bulletin*, *5*, 367–372.

Barnett, D. J. (1981). *Parole decision-making and the personalities of police, probation officers, and attorneys acting as decision-makers*. Unpublished doctoral dissertation, University of California at Los Angeles.

Bar-Tal, D., Goldberg, M., & Knaani, A. (1984). Causes of success and failure and their dimensions as a function of SES and gender: A phenomenological analysis. *British Journal of Educational Psychology*, *54*, 51–61.

Batson, C. D., Duncan, B., Ackerman, P., Buckley, T., & Birch, K. (1981). Is empathic emotion a source of altrustic motivation? *Journal of Personality and Social Psychology*, *40*, 290–302.

Beckman, L. J. (1979). Beliefs about the causes of alcohol-related problems among alcoholic and non-alcoholic women. *Journal of Clinical Psychology*, *35*, 663–670.

Bem, D. J. (1972). Self-perception theory. In L. Berkowitz (Ed.), *Advances in experimental social psychology* (Vol. 6, pp. 1–62). New York: Academic Press.

Berkowitz, L. (1969). Resistance to improper dependency relationships. *Journal of Experimental Social Psychology*, *5*, 283–294.

Berlyne, D. E. (1960). *Conflict, arousal, and curiosity*. New York: McGraw-Hill.

Berlyne, D. E. (1968). Behavior theory as personality theory. In E. F. Borgetta & W. W. Lambert (Eds.), *Handbook of personality theory and research* (pp. 629–690). Chicago: Rand McNally.

Bernstein, W. M., Stephan, W. G., & Davis, M. H. (1979). Explaining attributions for achievement: A path analytic approach. *Journal of Personality and Social Psychology*, *37*, 1810–1821.

Berscheid, E., Graziano, W., Monson, T., & Dermer, M. (1976). Outcome dependency: Attention, attribution, and attraction. *Journal of Personality and Social Psychology*, *34*, 978–989.

Betancourt, H. (1983). *Causal attributions, empathy, and emotions as determinants of helping behavior: An integrative approach*. Unpublished doctoral dissertation, University of California at Los Angeles.

Betancourt, H., & Weiner, B. (1982). Attributions for achievement-related events, expectancy, and sentiments: A study of success and failure in Chile and the United States. *Journal of Cross-Cultural Psychology*, *13*, 362–374.

Bettman, J. R., & Weitz, B. A. (1983). Attributions in the boardroom: Causal reasoning in corporate annual reports. *Administrative Science Quarterly, 28*, 165–183.

Block, J., & Lanning, K. (1984). Attribution therapy requestioned: A secondary analysis of the Wilson-Linville study. *Journal of Personality and Social Psychology, 46*, 705–708.

Bond, M. H. (1983). A proposal for cross-cultural studies of attribution. In M. Hewstone (Ed.), *Attribution theory* (pp. 144–156). Oxford: Basil Blackwell.

Bottenberg, E. H. (1975). Phenomenological and operational characterization of factor-analytically derived dimensions of emotion. *Psychological Reports, 37*, 1253–1254.

Bower, G. H., & Cohen, P. R. (1982). Emotional influences in memory and thinking: Data and theory. In M. S. Clark & S. T. Fiske (Eds.), *Affect and cognition: The 17th Annual Carnegie Symposium on Cognition* (pp. 291–332). Hillsdale, NJ: Erlbaum.

Braithwaite, R. B. (1959). *Scientific explanation: A study of the function of theory, probability, and law in science.* Cambridge, England: Cambridge University Press.

Brehm, J. W. (Ed.). (1966). *A theory of psychological reactance.* New York: Academic Press.

Brewin, C. R. (1984a). Attributions for industrial accidents: Their relationship to rehabilitation outcome. *Journal of Social and Clinical Psychology, 2*, 156–164.

Brewin, C. R. (1984b). Perceived controllability of life-events and willingness to prescribe psychotropic drugs. *British Journal of Social Psychology, 23*, 285–287.

Brewin, C. R. (1985). Depression and causal attributions: What is their relation? *Psychological Bulletin, 98*, 297–309.

Brophy, J. E., & Rohrkemper, M. M. (1981). The influence of problem ownership on teachers' perceptions of and strategies for coping with problem students. *Journal of Educational Psychology, 73*, 295–311.

Brown, J. (1984). Effects of induced mood on causal attributions for success and failure. *Motivation and Emotion, 8*, 343–354.

Brown, J., & Weiner, B. (1984). Affective consequences of ability versus effort ascriptions: Controversies, resolutions, and quandaries. *Journal of Educational Psychology, 76*, 146–158.

Brown, J. S. (1961). *The motivation of behavior.* New York: McGraw-Hill.

Brunson, B. I., & Matthews, K. A. (1981). The Type A coronary-prone behavior pattern and reactions to uncontrollable stress: An analysis of performance strategies, affect, and attributions during failure. *Journal of Personality and Social Psychology, 40*, 906–918.

Bryant, F. B., & Veroff, J. (1982). The structure of psychological well-being: A sociohistorical analysis. *Journal of Personality and Social Psychology, 43*, 653–673.

Bulman, R. J., & Wortman, C. B. (1977). Attributions of blame and coping in the "real world": Severe accident victims react to their lot. *Journal of Personality and Social Psychology, 35*, 351–363.

Burger, J. M., Cooper, H. M., & Good, T. L. (1982). Teacher attribution of student performance: Effects of outcome. *Personality and Social Psychology Bulletin, 4*, 685–690.

Burke, J. P. (1978). On causal attribution: The interactive relationship between self-esteem and task performance. *Social Behavior and Personality, 6*, 211–221.

Buss, A. R. (1978). On the relationship between reasons and causes. *Journal of Personality and Social Psychology, 36*, 1311–1321.

Carlsmith, J. M., & Gross, A. E. (1969). Some effects of guilt on compliance. *Journal of Personality and Social Psychology, 11*, 232–239.

Carroll, J. S. (1978). Causal attributions in expert parole decisions. *Journal of Personality and Social Psychology, 36*, 1501–1511.

Carroll, J. S., & Payne, J. W. (1976). The psychology of the parole decision process: A joint application of attribution theory and information processing psychology. In J. S. Carroll & J. W. Payne (Eds.), *Cognition and social behavior* (pp. 13–32). Hillside, NJ: Erlbaum.

Carroll, J. S., & Payne, J. W. (1977a). Judgments about crime and the criminal: A model and a method for investigating parole decisions. In B. D. Sales (Ed.), *Perspectives in law and psychology: Vol. 1. The criminal justice system* (pp. 191–240). New York: Plenum.

Carroll, J. S., & Payne, J. W. (1977b). Crime seriousness, recidivism risk, and causal attributions in judgments of prison term by students and experts. *Journal of Applied Psychology*, *62*, 595–602.

Carroll, J. S., & Wiener, R. L. (1982). Cognitive social psychology in court and beyond. In A. H. Hastorf & A. M. Isen (Eds.), *Cognitive social psychology* (pp. 213–254). New York: Elsevier/North Holland.

Chan, K., & Keogh, B. (1974). Interpretation of task interruption and feelings of responsibility for failure. *Journal of Special Education*, *8*, 175–178.

Chandler, T. A., & Spies, C. J. (1984). Semantic differential placement of attributions and dimensions in four different groups. *Journal of Educational Psychology*, *76*, 1119–1127.

Chapin, M., & Dyck, D. G. (1976). Persistence and children's reading behavior as a function of N-length and attribution retraining. *Journal of Abnormal Psychology*, *85*, 511–515.

Clary, E. G., & Tesser, A. (1983). Reactions to unexpected events: The naive scientist. *Personality and Social Psychology Bulletin*, *9*, 609–620.

Cochran, S. D., & Hammen, C. L. (1985). Perceptions of stressful life events and depression: A test of attributional models. *Journal of Personality and Social Psychology*, *48*, 1562–1571.

Cohen, J., & Hansel, C. E. (1956). *Risk and gambling*. London: Longmans Green.

Coke, J. S., Batson, C. D., & McDavis, K. (1978). Empathic mediating of helping: A two stage model. *Journal of Personality and Social Psychology*, *36*, 752–766.

Collins, B. E., Martin, J. C., Ashmore, R. D., & Ross, L. (1973). Some dimensions of the internal-external metaphor in theories of personality. *Journal of Personality*, *41*, 471–492.

Cooper, H. M., & Burger, J. M. (1980). How teachers explain students' academic performance: A categorization of free response academic attributions. *American Educational Research Journal*, *17*, 95–109.

Covington, M. V., & Omelich, C. L. (1979a). Are causal attributions causal? A path analysis of the cognitive model of achievement motivation. *Journal of Personality and Social Psychology*, *37*, 1487–1504.

Covington, M. V., & Omelich, C. L. (1979b). Effort: The double-edged sword in school achievement. *Journal of Educational Psychology*, *71*, 169–182.

Covington, M. V., & Omelich, C. L. (1984). An empirical examination of Weiner's critique of attributional research. *Journal of Educational Psychology*, *76*, 1214–1225.

Covington, M. V., Spratt, M. F., & Omelich, C. L. (1980). Is effort enough, or does diligence count too? Student and teacher reactions to effort stability in failure. *Journal of Educational Psychology*, *72*, 717–729.

Coyne, J., & Gotlib, I. (1983). The role of cognition in depression: A critical appraisal. *Psychological Bulletin*, *94*, 472–505.

Crittended, K. S., & Wiley, M. G. (1980). Causal attribution and behavioral response to failure. *Social Psychology Quarterly*, *43*, 353–358.

Cutrona, C. E. (1982). Transition to college: Loneliness and the process of social adjustment. In L. A. Peplau & D. Perlman (Eds.), *Loneliness* (pp. 291–309). New York: Wiley.

Cutrona, C. E., Russell, D., & Jones, R. D. (1985). Cross-situational consistency in causal attributions: Does attributional style exist? *Journal of Personality and Social Psychology*, *47*, 1043–1058.

Dalal, A., Weiner, B., & Brown, J. (1985). *Issues in the measurement of causal stability and the prediction of expectancy of success*. Unpublished manuscript, University of California at Los Angeles.

Davidson, D. (1963). Actions, reasons and causes. *Journal of Philosophy*, *60*, 685–700.

Davitz, J. R. (1969). *The language of emotion*. New York: Academic Press.

Day, V. H. (1982). Validity of an attributional model for a specific life event. *Psychological Reports*, *50*, 434.

De Charms, R. (1968). *Personal causation*. New York: Academic Press.

Deaux, K. (1984). From individual differences to social categories: Analysis of a decade's research on gender. *American Psychologist*, *39*, 105–116.

Deci, E. L. (1975). *Intrinsic motivation*. New York: Plenum.

DeJong, W. (1980). The stigma of obesity: The consequences of naive assumptions concerning the causes of physical deviance. *Journal of Health and Social Behavior, 21*, 75–87.

de Rivera, J. (1977). *A structural theory of emotions*. New York: International University Press.

Deutsch, F. (1974). Female preschoolers' perceptions of affective responses and interpersonal behavior in videotaped episodes. *Developmental Psychology, 10*, 733–740.

Diener, C. I., & Dweck, C. S. (1978). An analysis of learned helplessness: Continuous changes in performance, strategy, and achievement cognitions following failure. *Journal of Personality and Social Psychology, 36*, 451–462.

Diener, C. I., & Dweck, C. S. (1980). An analysis of learned helplessness: II. The processing of success. *Journal of Personality and Social Psychology, 39*, 940–952.

Diggory, J. C., Riley, E. J., & Blumenfeld, R. (1960). Estimated probability of success for a fixed goal. *American Journal of Psychology, 73*, 41–55.

DuCette, J., & Keane, A. (1984). "Why me?": An attributional analysis of a major illness. *Research in Nursing and Health, 7*, 257–264.

Dweck, C. S. (1975). The role of expectations and attributions in the alleviation of learned helplessness. *Journal of Personality and Social Psychology, 31*, 674–685.

Dweck, C. S., & Repucci, N. D. (1973). Learned helplessness and reinforcement responsibility in children. *Journal of Personality and Social Psychology, 25*, 109–116.

Eiser, J. R., Van der Pligt, J., Raw, M., & Sutton, S. R. (in press). Trying to stop smoking: Effects of perceived addiction, attributions for failure and expectancy of success. *Journal of Behavioral Medicine*.

Elig, T. W., & Frieze, I. H. (1979). Measuring causal attributions for success and failure. *Journal of Personality and Social Psychology, 37*, 621–634.

Ellis, A. (1975). *A new guide to rational living*. Englewood Cliffs, NJ: Prentice-Hall.

Enzle, M. E., & Shopflocher, D. (1978). Instigation of attribution processes by attribution questions. *Personality and Social Psychology Bulletin, 4*, 595–599.

Esware, H. S. (1972). Administration of rewards and punishment in relation to ability, effort, and performance. *Journal of Social Psychology, 87*, 139–140.

Etaugh, C., & Hadley, T. (1977). Causal attribution of male and female performance by young children. *Psychology of Women Quarterly, 2*, 16–23.

Eysenck, H. J. (1970). *The structure of human personality*. London: Methuen.

Falbo, T., & Beck, R. C. (1979). Naive psychology and the attributional model of achievement. *Journal of Personality, 47*, 185–195.

Fayans, L. J., Jr., & Maehr, M. L. (1979). Attributional style, task selection, and achievement. *Journal of Educational Psychology, 71*, 499–507.

Feather, N. T. (1974). Explanations of poverty in Australian and American samples: The person, society and fate? *Australian Journal of Psychology, 26*, 199–226.

Feather, N. T. (1983). Causal attributions for good and bad outcomes in achievement and affiliation situations. *Australian Journal of Psychology, 35*, 37–48.

Feather, N. T., & Davenport, P. (1981). Unemployment and depressive affect: A motivational and attributional analysis. *Journal of Personality and Social Psychology, 41*, 422–436.

Feather, N. T., & Simon, J. G. (1971). Causal attributions for success and failure in relation to expectations of success based upon selective or manipulative control. *Journal of Personality, 39*, 527–541.

Feather, N. T., & Simon, J. G. (1972). Attribution of responsibility and valence of outcome in relation to initial confidence and success and failure of self and other. *Journal of Personality and Social Psychology, 18*, 173–188.

Festinger, L. (1942). A theoretical interpretation of shifts in level of aspiration. *Psychological Review, 49*, 235–250.

Festinger, L. (1980). Looking back. In L. Festinger (Ed.), *Retrospections on social psychology* (pp. 236–254). New York: Holt, Rinehart & Winston.

Fincham, F. D., & Jaspers, J. M. (1980). Attribution of responsibility: From man the scientist to man as lawyer. In L. Berkowitz (Ed.), *Advances in experimental social psychology* (Vol. 13, pp. 82–139). New York: Academic Press.

Fishbein, M., & Ajzen, I. (1975). *Belief, attitude, intention and behavior: An introduction to theory and research*. Reading, MA: Addison-Wesley.

Fitch, G. (1970). Effects of self-esteem, perceived performance and choice on causal attributions. *Journal of Personality and Social Psychology, 16*, 311–315.

Foersterling, F. (1980a). A multivariate analysis of perceived causes for success and failure. *Archives of Psychology, 133*, 45–52.

Foersterling, F. (1980b). Attributional aspects of cognitive behavior modification: A theoretical approach and suggestions for techniques. *Cognitive Therapy and Research, 4*, 27–37.

Foersterling, F. (1985). Attributional retraining: A review. *Psychological Bulletin, 98*, 495–512.

Foersterling, F., & Engelken, R. (1981). Expectancies in relation to success and failure, causal attributions, and perceived task similarity. *Personality and Social Psychology Bulletin, 7*, 578–582.

Foersterling, F., & Groenvald, A. (1983). Ursachzuschreibungen für ein Wahlergebnis: Eine Uberprüfung von Hypothesen der Attributionstheorie in einer Feldstudie anhand die niedersächsischen Kommunalwahlen, 1981. (Attributions for election results: A study of attributional hypotheses in a field study of Lower Saxony community elections, 1981.) *Zeitschrift für Sozialpsychologie, 14*, 262–269.

Folkes, V. S. (1982). Communicating the causes of social rejection. *Journal of Experimental Social Psychology, 18*, 235–252.

Folkes, V. S. (1984). Consumer reactions to product failure: An attributional approach. *Journal of Consumer Research, 11*, 398–409.

Folkes, V. S. (1985). *Predicting reactions to service problems: The view from the departure lounge*. Unpublished manuscript, University of California at Los Angeles.

Folkes, V. S., & Marcoux, R. E. (1984). Beauty and the attributions of the beholder. *Journal of Experimental Social Psychology, 20*, 514–530.

Folkes, V. S., & Morgenstern, D. (1981). Account-giving and social perception. *Personality and Social Psychology Bulletin, 7*, 451–458.

Fontaine, G. (1974). Social comparison and some determinants of expected personal control and expected performance in a novel task situation. *Journal of Personality and Social Psychology, 29*, 487–496.

Forgas, J. P., Morris, S. L., & Furnham, A. (1982). Lay explanation of wealth: Attributions for economic success. *Journal of Applied Psychology, 12*, 381–397.

Forsyth, D. R. (1980). The function of attributions. *Social Psychology Quarterly, 43*, 184–189.

Forsyth, D. R., & McMillan, J. H. (1981). The attribution cube and reactions to educational outcomes. *Journal of Educational Psychology, 73*, 632–641.

Fowler, J. W., & Peterson, P. L. (1981). Increasing reading persistence and altering attributional style of learned helpless children. *Journal of Educational Psychology, 73*, 251–260.

Frank, J. D. (1935). Individual differences in certain aspects of the level of aspiration. *American Journal of Psychology, 47*, 119–128.

Freud, S. (1952). Beyond the pleasure principle (C. J. M. Hubback, Trans.). In R. M. Hutchins (Ed.), *Great books of the western world* (Vol. 54, pp. 639–663). Chicago: Encyclopaedia Brittanica. (Original work, published 1920).

Frieze, I. H. (1976). Causal attributions and information seeking to explain success and failure. *Journal of Research in Personality, 10*, 293–305.

Frieze, I. H. (1979). Perceptions of battered wives. In I. H. Frieze, D. Bar-Tal, & J. S. Carroll (Eds.), *New approaches to social problems* (pp. 79–108). San Francisco: Jossey-Bass.

Frieze, I. H., & Snyder, H. N. (1980). Children's beliefs about the causes of success and failure in school settings. *Journal of Educational Psychology, 72*, 186–196.

Frieze, I. H., & Weiner, B. (1971). Cue utilization and attributional judgments for success and failure. *Journal of Personality, 39*, 591–605.

Frieze, I. H., Whitley, B. E., Jr., Hanusa, B. H., & McHugh, M. C. (1982). Assessing the theoretical models for sex differences in causal attributions for success and failure. *Sex Roles, 8,* 333–343.

Fuller, T. (1642). *The holy state and the profane state.* Cambridge, England: University of Cambridge Press.

Furnham, A. (1982a). Why are the poor always with us? Explanations for poverty in Britain. *British Journal of Social Psychology, 21,* 311–322.

Furnham, A. (1982b). Explanations for unemployment in Britain. *European Journal of Social Psychology, 12,* 335–352.

Furnham, A. (1983). Attributions for affluence. *Personality and Individual Differences, 4,* 31–40.

Gatting-Stiller, I., Gerling, M., Stiller, K., Voss, B., & Wender, I. (1979). Änderungen der Kausalattribuierung und des Ausdauerverhaltens bei misserfolgsmotivierten Kindern durch Modellernen (Changing the causal attributions of failure-motivated children through models). *Zeitschrift für Entwicklungspsychologie und Pädagogische Psychologie, 11,* 300–312.

Gilmore, T. M., & Minton, H. L. (1974). Internal versus external attributions of task performance as a function of locus of control, initial confidence and success-failure outcome. *Journal of Personality, 42,* 159–174.

Gilovich, T. (1983). Biased evaluation and persistence in gambling. *Journal of Personality and Social Psychology, 44,* 1110–1126.

Gioia, D. A., & Sims, H. P., Sr. (1983). *Attribution and verbal behavior in organizational interactions.* Unpublished manuscript, Pennsylvania State University.

Goldstein, S., Gordon, J. R., & Marlatt, G. A. (1984, August). *Attributional processes and relapse following smoking cessation.* Paper presented at the 92nd Annual Convention of the American Psychological Association, Toronto, Ontario, Canada.

Gollwitzer, P. M., Earle, W. B., & Stephan, W. G. (1982). Affect as a determinant of egotism: Residual excitation and performance attributions. *Journal of Personality and Social Psychology, 43,* 702–709.

Goranson, R. E., & Berkowitz, L. (1966). Reciprocity and responsibility reactions to prior help. *Journal of Personality and Social Psychology, 3,* 227–232.

Graham, S. (1984). Communicated sympathy and anger to black and white children: The cognitive (attributional) consequences of affective cues. *Journal of Personality and Social Psychology, 47,* 40–54.

Graham, S., Doubleday, C., & Guarino, P. A. (1984). The development of relations between perceived controllability and the emotions of pity, anger, and guilt. *Child Development, 55,* 561–565.

Graybill, D. (1978). Effects of perceived freedom on the relationship of locus of control beliefs to typical shifts in expectancy. *Psychological Reports, 43,* 815–820.

Greenberg, M. S., & Frisch, D. M. (1972). Effect of intentionality on willingness to reciprocate a favor. *Journal of Experimental Social Psychology, 8,* 99–111.

Greenberg, M. S., Saxe, L., & Bar-Tal, D. (1978). Perceived stability of trait labels. *Personality and Social Psychology Bulletin, 4,* 59–62.

Halperin, M. S., & Abrams, D. L. (1978). Sex differences in predicting final examination grades: The influence of past performance, attributions, and achievement motivation. *Journal of Educational Psychology, 70,* 763–771.

Hamilton, V. L. (1980). Intuitive psychologist or intuitive lawyer? Alternative models of the attribution process. *Journal of Personality and Social Psychology, 39,* 767–772.

Harter, S. (1982). A cognitive-developmental approach to children's understanding of affect and trait labels. In F. C. Serafica (Ed.), *Social-cognitive development in context* (pp. 27–61). New York: Guilford Press.

Harter, S. (1983). Developmental perspectives on the self-system. In P. H. Mussen (Ed.), *Handbook of child psychology* (4th ed., Vol. 4, pp. 275–386). New York: Wiley.

Harvey, J. H., & Weary, G. (1981). *Perspectives on attributional processes.* Dubuque, IA: Wm. C. Brown.

Hastie, R. (1984). Causes and effects of causal attribution. *Journal of Personality and Social Psychology, 46,* 44–56.

Hastorf, A. H., Northcraft, G. B., & Picciotto, S. R. (1979). Helping the handicapped: How realistic is the performance feedback received by the physically handicapped? *Personality and Social Psychology Bulletin, 3,* 373–376.

Hayashi, T., & Yamauchi, H. (1974). Causal attributional judgments for achievement-related events. *Japanese Psychological Research, 16,* 40–49.

Heider, F. (1958). *The psychology of interpersonal relations.* New York: Wiley.

Heilman, M. E., & Guzzo, R. A. (1978). The perceived causes of work success as a mediator of sex discriminations in organizations. *Organizational Behavior and Human Performance, 21,* 346–357.

Hendrick, C., & Giesen, M. (1975). Effects of task success or failure on causal attributions and person perception. *Memory & Cognition, 3,* 363–369.

Higgins, E. T., Strauman, T., & Klein, R. (1985). Standards and the process of self-evaluation: Multiple affects from multiple stages. In R. M. Sorrentino & E. T. Higgins (Eds.), *Motivation and cognition: Foundations of social behavior.* New York: Guilford Press.

Hoffman, M. L. (1975). Developmental synthesis of affect and cognition and its implications for altruistic motivation. *Developmental Psychology, 11,* 607–622.

Hoffman, M. L. (1982). Development of prosocial motivation: Empathy and guilt. In N. Eisenberg-Berg (Ed.), *Development of prosocial behavior* (pp. 281–313). New York: Academic Press.

Holden, K. B., & Rotter, J. B. (1962). A nonverbal measure of extinction in skill and chance situations. *Journal of Experimental Psychology, 63,* 519–520.

Holtzworth-Munroe, A., & Jacobson, N. S. (1985). Causal attributions of married couples: When do they search for causes? What do they conclude when they do? *Journal of Personality and Social Psychology, 48,* 1398–1412.

Hull, C. L. (1943). *Principles of behavior.* New York: Appleton-Century-Crofts.

Ickes, W. J., & Layden, M. A. (1978). Attributional styles. In J. H. Harvey, W. J. Ickes, & R. F. Kidd (Eds.), *New directions in attribution research* (Vol. 2, pp. 121–152). Hillsdale, NJ: Erlbaum.

Ilgen, D. R., & Knowlton, W. A., Jr. (1980). Performance attributional effects on feedback from superiors. *Organizational Behavior and Human Performance, 25,* 441–456.

Inagi, T. (1977). Causal ascription and expectancy of success. *Japanese Psychological Research, 19,* 23–30.

Isen, A. M., & Shalker, T. E. (1982). The effect of feeling state on the evaluation of positive, neutral, and negative stimuli: When you "Accentuate the positive," do you "Eliminate the negative?" *Social Psychology Quarterly, 45,* 58–62.

Isenberg, A. (1980). Natural pride and natural shame. In A. O. Rorty (Ed.), *Explaining emotions* (pp. 355–384). Berkeley: University of California Press.

Iso-Ahola, S. (1977). Immediate attributional effects of success and failure in the field: Testing some laboratory hypotheses. *European Journal of Social Psychology, 7,* 275–296.

Izard, C. E. (1971). *The face of emotion.* New York: Appleton-Century-Crofts.

Izard, C. E. (1977). *Human emotions.* New York: Plenum.

Jagacinski, C., & Nicholls, J. G. (1984). Conception of ability and related affects in task involvement and ego involvement. *Journal of Educational Psychology, 76,* 909–919.

James, W. H., & Rotter, J. B. (1958). Partial and 100% reinforcement under chance and skill conditions. *Journal of Experimental Psychology, 55,* 397–403.

Janoff-Bulman, R. (1979). Characterological versus behavioral self-blame: Inquiries into depression and rape. *Journal of Personality and Social Psychology, 37,* 1798–1809.

Janoff-Bulman, R., & Brickman, P. (1982). Expectations and what people learn from failure. In N. T. Feather (Ed.), *Expectations and actions: Expectancy-value models in psychology* (pp. 207–240). Hillsdale, NJ: Erlbaum.

Jones, E. E., & Davis, K. E. (1965). From acts to dispositions: The attribution process in person perception. In L. Berkowitz (Ed.), *Advances in experimental social psychology* (Vol. 2, pp. 219–266). New York: Academic Press.

Jones, E. E., Farino, A., Hastorf, A. H., Markus, H., Miller, D. T., & Scott, R. A. (1984). *Social stigma*. New York: Freeman.

Kelley, H. H. (1967). Attribution theory in social psychology. In D. Levine (Ed.), *Nebraska symposium on motivation* (pp. 192–238). Lincoln: University of Nebraska Press.

Kelley, H. H. (1971). *Attributions in social interactions*. Morristown, NJ: General Learning Press.

Kelley, H. H. (1973). Causal schemata and the attribution process. *American Psychologist, 28*, 107–123.

Kelley, H. H. (1983). The situational origins of human tendencies: A further reason for the formal analysis of structures. *Personality and Social Psychology Bulletin, 9*, 8–30.

Kelley, H. H., & Michela, J. (1980). Attribution theory and research. *Annual Review of Psychology, 31*, 457–501.

Kelly, G. A. (1955). *The psychology of personal constructs*. New York: Norton.

Kent State University. (1981). [Untitled survey.] Unpublished raw data.

Kepka, E. J., & Brickman, P. (1971). Consistency versus discrepancy as clues in the attribution of intelligence and motivation. *Journal of Personality and Social Psychology, 20*, 223–229.

Kidd, R. F., & Amabile, T. M. (1981). Causal explanations in social interaction: Some dialogues on dialogue. In J. H. Harvey, W. Ickes, & R. F. Kidd (Eds.), *New directions in attribution research* (Vol. 3, pp. 307–328). Hillsdale, NJ: Erlbaum.

Kingdon, J. W. (1967). Politicians' beliefs about voters. *American Political Science Review, 14*, 137–145.

Knowlton, W. A., Jr., & Mitchell, T. R. (1980). Effects of causal attributions on a supervisor's evaluation of subordinate performance. *Journal of Applied Psychology, 65*, 459–466.

Kojima, M. (1984). A study of causal attribution in achievement-related behavior: An analysis both in the experimental and in the educational settings. *Journal of Child Development, 20*, 20–30.

Kovenklioglu, G., & Greenhaus, J. H. (1978). Causal attributions, expectations, and task performance. *Journal of Applied Psychology, 63*, 698–705.

Krebs, D. L. (1975). Empathy and altruism. *Journal of Personality and Social Psychology, 32*, 1134–1146.

Kruglanski, A. W. (1979). Causal explanation, teleological explanation: On radical particularism in attribution theory. *Journal of Personality and Social Psychology, 37*, 1447–1457.

Kukla, A. (1972). Attributional determinants of achievement-related behavior. *Journal of Personality and Social Psychology, 21*, 166–174.

Kun, A., & Weiner, B. (1973). Necessary versus sufficient causal schemata for success and failure. *Journal of Research in Personality, 7*, 197–207.

Langer, E. (1983). *The psychology of control*. Beverly Hills, CA: Sage.

Lau, R. R. (1984). Dynamics of the attribution process. *Journal of Personality and Social Psychology, 46*, 1017–1028.

Lau, R. R., & Hartman, K. (1983). Common sense representations of common illnesses. *Health Psychology, 2*, 167–185.

Lau, R. R., & Russell, D. (1980). Attributions in the sports pages: A field test of some current hypotheses in attribution research. *Journal of Personality and Social Psychology, 39*, 29–38.

Lawrence, D. H., & Festinger, L. (1962). *Deterrents and reinforcement*. Stanford, CA: Stanford University Press.

Lazarus, R. S. (1966). *Psychological stress and the coping process*. New York: McGraw-Hill.

Lee, Y. K. (1976). *Construct validation of a new locus of control scale by multidimensional unfolding*. Paper presented at the meeting of the Western Psychological Association, Los Angeles.

Lefcourt, H. M., von Baeyer, C. L., Ware, E. E., & Cox, D. J. (1979). The Multidimensional-Multiattributional Causality Scale: The development of a goal specific locus of control scale. *Canadian Journal of Behavioral Science*, *11*, 286–304.

Lepley, W. M. (1963). The maturity of the chances: A gambler's fallacy. *Journal of Psychology*, *56*, 69–72.

Lepper, M. R., Greene, D., & Nisbett, R. E. (1973). Undermining children's intrinsic interest with extrinsic reward: A test of the over-justification hypothesis. *Journal of Personality and Social Psychology*, *28*, 129–137.

Lewin, K. (1935). *A dynamic theory of personality*. New York: McGraw-Hill.

Lewin, K., Dembo, T., Festinger, L., & Sears, P. S. (1944). Level of aspiration. In J. McV. Hunt (Ed.), *Personality and the behavioral disorders* (Vol. 1, pp. 333–378). New York: Ronald Press.

Litman-Adizes, T. (1978). *An attributional model of depression: Laboratory and clinical investigations*. Unpublished doctoral dissertation, University of California at Los Angeles.

Locke, D., & Pennington, D. (1982). Reasons and other causes: Their role in attribution processes. *Journal of Personality and Social Psychology*, *42*, 212–223.

Lucas, J. D. (1952). The interactive effects of anxiety failure and interserial duplications. *American Journal of Psychology*, *65*, 59–66.

Luginbuhl, J. E. R., Crowe, D. H., & Kahan, J. P. (1975). Causal attributions for success and failure. *Journal of Personality and Social Psychology*, *31*, 86–93.

Mackenzie, M. (1984). *Fear of fat*. New York: Columbia University Press.

MacMillan, D., & Keogh, B. (1971). Normal and retarded children's expectancy for failure. *Developmental Psychology*, *4*, 343–348.

Major, B., Mueller, P., & Hilderbrandt, K. (1985). Attributions, expectations, and coping with abortion. *Journal of Personality and Social Psychology*, *48*, 585–599.

Mark, J., Williams, G., & Brewin, C. R. (1984). Cognitive mediators of reactions to a minor life event: The British Driving Test. *British Journal of Social Psychology*, *23*, 41–49.

Mark, M. M. (1985). Expectations, procedural justice, and alternative reactions to being deprived of a desired outcome. *Journal of Experimental Social Psychology*, *21*, 114–137.

Marlatt, G. A. (1985). Cognitive factors in the relapse process. In G. A. Marlatt & J. R. Gordon (Eds.), *Relapse prevention: Maintenance strategies in the treatment of addictive behaviors* (pp. 128–200). New York: Guilford Press.

Martinez, A. (1982, Nov. 1). Out-of-work lumbermen not out of the woods yet. *Los Angeles Times*, Pt. 5, p. 1.

McCaughan, L. R. (1978). Stability/instability and change of expectancy, a test for cognitive determinants of psychomotor performance. *Perceptual and Motor Skills*, *46*, 219–225.

McClelland, D. C. (1961). *The achieving society*. Princeton, NJ: Van Nostrand.

McHugh, M., Beckman, L., & Frieze, I. H. (1979). Analyzing alcoholism. In I. H. Frieze, D. Bar-Tal, & J. S. Carroll (Eds.), *New approaches to social problems* (pp. 168–208). San Francisco: Jossey-Bass.

McHugh, M. C., Frieze, I. H., & Hanusa, B. H. (1982). Attributions and sex differences in achievement: Problems and new perspectives. *Sex Roles*, *8*, 467–479.

McMahan, I. D. (1973). Relationships between causal attributions and expectancy of success. *Journal of Personality and Social Psychology*, *28*, 108–114.

Medway, F. J. (1979). Causal attributions for school-related problems: Teacher perceptions and teacher feedback. *Journal of Educational Psychology*, *71*, 809–818.

Medway, F. J., & Venino, G. R. (1982). The effects of effort-feedback and performance patterns on children's attributions and task persistence. *Contemporary Educational Psychology*, *7*, 26–34.

Menapace, R. H., & Doby, C. (1976). Causal attributions for success and failure for psychiatric rehabilitees and college students. *Journal of Personality and Social Psychology*, *34*, 447–454.

Metalsky, G. I., Abramson, L. Y., Seligman, M. E. P., Semmel, A., & Peterson, C. (1982). Attributional styles and life events in the classroom: Vulnerability and invulnerability to depressive mood reactions. *Journal of Personality and Social Psychology*, *43*, 612–617.

Meyer, J. P. (1980). Causal attributions for success and failure: A multivariate investigation of dimensionality, formation, and consequences. *Journal of Personality and Social Psychology, 38,* 704–715.

Meyer, J. P., & Koelbl, S. L. M. (1982). Dimensionality of students' causal attributions for test performance. *Personality and Social Psychology Bulletin, 8,* 31–36.

Meyer, J. P., & Mulherin, A. (1980). From attribution to helping: An analysis of the mediating effects of affect on expectancy. *Journal of Personality and Social Psychology, 39,* 201–210.

Meyer, W. U. (1970). *Selbstverantwortlichkeit und Leistungsmotivation. (Self-concept and achievement motivation).* Unpublished doctoral dissertation, Ruhr Universität, Bochum, Federal Republic of Germany.

Meyer, W. U. (1973). *Leistungmotiv und Ursachenerklärung von Erfolg und Misserfolg* (Achievement motivation and causal attributions for success and failure). Stuttgart: Ernst Klett.

Meyer, W. U., Bachmann, M., Biermann, U., Hempelmann, M., Ploeger, F. O., & Spiller, H. (1979). The information value of evaluative behavior: Influences of praise and blame on perceptions of ability. *Journal of Educational Psychology, 71,* 259–268.

Michela, J. L., Peplau, L. A., & Weeks, D. G. (1982). Perceived dimensions of attributions for loneliness. *Journal of Personality and Social Psychology, 43,* 929–936.

Mikula, G., & Schlamberger, K. (1985). What people think about an unjust event: Toward a better understanding of the phenomenology of experiences of injustice. *European Journal of Social Psychology, 15,* 37–49.

Miller, D. T., & Vidmar, N. (1981). The social psychology of punishment reactions. In M. Lerner & S. Lerner (Eds.), *The justice motive in social behavior* (pp. 145–172). New York: Plenum.

Miller, I. W., III, & Norman, W. H. (1979). Learned helplessness in humans: A review and attribution-theory model. *Psychological Bulletin, 86,* 93–118.

Mischel, W., Ebbesen, E. B., & Zeiss, A. R. (1973). Selective attention to the self: Situational and dispositional determinants. *Journal of Personality and Social Psychology, 27,* 129–142.

Montanelli, D. S., & Hill, K. T. (1969). Children's achievement expectations and performance as a function of two consecutive reinforcement experiences, sex of subject, and sex of experimenter. *Journal of Personality and Social Psychology, 13,* 115–128.

Mowrer, O. H. (1960). *Learning theory and symbolic processes.* New York: Wiley.

Musashi, M. (1974). *A book of five rings.* Woodstock, NY: Overlook. (Original work written in 1645).

Neale, J. M., & Friend, R. M. (1972). Attributional determinants of reactions to performance in academic situations. *Perceptual and Motor Skills, 34,* 35–40.

Nicholls, J. G. (1976). Effort is virtuous, but it's better to have ability: Evaluative responses to perceptions of effort and ability. *Journal of Research in Personality, 10,* 306–315.

Nicholls, J. G. (1979). Development of perception of own attainment and causal attributions for success and failure in reading. *Journal of Educational Psychology, 71,* 94–99.

Nisbett, R. E., Harvey, D., & Wilson, J. (1979). *"Epistemological" coding of the content of everyday social conversations.* Unpublished manuscript, University of Michigan.

Nisbett, R. E., & Ross, L. (1980). *Human inferences: Strategies and shortcomings of social judgment.* Englewood Cliffs, NJ: Appleton-Century-Crofts.

Nisbett, R. E., & Wilson, T. D. (1977). Telling more than we can know: Verbal reports on mental processes. *Psychological Review, 84,* 231–259.

Oatley, K., & Bolton, W. (1985). A social-cognitive theory of depression in reaction to life events. *Psychological Review, 92,* 372–388.

O'Brien, E. J., & Epstein, S. (1974). Naturally occurring changes in self-esteem. *Proceedings of the 82nd Annual Convention of the American Psychological Association,* Montreal, Canada.

Osgood, C., Suci, G. I., & Tannenbaum, P. H. (1957). *The measurement of meaning.* Urbana: University of Illinois Press.

Pancer, S. M. (1978). Causal attributions and anticipated future performance. *Personality and Social Psychology Bulletin*, *4*, 600–603.

Pancer, S. M., & Eiser, J. R. (1977). Expectations, aspirations, and evaluations as influenced by another's attributions for success and failure. *Canadian Journal of Behavioral Science*, *9*, 252–264.

Passer, M. W. (1977). *Perceiving the causes of success and failure revisited: A multidimensional scaling approach*. Unpublished doctoral dissertation, University of California, Los Angeles.

Passer, M. W., Kelley, H. H., & Michela, J. L. (1978). Multidimensional scaling of the causes for negative interpersonal behavior. *Journal of Personality and Social Psychology*, *36*, 951–962.

Pastore, N. (1952). The role of arbitrariness in the frustration-aggression hypothesis. *Journal of Abnormal and Social Psychology*, *47*, 728–732.

Pence, E. C., Pendleton, W. C., Dobbins, G. H., & Sgro, J. A. (1982). Effects of causal explanations and sex variables on recommendations for corrective actions following employee failure. *Organizational Behavior and Human Performance*, *29*, 227–240.

Peplau, L. A., Miceli, M., & Morasch, B. (1982). Loneliness and self evaluation. In L. A. Peplau & D. Perlman (Eds.), *Loneliness* (pp. 135–151). New York: Wiley.

Peplau, L. A., Russell, D., & Heim, M. (1979). The experience of loneliness. In I. H. Frieze, D. Bar-Tal, & J. S. Carroll (Eds.), *New approaches to social problems* (pp. 53–78). San Francisco: Jossey-Bass.

Peterson, C., Schwartz, S. M., & Seligman, M. E. P. (1981). Self-blame and depressive symptoms. *Journal of Personality and Social Psychology*, *41*, 253–259.

Peterson, C., & Seligman, M. E. P. (1984). Causal explanations as a risk factor for depression: Theory and evidence. *Psychological Review*, *91*, 347–374.

Peterson, C., Semmel, A., von Baeyer, C., Abramson, L. Y., Metalsky, G. I., & Seligman, M. E. P. (1982). The attributional style questionnaire. *Cognitive Therapy and Research*, *6*, 287–300.

Phares, E. J. (1957). Expectancy changes in skill and chance situations. *Journal of Abnormal and Social Psychology*, *54*, 339–342.

Phares, E. J. (1978). Locus of control. In H. London & J. E. Exner, Jr. (Eds.), *Dimensions of personality* (pp. 263–304). New York: Wiley.

Piliavin, I. M., Rodin, J., & Piliavin, J. A. (1969). Good Samaritanism: An underground phenomenon? *Journal of Personality and Social Psychology*, *13*, 289–299.

Porac, J. F. (1981). Causal loops and other intercausal perceptions of attributions for exam performance. *Journal of Educational Psychology*, *73*, 587–601.

Postman, L., & Brown, D. R. (1952). The perceptual consequences of success and failure. *Journal of Abnormal and Social Psychology*, *47*, 213–221.

Pyszczynski, T. A., & Greenberg, J. (1981). Role of disconfirmed expectancies in the instigation of attributional processing. *Journal of Personality and Social Psychology*, *40*, 31–38.

Reisenzein, R. (1986). A structural equation analysis of Weiner's attribution-affect model of helping behavior. *Journal of Personality and Social Psychology*, *50*, 1123–1133.

Rest, S. (1976). Schedules of reinforcement: An attributional analysis. In J. H. Harvey, W. J. Ickes, & R. F. Kidd (Eds.), *New directions in attribution research* (Vol. 1, pp. 97–120). Hillsdale, NJ: Erlbaum.

Rest, S., Nierenberg, R., Weiner, B., & Heckhausen, H. (1973). Further evidence concerning the effects of perceptions of effort and ability on achievement evaluation. *Journal of Personality and Social Psychology*, *28*, 187–191.

Richardson, S. A., Hastorf, A. H., Goodman, N., & Dornbusch, S. M. (1961). Cultural uniformity in reaction to physical disabilities. *American Sociological Review*, *26*, 241–247.

Riemer, B. S. (1975). Influence of causal beliefs on affect and expectancy. *Journal of Personality and Social Psychology*, *31*, 1163–1167.

Riesman, D., Glazer, N., & Denney, R. (1950). *The lonely crowd: A study of the changing American character*. New Haven: Yale University Press.

Robert, R. (1982, November 24). Malavasi questions character of some, says coaching is tough. *Los Angeles Times*, Pt. 3, p. 3.

Rodrigues, A. (1980). Causal ascription and evaluation of achievement related outcomes: A cross-cultural comparison. *International Journal of Intercultural Relations, 4*, 379–389.

Rogers, C. G. (1980). The development of sex differences in evaluation of others' successes and failures. *British Journal of Educational Psychology, 50*, 243–252.

Rohrkemper, M. (1985). Individual differences in students' perceptions of routine classroom events. *Journal of Educational Psychology, 77*, 29–44.

Ronis, D. L., Hansen, R. D., & O'Leary, V. E. (1983). Understanding the meaning of achievement attributions: A test of derived locus and stability scores. *Journal of Personality and Social Psychology, 44*, 702–711.

Rosenbaum, R. M. (1972). *A dimensional analysis of the perceived causes of success and failure*. Unpublished doctoral dissertation, University of California, Los Angeles.

Rosenfeld, D., & Stephan, W. G. (1978). Sex differences in attributions for sex-typed tasks. *Journal of Personality, 46*, 244–259.

Rotter, J. B. (1954). *Social learning and clinical psychology*. Englewood Cliffs, NJ: Prentice-Hall.

Rotter, J. B. (1966). Generalized expectancies for internal versus external control of reinforcement. *Psychological Monographs, 80*, 1–28.

Rotter, J. B., Chance, J. E., and Phares, E. J. (1972). An introduction to social learning theory. In J. B. Rotter, J. E. Chance, & E. J. Phares (Eds.), *Applications of a social learning theory of personality* (pp. 1–44). New York: Holt, Rinehart & Winston.

Rotter, J. B., & Hochreich, D. J. (1975). *Personality*. Glenview, IL: Scott Foresman.

Rotter, J. B., Liverant, S., & Crowne, D. P. (1961). The growth and extinction of expectancies in chance controlled and skilled tasks. *Journal of Psychology, 52*, 161–177.

Rotter, J. B., Seeman, M., & Liverant, S. (1962). Internal versus external control of reinforcement: A major variable in behavior theory. In N. F. Washbourne (Ed.), *Decisions, values, and groups* (Vol. 2, pp. 473–516). London: Pergamon Press.

Rudy, E. B. (1980). Patients' and spouses' causal explanations of myocardial infarction. *Nursing Research, 29*, 352–356.

Russell, D. (1982). The Causal Dimension Scale: A measure of how individuals perceive causes. *Journal of Personality and Social Psychology, 42*, 1137–1145.

Russell, D., Lenel, J. C., Spicer, C., Miller, J., Albrecht, J., & Rose, J. (1985). Evaluating the physically disabled. *Personality and Social Psychology Bulletin, 11*, 23–32.

Rychlak, J. F. (1968). *A philosophy of science for personality theory*. Boston: Houghton Mifflin.

Salancik, G. R., & Meindl, J. R. (1984). Corporate attributions as strategic illusions of management control. *Administrative Science Quarterly, 29*, 238–254.

Salili, F., Maehr, M. L., & Gilmore, G. (1976). Achievement and morality: A cross-cultural analysis of causal attribution and evaluation. *Journal of Personality and Social Psychology, 33*, 327–337.

Saulnier, K., & Perlman, D. (1981). The actor-observer bias is alive and well in prison: A sequel to Wells. *Personality and Social Psychology Bulletin, 7*, 559–564.

Schachter, S. (1964). The interaction of cognitive and physiological determinants of emotional state. In L. Berkowitz (Ed.), *Advances in experimental social psychology* (Vol. 1, pp. 49–80). New York: Academic Press.

Schachter, S. (1971). *Emotion, obesity, and crime*. New York: Academic Press.

Schachter, S., & Singer, J. E. (1962). Cognitive, social and physiological determinants of emotional state. *Psychological Review, 69*, 379–399.

Scherer, K. R. (1982). Emotion as process: Function, origin, and regulation. *Social Science Information, 21*, 555–570.

Schoeneman, T. J., Cheek, P. R., Fischer, K., Hollis, J. F., & Stevens, V. J. (1985, August). *Attributions for success and failure following smoking cessation treatment*. Paper presented at the American Psychological Association Convention, Los Angeles, CA.

Schoeneman, T. J., & Rubanowitz, D. E. (1983, August). *Attributions in the advice columns: Actors and observers, causes and reasons.* Paper presented at the American Psychological Association, Anaheim, CA.

Schoeneman, T. J., & Rubanowitz, D. E. (1985). Attributions in the advice columns: Actors and observers, causes and reasons. *Personality and Social Psychology Bulletin, 11,* 301–314.

Schopler, J., & Matthews, M. (1965). The influence of perceived causal locus on partner's dependence on the use of interpersonal power. *Journal of Personality and Social Psychology, 2,* 609–612.

Schunk, D. H. (1981). Modeling and attributional effects on children's achievement: A self-efficacy analysis. *Journal of Educational Psychology, 73,* 93–105.

Schunk, D. H. (1982). Effects of effort attributional feedback on children's perceived self-efficacy and achievement. *Journal of Educational Psychology, 74,* 548–556.

Schunk, D. H. (1983). Ability versus effort attributional feedback: Differential effects on self-efficacy and achievement. *Journal of Educational Psychology, 75,* 848–856.

Schunk, D. H. (1984). Sequential attributional feedback and children's achievement behaviors. *Journal of Educational Psychology, 76,* 1159–1169.

Schütz, A (1967). *Collected papers I: The problem of social reality.* The Hague: Martinus Nijhoff.

Seligman, M. E. P. (1975). *Helplessness: On depression, development, and death.* San Francisco: Freeman.

Shrauger, J. S., & Osberg, T. M. (1980). The relationship of time investment and task outcome to causal attributions and self-esteem. *Journal of Personality, 48,* 360–378.

Shultz, T. R., & Schleifer, M. (1983). Towards a refinement of attribution concepts. In J. Jaspers, F. D. Fincham, & M. Hewstone (Eds.), *Attribution theory and research: Conceptual, developmental, and social dimensions* (pp. 37–62). London: Academic Press.

Simon, J. G., & Feather, N. T. (1973). Causal attributions for success and failure at University examinations. *Journal of Educational Psychology, 64,* 46–56.

Singer, R. N., & McCaughan, L. R. (1978). Motivational effects of attributions, expectancy, and achievement motivation during learning of a novel motor task. *Journal of Motor Behavior, 10,* 245–253.

Smith, E. R., & Kluegel, J. R. (1982). Cognitive and social bases of emotional experience: Outcome, attribution, and affect. *Journal of Personality and Social Psychology, 43,* 1129–1141.

Smith, E. R., & Miller, F. (1983). Mediation among attributional inferences and comprehension processes: Initial findings and a general method. *Journal of Personality and Social Psychology, 44,* 492–505.

Sobel, M. P., Earn, B. M., Bennett, D., & Humphries, T. (1983). A categorical analysis of the social attributions of learning-disabled children. *Journal of Abnormal Child Psychology, 11,* 217–228.

Staff. (1926, April). Fifty and 100 years ago. *Scientific American,* p. 228.

Staffieri, J. R. (1967). A study of social stereotype of body image in children. *Journal of Personality and Social Psychology, 7,* 101–104.

Staton, J. J. (1984). *Acquired practical reasoning through teacher-student interactions in dialogue journals.* Unpublished doctoral dissertation, University of California, Los Angeles.

Steiner, I. D. (1970). Perceived freedom. In L. Berkowitz (Ed.), *Advances in experimental social psychology* (Vol. 5, pp. 187–248). New York: Academic Press.

Stephan, W. G., & Gollwitzer, P. M. (1981). Affect as a mediator of attributional egotism. *Journal of Experimental Social Psychology, 17,* 443–458.

Stephan, W. S., Rosenfield, D., & Stephan, C. (1976). Egotism in males and females. *Journal of Personality and Social Psychology, 34,* 1161–1167.

Stern, P. (1983). *A multimethod analysis of student perceptions of causal dimensions.* Unpublished doctoral dissertation, University of California, Los Angeles.

Stipek, D. J. (1983). A developmental analysis of pride and shame. *Human Development, 26,* 42–54.

Strenta, A., & Kleck, R. E. (1982). Perceptions of task feedback: Investigating "kind" treatment of the handicapped. *Personality and Social Psychology Bulletin, 8,* 706–711.

Taylor, S. E. (1983). Adjustment to threatening events. *American Psychologist, 38,* 1161–1173.

Tesser, A., Gatewood, R., & Driver, M. (1968). Some determinants of gratitude. *Journal of Personality and Social Psychology, 9,* 233–236.

Thompson, R. A., & Paris, S. G. (1981). *Children's inferences about the emotions of others.* Unpublished manuscript, University of Michigan.

Tolman, E. C. (1925). Purpose and cognition: The determinants of animal learning. *Psychological Review, 32,* 285–297.

Tolman, E. C. (1932). *Purposive behavior in animals and men.* New York: Appleton-Century-Crofts.

Tomkins, S. (1970). Affect as the primary motivational system. In M. B. Arnold (Ed.), *Feelings and emotions* (pp. 101–110). New York: Academic Press.

Triandis, H. C. (1972). *The analysis of subjective culture.* New York: Wiley-Interscience.

Trivers, R. L. (1971). The evolution of reciprocal altruism. *Quarterly Review of Biology, 46,* 35–57.

Valle, V. A. (1974). *Attributions of stability as a mediator in the changing of expectations.* Unpublished doctoral dissertation, University of Pittsburgh.

Valle, V. A., & Frieze, I. H. (1976). Stability of causal attributions as a mediator in changing expectations for success. *Journal of Personality and Social Psychology, 33,* 579–587.

Watson, J. S., & Ramey, C. G. (1972). Reactions to response-contingent stimulation in early infancy. *Merrill-Palmer Quarterly, 18,* 219–228.

Weary, G. B. (1978). Self-serving biases in the attribution process: A reexamination of the fact or fiction question. *Journal of Personality and Social Psychology, 36,* 56–71.

Weiner, B. (1972). *Theories of motivation.* Chicago: Rand McNally.

Weiner, B. (1979). A theory of motivation for some classroom experiences. *Journal of Educational Psychology, 71,* 3–25.

Weiner, B. (1980a). A cognitive (attributional)-emotion-action model of motivated behavior: An analysis of judgments of help-giving. *Journal of Personality and Social Psychology, 39,* 186–200.

Weiner, B. (1980b). May I borrow your class notes? An attributional analysis of judgments of help-giving in an achievement-related context. *Journal of Educational Psychology, 72,* 676–681.

Weiner, B (1980c). *Human motivation.* New York: Holt, Rinehart & Winston.

Weiner, B. (1983). Some methodological pitfalls in attributional research. *Journal of Educational Psychology, 75,* 530–543.

Weiner, B. (1985a). "Spontaneous" causal thinking. *Psychological Bulletin, 97,* 74–84.

Weiner, B. (1985b). An attributional theory of achievement motivation and emotion. *Psychological Review, 92,* 548–573.

Weiner, B., Amirkhan, J., Folkes, V. S., and Verette, J. A. (in press). *An attributional analysis of excuse giving: Studies of a naive theory of emotion. Journal of Personality and Social Psychology.*

Weiner, B., Frieze, I. H., Kukla, A., Reed, L., Rest, S., & Rosenbaum, R. M. (1971). *Perceiving the causes of success and failure.* Morristown, NJ: General Learning Press.

Weiner, B., Graham, S., & Chandler, C. C. (1982). Pity, anger, and guilt: An attributional analysis. *Personality and Social Psychology Bulletin, 8,* 226–232.

Weiner, B., Graham, S., Stern, P., & Lawson, M. E. (1982). Using affective cues to infer causal thoughts. *Developmental Psychology, 18,* 278–286.

Weiner, B., & Handel, S. (1985). Anticipated emotional consequences of causal communications and reported communication strategy. *Developmental Psychology, 21,* 102–107.

Weiner, B., Heckhausen, H., Meyer, W. U., & Cook, R. E. (1972). Causal ascription and achievement motivation. *Journal of Personality and Social Psychology, 21,* 239–248.

Weiner, B., & Kukla, A. (1970). An attributional analysis of achievement motivation. *Journal of Personality and Social Psychology, 15,* 1–20.

Weiner, B., Kun, A., & Benesh-Weiner, M. (1980). The development of mastery, emotions, and morality from an attributional perspective. In W. A. Collins (Ed.), *The Minnesota Symposium on Child Psychology* (Vol. 13, pp. 103–130). Hillsdale, NJ: Erlbaum.

Weiner, B., & Litman-Adizes, T. (1980). An attributional, expectancy-value analysis of learned helplessness and depression. In J. Garber and M. E. P. Seligman (Eds.), *Human helplessness* (pp. 35–58). New York: Academic Press.

Weiner, B., Nierenberg, R., & Goldstein, M. (1976). Social learning (locus of control) versus attributional (causal stability) interpretations of expectancy of success. *Journal of Personality, 44,* 52–68.

Weiner, B., & Peter, N. (1973). A cognitive developmental analysis of achievement and moral judgments. *Developmental Psychology, 9,* 290–309.

Weiner, B., & Potepan, P. A. (1970). Personality correlates and affective reactions towards exams of succeeding and failing college students. *Journal of Educational Psychology, 61,* 144–151.

Weiner, B., Russell, D., & Lerman, D. (1978). Affective consequences of causal ascriptions. In J. H. Harvey, W. J. Ickes, & R. F. Kidd (Eds.), *New directions in attribution research* (Vol. 2, pp. 59–88). Hillsdale, NJ: Erlbaum.

Weiner, B., Russell, D., & Lerman, D. (1979). The cognition-emotion process in achievement-related contexts. *Journal of Personality and Social Psychology, 37,* 1211–1220.

Weiner, B., & Sierad, J. (1975). Misattribution for failure and enhancement of achievement strivings. *Journal of Personality and Social Psychology, 31,* 415–421.

Whalen, C. K., & Henker, B. (1976). Psychostimulants and children: A review and analysis. *Psychological Bulletin, 83,* 1113–1130.

White, R. W. (1959). Motivation reconsidered: The concept of competence. *Psychological Review, 66,* 297–333.

Whitley, B. E., Jr., & Frieze, I. H. (1983). *The effects of question wording and situational context on success and failure attributions: A meta-analysis.* Unpublished manuscript, University of Pittsburgh.

Wicker, F. W., Payne, G. C., & Morgan, R. D. (1983). Participant descriptions of guilt and shame. *Motivation and Emotion, 7,* 25–39.

Wiley, M. G., Crittended, K. S., & Birg, L. D. (1979). Why a rejection? Causal attribution of a career achievement event. *Social Psychology Quarterly, 42,* 214–222.

Willson, V. L., & Palmer, D. J. (1983). Latent partition analysis of attributions for actual achievement. *American Educational Research Journal, 20,* 581–589.

Wilson, T. D., & Linville, P. W. (1982). Improving the academic performance of college freshmen: Attribution therapy revisited. *Journal of Personality and Social Psychology, 42,* 367–376.

Wilson, T. D., & Linville, P. W. (1985). Improving the performance of college freshmen with attributional techniques. *Journal of Personality and Social Psychology, 49,* 287–293.

Wimer, S., & Kelley, H. H. (1982). An investigation of the dimensions of causal attribution. *Journal of Personality and Social Psychology, 43,* 1142–1162.

Wine, J. D. (1971). Test anxiety and direction of attention. *Psychological Bulletin, 76,* 72–104.

Winter, L., & Uleman, J. S. (1984). When are social judgments made? Evidence for the spontaneousness of trait inferences. *Journal of Personality and Social Psychology, 47,* 237–252.

Wittig, M. A., Marks, G., & Jones, G. A. (1981). Luck versus effort attributions: Effect on reward allocations to self and other. *Personality and Social Psychology Bulletin, 7,* 71–78.

Wong, P. T. P. (1977). Partial reinforcement and the learning of a strategy in the rat. *American Journal of Psychology, 90,* 663–674.

Wong, P. T. P., & Weiner, B. (1981). When people ask "why" questions and the heuristics of attributional search. *Journal of Personality and Social Psychology, 40,* 650–663.

Wortman, C. B., & Dintzer, L. (1978). Is an attributional analysis of learned helplessness phenomena viable? A critique of the Abramson-Seligman-Teasdale reformulation. *Journal of Abnormal Psychology, 87,* 75–90.

Wright, B. A. (1983). *Physical disability—a psychological approach*. 2nd Edition. New York: Harper.

Wright, J., & Mischel, W. (1982). Influence of affect on cognitive social learning person variables. *Journal of Personality and Social Psychology, 43*, 901-914.

Zajonc, R. B., & Brickman, P. (1969). Expectancy and feedback as independent factors in task performance. *Journal of Personality and Social Psychology, 11*, 148-156.

Zoeller, C. J., Mahoney, G., & Weiner, B. (1983). Effects of attribution training on the assembly task performance of mentally retarded adults. *American Journal of Mental Deficiency, 88*, 109-112.

Zuckerman, M., Larrance, D. T., Porac, J. F. A., & Blanck, P. D. (1980). Effects of fear of success on intrinsic motivation, causal attributions, and choice behavior. *Journal of Personality and Social Psychology, 39*, 503-513.

Author Index

Kahan, J.P., 113
Kant, I., 13, 128, 205
Keane, A., 40
Kelley, H.H., 2, 23, 36, 52–54, 56, 59–
    61, 64, 66, 69, 78, 125–126, 244–246
Kelly, G.A., 44, 159
Keogh, B., 232
Kepka, E.J., 230
Kidd, R.F., 22, 123–124, 193–195, 197,
    204
Kington, J.W., 40
Kleck, R.E., 145
Klein, R., 127
Kluegel, J.R., 126, 129, 244
Knaani, A., 38–39, 74–75
Knowlton, W.A., 146–147
Koelbl, S.L.M., 52–56, 64, 66
Kojima, M., 88–89, 249
Kovenklioglu, G., 88–89
Krebs, D.L., 201
Kukla, A., 37, 44, 46, 51, 105, 111,
    114, 146–147, 169–170, 219, 245
Kruglanski, A.W., 22
Kun, A., 126, 246

Lanning, K., 183
Larrance, D.T., 113
Lau, R.R., 24–25, 34, 40
Lau, S., 205
Lawrence, D.H., 106
Lawson, M.E., 137, 235, 237, 246–247
Layden, M.A., 234
Lazarus, R.S., 119–120
Lee, Y.K., 52–53
Lefcourt, H.M., 221
Lenel, J.C., 145
Lepley, W.M., 83
Lerman, D., 122–126, 129, 153–154,
    235–236, 244, 246, 250
Lepper, M.R., 6, 45
Lewin, K., 5, 7–8, 10, 17, 80–82, 85,
    117, 243
Linville, P.W., 182–183, 187–188, 190
Litman-Adizes, T., 110, 154, 217
Liverant, S., 84–85, 106
Locke, D., 22
Lucas, J.D., 167–168, 179
Luginbuhl, J.E.R., 113

Mackenzie, M., 143
MacMillian, D., 232
Maehr, M.L., 147, 241
Mahoney, G., 182, 187
Major, B., 191, 216
Marcoux, R.E., 147
Mark, J., 40
Mark, M.M., 191
Marks, G., 147
Markus, H., 142, 145
Marlatt, G.A., 191, 210–211
Martin, J.C., 44–45
Maruyama, G.M., 113, 168, 174
Matthews, K.A., 27–28, 35
Matthews, M., 193
McCaughan, L.R., 88
McClelland, D.C., 24
McDavis, K., 201
McHugh, M.C., 191, 232
McMahan, I.D., 88–89, 233
Medway, F.J., 147, 185
Meindl, J.R., 26, 34
Menapace, R.H., 232
Metalsky, G.I., 174, 221
Meyer, J.P., 52–56, 64, 66, 200, 202,
    204–205
Meyer, W.U., 88, 90, 169–171, 174,
    177, 179–180, 246
Miceli, M., 191
Michela, J.L., 23, 36, 52–53, 56, 59–
    62, 64, 66–67, 69, 245
Mikula, G., 27, 29–31, 35, 245
Miller, D.T., 142, 145, 206
Miller, F., 23
Miller, I.W., 217
Miller, J., 145
Minton, H.L., 234
Mischel, W., 227
Mitchell, T.R., 147
Monson, T., 36
Montanelli, D.S., 82
Morasch, B., 191
Morgan, R.D., 150–152
Morgenstern, D., 241
Morris, S.L., 40
Mowrer, O.H., 154
Mueller, P., 191, 216
Mulherin, A., 200, 202, 204–205
Musashi, M., 1

Subject Index

Springer Series in Social Psychology

Attention and Self-Regulation: A Control-Theory Approach to Human Behavior
Charles S. Carver/Michael F. Scheier

Gender and Nonverbal Behavior
Clara Mayo/Nancy M. Henley (Editors)

Personality, Roles, and Social Behavior
William Ickes/Eric S. Knowles (Editors)

Toward Transformation in Social Knowledge
Kenneth J. Gergen

The Ethics of Social Research: Surveys and Experiments
Joan E. Sieber (Editor)

The Ethics of Social Research: Fieldwork, Regulation, and Publication
Joan E. Sieber (Editor)

Anger and Aggression: An Essay on Emotion
James R. Averill

The Social Psychology of Creativity
Teresa M. Amabile

Sports Violence
Jeffrey H. Goldstein (Editor)

Nonverbal Behavior: A Functional Perspective
Miles L. Patterson

Basic Group Processes
Paul B. Paulus (Editor)

Attitudinal Judgment
J. Richard Eiser (Editor)

Social Psychology of Aggression: From Individual Behavior to Social Interaction
Amélie Mummendey (Editor)

Directions in Soviet Social Psychology
Lloyd H. Strickland (Editor)

Sociophysiology
William M. Waid (Editor)

Compatible and Incompatible Relationships
William Ickes (Editor)

Facet Theory: Approaches to Social Research
David Canter (Editor)

Action Control: From Cognition to Behavior
Julius Kuhl/Jürgen Beckmann (Editors)

Springer Series in Social Psychology

The Social Construction of the Person
  Kenneth J. Gergen/Keith E. Davis (Editors)

Entrapment in Escalating Conflicts: A Social Psychological Analysis
  Joel Brockner/Jeffrey Z. Rubin

The Attribution of Blame: Causality, Responsibility, and Blameworthiness
  Kelly G. Shaver

Language and Social Situations
  Joseph P. Forgas (Editor)

Power, Dominance, and Nonverbal Behavior
  Steve L. Ellyson/John F. Dovidio (Editors)

Changing Conceptions of Crowd Mind and Behavior
  Carl F. Graumann/Serge Moscovici (Editors)

Changing Conceptions of Leadership
  Carl F. Graumann/Serge Moscovici (Editors)

Friendship and Social Interaction
  Valerian J. Derlega/Barbara A. Winstead (Editors)

An Attributional Theory of Motivation and Emotion
  Bernard Weiner

Public Self and Private Self
  Roy F. Baumeister (Editor)

Social Psychology and Dysfunctional Behavior: Origins, Diagnosis, and Treatment
  Mark R. Leary/Rowland S. Miller

Communication and Persuasion: Central and Peripheral Routes to Attitude Change
  Richard E. Petty/John T. Cacioppo

Theories of Group Behavior
  Brian Mullen/George R. Goethals (Editors)